Trails of Western Idaho

Cover: Green Lake (Lost River District, Challis National Forest)

Getting ready for Hells Canyon hiking

trails of
WESTERN IDAHO

From Sun Valley to Hells Canyon

by Margaret Fuller

Signpost Books

TRAILS OF WESTERN IDAHO
© 1982 by Signpost Books
All Rights Reserved

Back cover photo of author by Stuart Fuller.
All other photos by Margaret Fuller.

Signpost Books welcomes inquiries from authors about prospective
books. Suggestions for new titles also are welcome.
SIGNPOST BOOKS
8912 192nd SW
Edmonds, WA 98020

Library of Congress Cataloging in Publication Data

Fuller, Margaret.
   Trails of western Idaho.

   Bibliography: p. 258-260
   Includes index.
   1. Hiking—Idaho—Guide-books.   2. Trail riding—Idaho—
guide-books. 3. Idaho—Description and travel—1981-   —Guide-
books. I. Title.
GV199.42.I2F83   *917.92*   *82-5621*
ISBN 0-913140-44-9   *AACR2*

Foreword

Margaret Fuller has done it again. Her latest guide book to Idaho's hiking trails is a "must" for outdoor enthusiasts who desire an accurate description of an area or people who need suggestions of where they might visit.

The trails described range from easy to expert and from remote to urban. Whether you have one day or one month you will discover trails that were designed for you.

Idaho is dear to us and we hope our visitors will enjoy their time spent in our areas. We are blessed with many areas where, by following Margaret's suggestions, one can be alone for as long as they desire in an environment that will rejuvenate, while causing one to forget foreign travel. Beauty, solitude and the opportunity for enjoyment abound in Idaho. One only has to be properly prepared and by following Margaret's advice will experience a new world unfolding before your eyes with every step. All we ask is that you use the land, but that you don't abuse the land. Our resources are finite and there are many generations to come.

Cecil D. Andrus

Contents

TRIP LOCATION MAP

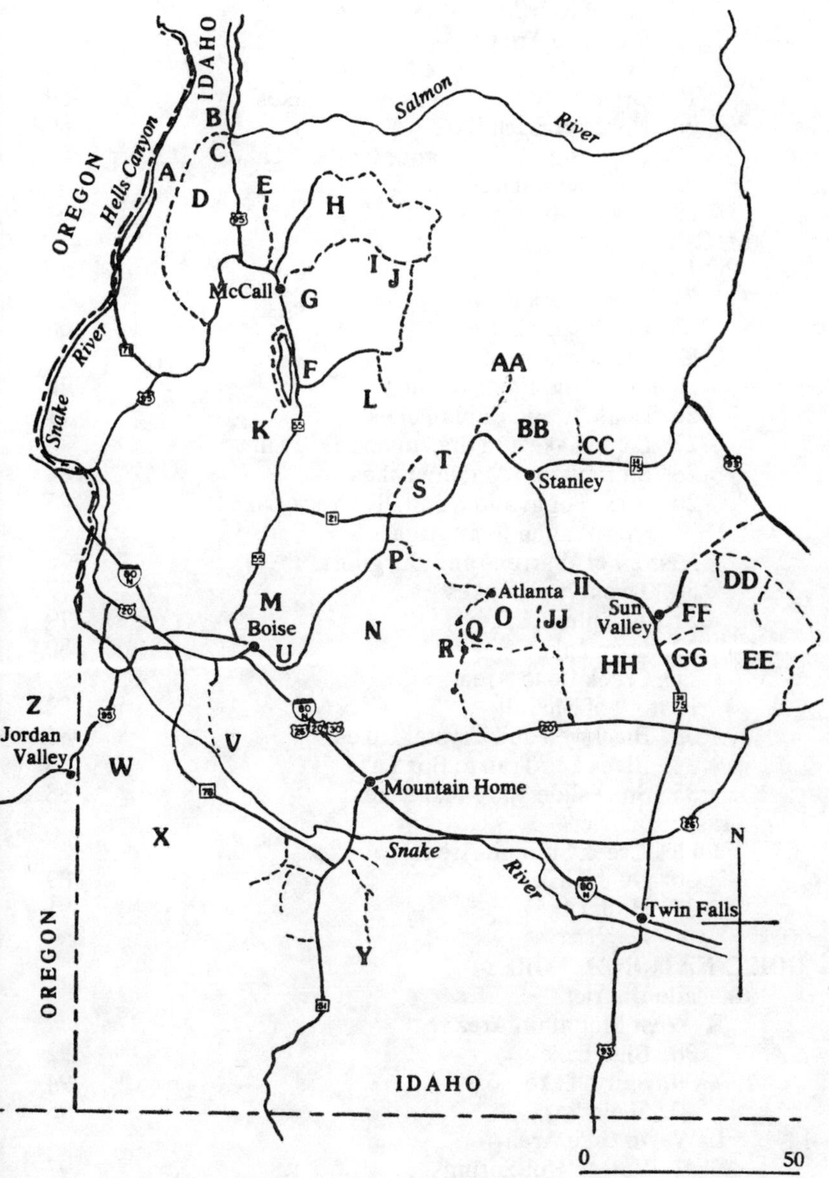

PAYETTE NATIONAL FOREST

BOISE NATIONAL FOREST

LEGEND FOR TRAIL MAPS

———————— paved road	
════════════ improved road	⚑ campground
‒‒‒‒‒‒‒‒‒‒‒‒ primitive road	
– – – – – – – described trail	⸗ marsh
–·–·–·–·–·– cross country route	
············· other trails	■ building
～～～～ creek	

Introduction

In southwestern Idaho, desert canyons so deep and narrow that the sun rarely reaches the bottom contrast with mountain meadows of spongy turf spangled with flowers. Aquamarine lakes fill hollows on the sides of slate-black lava peaks and fill basins below grey mountains streaked with white, rust, and rose.

An example of the contrast in this land is the Hells Canyon Wilderness Area. The Seven Devils Mountains of black basalt run for forty miles between the Little Salmon and Snake Rivers. The Snake River flows along the base of the Seven Devils through Hells Canyon, which is 7900 feet deep from the top of He Devil to the river. The canyon has the deepest gorge in the Western Hemisphere with twice the volume of the Colorado. Snow covers the mountains above the canyon during seven months of the year, but cactus grows along the river.

The Snake River begins near Yellowstone Park, flows south past the Tetons, then turns northwest into Idaho, where the river makes a great semi-circle across the southern part of the state. Along the western boundary of Idaho, the river flows north through Hells Canyon on its way to the Columbia. As the Snake turns north, it marks off a huge triangle of desert land in the southwestern corner of the state. The 8000-foot Owyhee Mountains with juniper and granite covered tops are in the northern corner of this triangle. Remnants of old mining settlements like Silver City hide among the hills.

Forested hills begin north and east of the irrigated and settled Boise Valley. This land of the Boise National Forest has sparkling lakes like the tiny Trinity and Red Mountain Lakes and has viewpoints of the Boise Valley and Long Valley near McCall. The glacier-scoured granite peaks, hanging valleys, and blue lakes of the mountains of the Payette National Forest near McCall create a hikers' playground.

East of the Boise National Forest are the gentle Smoky Mountains in the Sawtooth National Forest. In this green and beige range, colorful stripes etch cliffs on top of the peaks. North and east of the Smokies rise the Sawtooth, White Cloud, and Boulder Mountains of the Sawtooth National Recreation Area, which are described in *Trails of the Sawtooth and White Cloud Mountains* by the author.

East of Sun Valley and Hailey, the Pioneer Range features peaks that are the equal in beauty of any in Idaho. Here multicolored crags of metamorphic rock surround some of the thickest carpets of wildflowers in the state.

Northwest of Stanley the striped 1200-foot wall of Cabin Creek Peak and the brick-red top of Red Mountain highlight a little known section of the Salmon River Mountains. This group of peaks stretches along the southern boundary of the River of No Return Wilderness from the headwaters of Loon Creek to Soldier Lakes.

This book includes detailed descriptions of hikes from all of these areas. The Appendix summarizes some hikes not covered in detail. Since the Boise Valley touches the Oregon border, the guide includes three hikes at the edge of eastern Oregon.

Visitors to western Idaho and Idaho residents will be surprised at the rich variety of hiking opportunities and the solitude of the backcountry described in this guide. With a few exceptions, these areas get much less use than the Sawtooths and White Clouds.

The purpose of this book is to give hikers and horse riders an idea of the many trails in western Idaho. Information on many possible trails in an area and on alternate less-crowded areas will help distribute use, according to wilderness management specialists. The desert hikes in this book will help hikers extend the season for their sport from early spring to late fall. If more people become aware of the areas covered in this book, they will be able to fight effectively to save these areas as a recreation resource. Examples of threats to the backcountry are buildings, mining, logging, and careless recreation users.

HISTORY

A short history of each area is located with hikes for that area. These historical sections are not intended to be complete, but only to whet the interest of the reader in Idaho history. Many historical books on Idaho are listed in the Bibliography.

ROUTE DESCRIPTIONS

Basic information about each hike is listed at the top of the description. The round trip or through mileage and elevation gain or loss is listed at the top. A few have an additional note: "This section: x miles, y feet elevation gain". The miles for that section are given one-way. Also mentioned are the topographic maps needed, the time to allow if on foot, and the length and quality of the access road. The time is given for the round trip and includes 1 hour at the destination if the hike is a day hike. Hike mileage is given from the furthest point on the access road that a two-wheel drive truck can usually reach. Unless mentioned as having no

Baldy Lake (Seven Devils)

water, most trails have drinking water available from side streams that cross the trail.

ACCESS ROADS

Access roads for these hikes vary in quality, so the access roads are described as paved, gravel, dirt, or primitive. The heading also gives the number of miles on unpaved roads. Do not attempt to drive primitive roads in wet or snowy weather or before they have dried out in the spring. It is easy to get stuck or slide off the road. Also, traveling on these roads when they are wet damages them. Ask a ranger about access road conditions when uncertain. Primitive roads are not suitable for passenger cars, but do not require four-wheel drive unless noted. The gradation from gravel to dirt or dirt to primitive varies. Special maps called travel plan maps are available every year at each National Forest Office. These maps show which roads and trails are closed to motorized vehicles.

HIKING ABILITY

Hikes are classified by degree of difficulty. Easy hikes are less than 7 miles, with less than 1000 feet elevation gain, and require no cross-country travel. Moderate hikes are 7-10 miles, with 1000 to 2000 feet elevation gain, and require no cross-country travel. Notations are also included for hikes that require expert ability because of route-finding problems or treacherous footing, and for hikes requiring cross-country travel. Hikes not designated as easy, moderate, cross-country, or expert can be taken by most hikers in good condition. They are listed as strenuous because hikes of over 10 miles require the hiker to have a high energy level. Each section of a trip requiring several days is listed as strenuous. A list of easy, moderate, expert, and cross-country hikes is found in the Guide to Hikes.

MAPS

Topographic maps may be obtained from the Branch of Distribution, U. S. Geological Survey, Federal Center, Denver, Colorado 80225, or from office supply and mountaineering stores in Boise and Ketchum. A free map index and order forms for any state can be obtained by writing the above address. The index will help the hiker decide which maps to order for a particular area. The topographic maps needed for each hike in this book are listed at the beginning of the description. Topographic maps are less expensive if ordered directly from the Geological Survey. The Boise State University Library has a complete collection of Idaho topographic maps.

Standard topographic maps are 7½ minute size with 40-foot contour levels in a scale of 1 inch to 24,000 feet. Some of the older maps are 15 minute size with 80-foot contour levels in a scale of 1 inch to 62,500 feet. On a few maps of both scales, the contour lines are drawn at less than the above intervals. For these few cases the unusual contour interval is noted at the beginning of the description. Less detailed Forest Service maps which are indispensable for finding and following access roads can be obtained for a small charge at the Forest Service offices listed in the Appendix.

GLOSSARY

Switchback: a zigzag or to zigzag.

Talus: loose rocks or boulders with no dirt in between them.

Blaze: small letter "i" cut in bark of tree to mark official trail.

Rock bench: large flat or rounded solid rock outcropping.

Saddle: low point in a ridge.

Gully: miniature canyon, ravine.

Cairn: pile of rocks sometimes used as a trail marker.

Topo (topographic) map: very detailed map made by the U. S. Geological Survey. A topographic map shows the elevation differences of the ground as well as physical features. The U. S. Geological Survey omits apostrophes in all place names. This book follows that practice, even though these names may appear with apostrophes in other publications. (Examples: Hells Canyon, Hulls Gulch, Little Jacks Creek.)

LOW IMPACT CAMPING

Today when more and more people are discovering backpacking, those using the backcountry must learn how to use it without destroying some of the features that make wild areas such wonderful places.

Garbage along the trail or at a campsite offends most people. Who wants trash in their front yard? A campsite becomes the front yard and home of those camping there. Every year U. S. taxpayers pay heavily for the Forest and Park Services to pick up after backcountry visitors. Please carry out all unburnable trash, including leftover food and disposable diapers. Never bury garbage because animals will dig it up and scatter it. Foil freeze-dried food envelopes will not burn and must be carried out. Extra plastic bags will make carrying garbage easier.

The camper should select a campsite keeping both low impact and his own comfort in mind. Experience has shown that the low impact sites are often the most comfortable. Camp more than 100 feet away from a lake or stream even if other people have camped closer. Try to camp 200 feet away from water if possible and in a location that has already been used by others. Voluntary cooperation will avoid the need for implementing these measures by law enforcement. The best site is on pine needles or leaves with no vegetation underfoot to be trampled. A campsite should also be at least 100 feet from a trail. Avoid sites that have been overused.

Don't camp in meadows. Meadows are very fragile because of the short mountain growing season. Meadows are also damp, cold, full of mosquitoes, and lumpy. When camping in an area without previous campsites, try to return the area to its original appearance before leaving. Don't cut limbs or boughs from standing trees, dig ditches, or pound nails. It is illegal to cut standing trees, dead or alive, in wilderness areas and without a permit in National Forests. Before leaving put back stones which have been moved for any reason.

Use backpacking stoves as much as possible for cooking to prevent unsightly fire scars. Don't make a fire ring if a ring isn't already built. Build the fire on a non-burnable base of sand or earth from which all decaying vegetable matter has been removed. To avoid leaving a black mark, don't build fires on or against rocks.

Try not to pollute water with soap or food particles. Wash dishes in a container away from a lake or stream and dump the dishwater away from camp and away from the water source. Also wash clothes and bathe away from the lake or stream. Use special biodegradeable soap.

Wilderness use is a responsibility.

For disposing of human waste, dig a hole 6-8 inches deep (no deeper) and fill it in after use. The bacteria in the top layer of soil soon dispose of the waste. Do not overturn a rock and then replace it on top of the waste. For groups, dig a latrine at least 300 feet away from any water source. Burn fish guts rather than throwing them in a lake or burying them. When fires are not allowed, carry fish guts out in a double-layered plastic bag.

Travel on foot whenever possible, since horses leave more evidence of their passage than most foot travelers. When meeting horses on the trail, stand still quietly on the downhill side while they pass. If horse travel is necessary, use lightweight food and equipment so that fewer horses will be needed. Use alfalfa cubes or horse pellets for feed to prevent introducing weeds with hay and to prevent the horses from needing to graze. Grazing damages fragile high meadows. Because of the short growing season, scars last for years. Tie horses well away from campsites and don't tie them directly to trees unless the trees are protected with burlap or pieces of slit garden hose. Use the horse tie area if one is provided. Horses should be staked more than 100 feet from streams or lakes. Hitch racks and anything else the horse traveler constructs should be dismantled and stacked against a tree before leaving.

Train horses before they are taken into the mountains so they will be accustomed to the new things they will do. They should be conditioned to being picketed (staked or tied to a heavy but moveable log) or hobbled. Picket only one horse and hobble the rest to avoid damage to the grass. Condition the horses to strenuous exercise in advance and accustom them to the feed cubes or pellets. This pertains to mules and burros also.

Having an outfitter pack in gear to a base camp can make longer trips feasible for families with small children. To obtain a list of packers, write the Idaho Outfitters and Guides Association, P. O. Box 95, Boise, Idaho 83701.

The Forest Service recommends leaving dogs at home, but if the hiker wishes to take his dog, he should have it obey certain rules. A dog in the backcountry must obey instantly, so that it won't get into trouble. Never let a dog chase wildlife.....the wildlife might turn out to be a porcupine. Keep the dog from messing up the camp or trail.....clean up after it if necessary. Hold the dog if horses or other hikers are approaching. Keep the dog out of the drinking water source and away from the campsites of other people. It is preferable that dogs be kept on leashes at all times.

The hiker should leave historical and archeological objects as is for those doing research to observe and for other visitors to enjoy. On many trips, the hiker will see old log cabins, mine buildings, or Indian dwelling sites. The Antiquities Act protects historical sites by providing a large fine for people who remove or damage things. Under the 1979 Archeological Sites Protection Act, excavation or destruction of archeological sites is punishable by up to a $20,000 fine and two years in prison. Some sites are private property and should be respected as such. Because of high metal prices, people are working many of the old mine sites, so no one can be sure that the owner won't suddenly appear.

Another way for backcountry travelers to lessen their impact is to select the least-used trails within an area. A list of the little-used and well-used trails covered by this book is given in the Appendix. A ranger can provide further information. The hiker can select little-used areas and avoid well-known wildernesses. Those experienced with map and compass can go cross-country to trailless lakes. Small groups have less environmental impact, so try to travel in groups of less than 10 people. The use of trail shortcuts is a violation of Federal law. If backcountry users try to leave the land unchanged and try to distribute themselves over wide areas, they will delay the imposition of more regulations.

All wilderness areas are closed to motorized and mechanical use, so chainsaws, bicycles, motorcycles, and motorboats are prohibited. This book includes hikes in the Hells Canyon Wilderness and a few hikes at the southern border of the River of No Return Wilderness. Some other areas such as the Pioneer Mountains may be classified as wilderness in the future.

Where registration boxes and cards or forms are found at trailheads, please register, since this helps the Forest Service plan maintenance.

SAFETY

ALWAYS LEAVE WORD

The hiker should always leave information with someone at home telling in detail where he will be each day and when he will return. If far from home, leave word also at the nearest ranger station or Bureau of Land Management office. Be sure to check back with this office upon return from the trip.

HYPOTHERMIA

Beware of hypothermia, which is the lowering of the body temperature in cold and wet conditions. Hypothermia is the biggest danger when outdoors, even in the desert, and can occur even in temperatures above freezing.

To prevent hypothermia, warm clothing and shelter are important. Wear warm clothes, including a wool hat and gloves, keep dry, and eat regularly. An uncovered head can lose up to 50% of the body's heat production at 40 degrees and up to 75% of the heat at 5 degrees. Raingear is essential. Wet clothing can take heat from the body up to 32 times faster than dry clothing. Wool, polarguard, or synthetic pile clothing stays warmer than down or cotton when wet. Down collapses and becomes useless if wet. Wear fabrics that "breathe" so water vapor won't condense in clothing. Sweat dampens clothing, so remove extra clothes when active to avoid sweating; replace the clothing immediately when resting.

The wind chill factor dramatically lowers the effective temperature, so wear windproof clothes or stay out of the wind. The higher the wind velocity, the greater the heat loss. When conditions first become threateningly cold, make camp and build a fire. Be sure to carry an emergency shelter (such as a tube tent and 20 feet of nylon cord for it) on a day hike. In camp remember that sitting on cold rock causes heat loss. Skin contact with super-cooled liquid stove fuel can cause hypothermia and frostbite. Most hypothermia fatalities result from cold, wet, and windy conditions.

Persistent shivering is the first danger signal of hypothermia. This is closely followed by confusion and stumbling. The shivering person's wet clothes must be changed and he or she must be put into a warm sleeping bag. If the person is only semi-conscious, he must be stripped and placed in the sleeping bag with another stripped person in order to be warmed as quickly as possible. Hypothermia can be fatal and is caused partly by the hiker's own lack of awareness of danger.

HIKER'S DANGER TO HIMSELF

Not all injuries can be prevented, but sensible precautions can reduce the number. The hiker can help prevent falls by some of

the following measures.
- Do not run or allow children to run on rocky, uneven ground.
- Wear hiking boots with non-slip soles.
- Use special care when there is gravel on rock pavement because the gravel acts like ball bearings.
- Be sure packs are not loaded so high above the head that they tend to unbalance the hiker.
- Leave rock climbing to trained mountaineers.
- Tie markers to tent guylines or use white guylines.
- If the trail or route is lost, it is safer for the hiker to turn back than to go cross-country or off route unless a member of the party is an expert with map and compass.

There are several other dangers to the hiker including axes, hunting knives, and guns. Only hunters in hunting season need guns and hunting knives. Otherwise they are an unnecessary hazard. Usually an ample supply of firewood can be found on the ground within walking distance of camp, so the hiker will not need an axe. Preschool children should be watched constantly, especially near water.

FIRST AID

Someone in the party should have had a course in first aid, or at least have thoroughly read and have with him the Red Cross text-book on first aid. In the event someone is injured, the Red Cross says first to be sure the victim is breathing. If not, be sure he has an open airway and then give mouth-to-mouth resuscitation. Next, control bleeding. Don't move the victim unless it is necessary to keep him from further injury. Cover the victim with a sleeping bag or jackets and treat for shock.

Then after deciding what seems to be the matter, the leader can determine what to do. The action taken will depend on the seriousness of the injury, size of the party, and distance from a trailhead. In case of serious injury, send for help. It is best to have a party of at least three people, so that one can stay with the victim while the other goes for help. If the party is large enough, a person who is unable to walk can be carried out on a litter made of poles inserted into a sleeping bag, which has the stitching ripped out at the foot. A person with a suspected back or neck injury should only be moved by professional rescuers.

CROSS-COUNTRY TRAVEL

To gain the necessary skill for cross-country travel, hikers should practice several days with topographic map and compass while following trails. Off-trail hiking is an excellent way for experienced hikers to avoid crowds and disperse use. Some off-trail areas may be closed to horse travel, so if planning off-trail travel with horses, check with a ranger first.

TRAVELING WITH THE COMPASS

Every trail traveler should have with him the U. S. Geological Survey topographic map or maps for the area. Be sure to check with a ranger in advance of the trip on trail conditions, since some trails (and roads) shown on the older topo maps no longer exist. In addition, some current trails do not appear on the topographic maps. With the detailed topographic maps, a person can concentrate at all times on knowing where he is. A hiker who knows his location on the map will usually not get confused or lost.

Before starting on the trail, orient the topographic map by placing the compass on the map so that the north-pointing compass needle is parallel with the side edge of the map. (Top of the map should be to the north.) Check the angle of declination shown at the bottom of the map (about 19 degrees in Idaho). Turn the compass dial this 19 degrees counter-clockwise. Now the compass needle will be pointing 19 degrees east of north, but the north mark on the dial will be pointing north. Turn the map so the side edges parallel the north-south line on the compass dial. Along the trail, the hiker should know where he is on the map. Remember that panic can kill, so if lost, stay put, build a fire, and make camp. With the map, calmly try to figure out your location. If unable to do this, wait for rescue.

MINE SHAFTS

There are many old mine shafts and tunnels in Idaho's back-country. Stay away from these and watch children closely near the shafts and tunnels. Mine shafts may not always be evident on the surface. For example, a shaft may be hidden under the apparent ruins of an old cabin.

HIKING ALONE

Hiking alone always has an element of danger. No one can be sure he won't break a leg or cut an artery so he needs someone to treat him for shock or bleeding and go for help. Experienced hikers occasionally do go alone. Special precautions should be taken by a solo traveler, such as carrying food for a few extra days, taking plenty of warm clothes, and carrying water. A person will die much sooner from lack of water than from lack of food. The length of time varies with the person, his physical activity, and the temperature and weather. If a hiker is injured, he may not be able to get to water. Even on a day hike, the lone hiker should take a tent, stove and fuel, sleeping bag, signal flares, and survival kit if the area gets little travel. Avoid going cross-country alone; if injured in thick forest, a hiker might never be found.

TEN ESSENTIALS

Every hiker should always carry these ten things:
1. Extra clothes (long pants, sweater, quilted parka, rain jacket or poncho and rain pants or chaps, wool hat, wool gloves)
2. Extra food beyond the needs of the trip
3. Pocket knife
4. Waterproof matches or butane lighter
5. Firestarter (purchased stick or jelly type, or homemade from paraffin and corrugated cardboard)
6. First aid kit including prescription pain medication
7. Flashlight with extra bulb and batteries
8. Topographic map
9. Compass and knowledge of how to use it
10. Sunglasses

CONDITIONING

A physical exam and several weeks of regular exercise should precede the first trip of the summer. The conditioning should include aerobic exercise such as running or swimming. Three days at the trailhead should be allowed to get accustomed to the altitude if possible. Respiratory and biochemical adjustments for altitude are completed by the body in eight days. Red blood cell increase to adapt to a higher altitude takes several weeks. Those living at 2500 feet and above will need less time to adjust than those living at sea level. Altitude sickness can cause headache, nausea, and even life-threatening pulmonary edema.

The fatigue of those out of condition can lead to accidents. Lack of conditioning and trying to hike too far and too fast can cause altitude sickness and even a heart attack. For optimum safety on the trail, the hiker should keep his pulse under 130. If chest pains occur in the mountains, they aren't necessarily caused by heart problems, but should be investigated by a doctor. Another cause can be inflamed rib joints caused by the deep breathing of vigorous exercise. Digestive disturbances can also cause chest pains.

STREAM CROSSING

Crossing a stream or river is often the most dangerous part of wilderness travel. If there is any doubt whether a crossing is safe, detour upstream to cross where the stream is smaller, turn back, or change the destination. If detouring, remember that cross-country travel takes 1½ to 2 times as much time and energy as trail travel. When detouring do not attempt to pass cliffs at the edge of the stream. Logs floating down the creek indicate dangerously high water. Large mountain creeks are often not safe until after July 15 in an average year. Check the topographic map in advance for possible problem stream crossings. Then check beforehand with a ranger to be sure of probable conditions at these crossings. Desert creeks may not be safe until after June 15. Rivers are rarely ever safe. If a stream is snow-fed, the water will be lowest in early morning.

Wading across on gravel in a wide part of the stream is the safest crossing. Rocks or logs can be very slippery. Keep boots and socks on when wading to prevent injury to feet numbed by cold water and to help with footing. If wearing a backpack, unfasten the hip belt. Face upstream and lean into the current. Use a stick to help with balance, placing it upstream with each step. Move one foot at a time sideways. First find secure footing for the lead foot and step onto it. Then place the stick in a new position. Move the following foot last. This way there are always two points of support. (Walking sticks are needed in the backcountry only to help with stream crossings and not for normal travel.) Change to dry socks once across the stream to prevent blisters.

WATER

The only way to be sure water is safe to drink is to boil it for at least five minutes at a *full rolling boil,* because pure mountain water can become contaminated at any time.   The purification method using drops of an iodine solution, obtained by mixing water with iodine crystals, kills most bacteria and viruses, but takes 20 to 30 minutes. This method will not kill the protozoal cysts of giardia lamblia, and may not kill the cysts of amoebic dysentery.

Diarrhea caused by giardia is becoming more common in Idaho because of increased backcountry use. Giardiasis, although not serious, is miserable. Up to 20% of the population may be carriers who have no symptoms. The incubation period is from 6 days to 4 weeks. This protozoa is also found in dogs, antelope, beaver, and bighorn sheep. There were 45 reported cases in the first nine months of 1979 in southwestern Idaho. When car camping or day hiking, it will probably be easiest to bring water from home.

In desert areas the only safe and practical course is to carry all water needed.   Thus in desert hiking, canned goods become practical if the contents are consumed juice and all. Of course, the empty cans must be carried out. In desert areas, water sources may be dried up, or they may be contaminated with alkali, mud, or minerals like mercury from old mine tailings.

BEARS

The black bear is the only bear found in the areas of Idaho covered by this book. However the Idaho Fish and Game Department reports that there have been sightings of grizzlies recently in the Hells Canyon Wilderness and the Salmon National Forest. Black bears may be any color from black to blonde, but have no

Taking a few moments for fishing near Kane Lake (Challis N.F.)

shoulder hump like grizzlies, and their claws are black. Few bears in remote areas will come near humans or campsites.

To prevent any possibility of bear problems, it is best to hang all food in a tree at night and keep food away from sleeping areas. Hang the food in a heavy closed plastic bag inside a stout cloth sack at least 12 feet from the ground, 5 to 10 feet from the tree trunk, and 5 feet below any branch. Keep the campsite clean. Burn all scraps and fish guts and hang any garbage including empty food packets with the food. Burn tampons and sanitary napkins. If a campsite is dirty, choose a different one or clean it up. Keep food out of tents, and pitch tents at a distance from the cooking area.

If a bear is encountered, give it room, walk slowly, and talk calmly. The bear will probably soon leave. Mother black bears with cubs can be dangerous. It should be obvious that feeding bears is very foolish. The main problem the hiker is likely to have in southwestern Idaho with bears is their getting into food, and this seldom happens.

SNAKES

The western rattlesnake *(croatalus viridis)* is found in Idaho desert areas, usually but not always at elevations lower than 5200 feet and rarely above 7000 feet. This snake has different background colors in different locations: pink, grey, green, or brown. The snake has diamond or hexagonal brown to black splotches. When hiking in the desert wear boots and long pants and look carefully before stepping or placing hands. This snake will usually crawl away when a person comes near it and strikes only when cornered or unusually frightened. The snake won't necessarily crawl away at once. Rattlesnakes often come out at night in the hot summer months. They like temperatures between 80 degrees and 90 degrees best, but are often active at higher and lower temperatures. Night temperatures near and below freezing in the spring and fall greatly reduce rattlesnake activity, however.

Do not attempt to treat a bite except with a constricting band (not a tourniquet) and bed rest. Most doctors do not recommend use of antivenin in the field because of the danger of allergic reaction. Studies have shown that the use of ice causes more tissue damage than the old fashioned cut and suck method. The cut and suck method often damages tendons, blood vessels, or nerves, especially in the hand and foot areas. This method usually causes more damage than benefit. In about half the snake bites, little or no venom is injected anyway.

SCORPIONS

Scorpions are found under rocks in the Idaho desert and come out at night. The variety found here stings a little more strongly than a bee and a bite should be treated as a bee sting.

TICKS

Ticks are found in the spring and early summer in all Idaho areas. They look similar to small watermelon seeds. In season a hiker should examine himself at least once a day for ticks. Long pants and long-sleeved shirts with tight cuffs will help keep off ticks. Ticks can carry Rocky Mountain Spotted Fever or tularemia, both of which can be cured by antibiotics.

Ticks crawl around on a person for several hours before starting to bite. When they do bite, they burrow painlessly into the skin. Ticks can be encouraged to back out by applying insect repellent, white gas, or a just-extinguished match. It may be necessary to pull the tick out with tweezers. In that case, consult a doctor after the trip.

BUBONIC PLAGUE

In Idaho, bubonic plague is endemic in rodents, whose fleas carry the germs. Therefore, do not handle chipmunks or ground squirrels.

POISON IVY OR OAK

Rhus radicans, correctly called poison ivy, is the only species of poison ivy or oak in Idaho. Locally, people may call the plant either poison ivy or poison oak. In Idaho, poison ivy appears either as a shrub or a plant and grows mainly in desert canyons. The shrub can be identified by its shiny leaflets occurring in groups of three. Another species, *rhus diversiloba* or poison oak, appears only along the Pacific Coast and not in Idaho.

All species have the same poison and will cause the same blisters and itching. Scrub with strong soap and cold water immediately after exposure to avoid the effects. The best prevention is to avoid the plant. If blisters appear, cortisone ointment may help relieve the itching.

SPECIAL PRECAUTIONS FOR DESERT AREAS

GETTING STUCK

Be sure that the vehicle to be used is in excellent condition. If planning to drive on dirt roads, take a Bureau of Land Management map, topographic maps, and a compass. Also take a shovel, pick, tow chain, 50 feet of tow rope, instant tire repair kit, axe, duct tape, water, spare parts (such as a fan belt), and tools. Stay on the main roads and don't drive on desert primitive roads until about May 1. Rain makes these roads like grease, so don't drive primitive roads in threatening weather. (High mountain primitive roads are often not passable until July 15.) Leave word at home of the destination and timetable and stick to the route. It is wise to explore bad roads only uphill, never downhill. Check washes and fords on foot in advance.

A high wheelbase vehicle, such as a pickup, is recommended for primitive roads. Such roads tend to damage passenger cars. A vehicle with four-wheel drive and a winch would be ideal. Most small four-wheel drive vehicles don't have a high enough wheelbase for some of these roads. If the vehicle becomes stuck, wait in it for rescue unless in a very remote area. Owyhee County is 7600 square miles and has only one sheriff and about two deputies. They do patrol by air, however.

To be prepared to wait for rescue, take plenty of food and water, jackets and sleeping bags. Hypothermia can occur in the desert, too, especially in spring and fall, since desert nights are cold.

Avoid traveling Idaho desert areas in July and August because of high temperatures.

SUNSTROKE

Sunstroke is a life-threatening emergency, and should be treated by immersing the victim in cold water if possible, or covering him with cool, wet cloths. Symptoms of sunstroke are: no sweating, hot dry skin, temperature above 105 degrees, and possibly unconsciousness. Get the person to a doctor as soon as possible. Sunstroke can be prevented by drinking enough water and consuming enough salt, resting in the shade in the hottest part of the day, and wearing a hat.

HEAT EXHAUSTION

The person suffering from heat exhaustion has pale, moist, cool skin and a low temperature. He may vomit or faint. Treatment consists of having him drink slightly salted water and lie down.

DEHYDRATION

Dehydration can cause serious symptoms such as delirium, which may cause a person to wander away and become lost. A gallon of water a day should be consumed during spring and fall desert hiking. The party should carry this water, as water sources are uncertain and may be alkaline. Symptoms of dehydration are thirst, slow motion, lack of appetite, drowsiness, and high temperature. Water is more important than salt. Don't consume salt unless water is available. Don't rely on making a solar still or finding water by digging in a dry streambed. Solar stills make only about a pint of water a day when they work, and in unskilled hands they often don't work at all. Dehydration in cold weather reduces blood flow to the extremities and increases the danger of frostbite.

GEOLOGY

The basic feature of the geology of Idaho's mountains is the Idaho batholith, which stretches from the Boise Ridge north to Kellogg and is one of the largest batholiths in the world. A batholith is a large mass of igneous rock which formed under the surface of the ground. Idaho's 100-mile wide by 300-mile long block of quartz mixed with granodiorite and basalt is a remnant of the original Rocky Mountains. These mountains arose in the Cretaceous geological period at the end of the Mesozoic era 100 million years ago. This was the first major change in Idaho's geology.

Before the batholith formed, Idaho was mainly a region of seas and swamps. However, the Seven Devils volcanics, underlying that mountain range, formed earlier, in the Permian period about 260 million years ago. Also mountain formation called the Nevada uplift occurred in the western Snake River region in the Jurassic period.

During the cooling of the hot magma of the Idaho batholith, molten minerals flowed from the cooling liquid into nearby rocks to form many ore deposits. At the end of the Cretaceous period after the 25,000-foot high original Rockies formed, the temperature of the earth dropped six degrees for an unknown reason. Most of the animals then alive, such as the dinosaurs, became extinct.

The Cenezoic era began 70 million years ago and consisted of the Paleocene, Eocene, Oligocene, Miocene, and Pliocene epochs of the Tertiary period and the Pleistocene epoch of the Quaternary period. During the Eocene epoch, erosion of the original Rockies was completed. Volcanoes began to erupt while lava flowed from cracks in the earth. This volcanic activity has continued to the present time. Redwood trees grew here in the Eocene, because no western mountains then blocked the rain clouds when they came in from the Pacific. Therefore, the climate was much wetter than it is today. At this time, the Sawtooth batholith pushed up under the older Idaho batholith rocks in the Sawtooth range. Mountain ranges that run north and south (the Lost River Range, Pioneers, and Sawtooths) were uplifted by block-faulting of Paleozoic sediments and Cretaceous granite. The Challis volcanics of the Oligocene covered most of these original ranges before uplift continued.

Three million years ago in the Miocene epoch, the Columbia River basalts poured over the Snake River plain, damming rivers into huge lakes. One of these was geologic Payette Lake, which filled the Boise Valley and created the sand for the Bruneau Sand Dunes. Table Rock just above Boise is the remains of a lake terrace of this lake. The vast sheets of lava covered an area 30 by 60 miles. Elephants roamed among hardwood forests around the sheets of lava. Mountains gradually rose around the drainage of the Snake River to become the Bitterroots and the Wallowas. In the Cretaceous, granitic rocks intruded into Permian volcanics and sediments of the Seven Devils. Then these were eroded, folded, and covered by Columbia River basalts of the Miocene. Later the peaks were lifted up by block faulting and sculptured by erosion.

In the Pliocene epoch, the Snake River Valley sank 300 to 400 feet in a crescent shape along earthquake faults. The Continental Divide, the Blue Mountains, and Seven Devils Mountains arose. Lava flows, called the Snake River basalts, continued in the Snake River plain and created the final course of the river. Tributaries flowing from the north into the river became ''lost'' in the fissured lava and formed the Snake River

Indian Bathtub (Boise District, Bureau of Land Management)

aquifer, one of the largest underground reservoirs in the world. The rivers emerge into the Snake at Thousand Springs near Buhl. Vegetation gradually became much more like the present, as the area became drier when the Cascades were created.

In the Pleistocene, the climate became wetter and cooler, which caused glaciers to form on four occasions. The Stanley Basin was full of ice, while even the Owyhees felt the nibble of small summit glaciers. Glaciers scooped out most of Idaho's mountain lakes and formed hanging valleys like that at Hum Lake near McCall. During this epoch, more minerals were deposited in rock fractures. The mountains in Idaho are so high now that a long-term drop of only a few degrees in temperature would create glaciers again.

The Snake River is 20 million years old. Man probably came to Idaho 30,000 years ago by way of Canada and Alaska over a land or ice bridge. About 20,000 years ago, geologic Lake Bonneville in Utah overflowed and washed huge boulders from the canyon walls along the Snake River in its flood water. These boulders scattered as far west as Homedale, Idaho. The most recent volcanic activity in Idaho was at Craters of the Moon about 2000 years ago. Sudden geologic events still occur such as the forming of a lake out of the town of Roosevelt by a landslide in 1909, the creating of "Sinking Canyon" near Buhl in the 1930s when a bubble in volcanic rocks collapsed, and the deposition of volcanic ash in northern Idaho from the 1980 eruption of Mt. St. Helens in Washington.

In the Hells Canyon area, the Columbia River basalts filled depressions up to 2000 feet deep. The exact origin of Hells Canyon is unknown. Some geologists theorize that the canyon was the outlet of a huge lake formed on the Snake plain by the Columbia River basalts. They think this outlet cut the deep canyon as mountains were uplifted about it. Another theory is that the original canyon was cut by another river, such as a tributary of the Salmon, which by erosion intersected the Snake and diverted its water.

Besides metals, Idaho has many precious and semi-precious stones such as jasper, opal, agate, petrified wood, garnet, sapphire, quartz crystal, amethyst, and ruby. From these riches, Idaho has been nicknamed the "Gem State". Many of these gems occur in the area covered by this book. For information about rock hunting sites, consult *Gem Minerals of Idaho* by John Beckwith. Some are on private land or mining claims not open to the public.

BOTANY

Idaho has a wide variety of trees, shrubs, and plants due to its diverse terrain. The state flower is the syringa (*Philadelphus lewsii*). This spring-blooming shrub grows up to 10 feet tall and has ½ inch wide four-petalled white flowers with a fragrant odor. Whole hillsides bloom with syringa during the month of June.

The state tree is the white pine (*pinus monticola*), well-known for its soft white wood that is unusually free of knots. The white pine is the most valuable timber tree in Idaho. Needles in groups of five and slender cones 5 to 8 inches long identify this tree.

To know the plants and trees of Idaho, books such as *Rocky Mountain Trees* by Richard Preston, Jr. and *Field Guide to Rocky Mountain Wildflowers* by John Craighead, Frank Craighead, and Ray Davis are helpful.

The life zone names such as Upper Sonoran, Transition, and Canadian often used in other states become confusing in Idaho because of the varied terrain. Therefore in Idaho, zones are named for their typical plants or trees. Because of the varied landscape and the difference in sun exposure between south and north facing slopes, the life zones in Idaho may not all be present as altitude increases.

IDAHO PLANT ZONES

1. *Sagebrush-grass:* big sagebrush, buckbrush, horsebrush, grasses, greasewood, hop sage, shadscale, winterfat, rabbitbrush.

2. *Wheatgrass-bluegrass:* Bluebunch wheatgrass, Idaho fescue, Sandberg's bluegrass; few flowering plants, no wild rose or snowberry. This is prairie land found now in the Salmon, Clearwater, and Snake River Valleys.

3. *Fescue-wheatgrass:* little sunflower, balsamroot, paint-

brush, sego lily, lupine, geranium. In northern Idaho: wild rose, snowberry, chokecherry, cottonwood, hawthorn. This also is prairie, so shrubs tend to be dwarfed. There are mostly plants and grasses.

4. *Oak-mountain mahogany:* mountain mahogany, bitterbrush, serviceberry, buckbrush. No conifers. Mainly southeast Idaho. There are no oaks in this zone in Idaho.

5. *Pinyon-juniper:* juniper, pinyon pine, limber pine. No ponderosa pine. South of Snake River.

6. *Ponderosa (yellow) pine:* No other conifers. Grasses and plants, ninebark, spirea, wild rose, serviceberry. This is the lowest forest zone north of the Snake River.

7. *Douglas fir:* pine grass, elk sedge, serviceberry, bitter cherry, wild rose, buckbrush, mountain spray. Lodgepole and larch invade after a fire. No grand fir, spruce, or subalpine fir. Next higher forest zone above ponderosa.

8. *Arbor vitae (red cedar)-hemlock:* Only north of the Salmon River so not found in areas covered by this book. Grand fir, yew, western white pine; spruce and fir uncommon.

9. *Spruce-fir:* subalpine fir, fool's huckleberry, Engelmann spruce, grouse whortleberry, white-flowered rhododendron, woodrush. In southern Idaho, Douglas fir and lodgepole pine are the most common trees in this zone. This is the next higher forest zone above the Douglas fir zone.

10. *Alpine:* No true alpine zone in Idaho. Only a few crevice plants and lichens: mountain sorrel, mountain avens, alpine timothy, moss campion, dwarf willow, saxifrage. Misshapen whitebark and limber pine grow just below timberline which is at 10,000 feet in southern Idaho, and decreases to 7,000 feet at the Canadian border.

WILDLIFE

Idaho is not well-marked geographically, so it borrows types of wildlife from neighboring areas as well as having some unique subspecies. The state has many species of waterfowl, 24 species of game birds and animals, and 20 species of game fish. Idaho has some of the best deer and elk hunting in the United States.

Mammals typical of certain Idaho areas are as follows:

low sagebrush deserts: pocket mouse, sagebrush chipmunk, Townsend's ground squirrel, black-tailed jackrabbit

grassland: pocket gopher, meadow mouse, antelope, white-tailed jackrabbit

ponderosa pine forest: red squirrel, mule deer

spruce-fir forest: flying squirrel, red-backed mouse, snowshoe hare *subalpine forests and meadows:*   pika, golden mantle ground squirrel

rocky peaks and cliffs: mountain goat, bighorn sheep

Craters of the Moon: blackish chipmunks and pocket mice to match the black rocks

Some of Idaho's animals are interesting or unique such as the Idaho ground squirrel, found only in Idaho. This squirrel is dappled grey-brown on its upper parts and lives on dry, rocky open ridges in Adams and Washington counties. The buds of wild onions are its favorite food.

The pronghorn antelope is interesting because its white rump patch forms a signalling device. The antelope can raise and spread these hairs to form a type of reflector.

Idaho's bighorn sheep have caused controversy. In 1972 a researcher went into the Salmon River range in central Idaho to see why 50% of the bighorn sheep there had disappeared in ten years. When he announced that his study showed that the cause was overgrazing by stock, people tried to shoot him. California bighorn used to roam the Owyhees but had been gone from the area for 100 years when the BLM transplanted some to re-establish herds. Recently the nearness of the largest bighorn sheep herd in Idaho to the largest cobalt deposit in the nation caused conflict in establishing the River of No Return Wilderness Area.

The Birds of Prey Area has the largest concentration of raptors in North America. Bald and golden eagles, peregrine falcons (an endangered species), prairie falcons (a rare species), and various hawks all live here.

Another bird, the greater sandhill crane (a rare species) lives in marshes remote from man in the Boise, Challis, and Sawtooth forests. The bird is grey, long-necked, and long-legged with a red crown and trumpet-like cry. The sandhill crane can injure or blind a person with its heavy bill if provoked.

Two of Idaho's fish are especially interesting. The kokanee is a true salmon, but lives only in fresh water, returning to lakes rather than the ocean. There are two types of kokanee. One is the type found in Redfish Lake. This is a native fish and has bright red flesh. The kokanee found in the large lakes of northern Idaho migrated there from Flathead Lake and has paler flesh. This fish is an important food for the enormous kamloops and mackinaw lake trout found in the big northern Idaho lakes.

Another fish, the white sturgeon, lives in Idaho only in the Snake River and is the largest freshwater fish in North America. It can grow up to 13 feet. It looks like a shark but has no teeth. The sturgeon eats insect larvae, crayfish, clams and snails from the river bottom through a mouth that resembles a vacuum cleaner attachment. A catch and release program now protects sturgeon.

Devils Tooth, (Seven Devils area)

HELLS CANYON NATIONAL RECREATION AND WILDERNESS AREAS

HELLS CANYON AREA

HISTORY OF SEVEN DEVILS —

NAMES

Early trappers indirectly named the Snake River when they called the Shoshoni Indians the "Snake Indians". Some say the name was a misinterpretation of Shoshoni sign language for "weavers of grass lodges". Other writers say the Plains Indians named the Shoshoni for the sticks painted with snakes that they used to frighten neighboring tribes. Early maps labeled Hells Canyon the Grand Canyon of the Snake. Some early travelers referred to it as Box Canyon.

Early boatmen likened the passage through Hells Canyon to a trip through hell. However, this name wasn't widely used until a controversy over dams surfaced in the 1950s.

The exact origin of the name Seven Devils is lost in time. One version says that Indians gave the peaks that name from a legend which told of a lost Indian who saw devils in the mountains.

INDIANS

The Indians of the area were of the Nez Perce tribe. The name Nez Perce meaning "pierced nose" was given by the French trappers. The tribe, however, has no tradition of nose piercing. A small group of Nez Perce controlled Hells Canyon from the Imnaha to the upper end at the time settlers began to come into the area. Along the river, petroglyphs and pictographs line the rocks, and Indian rock shelter remnants lie scattered. The most interesting Indian trail is the Old Boise Trail, the trail along the eastern side of the Seven Devils. This route is still in use today, even though much of it has been rerouted.

The Nez Perce Indians who lived in the Wallowa Valley under Chief Joseph crossed the Snake River during spring flood in 1877 at Dug Bar. They were on their way to the Lapwai Reservation upon General Oliver Howard's orders. Members of another band of Nez Perces, under White Bird, murdered some settlers, so

General Howard sent troops. These troops met the Indians' white flag of truce with bullets. Thus began the dramatic saga of the 1000-mile flight of Chief Joseph and White Bird and their people to escape to freedom in Canada. The journey ended in tragedy and surrender on Joseph's part just south of the Canadian border, although White Bird and his band escaped.

EARLY EXPLORERS

Although part of Lewis and Clark's party fished the lower end of the canyon in 1806, guided by Indians, the members of the Wilson Price Hunt party in 1811 were the first white men to see the rougher, upper section of Hells Canyon. The Hunt party entered the canyon at Manns Creek, but were turned back from following it by the cliffs. Part of their group traveled from the Oxbow to the Salmon-Snake confluence by way of Six Lake Basin and Rapid River. One of the members of the expedition was Donald Mackenzie, a huge and powerful man.

In March 1819, Mackenzie and his party dragged a barge UP Hells Canyon as far as what he called Point Successful, believed to be close to the present Hells Canyon Dam. The boats of his Northwest Company never used his route since the company found it easier to ship materials across the Blue Mountains by pack train.

Another famous early explorer who entered Hells Canyon was Captain Bonneville. His party went down the river in 1833 on horseback as far as Thirty-two Point Creek and then out up the Imnaha River.

MINING

Levi Allen of the Stubadore Company began the mining history of the area by discovering the Peacock Copper Lode southwest of Cuprum in 1862 on a prospecting trip. No one mined the lode until Albert Kleinschmidt bought the claim in 1885. A settlement, Helena, grew up below the mine. Other mines in the area, such as the Blue Jacket, were opened both by Kleinschmidt's company and others. Towns like Landore, Decorah, and Cuprum sprang up at these mines.

Kleinschmidt had a great plan to ship ore from his mines down the river to Lewiston by boat, so in 1889 he had a road built from the mines down to the river. When the road was completed in 1891, he had a paddlewheel steamboat built, the *Norma*, to carry the ore. She made only two runs because Kleinschmidt sold his stock for shares in a new mining company. The new company became involved in lawsuits just as the price of copper fell. Finally Captain William Gray in 1895 took the ship down river to Portland.

After Kleinschmidt, the other miners in the area hoped that the railroad would reach Helena or Landore. By the time the railroad was built, the copper boom had faded, so the route was changed to reach New Meadows in 1911. A smelter was built at Landore in 1904 but lost money due to poor design. There is still an active copper mine at Cuprum, the site of another early smelter.

Other mining settlements were at Black Lake, Placer Basin, and Rankin Mill. An aerial tramway crossed Black Lake from the mine high above the lake to the mill below. The mill and town below it were scrapped and burned during World War II. A mill for the Placer Basin Mine was built in the 1930s and took out $3 million in gold. The foundations of this mill still stand beside the Black Lake Road near Smith Mountain. Rankin Mill on Rapid River was the site of a mill and a nitric acid factory, both of which failed.

People worked various mines and prospects along the river in Hells Canyon, such as the gold mine at Battle Creek, from time to time. The developers of a mining camp called Eureka at the mouth of the Imnaha in 1902 kept secret the fact that there was no valuable ore in the area. In the spring of 1887, thirty-two Chinese miners were murdered, probably for their gold, at the mouth of Deep Creek. The murders were discovered when the bodies washed down to Lewiston. Three of six men indicted by a grand jury were tried, but finally were acquitted. Years later, someone found a flask of gold at Deep Creek.

NAVIGATION

The first attempt at navigation was made by the 136-foot paddlewheel steamship, *Shoshone*, which was built at Old Fort Boise in 1866. The ship made runs up to Owyhee Ferry and down to Olds Ferry. However, that winter it was impossible to get enough wood to power the boilers. By spring the railroad was completed to Winnemucca, so Idaho travelers no longer had to go by way of Portland. Captain Silas Smith piloted the boat down the Snake as far as Lime Point in 1869. Sebastian Miller took her the rest of the way to the Columbia in April 1870. She lost eight feet of the bow going down Copper Creek Falls, but successfully reached the Columbia.

An attempt at regular river transportation on the lower river was made in 1903-1904 when the *Imnaha* went up and down the canyon from Lewiston to the mines at the mouth of the Imnaha. The boatmen used cables attached to rings in the rock on the side of the canyon to pass rapids. Even though they had blasted rock at Mt. Sheep Rapids to make a wider passage, the boat sank there in 1904 when the lining cable became entangled with the paddlewheel. Successful navigation began in 1910 when Ed McFarlane started a boat transportation service on the Snake with the 36-foot gas powered *Flyer* which went from Asotin to Pittsburg Landing.

RIVER RUNNING

It wasn't long before people were braving the rapids in small boats and rafts. Amos Burg ran the river with John Mullen in a canoe in 1925, although they lined three rapids. In 1939 Buzz Holmstrom took a woman, Edith Clegg, through the canyon as part of a trans-continental trip by river. They used 14-foot flat-bottomed wooden boats. Five parties ran the river in the 1940s. The first river runners used wooden boats and the later ones used rubber rafts.

In 1954, Georgie White, a woman, started a river running business in the canyon. Other commercial river runners soon followed, as well as service by jet boats. Jet boats fare better than conventional motor boats in rapids because their working parts are inside the boat.

SETTLERS

Many of the people who lived in the canyon and in the Seven Devils were colorful characters. In the early 1870s, Hannibal Johnson came to the Seven Devils to mine. His poems, which were published in book form in 1895, reflect the flavor and humor of the mining camps and the beauty of the mountains. He was also an early-day legislator.

One of the most interesting ranchers was Martin Hibbs who moved to Granite Creek in 1902 with his wife and six children. His wife, Ellen, once had to be taken out to a doctor. To do this she was strapped to a log stretcher between two mules. Someone murdered Hibbs on the site many years later and burned his cabin. The body of an itinerant prospector was found in the ashes. A second prospector was suspected of the murder. Hibbs was Ace Barton's grandfather. Ace is a co-author of the fascinating book of history on Hells Canyon called *Snake River of Hells Canyon.*

Then there was Len Jordan, Idaho governor and U. S. senator, who lived at Kirkwood Bar during the Depression with his wife, Grace, and their three children. Grace told of their life in her book *Home Below Hells Canyon.*

DAMS IN HELLS CANYON

As soon as Idaho Power Company was formed in 1915, it began to try to get permission to build dams in Hells Canyon. The Army Corps of Engineers advocated a "high dam" of 600 feet. Idaho Congresswoman Gracie Pfost earned the nickname "Hell's Belle" when she introduced legislation in the 1950s for a high federal dam and fought for it. Idaho Power eventually obtained permits for three low dams: Brownlee, Oxbow, and Hells Canyon. Hells Canyon, the last built, was completed in 1968. These three dams erased the most difficult of the rapids, including Buck Creek and

Stone cabin at Bills Creek

Copper Ledge Falls. The dams also destroyed the Snake River salmon and steelhead runs when fish ladders proved inadequate.

HELLS CANYON NATIONAL RECREATION AREA

Attempts to get permits for dams in the lower canyon led to the formation of the Hells Canyon National Recreation Area. Four private utility companies formed Pacific Northwest Power Company and 18 city power systems consolidated into Washington Public Power Supply System. Both began applying for permits to build dams on the lower part of the canyon in the mid-1950s. Finally in 1964 the Federal Power Commission granted a permit to Pacific Northwest Power for the High Mt. Sheep Dam. The Interior Department, which favored a federal dam, and WPPSS took the case to the U. S. Supreme Court. The matter was remanded for rehearing in 1967. At that time the Hells Canyon Preservation Council was formed. Senators Frank Church and Len Jordan introduced a bill to create a ten year moratorium on dam construction on the Snake River in 1968.

In 1969 the new Secretary of the Interior, Walter Hickel, changed the position of the department to oppose any dams in the canyon. In 1972, the Senate appropriated $4 million to the Forest Service to buy private land in the canyon, which was endangered by developers. In 1973 Idaho and Oregon senators introduced the Hells Canyon National Recreation Area Bill, which was finally passed in 1975.

HELLS CANYON NATIONAL RECREATION TRAIL

HELLS CANYON:
Birch Springs (Butler Bar) to Bernard Creek

1

One-way distance: 10 miles
Elevation gain: 1100 feet estimated
Elevation loss: 1180 feet estimated
Highest point: 2000 feet
Topo map: He Devil (15′)
Time: 7 hours (part of four day through trip)
Access: Drive 64 miles northwest of Cambridge, Idaho on paved
   Hwy. 71 to Hells Canyon Dam. Take jet boat 3.5 miles to Brush
   Creek. Walk or take jet boat 3 more miles to Birch Springs.
Difficulty: Strenuous

In Hells Canyon, rust brown and dark grey cliffs leap out of the
yellow-green Snake River and terrace upward thousands of feet. A
mantle of soft grass, green in the spring, and golden the rest of the
year, covers the slopes between the cliffs. The river swirls along in
eddies under the cliffs, then breaks into the uproar of rapids.
Occasionally a flat river terrace, called a bar, green with grass and
parklike with ponderosa pines, edges the river. Larger fan-shaped
bars mark the entry of side creeks. Granite and Bernard Creeks,
which tumble 5500 feet out of the Seven Devils in less than 5 miles,
roar down little canyons through a tangle of netleaf hackberry,
chokecherry, and syringa.

In May, the 1½-inch white flowers of the Bartonberry, a
thornless raspberry that grows only in Hells Canyon, decorate the
trail. This bush is named after Ace Barton's mother, who first
brought the plant to the attention of botanists. In early spring
pastel flowers like pink grass widows and blue hyacincths
embroider the grass. Between them grow tiny "belly flowers"
(flowers so small the viewer can see them best while lying on his
belly). Side canyons mold triangular hills out of the canyon walls.
Sagebrush grows in most desert areas in Idaho but no sagebrush is
found in Hells Canyon. Especially in the spring the hiker may see
mountain goats and bighorn sheep on ledges high above the trail
between Granite and Bernard Creeks, so binoculars may be useful.

To reach Hells Canyon Dam, drive 29 miles northwest of
Cambridge, Idaho, over paved but winding Highway 71 to
Brownlee Dam. The road crosses the river and winds 12 miles to
Oxbow Dam. Then the route crosses back to the Idaho side and

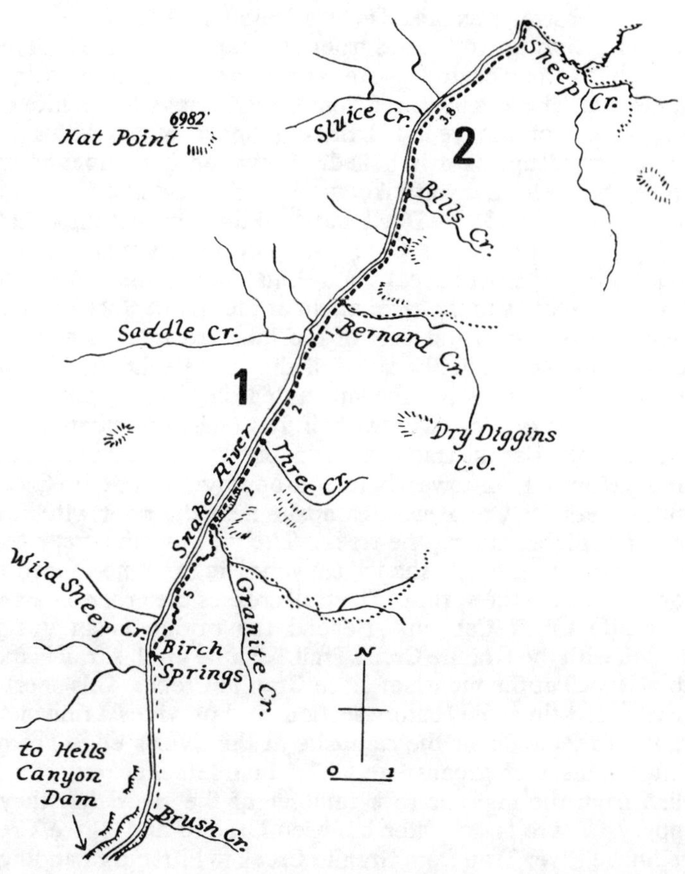

goes 23 miles more along Oxbow and Hells Canyon Reservoirs to the dam. At Hells Canyon Dam, 64 miles from Cambridge, drive across the dam, down a gravel road, and up to a parking area for the boat launch. Cliffs wall the river for the first 2 miles, so a commercial jet boat ride is necessary to get through this trailless section. Jim Zanelli (Box 145, Oxbow, Oregon 97840 (503/785-3352) has the only jet boat service here, so reservations are advisable.

The trail from Lamont Springs past Brush Creek to Birch Springs gets very little use and thus is hard to follow. Birch Springs is also known as Butler Bar, as Lee Butler drowned there in 1923. Two parts of this trail section are often underwater even before high water in late May and June. From the boat launch to Birch Springs, the river passes campsites in little flats such as Lamont Springs and Chimney Bar. .5 mile before Birch Springs the river passes Battle Creek on the Oregon side. An old cabin where Ace Barton was raised is on a fan-shaped bar.

At Birch Springs, 6.5 miles from the launch site, the trail leaves a section that may be underwater and climbs 300 feet up the side of the canyon. There is no water from Birch Springs to Granite Creek during most of the year. Drinking Snake River water is not recommended unless it is boiled. Elevation gains for the upper part of the Hells Canyon hike were hard to calculate due to the small scale of the 15' He Devil map and the fact that the trail from the beginning to Granite Creek was not on this map. Just past Birch Springs the river breaks into Wild Sheep Rapids. At 2 miles, the path descends to the river again at the flat of Rocky Bar. The canyon walls in the first part of the hike are much steeper than they become later on. Because of the low elevation, hiking the Hells Canyon Trail is not recommended during July and August. No open fires are allowed between July 1 and September 15.

After Rocky Bar the trail climbs again 500 feet and passes under a rust-colored rock tower before dropping to Granite Creek at 5 miles. Granite Creek has a campsite near the river with several sandy flat places among the trees. The view up the creek from a grassy flat here is of a V-shaped canyon rising to pine-topped hills, snow-covered in the spring. The trail crosses the creek on a bridge in Granite Creek Canyon. Beyond the bridge is an unsigned junction with the Granite Creek Trail. .6 mile up this trail is the old Hibbs Ranch at the mouth of Little Granite Creek. This short side trip is interesting (see History section) and provides a fine view up Granite Creek. Below the campsite at the river's edge are great shiny boulders of greenstone. The boulders have such a high polish from the gigantic rock tumbler of the river that they are slippery. There is no water between Granite and Three Creeks. The Snake River Trail from Granite Creek to Pittsburg Landing has been designated a National Recreation Trail.

Just past Granite Creek the trail cuts right down to the water and runs under an overhanging cliff. This section is called the "Tight Squeeze". At high water the trail will be under water here. If it is, go back and climb the Granite Creek Trail .5 mile (600 feet in elevation) to a rough side trail signed "High Water Trail". Before the hiker starts climbing, some fine petroglyphs are located 200 feet beyond the "Tight Squeeze". Alongside them Granite Creek Rapids churn the river. This is one of the last remaining large rapids.

Beyond the Tight Squeeze, the main trail climbs again 150 feet. At 5.5 miles Cache Creek enters on the Oregon side. At 6 miles the route descends again, then once more climbs 150 feet. At 7 miles, the path descends to ford Three Creek. There is no water between Three and Bernard Creeks. Beyond Three Creek the trail continues high above the river. Across the way is the long narrow, pine-studded bar of Two Bars. At 8 miles the trail comes to the flat high bar of Dry Gulch.

At 9 miles, on the Oregon side the green chasms of Saddle Creek and Hat Creek come down from the west. A large bar of rounded river stones lies in the river between the two creeks. In early spring, this bar is an island.

From here the trail runs along the canyon wall to the big green flat of Bernard Creek at 10 miles. Here a dilapidated, unpainted cabin squats amid pieces of rusty machinery. Rock towers top pine and snow-covered hills at the head of Bernard Creek Canyon. The best campsite is across the bridged creek on a high bar. Beyond the campsite on the river are two tiny sand beaches.

HELLS CANYON:
Bernard Creek to Sheep Creek

2

One-way distance: 6 miles
Elevation gain: 480 feet
Elevation loss: 560 feet
Highest point: 1600 feet
Topo map: He Devil (15′)
Time: 5½ hours (second section of four day through trip)
Access: see Birch Springs to Bernard Creek
Difficulty: Strenuous

Beyond Bernard Creek the Snake River Canyon widens out so that the river bars, tufted with bunch grass, are up to 200 yards across and .2 mile long. Across from Sluice Creek rise tiers of Columbia basalt with conifers growing between the layers. On the top of the basalt layers, Hat Point Lookout stands on stilts among the pines. From the bar beyond Bills Creek, the hiker can look up to the forested knoll upon which Dry Diggins Lookout sits. Gentle canyons wind up from the river in this section instead of steep gulches. From among the grass on Bills Creek and Johnson Bars, small prickly pear cacti peep. Sheep Creek thunders down under bronze-barked water birch beside the renovated McGaffee house and barn.

From Bernard Creek the trail climbs 300 feet above the river. The route passes along cliffs above No Name Rapids. Beside the trail at 1.5 miles is a water-sculptured pothole that is 4 feet across and 6 feet deep. There is no water from Bernard Creek to Bills Creek. The path descends 50 feet, then climbs again 200 feet to a long grass shelf that has cactus and sumac. Beyond here foam Waterspout Rapids.

At 2.2 miles the trail curves into the little canyon of Bills Creek, near a roofless stone house and corral. Silas Bullock built this cabin on his homestead in 1906. There is no water between Bills and Sheep Creeks. Next the trail strides .5 mile along the flat grass of Bills Creek Bar, elevation 1250 feet, where Dry Diggins Point, elevation 7900 feet, can be seen upriver. At the end of the bar, the trail continues on an alluvial fan. At 3.5 miles the hiker can look up Sluice Creek to Hat Point. Sluice Creek Rapids seethe below a landing strip marked with painted white rocks.

Across from Rush Creek at 4 miles, the trail wanders along immense Johnson Bar, which is 1.2 miles long and .2 mile wide. The ruins of an old stone house, the Bullock-Barton Cabin, stand at the upper side. Pointed green peaks sprinkled with forest climb the canyon of Rush Creek. At the end of Johnson Bar, the trail descends to a big sandy beach and campsite at 5.2 miles.

Near Sheep Creek, slanting solid rock walls close in on the river. The trail climbs 50 feet and skirts along cliffs before dropping to a grassy bar split by Sheep Creek at 6 miles. Campsites are located on the bars and in little flats along the creek, just across the wooden bridge. Cliffs and ledges flank the canyon of Sheep Creek and rise to the hidden tops of Old Timer Mountain and Stormy Point. On the north side of Sheep Creek near the McGaffee house, the Stormy Point Trail goes 6 miles to the end of a road at Low Saddle. Seven Devils Guard Station is 14 miles distant via this trail and the East Fork of Sheep Creek Trail.

Bill McLeod, a Scotsman, homesteaded at Sheep Creek in 1884. He was probably the earliest settler in this part of the canyon. He built a rock dugout alongside the trail just below the present cabin. From 1935 until 1952, Ace Barton lived in the McGaffee house, remodeled it, and constructed the outbuildings.

HELLS CANYON:
Sheep Creek to Kirkwood Creek

3

One-way distance: 10 miles
Elevation gain: 1100 feet
Elevation loss: 1200 feet
Highest point: 1500 feet
Topo maps: He Devil (15'), Kernan Point (15'), Kirkwood Bar
Time: 7 hours (third section of four day through trip)
Access: see Birch Springs to Bernard Creek
Difficulty: Strenuous

Hells Canyon below Sheep Creek has rounder hills, less cliffs, and bigger and higher bars. The route passes the red barns and broad pastures of a modern ranch on the Oregon side. At Kirk-

Hells Canyon

wood Creek sits Len Jordan's old white clapboard house which has a bathtub and sink that he built himself out of cement. The Forest Service has a living history interpretive center here, which is open most of the week during the summer. The trail climbs the sides of two inner-canyon peaks. At the largest, Suicide Point, where the trail ascends 400 feet above the river, the hiker looks straight down into the water. Below Sheep Creek there is boating traffic, since the river from this point is considered navigable. The big grove of ponderosa pines at Pine Bar seems like a bit of forest transplanted from a higher elevation. Mile signs, especially noticeable in this section, refer to distance from Pittsburg Landing.

Beyond Sheep Creek there is no water until Meyer Creek. From Sheep Creek the trail passes the McGaffee ranch house, then skirts the base of cliffs at the edge of the river above a sign that says "End of navigable waters". At .5 mile the path crosses Steep Creek, a small creek flowing down a canyon that rises 600 feet from the river in .2 mile. This creek marks the northern boundary for the Bartonberry.

At 1 mile, the trail traverses a grassy hillside scattered with boulders and hackberries and then climbs 100 feet above the river along a cliff. Across the river at 1.5 miles, a building in the middle of a high bar stands at Sand Creek. This building is used by the Oregon Fish and Game Commission. The trail then drops to the tiny canyon of Willow Creek at 2 miles, which runs through birches and hackberries. Indian ruins lie along both sides of the trail just north of Willow Creek. They are the remains of "pit houses", shaped like basins 12 to 16 feet in diameter and 2 to 3 feet deep. After this the path climbs 100 feet again along a cliff. The trail is steep with several imbedded cement steps to assist the hiker.

Beyond here the route winds into the streamless canyon of Pine Bar after passing a campsite near the river. The ground under the large grove of pines is orange and has been eroded into gullies between the trees. Behind the grove, erosion continues up the mountain to a badlands of orange outcrops and gravel. Then the trail wanders across the bar, rounds a few outcrops, and reaches a large rolling bar, called High Bar, at 3 miles. At one point the trail crosses an ancient pit house. High Bar affords a last glimpse of the top of Dry Diggins. About halfway between Pine and High Bars, the hiker can see pictographs beside the trail. Beyond the middle of High Bar, the view ahead includes Big Bar and the point where Duncans Tunnel lies. Here rock outcrops and small cliffs dot high grassy hills. Big cliffs occur only next to the river. A small creek from Hutton Gulch intersects the trail at about 4 miles. Next Caribou Creek joins the river at Little Bar, which is a steep grassy hillside. Below an old mortared stone cellar that is built like a dugout is a sign for the Caribou Creek Trail.

The river trail continues along a grassy hillside 200 feet above the water and curves into a dry gulch. Across the river is the end of a huge pasture belonging to a ranch. Next the path runs back into the deep canyon of Meyer Creek. The next water is at Kirkwood Creek. Across the creek an old pipe winds along the rocky point into Duncans Tunnel. The trail climbs over this knoll 200 feet above the river, then comes down to the vast expanse of Big Bar near a brown cabin at 6 miles.

Across from Suicide Point at 8 miles, a cabin stands above a big sandbar beach at Salt Creek. A short time later, the trail climbs across the face of Suicide Point, and comes down onto a steep, grassy slope. A sand beach curves in to mark Half Moon Bar at 9 miles. 300 yards south of the 9 mile marker, a lizard pictograph is on a rock overhang above the trail. Before Kirkwood Creek, the trail circles the base of a smaller rock similar to Suicide Point.

A large grassy bar, split by Kirkwood Creek at 10 miles, contains a set of old lambing sheds. Across the creek from the Jordan House and a modern log cabin stands a sturdy white-washed fence and corral. A jeep trail leads 12 miles to Lucile. This jeep track is very rough and is impassable in wet weather. The bar continues beyond the corral to a camping area. Pointed knolls of rock and grass guard both sides of Kirkwood Creek. Across the river looms the shadowy recess of Slaughter Gulch. Solid rock walls squeeze the river at Kirkwood Creek into a narrower channel.

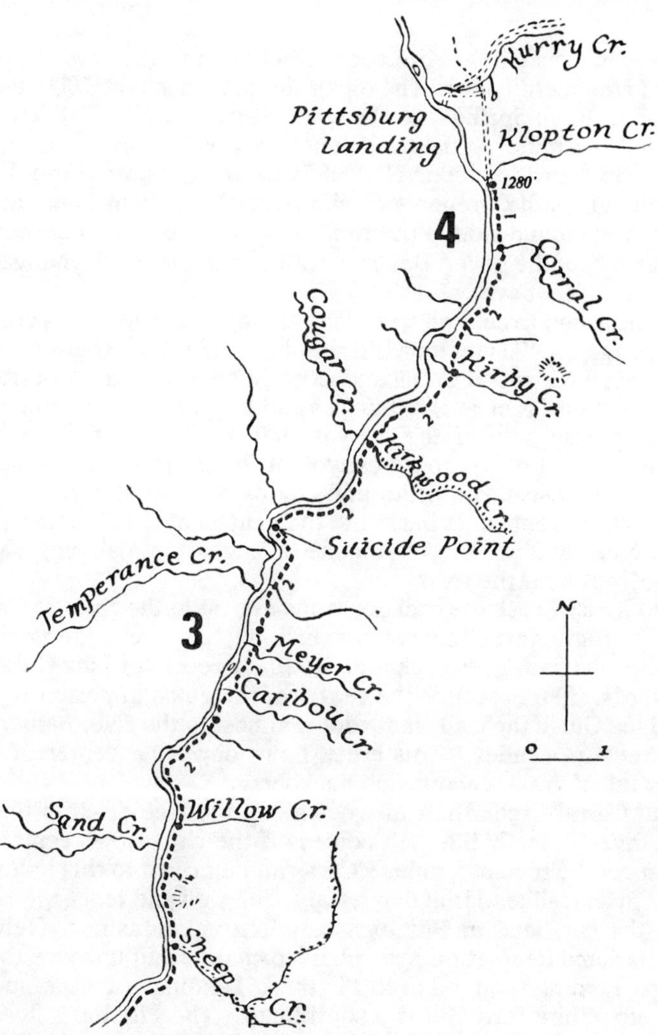

HELLS CANYON:
Kirkwood Creek to Pittsburg Landing

4

One-way distance: 6 miles
Elevation gain: 800 feet
Elevation loss: 720 feet
Highest point: 1600 feet
Topo maps: Kirkwood Bar, Grave Point
Time: 5 hours (fourth section of four day through trip)
Access: see Birch Springs to Bernard Creek
Difficulty: Strenuous

The canyon closes in at Kirkwood Creek with fewer bars, more cliffs, and steeper hillsides. The top of the canyon is now 2000 feet lower than at Birch Springs, so the whole canyon wall is visible up to pine-clad summits. At the trail's end the traveler leaves a gorge and goes into the wide green valley of Pittsburg Landing. Here the top of a big hill on the Oregon side shows black bands of Columbia basalt. On the Idaho side is the first view of the contact between the older rocks of the Seven Devils volcanics and the much younger Columbia basalts above.

From Kirkwood Creek the trail goes along the bar for 200 yards before zigzagging 400 feet up a big rock hill in .5 mile. There is no water between Kirkwood Creek and Corral Creek, and from Corral Creek to Klopton Creek at Pittsburg Landing. The route continues along the grassy side of the canyon 400 feet above the river, curving in and out of the rocky canyon of Royal Gorge at 1 mile. The path then descends a little, and climbs 50 feet up through a notch. Next the route cuts back into the canyon of Kirby Creek to cross the creek at 2 miles. A campsite is located on a sloping bar on Kirby Creek near the river.

Beyond Kirby Creek the trail descends almost to the river at Cat Gulch. The route next climbs along cliffs 200 feet above the river. At 3.5 miles the path goes back into the shady recess of Line Gulch for 150 yards, then descends the center of the gulch in poison ivy. Beyond Line Gulch the trail slants down almost to the river bank at Corral Creek at 4 miles. This creek flows down the center of a rocky bar full of grass, cactus, and hackberry.

Beyond Corral Creek the trail goes along the face of cliffs that edge the river. Finally the path comes off the cliffs down cement steps to meet the road at 5 miles. Cars can be driven to this point. but the official trailhead is at 6 miles at a trail sign and fence.

Thus, the trailhead at Pittsburg Landing is confusing. Hells Canyon National Recreation Area plans to change and improve the trailhead. Finding the road in to Pittsburg Landing from the new highway up White Bird Hill is also difficult. The Pittsburg Road turns off old U. S. 95 south of White Bird. When the gravel road crosses pine-covered Pittsburg Saddle, the surface becomes rough and rocky. The track drops in hairpin turns to Kurry Creek and then down the creek to a junction at 14.5 miles. Three roads branch here. The left branch leads 1 mile south to the trailhead. On the way the road passes an abandoned farm and fords Klopton Creek. The center road leads down to the river at Lower Pittsburg Landing. The right branch is a jeep trail that goes north to Big Canyon Creek. Some of the roads shown on the topo map don't exist. Upper Pittsburg Landing is not in the location shown on the map. Instead the trail begins just south of Klopton Creek. There are no services at Pittsburg Landing.

Driving from the trailhead to White Bird takes 1 hour. Since driving from Cambridge to Hells Canyon takes 1½ hours, retrieving a car on a through trip is time-consuming. It would save time and gasoline for half a group to start hiking from Pittsburg Landing and half from Hells Canyon Dam and then exchange car keys when they meet in the middle. The group would have to make arrangements for the jet boat to meet those who started from Pittsburg Landing.

RIGGINS AREA

WEST FORK OF RAPID RIVER TRAIL

5

Round trip: 9 to 16 miles
Elevation gain: 600 to 1800 feet
Highest point: 2800 to 4000 feet
Topo map: Heavens Gate
Time: 6 to 11 hours
Access: 5 miles south of Riggins on U. S. 95 turn west on gravel
    road; drive 2.5 miles to Rapid River Fish Hatchery.
Difficulty: Moderate

This trail punches through a jungle of shrubs and trees that hides the canyon walls. Above 400-foot cliffs, grassy hills dotted with firs watch the canyon. Chest-high grass, elderberry, wild rose, water birch, Douglas fir, and Pacific yew help create the jungle. The river rushes along in the spring with such force that near the junction of the main Rapid River with the West Fork, the water is completely white. Up the West Fork, the white water plunges down in interlacing ribbons like macrame. A little ridge with a rock knoll at the end juts out between the main river and West Fork at their junction. Since the rock knoll blocks the main river's sound from one direction, someone sitting on the ridge hears the West Fork in one ear and the main river in the other.

This hike is excellent for early spring and late fall because the 2.5 mile access road is an all weather road and the river crossings are bridged. Few people hike the canyon, although lots of hikers could use the area and never be seen because it is so wooded. Poison ivy and rattlesnakes both live in this canyon although there isn't enough poison ivy to be a problem.

To reach the trailhead, drive 2.5 miles to the Rapid River Fish Hatchery picnic area on a gravel road that turns west from U. S. 95 5 miles south of Riggins. Idaho Power Company funds the hatchery because their Hells Canyon dams destroyed the Snake River salmon runs. The short stretch of the Rapid River below the hatchery is designated by treaty as Nez Perce Indian salmon

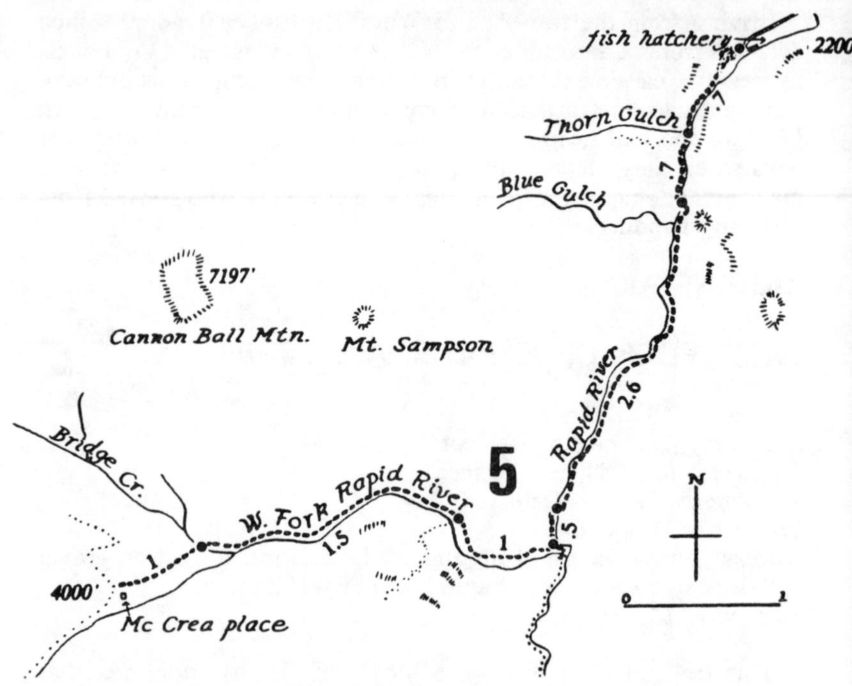

fishing grounds. In the last few years, controversy has resulted when the Idaho Fish and Game Department closed the river to all fishing below the hatchery due to extremely low salmon runs caused by the 1977 drought.

On the southeast at the mouth of the canyon, a triangular hill covered with firs and grey-green mountain mahogany is tiered with cliffs. The trailhead is located where the road curves into the picnic area (day use only). Two dirt roads lead up the river from here. The right-hand one, with the trail sign, has a locked gate 50 yards up the road. Walk along the river on the unsigned left road, which has an unlocked gate. This road ends at 150 yards. At the far end of the flat area, a path leads 100 yards up a steep hillside to join the trail. The trail then winds across an open hillside and along cliffs above the river for .5 mile. This hike is not suitable for small children because of these dropoffs. Across from a pale-orange overhanging cliff full of miniature caves, an unsigned trail for Cannon Ball Mountain leads from the river to the right (west).

At .7 mile the trail passes a trickle of water in Thorn Gulch, then drops to run along the edge of the creek. At 1.4 miles the route crosses the river to the east side on a sturdy bridge. At 1.5 miles, the wooded chasm of Blue Gulch rises across the river. Here the canyon widens so the path parts chest-high grass in a green jungle. At 2.2 miles the trail climbs across a rocky area, then at 2.7 miles leads up 150 feet on a shrubby hillside. The trail returns to the creek at 3.2 miles where red-barked Pacific yew grows.

The way next passes under moss-draped cliffs. At 4 miles the trail crosses back to the west side of the creek at a narrows. At 4.5 miles the path crosses a grassy hillside at the base of a spur between the rivers where the Main and West Fork Trails join. The first possible campsite is on a grassy flat next to the West Fork. A good lunch place is at the West Fork Bridge on the Main Rapid River Trail 150 yards below the junction.

The trail up the West Fork climbs 400 feet in .5 mile across a flower-studded hillside that is cut by short grey cliffs and has a view of the cascades of the West Fork. As the trail enters the trees again, a wooden gravestone honors a man killed in an early day mining accident. The route continues through shrubs and trees in a flat area beside the now placid creek. The area is named Potter Flat for George Potter, an early prospector and homesteader.

At 5.5 miles at a junction with the Potter Cabin Trail is a campsite suitable for a large party. From here the trail continues for 1.5 miles through the wooded creek bottom with light grey cliffs and rocky points visible through a curtain of greenery. At 7 miles the trail fords Bridge Creek. This crossing may be dangerous during high water. The trail climbs 400 feet along the base of an open hillside to the old McCrea Ranch at 8 miles.

Beyond the ranch, the trail continues up the wooded canyon of the West Fork, crossing Deep Creek and Hanson Creek. At the Oxbow Bridge junction at 9.7 miles, one trail climbs west 2.5 miles up Dog Ridge to the Boise Trail and another ascends Oxbow Creek to Bryan Mountain, 6 miles distant. From this junction the West Fork Trail continues past Dog and Horse Heaven Creeks into the Payette National Forest. North of Mill Creek .2 mile, the trail comes to the ruins of the old Rankin Mill. This is just before reaching junctions with the Jackley Mountain and Horse Heaven Trails at about 13 miles.

WINDY SADDLE AREA — Northern Seven Devils Loop

BOISE TRAIL:
Seven Devils Guard Station to Cannon Ck.;
Cannon Creek Trail to Cannon Lake

6

Round trip: 7.6 miles (Seven Devils Guard Station to Cannon Creek: 3 miles; Cannon Creek to Cannon Lake: .8 mile)
Elevation gain: 480 feet
Elevation loss: 680 feet (return climb)
Highest point: 7200 feet
Topo map: He Devil (15')
Time: 4 hours (this section one-way)
Access: Turn west just south of Riggins off of U. S. 95. Drive 15 miles on gravel and dirt road to Windy Saddle trailhead. Walk southeast downhill .2 mile to Seven Devils Guard Station.
Difficulty: Moderate

A silvered forest of trees, dead from a forest fire, surrounds miniature green Cannon Lake. Black peaks splashed with lichen hang above like the underworld spirits for which they are named: The Goblin, The Ogre and She Devil. When the wind blows, the dead trees howl in a high-pitched tone like an eerie army of ghosts.

The easiest way to reach the trailhead for Cannon Lake is to drive in on the road from Riggins to Windy Saddle. Before driving up this road, stop at the Hells Canyon National Recreation Area office in Riggins for information. The signed gravel road turns west just south of Riggins off U. S. 95. The route first winds along Squaw Creek; then at 2 miles, it turns up Papoose Creek, and becomes dirt. At 8 miles the road winds up McClinery Ridge, and passes a dead-end road to the left.

The road enters a high meadow at 14 miles with a view of the Salmon River Canyon, and the track hairpins to the west. In a few yards, a side road to the left signed "Administrative use, no public parking" turns off downhill. This is the road to the guard station. Continue on the main road a short distance to the Windy Saddle trailhead and parking area at 15 miles. Park here and walk straight downhill to the southeast for .2 mile on a path to the guard station.

From the guard station, the Boise Trail first switchbacks down in the open. The path goes into the trees at .2 mile, then joins another trail at a gate. This unsigned trail turns and follows the fence downhill to the east. This is the trail to Saddle Camp and

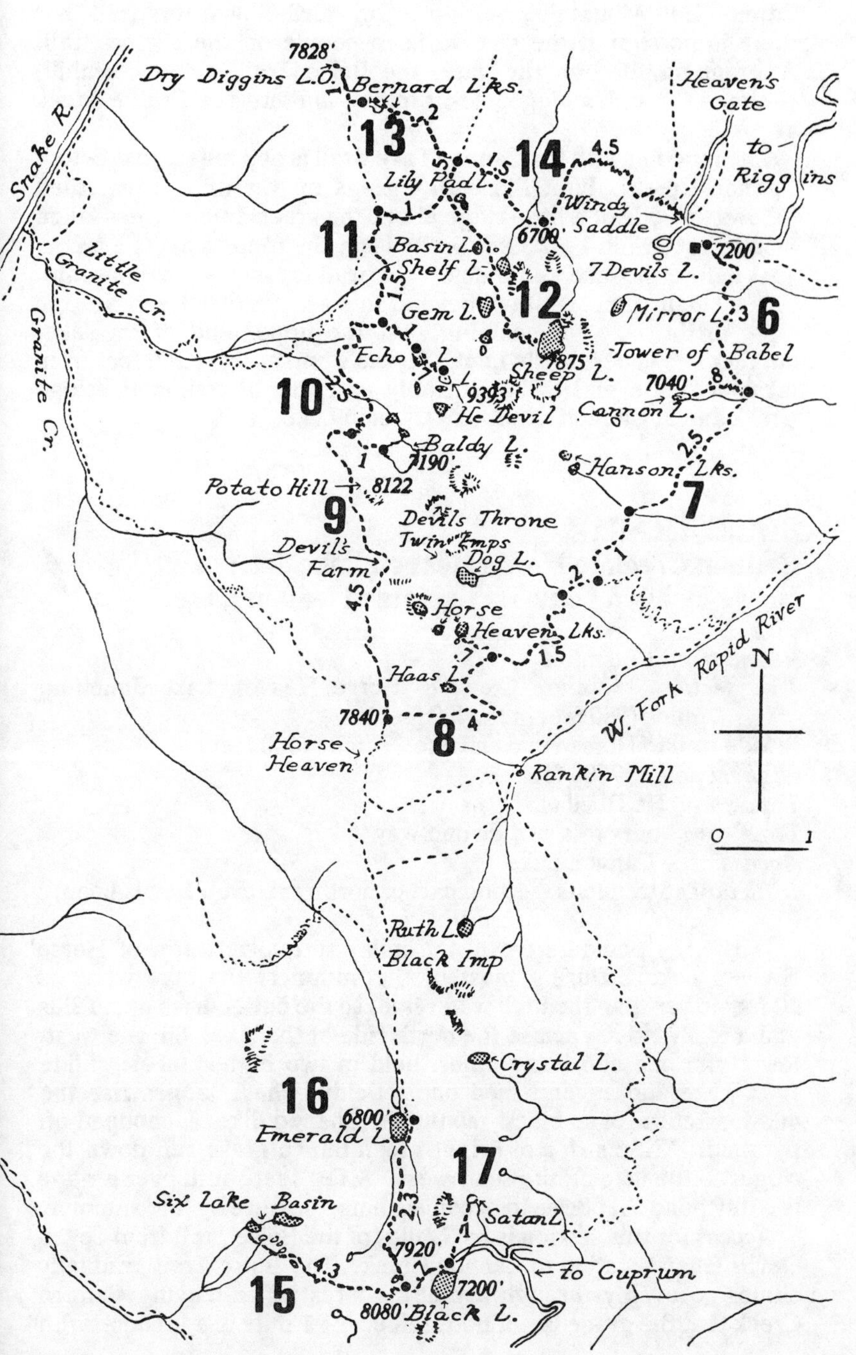
Snake R.
7828'
Dry Diggins L.O.
Bernard Lks.
Heaven's Gate
to Riggins
13
2
14
4.5
1.5
Lily Pad L.
Windy Saddle
6700'
7200'
11
Basin L.
Shelf L.
7 Devils L.
Little Granite Cr.
Gem L.
12
Mirror L.
3
6
Echo L.
7875'
Tower of Babel
Sheep L.
7040'
8
Granite Cr.
He Devil
9393
Cannon L.
10
2.5
Baldy L.
1
7190'
Hanson Lks.
Potato Hill
8122
7
Devils Throne
9
Twin Imps
Dog L.
Devil's Farm
2
4.5
Horse
1
Horse Heaven Lks.
.7
1.5
Haas L.
W. Fork Rapid River
7840'
8
4
N
Horse Heaven
Rankin Mill
0   1
Ruth L.
Black Imp
Crystal L.
16
6800'
Emerald L.
17
Six Lake Basin
Satan L.
2.3
7920'
to Cuprum
4.3
.7
15
7200'
8080' Black L.

Cannon Ball Mountain. A sign is 200 yards down this trail, but there is no sign at the gate to keep people on the correct trail. After going through the gate, the Boise Trail winds downhill, contours through a lodgepole-fir forest, and crosses Bridge Creek at 1 mile.

The junction with the Cannon Lake Trail is at 3 miles, just before Cannon Creek. First the path zigzags up through forest, then follows the side of a little ridge above the creek among trees killed by a forest fire in 1962. Below the lake, the route crosses a creek. Just before the lake at 3.8 miles, the trail crosses a small swamp. Three small campsites just beyond this are overused and are too close to the lake for camping. At the upper end of the lake, another site is beside the inlet. Please camp at least 200 feet from lakes in the Seven Devils. The only water on the trail is at Bridge Creek and at Cannon Creek and Cannon Lake.

BOISE TRAIL:
Cannon Creek to Horse Heaven Lake Jct.;
Horse Heaven Lake Tr. to Horse Heaven Lake

7

Round trip: 17.8 miles
This section: Cannon Creek to Horse Heaven Lake Junction:
    5.2 miles (980 feet gain, 400 feet loss)
   Side trail to Horse Heaven Lake: .7 mile (400 feet gain)
Highest point: 7600 feet
Topo map: He Devil (15')
Time: 5½ hours this section one-way
Access: see Cannon Lake
Difficulty: Strenuous (second part of northern Seven Devils Loop)

Dark grey boulders crowd the milky turquoise water of Horse Heaven Lake. During most of the summer, the lake water is 20 feet lower than the high water line, so the outlet dries up. Talus and a rocky ridge enclose the north side of the lake. On the west, low cliffs, one above the other, hold in two higher lakes: Slide Rock Lake and an unnamed one. Behind these ledges rise the 400-foot cliffs of a black mountain, shaped like a chopped-off pyramid. Wide strips of bright green bunch grass run down the ridges to the lake on the southwest. A few feet south over a ridge is a tiny pond that dries to become a horse pasture by late summer.

Access for this section is by 3 miles of the Boise Trail from Seven Devils Guard Station to Cannon Creek. The Boise Trail gradually climbs so evenly through a pine-fir forest after leaving Cannon Creek that the grade is not noticeable. At 1 mile is a junction with a trail to Rapid River. At 2 miles, the path circles in to the head of the canyon of Hanson Creek and crosses the creek at 2.5 miles. At this point the hiker can follow the creek up 1.5 miles cross-country to Lower Hanson Lake.

Next the Boise Trail winds gently up a ridge on the other side of the creek. At 3.5 miles the route meets the West Fork of Rapid River-Dog Ridge Trail. The West Fork Trail is 2.5 miles downhill from this junction, and leads 3 more miles up the river to the early day Rankin Mill.

After this junction the Boise Trail rounds the end of the ridge and heads up the canyon of Dog Creek in the open. From here look up the canyon of Dog Creek to black peaks encircling Dog Lake. At Hanson Creek (2.5 miles) and at Dog Creek (3.7 miles) are large shady campsites. The hiker can leave the trail 75 yards north of Dog Creek and take an unsigned trail 2 miles to Dog Lake.

Beyond Dog Creek the trail winds along in the woods. At 5 miles the path makes a sharp hairpin and enters a grassy hillside. At 5.2 miles, after the Boise Trail has descended 200 feet, an unsigned trail to Horse Heaven Lake turns northwest. This path is in the trees just beyond a sandy stream (usually dry) and campsite. The route gains 400 feet and passes through forest, rock benches, and a meadowed hillside to reach the lake in .7 mile.

From Horse Heaven Lake the hiker can climb west to a dry lake, then go northwest up to Slide Rock Lake which is 1 mile from Horse Heaven Lake. From Slide Rock Lake, he can look west up to the Twin Imps. This route is cross-country.

BOISE TRAIL:
Horse Heaven Lake Junction to Junction with Potato Hill Trail near Horse Heaven

8

Round trip: 25.8 miles
This section: 4 miles (800 feet gain)
Highest point: 7840 feet
Topo map: He Devil (15')
Time: 3 hours this section one-way
Access: see Cannon Lake and Horse Heaven Lake
Difficulty: Strenuous (third section of northern Seven Devils Loop)

Along this section of the Boise Trail, the green grassy hill of Horse Heaven beckons from the distance. A few trees dot this hill, which is as high as nearby peaks. Among these rugged mountains, Horse Heaven seems like a misplaced golf course.

Access for this section is by 8.2 miles of the Boise Trail from **Seven Devils Guard Station. The trail from the Horse Heaven Lake**

Junction climbs gradually through forest. At .7 mile, the trail passes a rock slide just below Haas Lake. Then the path climbs a long switchback up the side of a wooded ridge. At 1.5 miles, the route hairpins back and comes onto an open ridge that leads toward Horse Heaven. To the south, black hills north of Black Lake sweep up to sharp peaks, accented by a black spire, the Black Imp.

At 2.5 miles the trail makes several switchbacks up a boulder field to the Horse Heaven-Potato Hill Trail Junction, which is amid rocks and sulphur flowers at 4 miles. There is no evidence of the trail shown on the topo map going 9 miles from this junction down **Two Creek, Devils Farm Creek, and Granite Creek to the Snake River.** From the junction, the distance on the Potato Hill Trail to the Baldy Lake Junction is 5.5 miles. The entire trail from the Seven Devils Guard Station to this junction was rerouted by construction started in 1958 and completed in 1964, so it differs from the map. The new route parallels the original Old Boise Indian Trail much of the way.

POTATO HILL TRAIL:
Junction with Boise Trail to Baldy Lake Jct.
BALDY LAKE TRAIL:
Junction with Potato Hill Trail to Baldy Lake

9

Round trip: 24 miles by Little Granite Creek Trail
This section: Potato Hill Trail from junction with Boise Trail to
    Baldy Lake Junction: 4.5 miles (320 feet gain, 1200 feet loss)
   Side trail to Baldy Lake: 1 mile (240 feet gain)
Highest point: 7920 feet
Topo map: He Devil (15′)
Time: 4 hours for this section one-way
Access: see Cannon Lake, Horse Heaven Lake, Potato Hill
    Junction, and Iron Phone Junction
Difficulty: Strenuous (fourth part of northern Seven Devils loop)

Baldy Lake is .5 mile wide and fills a basin of grey rock hills backed by jumbled black peaks. Between the two summits on the left peers He Devil, the highest mountain in the Seven Devils. In the center, the Devils Throne sweeps up in tiers to a rounded top. To the right, four sharp jagged summits all point left and stairstep to a furrowed peak. Around Baldy Lake, dead trees toothpick from a 1945 man-caused fire. Young lodgepoles now 20 feet tall blanket the shore between the dead trees.

The route from the junction near Horse Heaven first runs along green Haas Flat with a 5000-foot view down into Hells Canyon. Later the trail passes jumbled black boulders and pinnacles of the Devils Farm below overshadowing black peaks. In a level area above the trail, the boulders form mounds, to create the farmer's "field". On the topo map, Devils Farm is not labeled in the right place. The Nez Perce Forest map shows the right location.

The Potato Hill Trail beyond its junction with the Boise Trail first gently climbs meadows with Hells Canyon on the west. At .5 mile, look up to the right and note clumps of bluebells and false hellbore. These mark the location of Haas Flat Spring, which is the last water until the trail crosses the South Fork of Little Granite Creek below Baldy Lake at 4.5 miles.   At .7 mile, the trail corkscrews down across talus 400 feet in .5 mile.   From here, grassy slopes, boulders, aspens, and forest alternate. At 2 miles, the path contours into the canyon of the Devils Farm. After that the trail skirts under Potato Hill (not seen) and heads back to the east through trees to the Baldy Lake Junction at 4.5 miles.

The 1 mile trail to Baldy Lake crosses two small ridges with rocks and trees in a 240-foot climb. Just below Baldy Lake along the outlet creek rest two tiny Little Baldy Lakes.

POTATO HILL TRAIL:
Baldy Lake Junction to Echo Lake Junction; Echo Lake Trail to Echo and He Devil Lakes

10

Round trip: 20.4 miles
This section: Baldy Lake Jct. to Echo Lake Jct.: 2.5 miles (320 feet gain, 800 feet loss)
    Echo Lake Trail to Echo Lake: 1 mile (400 feet gain);
    Echo Lake to He Devil Lake: .7 mile (200 feet gain)
Highest point: 7920 feet
Topo map: He Devil (15′)
Time: 3½ hours (this section including lakes one-way)
Access: see Cannon Lake, Iron Phone Junction, etc.
Difficulty: Strenuous (fifth section of northern Seven Devils Loop)

Black peaks wait up the canyon above the forest surrounding oval green Echo Lake. From the trail to He Devil Lake, Echo Lake, accented by a rock and tree-covered hill, seems to hang at the edge of Hells Canyon. Above the east shore of He Devil Lake, talus rises to a 600-foot black cliff. At the southeast end of this lake, He Devil supervises his domain which includes a round island, sprouting trees from a bald rock surface, in the lake. To the right of He Devil, a humped black mountain defends a jagged low ridge of summits.

Access for this section is either by 16.7 miles of the Boise and Potato Hill Trails from Seven Devils Guard Station or by 8.5 miles of trail from Windy Saddle around the north end of the loop trail. The Potato Hill Trail from the Baldy Lake Junction to the South Fork of Little Granite Creek hairpins 800 feet down through woods to cross the creek at 1 mile. Once across the creek the trail climbs 150 feet up a boulder field, then contours along in the trees. Finally, the route turns sharply east and runs back into a wooded canyon to cross the Middle Fork of Granite Creek. At 2.5 miles in a clearing, the trail turns abruptly northwest just before the Echo Lake Junction.

The side trail to Echo Lake winds up a rocky hillside 1 mile to the lake. From there the route skirts the left side of Echo Lake and corkscrews .7 mile up to He Devil Lake. From He Devil Lake, the hiker can continue cross-country south .2 mile to Triangle Lake. From there, go uphill to the southeast .5 mile to Purgatory Lake.

POTATO HILL TRAIL:
Echo Lake Junction to junction with Little Granite Creek Trail near Hibbs Cow Camp
LITTLE GRANITE CREEK TRAIL:
Jct. with Potato Hill Tr. to Sheep Lake Tr.

11

Round trip: 17 miles
This section: Echo Lake Jct. to Little Granite Creek Jct.: 1.5 miles (800 feet gain)
   Potato Hill Trail Jct. to Sheep Lake Jct.: 1 mile (160 feet loss)
Highest point: 7600 feet
Topo map: He Devil (15′)
Time: 2½ hours for this section one-way
Access: see Cannon Lake and Iron Phone Junction
Difficulty: Strenuous (sixth section of northern Seven Devils loop)

This trail first climbs a 800-foot grassy hill from the Echo Lake Junction to a junction with the Little Granite Creek Trail near Hibbs Cow Camp. From this part of the trail, there is a magnificent view of Hells Canyon and black peaks above Echo and He Devil Lakes. One peak looks like a black ogre wearing a hood.

Access for this section is by 19.2 miles of the Boise and Potato Hill Trails from Seven Devils Guard Station or by 6.7 miles of trail from Windy Saddle. The first part of this section of the Potato Hill Trail climbs a hot, open slope until trees close in and provide shade. At .7 mile, the trail crosses the North Fork of Little Granite Creek at a refreshing meadow. Beyond at 1.2 miles, the route

Baldy Lake (Seven Devils)

reaches a junction with the trail down Little Granite Creek past
Hibbs Cow Camp. There are two junctions for it 50 yards apart;
both are signed. It is 6.5 miles from here down to the Snake River.

On the main loop trail 200 yards beyond the junction of the
Potato Hill and Little Granite Creek Trails is an unmarked junction
in an open area.   Keep left here and go 300 yards up a sandy hillside to the junction of the Little Granite Creek Trail with the Dry
Diggins Lookout Trail at 1.5 miles. The route leads along an open
ridge and then drops down a grassy hill and along through trees to
the Sheep Lake Trail, 1 mile from the Dry Diggins Lookout Trail
junction.

SHEEP LAKE TRAIL:
Basin, Shelf, Gem and Sheep Lakes   12

Round trip: 19.4 miles
This section: Sheep Lake Trail from jct. with Little Granite Creek
  Trail to Sheep Lake: 3.7 miles (1040 feet gain, 560 feet loss)
Highest point: 8320 feet
Topo map: He Devil (15′)
Time: 4 hours this section one-way
Access: see Cannon Lake and Iron Phone Junction
Difficulty: Strenuous (seventh part of northern Seven Devils loop)

Black talus drips from a solid rock hill above shallow green Basin Lake, the first lake on this trail. Two black skyscraper-shaped mountains with a deep notch between them guard the canyon above Shelf Lake, the second lake. Below these peaks the inlet splashes down in an inviting waterfall into the upper end of the lake. East of and behind the double peak juts the rough square top of He Devil. Above the south end of blue-green Gem Lake (the third lake), a mountain like a huge black front tooth gnaws a 100-foot cliff. On the east side an enormous flat rock makes a fine fishing platform. Towers march along a fluted wall to the west.

From the south, the broad 1000-foot black face of the She Devil frowns over the south end of the fourth lake, Sheep Lake, which is deep blue and shaped like one of the She Devil's tears. Yellow-green lichen makes the She Devil look moldy.   A meadow blanketed with wildflowers adjoins the end of the .5 mile long lake beside lodgepoles and firs. Above the meadow, He Devil's ugly features are silhouetted against the skyline. Between the two devils a snow-filled couloir runs up to the ridge top. Islands and peninsulas reach out from the west shore of the lake, towards the east where a crag named the Tower of Babel resembles the battlements of a castle. Some of the castle towers have fallen; some have been nibbled by time. Beyond the lower end of the lake, Sheep Creek falls into the canyon below. These four lakes are heavily used and are not recommended for the solitude seeker.

Access for the Sheep Lake Trail is by 6.7 miles of trail from Windy Saddle or by 20.7 miles of the Boise Trail. The Sheep Lake Trail turns east from the Little Granite Creek Trail at a Sheep Lake Trail sign 1 mile from the junction of the Little Granite Creek and Dry Diggins Lookout Trails. At .2 mile, the trail comes to tiny Lily Pad Lake.

The Sheep Lake Trail then climbs over a little ridge to Basin Lake at 1 mile. Then it goes over a rocky ridge to Shelf Lake at 1.5 miles. Campsites along the lakeshore are overused. Please camp at least 200 feet from the lakes in the Seven Devils.

Beyond Shelf Lake the trail climbs the inlet, threading rock benches and alpine gardens for .2 mile to a junction with a .2 mile trail to Gem Lake. The only places to camp near Gem Lake would be between the rock benches 100 vertical feet above the east side of the lake. To see Gem Lake and then go on to Sheep Lake, go cross-country up the rock benches half way along Gem Lake and intersect the Sheep Lake Trail just below the two skyscraper peaks.

From the Gem Lake junction, the trail on to Sheep Lake corkscrews up past rock outcrops and flowers, then skirts underneath the two peaks. From here these lava teeth have several cavities and green stains. Beyond this the trail passes a snow pond and then winds up to a saddle at 3.2 miles, 800 feet above Shelf Lake. At this snow pond, the hiker can go west 200 yards and see Rock Island and Appendix Lakes below. On the way to the saddle, the hiker can look across to Dry Diggins Lookout. From the saddle Sheep Lake is spread out below the menacing He Devil. The route then drops 400 feet to the lake at 3.7 miles. Be sure to camp at least 200 feet from the lake. There are many possible sites.

LITTLE GRANITE CREEK TRAIL: **13**
Sheep Lake Trail to Iron Phone Junction
DRY DIGGINS TRAIL: Iron Phone Jct.
to Bernard Lakes and Dry Diggins Lookout

Round trip: 18 miles
This section: Sheep Lake Trail to Iron Phone Junction: .5 mile
    (80 feet loss)
   Dry Diggins Trail from junction to Bernard Lakes: 2 miles
    (320 feet gain, 320 feet loss)
   Bernard Lakes to Dry Diggins Lookout: 1 mile (640 feet gain)
Highest point: 7828 feet
Topo map: He Devil (15')
Time: 3½ hours for this section one-way
Access: see Cannon Lake and Windy Saddle to Iron Phone Jct.
Difficulty: Strenuous (eighth part of northern Seven Devils loop)

Grass edges Bernard Lakes, which are small green lakes set in woods below rounded black ridges. A large grey rock outcrop crowds the trail along the lower lake near lodgepoles choked by dark strands of elk moss. Yellow water lilies float along the shore of the upper lake, which is chaperoned by the lookout. Camping is limited near both lakes; be sure to camp 200 feet from the lakes.

Dry Diggins Lookout perches 6000 feet above Hells Canyon. Black rocks and gnarled trees line the edge of the abyss. Over the edge brown grass, trees, and cliffs plunge to the river. White rapids embroider the dark blue ribbon of river that threads the bottom of the canyon. The banks are blued by distance and by the haze that often fills the whole canyon. A succession of points marks side canyons up and down the river. Ghostly shapes of the Wallowas loom beyond the canyon to the southwest. The Tower of Babel, She Devil, and He Devil lurk on the southeastern horizon. A firespotter mans the lookout.

To reach Bernard Lakes from the Sheep Lake Trail Junction, first walk north .5 mile on the Little Granite Creek Trail to the Iron Phone Junction. The .5 mile of the Little Granite Creek Trail from the Sheep Lake Trail to the Iron Phone Junction runs through grassy areas. This trail drops just before this four-way junction on top of Dry Diggins Ridge.

To reach Bernard Lakes, take the Bernard Lakes Trail west along the wire from the old telephone at the junction. From here the trail switchbacks down 400 feet into the cool canyon of Bernard Creek. The route passes right under a 100-foot cliff and at the bottom crosses Bernard Creek. Then the path zigzags 320 feet up past rock benches and a lily pond to the first lake at 2 miles and the second lake at 2.1 miles.

The trail winds past the lakes and a lily pond above the upper lake before leaping up a dry, rocky hillside. At 3 miles is a junction with the Dry Diggins Lookout Trail which runs south 2 miles to intersect the Little Granite Creek Trail .5 mile north of the Potato Hill Trail Junction. Continuing to the lookout, the hillside levels off and trees resume until the trail reaches the rocks of the lookout plateau at 3 miles. From the north end of the last switchback before the lookout, the hiker can look down to the Snake River at Bills Creek Bar. Along the trail, the first summit southeast of the lookout, Three Creek Point, provides a wonderful view down Three Creek to the Snake River. Go 150 yards west off the trail here to see it.

WINDY SADDLE TO IRON PHONE JCT. ON DRY DIGGINS RIDGE   14

Round trip: 12 miles
Elevation gain: 1440 feet
Elevation loss: 1780 feet
Highest point: 8000 feet
Topo map: He Devil (15′)
Time: 7 hours this section one-way
Access: see Cannon Lake
Difficulty: Strenuous (ninth part of northern Seven Devils loop)

Spectacular views occur along the trail from Windy Saddle to the Iron Phone Junction on Dry Diggins Ridge since the route goes down and up and down 1000 feet at a time into and out of deep canyons. From the trail down into the canyon of Sheep Creek, the Devils Tooth waits in front of the dark masses of He Devil, She Devil, and the Tower of Babel. Near the Tooth, the hiker can look back across at Dry Diggins Lookout and north down the canyon of Sheep Creek almost to Hells Canyon.

For access and directions, see Seven Devils Guard Station to Cannon Lake. Windy Saddle is .2 mile by a path from the Seven Devils Guard Station. Directions are given here from Windy

View from Dry Diggins Lookout

Saddle to the Iron Phone Junction. However, this is the final section of the northern Seven Devils loop description that started at Seven Devils Guard Station.

The trail at Windy Saddle starts by dropping 480 feet to the tiny East Fork of Sheep Creek. The path skirts under a rock wall and climbs 1000 feet up the other side of the canyon where the hiker can look back to the ridge of Windy Saddle and Heavens Gate Lookout.

At 2.5 miles the path rounds a spur in the ridge, contours along to the end of the ridge and begins a 1300-foot drop to Sheep Creek. At 3 miles the trail hairpins down under 100-foot black rock towers, then cuts across a grey rockslide that is dappled with olive green, russet, rose, and white, and sprinkled in season with pungent purple horsemint.

At Sheep Creek at 4.5 miles, a waterfall nearby splashes down after running under a curving overhang of moss-topped rock. (Sheep Creek is too steep to use as a route to Sheep Lake.) The trail crosses two sections of Shelf Creek at 5 miles. Beyond Shelf Creek the path circles the head of the canyon and switchbacks 560 feet up a huge boulder field to Dry Diggins Ridge and the Iron Phone Junction at 6 miles.

Because of the large changes in elevation, the hiker will probably prefer to begin a loop trip by taking the Boise Trail to Cannon Lake instead of this entrance.

From Windy Saddle Campground at the trailhead, an unsigned road to the southwest leads down to Seven Devils Campground where a sign at the back of the loop road points 150 yards to Seven Devils Lake. This emerald tarn clings beneath an 800-foot black rock wall. Another road from Windy Saddle leads northwest 2 miles to Heavens Gate Lookout, which has a view of three states, and a .2 mile foot trail to an observation point. This trail is a National Recreation Trail.

BLACK LAKE AREA (Seven Devils)

SIX LAKE BASIN

15

Round trip: 10 miles
Elevation gain: 1100 feet
Elevation loss: 920 feet (return climb)
Highest point: 8080 feet
Topo map: Cuprum (15′)
Time: 8 hours
Access: From Council, drive 10 miles on pavement and 20 miles
    on gravel to Bear. 4.5 miles beyond Bear, take the left (north)
    fork and drive 15 miles to Black Lake on primitive road.
Difficulty: Moderate

Hills of light green grass and dark green firs roll across this basin beside emerald green lakes. The lakes reflect dark grey cliffs and boulders of peaks above. Fields of paintbrush, lupine, cream-colored umbrella plant, purple horsemint, and bright blue-flax accent the hillsides along the trail. From the first saddle on the trail, the green mound of Horse Heaven glows to the north below the high black peaks of the northern Seven Devils. The pale shapes of the Wallowa Mountains drift in the distance beyond Joes Gap across Hells Canyon.

Black Lake, where the hike begins, is a dark green lake nestled in a circle of light green ridges and black cliffs. In the heyday of Seven Devils mining, a tramway was built to carry ore from a mine above cliffs across the lake to a mill below. A short detour from the trail allows a view of one wooden tramway tower still standing at the brink of a cliff above the lake. Twisted, rusty cables, ore buckets, and an immense wheel that carried the cables are scattered below the tunnel of the mine.

To reach the trailhead, first drive 30 miles from Council to Bear. The first 10 miles are paved and the rest is gravel. There are no services in Bear, but there is a Forest Service guard station just beyond. About 4.5 miles beyond Bear is the Black Lake Junction. Take the left (north) fork here. This primitive road climbs 2400 feet in 7 miles over the side of Smith Mountain near a look-out, then winds across Lost Basin for 1 mile before plunging over the edge of "High Dive". Here the road appears to dive over the edge of a cliff but turns and drives along the side of it. Then the route traverses the canyon wall and finally turns up a second canyon to the lake at 15 miles. The Black Lake Road is airy, steep, and extremely rocky. Even though four-wheel drive isn't needed, passenger cars are not recommended. The road to the lake is usually not open until after July 15 because of snow beyond High Dive.

The trail to Six Lake Basin and Emerald Lake leaves Black Lake on the north side near the campground. The trail, a former mining road, climbs west behind the campground. At .2 mile the route passes beneath a 30-foot boulder below cliffs. A crust of green malachite (copper ore) spots some of the big rocks here. At .5 mile the trail makes a switchback to the right. Here a path to the left (southeast) from the end of the switchback detours to the mine and tramway. Walk to the top of the rock bluff to see the tram tower, then follow the cables southwest to the mine.

After rejoining the main trail, the way leads northwest up a grassy slope to a pond at .7 mile. In a gully below the pond is an unsigned trail junction. The left branch leads to the southwest corner of the pond where a post sticks out of a rock cairn. Here the trail to Six Lake Basin turns south and zigzags up a hillside that is covered thickly with 3-foot tall plants of curly dock. The trail reaches a saddle at 1 mile. (The right branch of the trail at the pond leads north over Purgatory Saddle to Emerald Lake.)

Near the unnamed saddle at 1 mile on the Six Lake Basin Trail, the main Seven Devils appear to the north. Beyond the saddle are the grass hills and dead trees of Horse Pasture Basin. A green horseshoe-shaped lake nestles under a dark peak at the upper end of Horse Pasture Basin.

From here the trail zigzags down the side of the ridge, and heads west towards Joes Gap, 1.5 miles distant. The route first drops 320 feet, then climbs 160 feet through wildflower gardens to the gap at 2.5 miles. From the gap, the trail switchbacks down talus to the first blue-green lake at 3 miles.

Below the first lake the trail winds down through woods 200 feet, then cuts over to cross the outlet at 3.5 miles. At 4 miles the path passes the second shallow green lake in woods below tree-dotted ridges. The third lake is just east of the second lake and is not seen from the trail. The trail then climbs around the end of an open ridge and heads north to the fourth tea-colored lake. The route continues on to the fifth lake, but this path isn't shown on the topo map. The trail climbs a grassy hill, gradually turns east, and at 4.5 miles intersects trails to Deep and Granite Creeks. Beyond this signed junction is a large camp and horse area. At 5 miles the path reaches the fifth lake, largest of the six lakes. (The sixth lake is a tiny pond .2 mile off the trail below the third lake.)   Small peninsulas extend from the south shore into the long blue-green lake. Above the far end rise the dark cliffs of three round grey peaks that are left of Joes Gap.

EMERALD LAKE

16

Round trip: 6 miles
Elevation gain: 720 feet
Elevation loss: 1120 feet (return climb)
Highest point: 7920 feet
Topo map: Cuprum (15')
Time: 6 hours
Access: From Council, drive 10 miles on pavement and 20 miles on gravel to Bear. 4.5 miles beyond Bear, take left (north) fork and drive 15 miles to Black Lake on primitive road.
Difficulty: Moderate

Emerald Lake gleams in a deep canyon between black walls. On the west, among green grass, slices of dark lava lie in stacks below the fluted top of a wall. Left of this a triangular peak with a ski jump nose resembles a man's head lying back looking at the sky. The marsh at the upper end of the lake thins out into a narrow strip of grass around the entire shoreline. Monument Peak on the east wall of the canyon has a great dark protruding cliff with lines on it that look like writing. Along the trail Purgatory Saddle gives an excellent view of the shadowed canyon of Emerald Lake, the green dome of Horse Heaven, and the northern Seven Devils peaks.

The first .7 mile of this hike is along the same trail that leads to Six Lake Basin, so for access and directions for hiking to the pond at .7 mile, see that hike. At .7 mile the Emerald Lake Trail circles the east side of the pond and climbs to Purgatory Saddle, a notch in a line of dark grey cliffs. North of the saddle at 1 mile, the path zigzags down a headwall to return to grass and forest at 1.5 miles. The route continues straight down the canyon, switchbacks twice and crosses a little stream on two occasions. At 2 miles the trail runs through dense woods along the ravine of the main creek. The route reaches the upper end of the lake at 3 miles. From here it is 5 miles to Horse Heaven.

The trail continues around the east side of the lake. The largest campsite is at the upper end, but there are several others. About 200 yards around the lake is a big rock bench and a second inlet. The elevation loss from Purgatory Saddle to the lake is 1120 feet, so consider this in planning the return.

Mine above Black Lake

SATAN LAKE

17

Round trip: 2 miles (cross-country)
Elevation gain: 320 feet
Elevation loss: 160 feet (return climb)
Highest point: 7360 feet
Topo map: Cuprum (15′)
Time: 2 hours
Access: From Council, drive 10 miles on pavement, and 20 miles on gravel to Bear. 4.5 miles beyond Bear, take the left (north) fork and drive 15 miles to Black Lake on primitive road.
Route: Cross-country

The color of Satan Lake is a deep olive green, almost black. The lake nestles in a pocket in the cliffs about 1 mile from Black Lake. On the west side, dark cliffs spill down to the water. Behind a meadow at the north end, talus rises to a black rock point. On the east, orange talus separates black outcrops. A grey rock bench covered with firs, lodgepoles, and grouse whortleberry holds in the lake. From this bench the view of Black Lake and the surrounding peaks is excellent. The outlet splashes down a ravine into a meadow hundreds of feet below.

To reach the trailhead, drive to Bear from Council. The first

10 miles are paved, the next 20 miles are gravel. 4.5 miles beyond Bear is the Black Lake Junction. Here take the left (north) fork of the road and drive 15 miles on a primitive, but spectacular, road to Black Lake. Just below a side road leading left (southeast) to campsites by the outlet of Black Lake, another road goes right (north). Walk along this road for 100 yards. Just before this road ends, go to the right downhill off the edge of the road. There is no trail to Satan Lake, so a topographic map and compass are needed.

Angle north downhill keeping close to the cliffs. Beyond a meadow, cross a belt of thick forest. At .5 mile, the hiker should come out of the trees onto a steep talus slope below cliffs. Angle northeast towards the apparent head of the deep canyon of Satan Creek. At .7 mile, a light-colored rock bench clings to the left side of the canyon ahead. Go up the left side of this outcrop to the lake at 1 mile.

PAYETTE NATIONAL FOREST

NEW MEADOWS DISTRICT — Hazard Lake Area

EARLY HISTORY OF LONG VALLEY

In an unpublished account, Lizzie Sisk, one of the early settlers in Long Valley, gave an example of how women pioneers gradually became accustomed to dangers. She said she was so afraid of wild animals at first that she never went very far from the house except on horseback. Eventually Lizzie worked up enough courage to take her children on foot into the woods to gather huckleberries.

Long Valley is the mountain valley that reaches more than 30 miles from Cascade to McCall at an elevation of 4500 feet. Before the Sisk family arrived in 1884, there had been several other settlers. James Horner and the John Horenberger family settled in Long Valley in September 1883. Several others wintered there that year, but by the time the Sisks came, most of the early settlers had left. By 1886, settlers mainly came to homestead, although some mined at Paddy Flat and on Gold Fork and Boulder Creeks.

Early life in Long Valley was rough. The winters were long and cold. The mourners traveled to the first funeral, in 1889, on skis. Other difficulties included frontier disputes. In 1890 a cattle war occurred between settled cattlemen and newcomers in which hundreds of cattle belonging to the newcomers were shot. Three men were defended by William Borah, who proved that the men had been framed.

Most of the early settlement in Long Valley was near a post office named Roseberry. The Finns built a church and community hall here. By 1910, Roseberry had a flour mill, several stores, three churches, a bank, and a hotel. In 1914 when the railroad bypassed Roseberry, the town died. A new town, Donnelly, grew up next to the railroad.

Cascade was established in 1890 as Crawford and renamed Cascade in 1915. Crawford was in a bend on the banks of the Payette at The Falls, and became the center of settlement. Three men, William Monday, Jake Grosclose, and John Healy, had been killed by Indian ambush here in 1878.

Two other villages began near Cascade, but no longer exist. Thunder City, a village 6 miles southeast of Cascade, was a supply point for the Thunder Mountain mines. Van Wyck, which was established in 1888 with 300 people, now is under the waters of Cascade Reservoir. The reservoir, a federal reclamation project completed in 1948, eliminated the rapids for which the town was named.

Henry Hawksley started a hog ranch in Round Valley in 1886. Round Valley is the little valley where Smiths Ferry is located, south of Long Valley. By the early 1900s, Smiths Ferry was a logging headquarters. After the railroad was built in 1913, Hank Gowel constructed a swinging bridge. Railroad passengers could then cross the river to his Swinging Bridge Inn, which was located where Ferncroft used to be.

HISTORY OF NEW MEADOWS

The first permanent settlers in the New Meadows area were Bill Jolley and the Calvin White family in 1877. In 1880 the Clay family from Warren settled in Meadows Valley. White Bird's Indians had killed Mrs. Clay's first husband, Edward Osburn, on the Salmon River.

At New Meadows the Clays first lived in Packer John's cabin. John Welch had built the cabin in 1862 for storing goods on the road to the Boise Basin from Lewiston. Idaho's first Territorial Democratic Convention was held in that cabin in 1863. The cabin and land around it is now a state park.

One of Mrs. Clay's daughters, Caroline, married Charles Campbell who started the Circle C Ranch. It became one of the largest cattle ranches in the United States after beginning in 1888 with three cows and $500.

The railroad arrived in Meadows Valley in 1911. The terminal was the end of the line and led to the moving of the business section of town about 2 miles west to the present location of New Meadows.

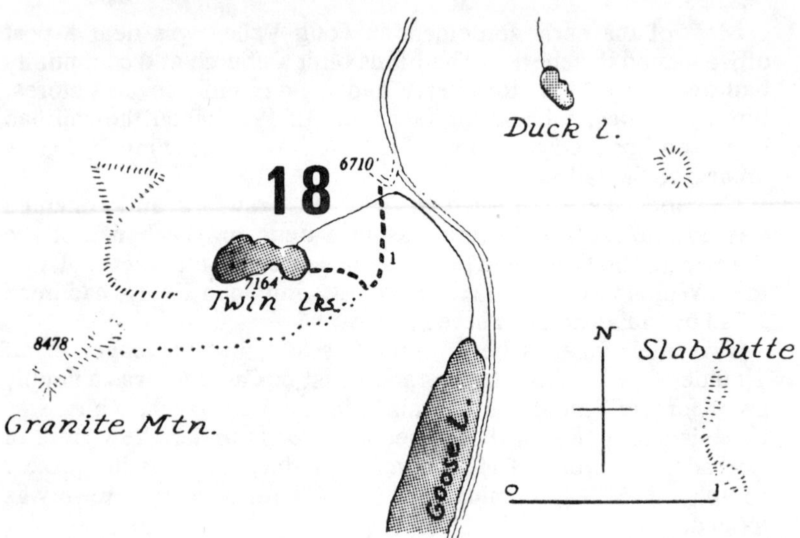

TWIN LAKES
(Granite Mountain Trail)

18

Round trip: 2 miles
Elevation gain: 450 feet
Highest point: 7164 feet
Topo map: Brundage Mountain
Time: 2½ hours
Access: Turn right (north) 5 miles northwest of McCall off Highway 55 on graveled Hazard Lake Road. Drive 2.8 miles past Goose Lake to trailhead at 12.9 miles.
Difficulty: Easy

Glacier-carved Granite Mountain bulges over Twin Lakes and is still covered in early July by a network of snow. A row of short cliffs finishes off the summit ridge. Between trees, rock benches drop 20 feet into the water of the upper lake. Since the lower lake is dammed, this hike is best for early season. In July the water is so high there is only one lake. Late in the summer when the water drops, two lakes form with dead logs littering muddy shores.

To reach the trailhead, turn right (north) off Highway 55 onto the graveled Hazard Lake Road 5 miles northwest of McCall. This road passes a turnoff for Brundage Mountain Ski Area. An overlook provides a view south to Council Mountain. At 6.2 miles the route passes the end of Brundage Reservoir. At 10.1 miles the road edges Goose Lake Reservoir and reaches the trailhead in a meadow at 12.9 miles. A dirt road turns left at a sign for Granite Mountain Trail and stops beside a small creek.

Follow the trail across the creek into a fir forest full of logging slash. The trail isn't quite the same as on the topographic map. Follow the blazes left (south); in 100 yards cross the outlet of the lower lake and find a more definite trail that is an old jeep road. At .5 mile the jeep track makes a big switchback to the northwest. Beyond, the track climbs gently to the lower lake at 1 mile. From this part of the trail the hiker can look across the canyon to the face of Slab Butte east of Goose Lake. Cattle have been pastured at Twin Lakes, so drinking water must be boiled.

GRASSY TWIN AND COFFEE CUP LAKES **19**

Round trip: 6.4 miles
Elevation gain: 840 feet
Elevation loss: 520 feet (return climb)
Highest point: 7800 feet
Topo map: Hazard Lake
Time: 6 hours
Access: Turn right (north) 5 miles northwest of McCall off Highway 55 onto graveled Hazard Lake Road. Drive 10 miles on gravel and 8 miles on dirt to Vance Creek Trail.
Difficulty: Moderate

From a grassy saddle above brownish-green Coffee Cup Lake, shapes of the Seven Devils Mountains billow to the northwest. To the north dips the indentation of the Salmon River Canyon. East across the canyon of Hard Creek, glaciers have carved granite hills near Bruin Mountain. Meadows dotted with wildflowers slope into both Grassy Twin Lakes. In July these meadows are golden carpets of buttercups and dogtooth violets. Slabs, talus, and firs slide into the lakes from a pointed granite knoll 600 feet above. The lower lake has a small rocky island near the far shore.

To reach the trailhead, turn right (north) on the graveled Hazard Lake Road 5 miles northwest of McCall. Drive beyond Goose Lake to the Vance Creek Trail at 18 miles, just below the Hard Creek Guard Station. (After 10 miles the road becomes dirt.) The trail starts closer to the bend in the road than is shown on the map.

At first the trail is a jeep track. At 200 yards the path intersects another track. At .3 mile the Vance Creek Trail joins the Grassy Mountain Trail. Turn left (west) here on the Grassy Mountain Trail, which diagonally climbs an open slope that is clumped with subalpine firs and aspens. At .7 mile the trail dips before climbing through forest. At 1.5 miles the route splits at a sign for Grassy Twin Lakes (called Grass Mountain Lakes on the topo map). The first lake is .2 mile down a path over the meadow. The main trail to

Grassy Twin Lakes

Coffee Cup Lake leads straight ahead here for 200 yards across the unmarked grass to blazed trees. Most people will want to take the path that runs closer to Grassy Twin Lakes. On this path, beyond the lakes a rocky trail leads east to meet the main trail near a saddle at 2.2 miles, where a sign points ahead along the ridge to Coffee Cup Lake. The trail runs along the side of this open ridge, then drops to a notch just above the lake. The path descends .2 mile down a fir-filled gully to the shore at 3 miles.

UPPER HAZARD LAKE   20

Round trip: 4 miles
Elevation gain: 360 feet
Highest point: 7428 feet
Topo map: Hazard Lake
Time: 3½ hours
Access: Turn right (north) 5 miles northwest of McCall from Highway 55 onto graveled Hazard Lake Road. Drive 10 miles on gravel and 12 miles on dirt to Hazard Lake.
Difficulty: Easy

Meadows filled in July with yellow and white flowers creep into blue Upper Hazard Lake across from a ridge of granite slabs. Fissures in the slabs angle to the east to the rounded summit of the ridge. The ridge looks like a lurking grizzly with a hump on its

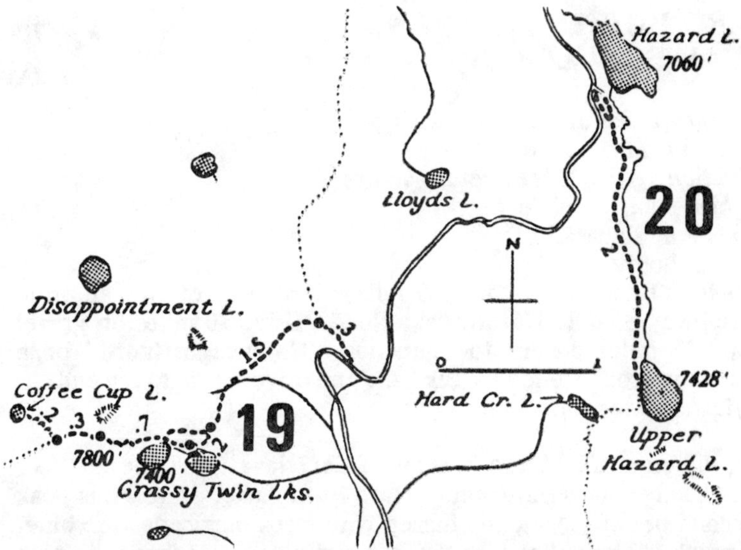

back, thus the name Bruin Mountain. Talus drops into the lake below the slabs, and trees edge the lake on both sides.

To reach the trailhead, turn north 5 miles northwest of McCall from Highway 55 onto the Hazard Lake Road and drive 22 miles to Hazard Lake. The gravel road turns to dirt at 10 miles. The road passes a sign for the other end of the Upper Hazard Lake Trail at 19 miles. At 22 miles is a sign for the Upper Hazard Lake Trail, which can also be reached from the campground. The road into the Hazard Lake Campground turns right (east) from the main road a few yards past the trail sign. Park at the sign at the main road, where the trail leads to the right (southeast) and intersects a second path from the main road. Turn left (east) at this intersection and hike 100 yards to the campground.

At another sign for Upper Hazard Lake at the edge of the campground, turn right (south) and follow the trail along the edge of a big meadow in the firs. Beyond the meadow the trail leads through a fir forest to a second meadow at 1.2 miles. The trail goes through this meadow instead of above it as is shown on the topo map. When the trail levels in a small clearing, the lake shines through the trees ahead. Here a side path leads through another grassy area to the lake at 2 miles. Campsites are on the west side.

The trail continues along the lake above the west shore. At 2.5 miles the route turns west and climbs 120 feet over a rise and down the same distance to small, narrow Hard Creek Lake in the woods. The hiker may make a through trip of 5 miles to the sign at 19 miles for Upper Hazard Lake on the main road by continuing on this trail or he can return the way he came.

HARD BUTTE, TWIN, AND RAINBOW LAKES

21

Round trip: 9.3 miles
Elevation gain: 600 feet
Elevation loss: 520 feet (return climb)
Highest point: 7760 feet
Topo map: Patrick Butte
Time: 7 hours
Access: Turn right (north) 5 miles northwest of McCall from Highway 55 onto Hazard Lake Road. Drive 10 miles on gravel and 15 miles on dirt to a junction. Go straight (north) on a primitive road signed for Elk Lake and drive 1 mile to the end.
Difficulty: Moderate

A ribbed knife edge and spire of dark lava flank the 200-foot black hood of Hard Butte above Hard Butte Lake. Below this peak a second tier of black cliffs fuzzed with trees barricades the blue-green lake. The outlet runs through a meadow splashed with pink mountain heath. Hard Butte Lookout perches on a rounded wooded summit above the upper Twin Lake.

North of the main trail below these lakes, dark lava cliffs and pillars sit beside the black lava face of a triangular wooded peak. To the right of these, blue hills fall away into the Salmon River Canyon. Further east Hershey Point Lookout commands a tree-dotted hill. South of Hershey Point, a 300-foot square blob of black lava forms part of Lava Ridge. Shooting stars cover grass at the edge of Rainbow Lake. Here granite cliffs separated by light green strips of bushes form a hill that reaches nearly to the skyline. Behind, a slanting wall of light granite dips and rises along to Hard Butte Lookout at the north end. East of this, a knoll of dark slabs divided by evergreens finishes the backdrop of the lake.

To reach the trailhead, turn north 5 miles northwest of McCall off Highway 55 and drive 25 miles up the Hazard Lake Road. This gravel road turns to dirt at 10 miles. The continuation of the road beyond Hazard Lake is not shown on any maps. 3.1 miles north of the Hazard Lake Campground, the road forks. The right (east) branch goes to Elk Meadows. Here take a primitive road straight ahead (north) 1.2 miles to its end. Two trails start here: the Clay-burn Trail to Lava Ridge and Hershey Point, and the Elk Lake Trail. (The hike to Lava Butte Lakes begins at the other end of the Clayburn Trail.)

Take the Elk Lake Trail north across meadows filled with flowers like blue sky pilot and yellow paintbrush. The trail, a jeep road

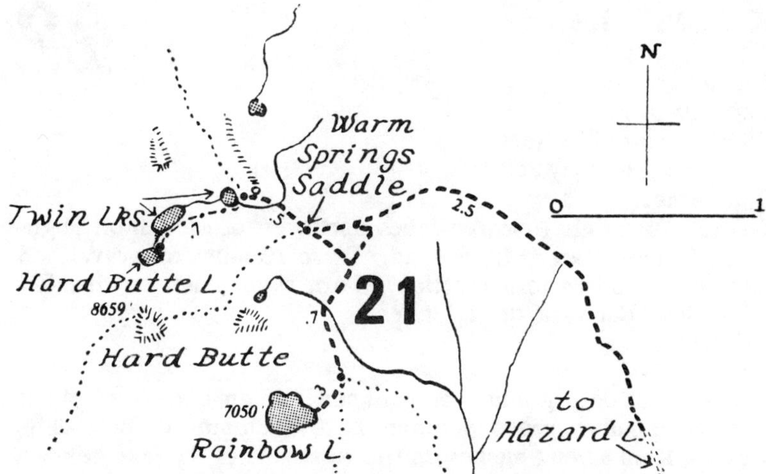

closed to motor vehicles, goes gently downhill. At 1 mile the route crosses a side stream. At 2 miles another jeep track splits to the left. At 2.2 miles the Partridge Creek Trail towards the Salmon River leads right (north).

At 2.5 miles, beyond a low point called Warm Springs Saddle on a flat ridge, is a three-way junction. The left branch drops south 1 mile to Rainbow Lake. The middle trail climbs 2 miles southwest to the top of Hard Butte. The right trail leads northwest to Elk Lake. .3 mile beyond the junction, the Elk Lake Trail crosses the outlet of Twin Lakes. A tiny pond is on the right 200 yards beyond the outlet. Turn left (west) here and walk 100 yards to Lower Twin Lake, 3 miles from the trailhead.

To reach the upper lakes, go left (south) and cross the outlet. A good path leads around the lake and up a little ridge beside the inlet to Upper Twin Lake. The path continues up the inlet to Hard Butte Lake at 3.7 miles.

To reach Rainbow Lake, at the three-way junction take the Rainbow Lake Trail southeast. The track drops across meadows and through bits of forest to a cabin covered with shiny metal that is still used by the Cattle Grazing Association. Beyond here the jeep track becomes a trail and continues uphill. .7 mile along the Rainbow Lake Trail a path turns off and goes .3 mile southwest to the lake. The total elevation loss from the junction to Rainbow Lake is about 240 feet. There are large campsites in the trees on the east side of Rainbow Lake. The main trail below Rainbow Lake continues on to Hazard Creek and to Black, Eden, and Buck Lakes.

On the return, .5 mile can be saved by taking a jeep track which branches northeast at the shiny cabin. This eliminates 2 sides of a triangle in going back to the trailhead.

SCRIBNER LAKE   22

Round trip: 1 mile
Elevation gain: 160 feet
Highest point: 7154 feet
Topo map: Hershey Point
Time: 1 hour
Access: Turn right (north) 5 miles northwest of McCall off High-
   way 55 onto Hazard Lake Road. Drive 10 miles on gravel and
   15 miles on dirt to a junction. Turn right (east) on dirt Elk
   Meadows Road and drive 7 miles.
Difficulty: Easy

A 400-foot dark granite face shaped like an earless elephant
overlooks shallow green Scribner Lake. Clumps of pale cliffs
stick out from among bushes on the west side of the lake below a
high grass-green ridge.

To reach the trail, turn north off Highway 55 onto the Hazard
Lake Road 5 miles northwest of McCall. Drive 10 miles on gravel
and 15 miles on dirt to a junction. Turn right (east) on the Elk
Meadows Road and go 7 miles to a sign for Scribner Lake.

The trail climbs through a fir forest underlain by wildflowers.
Then the route edges a jumble of enormous boulders. The path
continues level through scattered boulders and trees to the lake at
.5 mile. This hike is an easy side trip for those planning to hike to
Lava Butte Lakes the same day.

LAVA BUTTE LAKES
(National Recreation Trail)   23

Round trip: 6 miles (includes 4 mile loop)
Elevation gain: 1120 feet
Elevation loss: 400 feet
Highest point: 7900 feet
Topo maps: Patrick Butte, Hershey Point
Time: 5 hours
Access: Turn right (north) 5 miles northwest of McCall from
   Highway 55 onto Hazard Lake Road. Drive 10 miles on gravel
   and 15 miles on dirt to a junction. Turn right (east) on dirt Elk
   Meadows Road and drive 8 miles to Clayburn Trail sign.
Difficulty: Moderate

A crumbled lava face near the two lower Lava Butte Lakes
resembles a decaying castle overgrown by fungus. As seen from
the highest lake, a tiny milky aqua gem, this set of lava cliffs forms

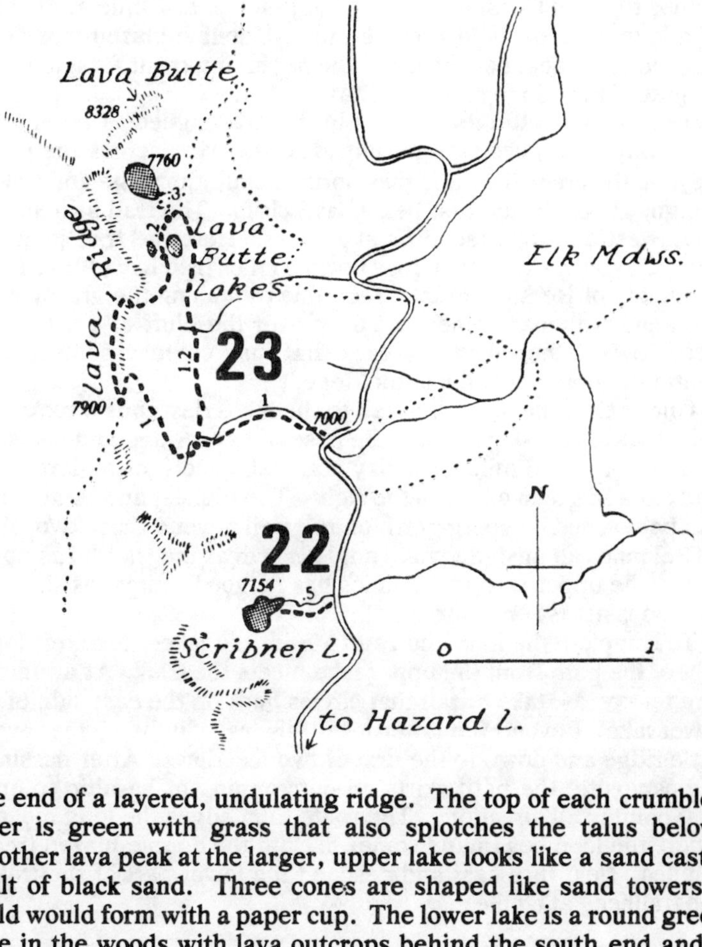

one end of a layered, undulating ridge. The top of each crumbled
layer is green with grass that also splotches the talus below.
Another lava peak at the larger, upper lake looks like a sand castle
built of black sand. Three cones are shaped like sand towers a
child would form with a paper cup. The lower lake is a round green
lake in the woods with lava outcrops behind the south end and a
veiled view of Lava Ridge on the west.

To reach the trailhead, turn right (north) off Highway 55 onto
the Hazard Lake Road 5 miles northwest of McCall. Drive 10 miles
on gravel, then 15 miles on dirt to a junction. Turn right (east) on a
dirt road signed for Elk Meadows. This road is sometimes closed
weekdays for logging. At .6 mile the road comes to a sign "Lava
Ridge Trail". Beyond this the road climbs south along a ridge
above Big Hazard Lake.

The road rounds the end of the ridge at 3.5 miles and runs back
to the north along the other side of the ridge. At 8 miles, just
beyond a bend in the road, the Clayburn Trail begins as a jeep
track that turns to a trail at a creek crossing in 100 yards. (Park by
the main road, since the jeep track is often muddy.) The trail

climbs through forest to an unsigned junction at 1 mile at the edge of a long meadow below lava bluffs. A double-blazed tree at the near edge of the meadow marks the beginning point for a loop that includes Lava Ridge and Lava Butte Lakes.

To go up Lava Ridge, take the blazed trail signed "Center Stock Driveway". It goes straight ahead to the west across the creek. Beyond the creek the path goes northwest up the ridge and follows a high, grassy bench just below lava cliffs. The trail switchbacks southwest and tops the cliffs at 2 miles. Here the trail joins one from Clayburn Creek that goes north 6 miles past Lava Butte Lakes to the top of Hershey Point. Take this trail along the grassy ridge top amid whitebark pines and drop over the bluff at 2.5 miles to head toward the lakes. A path that may confuse some people continues along the crest of the ridge.

Once below the bluff, the trail to the lakes descends a rocky hillside. The route skirts under the nose of Lava Ridge and crosses a bed of lava. At 3 miles, a milky aqua lake is off to the left (west) and a round green one is to the right. The highest and largest lake can be reached by going north on the trail beyond these two lakes. At 3.2 miles an unsigned path angles north as the trail turns northeast. The upper lake at 3.5 miles has no good campsites since the ground is grassy or lumpy.

To complete the loop and return from the lakes, turn left (east) where the path from the upper lake meets the trail. At a junction in a few yards, take a trail that circles back on the east side of the lower lake. Beyond the lower lake, this trail climbs 40 feet over a little ridge and down to the first of two meadows. After passing a big campsite, the path skirts an outcropping of basaltic columns that point in all directions. The route then edges the long meadow where the loop began and comes back to the double-blazed tree at 5 miles. Next turn east and descend the lower part of the trail to the trailhead at 6 miles.

McCALL DISTRICT — Paddy Flat Area

NORTH FORK KENNALLY CREEK TRAIL
(National Recreation Trail)

24

Round trip: 5 miles (18 miles to lakes)
Elevation gain: 200 feet (1600 feet to lakes)
Elevation loss: 120 feet (return climb)
Highest point: 7240 feet at lakes
Topo maps: Blackmare and Paddy Flat
Time: 4 hours (2 days for lakes)
Access: Between Donnelly and Lakefork, turn right (east) off Highway 55 onto graveled and dirt Paddy Flat Road. Following signs, drive 14.1 miles to Kennally Creek Campground.
Difficulty: Easy to creek crossing

At first, Kennally Creek froths over granite boulders beside dense lodgepoles, larches, and firs. Further up on the North Fork, transparent water flows over golden sand under banks of tall grass and flowers. Foot-long white flower clusters of beargrass shine like lacy lanterns when the sunlight strikes them from behind. The trail climbs gently up the wooded canyon to Kennally Creek Lakes at 9 miles. The first part of the trail to a creek crossing at 2.5 miles makes a pleasant day hike.

To reach the trailhead, turn east on the graveled Paddy Flat Road between Donnelly and Lakefork on Highway 55. Drive 10.5 miles to the junction of the Paddy Flat and Kennally Creek Roads. Turn left (east) on the dirt Kennally Creek Road, drive 2 miles to a junction with Sloans Point Lookout Road and turn left. Go east 1.6 miles to the Kennally Creek Campground.

The East Fork of Kennally Creek Trail leads to the North Fork Trail. The East Fork Trail begins at the far end of the campground and climbs 100 feet along the creek in the first .7 mile. At .7 mile the path crosses the North Fork on a wooden bridge and at 1 mile joins the North Fork Trail. On the East Fork Trail, the Needles Trail branches south 1 mile beyond the North Fork Trail Junction.

Turn left (north) on the North Fork Trail at the 1 mile junction. The trail edges a swamp near the stream. There are a few small clearings but no big meadow. At 2 miles the trail leaves the creek and climbs over a 100-foot hill. At 2.5 miles the route fords the creek. Above the trail, hidden by trees, light green chapparal and grey granite outcrops punctuate the wooded canyon walls. The

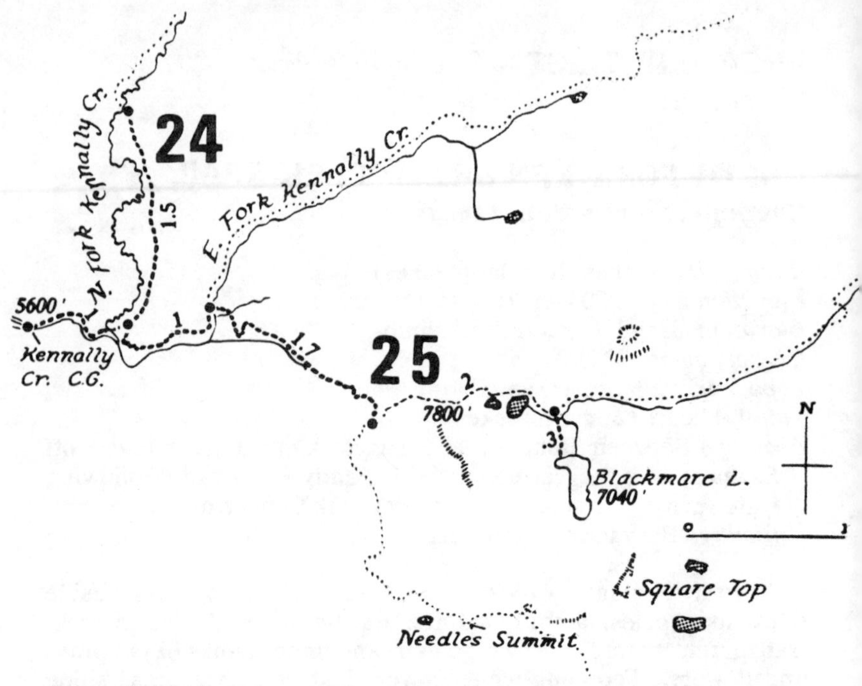

route up the canyon to the lakes is much the same except that the
trail steepens for the last 2 miles.

BLACKMARE LAKE

25

Round trip: 12 miles
Elevation gain: 2280 feet
Elevation loss: 1040 feet (return climb)
Highest point: 7800 feet
Topo map: Blackmare
Time: 10 hours
Access: Turn east on Paddy Flat Road off Highway 55 between
  Donnelly and Lakefork; following signs, drive 14.1 miles to
  Kennally Creek Campground.
Ability: Expert

A huge floating platform of driftwood hugs the lower end of
blue-green Blackmare Lake. At the upper end, a narrow, high rock
knoll sits below a pointed mountain of crumbled granite cliffs. A
long ridge of talus and slabs borders the east side of the lake.
Trees stripe the ridge diagonally. West of a bay at the north end of

Blackmare Lake

the lake rise tiers of granite divided by trees.

The route from Kennally Creek on an unofficial trail drops 1000 feet from a saddle, so this must be climbed on the way back. Another route gains 2800 feet in 11 miles from the South Fork of the Salmon. An unnamed lake 700 feet above Blackmare Lake on the Kennally Creek route is a fine destination itself. On the west side of this tiny lake, a 40-foot cliff slants out of the water towards a wall of cliffs on the ridge above.

To reach the trail, turn east on the Paddy Flat Road off Highway 55 between Donnelly and Lakefork. Follow the signs and drive 14.1 miles to Kennally Creek Campground on a gravel road that turns to dirt at about 12.5 miles. From the campground, take the East Fork of Kennally Creek Trail. The first two miles follow along Kennally Creek through larches and firs. At 1 mile the North Fork of Kennally Creek Trail branches off. The East Fork Trail above this junction zigzags 500 vertical feet up a wooded rocky slope.

At 1.7 miles the trail turns left (north) and reaches a junction with the Needles Trail at 2 miles. Turn right (east) on the Needles Trail, which crosses the East Fork on a log. The path angles through thick forest beside beargrass, and runs beside but doesn't cross Kennally Creek at 2.5 miles. At 3 miles the route goes through a flat wooded area. At 3.7 miles a sign points uphill indicating "Blackmare Lake 1½ - No trail". It is really 2.2 miles from this point to the lake. A well-trodden path that is easy for the experienced hiker to follow leads straight up the ridge from here.

After going up, the path angles over to the crest of a fold in the canyon wall at 4.2 miles. From here look back and see Cascade Reservoir. Next the path drops over the fold and heads east up a small side canyon. At a boulder field, the route moves northeast and switchbacks to the top of a small wooded ridge at the head of the canyon at 4.7 miles, 600 feet above where the path left the official trail.

The route drops northeast, passes below rectangular blocks of talus, and descends to a tiny pond. The path skirts the pond on the north to reach the small, unnamed lake at 5.5 miles. The track continues around the north side of this lake, then plunges down the north side of its outlet to meet the Blackmare Creek Trail at 5.7 miles. This trail shows much less use below this intersection than above it. The trail crosses the outlet of Black-mare Lake, then climbs a brushy hillside to the lake at 6 miles.

McCALL DISTRICT — Boulder Creek Area (Lake Fork)

THE FINNS IN LONG VALLEY

Many of the first Long Valley settlers were from Finland by way of the Wyoming mines. At first the men went back to these mines in the winter to earn money. Later they worked nearby at the Thunder Mountain mines. The first Finnish families were those of Matt Koskella, John Lahti, and John Haarola, who settled in Arling and Roseberry in 1895. The writing of Andrew Campula in Finnish newspapers in the United States influenced settlers to come to Long Valley. By 1902 the valley was a Finnish community, and by 1908, there were 95 homesteads.

Few of the Finnish settlers were sure if they would stay in the U. S. permanently, so they made an effort to keep Finnish customs like the sauna. The original saunas had no smokestacks, so the bathers got sooty as well as sweaty. The Finns didn't go out afterwards and jump in an icy creek or roll in the snow; they just took baths in warm water. The first school for Finnish settlers was held in the village of Elo, which was near Lakefork. The school was taught in English, so the pupils were able to teach their parents English in the evenings.

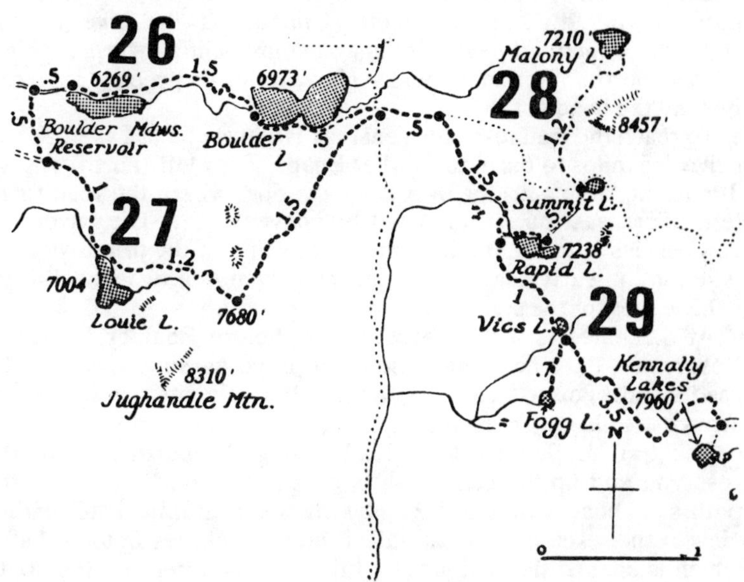

BOULDER CREEK TRAIL TO BOULDER LAKE AND RAPID LAKE
26

Round trip: 8 miles
Elevation gain: 1120 feet
Elevation loss: 320 feet (return climb)
Highest point: 7280 feet
Topo map: Paddy Flat
Time: 6½ hours
Access: Turn east off Highway 55 at Lakefork. Go 1.5 miles to Farm to Market Road. Turn left and go 3 miles north to a bridge over Lake Fork. Turn east here on a paved road; go 1 mile to end of pavement, and then 3.2 miles on primitive road to Boulder Meadows Reservoir.
Difficulty: Moderate

At the head of Rapid Lake, small firs and brush climb grey and white 200-foot cliffs trying to reach the green grass growing among the rocks on top. Blue and red dragonflies flit above the shore like miniature helicopters, while fat frogs plop in and out of the water. Yellow pond lilies float near the edge next to marsh grass. A peninsula nearly cuts the green lake in two. On the peninsula, the tiny white flowers of beargrass cluster on long stalks. Boulder

Lake is .7 mile long and has had its level raised by an 8-foot rock dam, so muddy sand completely surrounds the lake in late summer. A pointed peak with charcoal grey cliffs dwarfs the dam on the north. Rounded peaks above hills of green grass rise beyond the head of the lake.

To reach the trailhead, turn east off Highway 55 at Lakefork and drive 1.5 miles to Farm to Market Road. Turn left (north) and go 3 miles north to a bridge over the Lake Fork where the road turns left. Turn east on an unsigned but paved road. The pavement ends in less than 1 mile. Beyond the pavement, the primitive road is muddy in early season, but can be driven in a two-wheel drive vehicle most of the summer.

At 3.2 miles is a campground just before Boulder Meadows Reservoir. Park here, because there is no parking space at the road's end. Pointed grey Jughandle Mountain sits across the log-strewn .5 mile long reservoir.

The trail to Boulder Lake leads along the north side of the reservoir and up the canyon through thick forest. At 1 mile the path switchbacks and at 1.2 miles' passes a granite knoll with a view of the reservoir. At 1.5 miles the trail reaches Boulder Lake, which is shaped like a figure eight. The route borders the south side of the lake. Beside the upper half of the lake, a detour, marked "Horse Trail", skirts above a muddy area.

Beyond the lake at 2.5 miles near a tiny pond, the path reaches a junction with the Paddy Flat-Lake Fork Trail. 100 yards before this junction, a small sign points southwest to the Jughandle Trail.

The Rapid Lake route winds through open meadows, full of wild-flowers in season, to a junction with the Buckhorn Trail to Summit Lake at 3 miles. The Rapid Lake Trail continues southeast across the side of a grassy hill with a view of Jughandle Mountain. Then the path descends through trees to a swamp at 3.5 miles. The trail may be hard to find through the swamp, but beyond the swamp, it runs along the north side of the creek, then crosses it at 3.7 miles. From the creek the route heads south up a hill to a junction with a path to Rapid Lake. Walk 200 yards east on this path to the .2 mile long lake at 4 miles. Campsites are just beyond the outlet and on and near the peninsula on the north side of the lake.

LOUIE LAKE
AND THE JUGHANDLE TRAIL
27

Loop trip: 6.7 miles via Boulder Lake
One-way: 1.5 miles to Louie Lake
Elevation gain: 1480 feet
Highest point: 7680 feet
Topo map: Paddy Flat
Time: 6 hours for loop trip
Access: Turn east off Highway 55 at Lakefork, and go 1.5 miles to
Farm to Market Road. Turn left (north) and go 3 miles to bridge
over Lake Fork. Turn east on paved road and drive 1 mile to end
of pavement and 3.2 miles on primitive road.
Difficulty: Easy to Louie Lake; expert ability needed for Jughandle

Aspens frame dark blue Louie Lake, which is shaped like a
witch's hat. Grey cliffs of pointed Jughandle Mountain overlook
the lake and two dark granite islands. A tipsy log cabin sits near
the 8-foot earth dam. From the Jughandle Trail above Louie Lake,
Payette and Little Payette Lakes spread robin's egg blue arms
among green-black forest. Brundage and Granite Mountains
frame one side of a view that stretches to the Seven Devils. From
this trail Jughandle's cliffs look like the back of a grey elephant
chopped in half. From the Rapid Creek side of the Jughandle
Trail, the hiker views cliff-covered peaks behind Rapid and
Summit Lakes.

To reach the trail, turn east off Highway 55 at Lakefork and go
1.5 miles to Farm to Market Road. Turn left (north) and go 3 miles
to a left turn in the road just before a bridge over the Lake Fork.
Turn right (east) on an unsigned, paved road (the Boulder Creek
Road). Pavement ends in 1 mile; continue 3.2 miles on primitive
road to the Louie Lake Trail below Boulder Meadows Reservoir.

Walk along the trail as it crosses Boulder Creek on logs. Then
the route climbs 300 feet south up a ridge to intersect the Louie
Lake Jeep Trail at .5 mile. Walk east (left) up the jeep trail, which
jogs north at .7 mile. At this point the track goes straight up
through jack-o-lantern-sized boulders. The route continues
through forest to the .4 mile long lake at 1.5 miles. A dam has
raised the lake level 15 feet. Best campsites are around the lake
away from the jeep road and trail.

The Jughandle Trail turns southeast from the dam and follows
the lakeshore for a short distance before climbing a low ridge east
of the lake. The Jughandle Trail is not maintained, but is marked
with rock cairns from Louie Lake to the saddle. The path zigzags
up through rock outcrops and skirts cliffs of Twin Peaks just below
the saddle. Beyond the saddle at 2.7 miles, the trail is difficult to

follow through fallen timber and grassy places, so a topographic map is essential.

From the saddle the Jughandle Trail skirts along the east side of Twin Peaks up to another saddle at 3.2 miles. From here the route follows the wooded crest of a ridge that runs northeast. Then the path starts down a grassy gully at 3.5 miles. Even though early in the season a spring bubbles at the head of the gully, for most of the summer the only water on the trail is at the lakes. Below the gully the path follows a ridge down to the Boulder Lake Trail at 4.2 miles. This junction, 100 yards west of the Paddy Flat-Lake Fork Trail Junction, is marked with a small sign on a tree facing east. The trailhead at Boulder Meadows Reservoir is 2.5 miles down the Boulder Lake Trail.

SUMMIT LAKE AND MALONY LAKE FROM RAPID LAKE   28

Round trip: 11.4 miles
This section: 880 feet gain and 910 feet loss (return climb)
Highest point: 8120 feet
Topo map: Paddy Flat
Time: 4 hours for this section, one-way
Access: from Rapid Lake (see Boulder Creek Trail)
Route: Cross-country

The 800-foot grey cliffs of Buckhorn Mountain hang at the head of a talus-filled canyon above Malony Lake. The lake is milky blue-green with a shoreline of silvered logs below forest and cliffs. On the east side of the lake, a rocky peak resembles a one-humped camel. Bunch grass and flowers cover a saddle between Malony and Summit Lakes beside Buckhorn Mountain. In the distance to the north from the saddle are white peaks along the Lick Creek Road and to the northwest lurk the black shapes of the Seven Devils. The splintered cliffs of Rapid Peak rise to the southeast. To the south below the saddle, pale blue Cascade Reservoir floats like a mirage. Below Buckhorn Mountain, grass and lilies fringe 300-yard Summit Lake.

Most people who visit Summit Lake do so as a side trip from Rapid Lake, for the Buckhorn Trail to the lake is poor. For access and directions for reaching Rapid Lake, see the hike description for the Boulder Creek Trail. To reach Summit Lake, .5 mile from Rapid Lake, just beyond the peninsula of Rapid Lake ascend the left side of the inlet stream. There's a hint of a path some of the way. Campsites beside this lake consist of lumpy grass. To get to the saddle on the side of Buckhorn Mountain, climb cross-country up a low ridge west of Summit Lake and go north until the ridge merges with the mountain above. Walk east to the saddle, which is 1 mile from Rapid Lake.

From the saddle, the hiker can reach Malony Lake by first walking northeast to the edge of a dropoff beside Buckhorn Mountain. Then turn left (north) and walk 100 yards along a ridge perpendicular to the saddle. Climb northeast down a green gap between the sloping granite slabs to a tiny pond at 1.5 miles. Just above the pond the gap is steep, so be careful. Beyond the pond descend a gully to a rock knoll that overlooks the lake. Just before the knoll another gully turns east down into the canyon at the head of the lake. Take this gully down to the canyon. This route avoids the talus that chokes the upper end of the canyon. From here it is an easy walk down to Malony Lake, 1.2 miles from Summit Lake and 1.7 miles from Rapid Lake.

VICS LAKE, FOGG LAKE, AND KENNALLY CREEK LAKES FROM RAPID LAKE **29**

Round trip: 16 miles
Elevation gain: 1760 feet
Elevation loss: 1400 feet (return climb)
This section: 4 miles, 640 feet gain, 1080 feet loss (return climb)
Highest point: 8000 feet
Time: 3½ hours for this section one-way
Topo map: Paddy Flat
Access: from Rapid Lake (see Boulder Creek Trail)
Difficulty: Strenuous

Water lilies cover 150-yard long Vics Lake beside white boulders, trees, and wildflowers. Fogg Lake is about the same size, but is deeper and has only a few lily pads. Fogg Lake sits in a little pocket in the woods with a few granite outcrops that provide fishing platforms. South of Kennally Creek Summit, a granite hogback bristles with pinnacles. The pointed green top of Green Mountain is to the southeast. The Seven Devils are northwest and peer from behind granite slopes of Jughandle Mountain. The largest Kennally Lake is in the woods surrounded by grass with a view back to the hogback. The other three tiny marshy lakes cling to a small rocky ridge.

For access and directions for reaching Rapid Lake, see Boulder Creek Trail. The trail from the Rapid Lake Junction on to Vics Lake and Kennally Creek Lakes climbs over the crest of a ridge and drops 50 feet to Vics Lake at 1 mile. The trail skirts the lake on the west and crosses the outlet. Just beyond the outlet is a signed spur trail for Fogg Lake. The trail to Fogg Lake drops through trees about .7 mile to a large campsite. Few hikers use the trail to Kennally Creek Summit at 2 miles. This path climbs through pines, firs, and grassy clearings dotted with gentians in season.

Below the summit the trail descends towards Kennally Creek Lakes in the open just under the hogback ridge and turns into the forest at 2.2 miles. At 2.7 miles the path crosses Kennally Creek to the north and at 3.5 miles goes back again to the south. At this crossing, head cross-country southwest down to the forested largest lake at 4 miles.

McCALL   DISTRICT — Warren Wagon Road Area

HISTORY OF WARRENS AND BURGDORF

When James Warren, Matthew Bledsoe, and others discovered gold on the South Fork of the Salmon in 1862, the original settlement was called Richmond. Miners loyal to the Union moved 1 mile downstream and called their settlement Washington, which became the county seat of Idaho County. In 1875 Washington lost the county seat to Mt. Idaho, and then Washington was known as Warrens. Warrens is now known as Warren.

Warrens was too isolated for the residents to expect entertainers to come there, so the miners started their own theatrical society with a unique rule: neither the audience nor the performers could smile. One cheerful and persistant person in Warrens was Polly Bemis, a Chinese girl who had been sold to a bandit in China as a young girl. She was owned by a man named Big Jim who brought her to Warrens as a prostitute. When her owner died, Polly opened a restaurant. A saloon keeper, Charlie Bemis, was shot on the porch of her restaurant. She nursed him back to health and lived with him for twenty years before becoming his legal wife. However, another version of this story says Bemis won her in a poker game.

At that time the main north-south road went from Lewiston up French Creek Grade from the Salmon River to Boise Basin by way of Warrens. The road detoured to a hot springs en route. These springs were discovered in 1863 and called Warm Springs. Fritz Burgdorf from Warrens homesteaded there and provided travelers with hot baths and beef. In 1870 Burgdorf built a hotel which became a social center called Resort. Burgdorf married a singer who was on her way to Warrens for a performance. In 1914, Mrs. Burgdorf had the post office renamed in honor of her husband.

East Twentymile Lake

TWENTYMILE LAKES

30

Round trip: 13.5 miles to see all four lakes
Elevation gain: 2360 feet
Highest point: 7960 feet
Topo maps: Black Tip, Victor Peak, Box Lake
Time: 10 hours
Access: Drive 12.5 miles north of McCall on paved Warren Wagon
   Road. Trailhead is at the upper end of Upper Payette Lake.
Difficulty: Strenuous; cross-country to see upper lakes

A row of fissured 400-foot grey cliffs unfolds behind blue East Twentymile Lake. To the right of this, a buff-colored rock wall sweeps up to a point. Further right (west), fractured cliffs sprinkled with trees form a high cone-shaped peak. Red mountain heath and yellow buttercups grow among moss on the shore. The cone-shaped peak dominates South Twentymile Lake above a waterfall that sneaks down a crevice to the lake.

North Twentymile Lake, at the trail's end, has a band of trees between the lake and the fluted cliffs. Deep blue Long Lake gleams among white boulders and granite outcrops. The trail gains more than 1800 feet between the junction with the Duck Lake Trail at 3 miles and North Twentymile Lake at 6 miles. This stretch

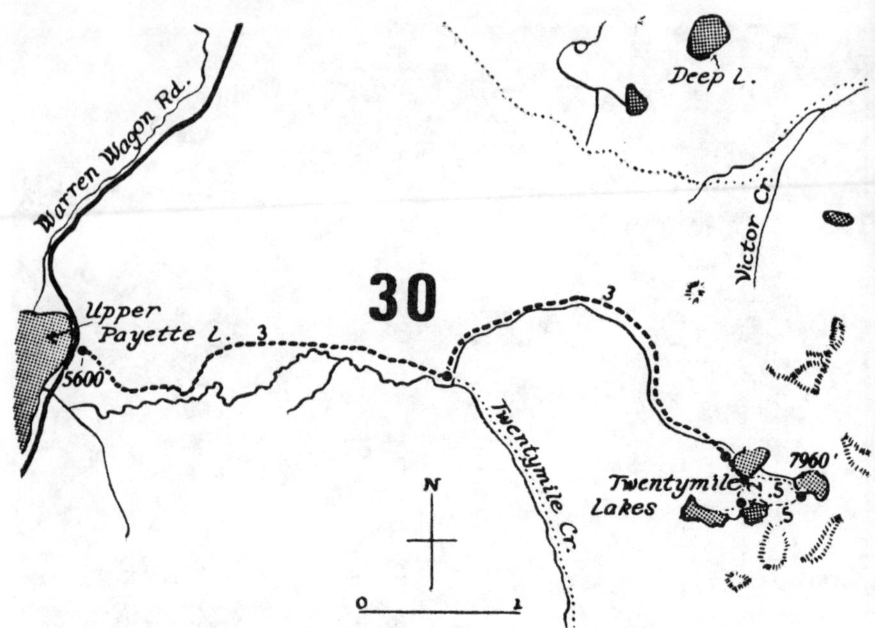

may seem like 20 miles on a hot day! In two places, the trail climbs 200 feet in 200 yards.

To reach the trailhead, drive north of McCall on the paved Warren Wagon Road. The Twentymile Lakes Trail begins 1.5 miles north of the turnoff to the campground at Upper Payette Lake.

The trail climbs only 280 feet in the first 3 miles through a forest of firs and lodgepoles carpeted with grouse whortleberry and beargrass. At 3 miles, the Twentymile Lakes Trail turns off of the Twentymile Creek Trail which continues 9 miles to Duck Lake.

The trail to the lakes climbs 200 vertical feet right beside the North Fork of Twentymile Creek before the grade lessens. At 3.5 miles from the beginning of the trail, the route crosses a tiny side stream. At 4.5 miles the trail passes through open grassy areas that extend up the wooded ridge on the north. At 5 miles the path again climbs 200 feet in 200 yards before flattening out to run along the creek to North Twentymile Lake. The topo map shows the trail crossing the creek and going up to Long Lake, but the route leads to North Twentymile Lake first. Just before the north lake at 6 miles, the path crosses the creek in a swamp.

To see the other lakes, go about .2 mile south from North Twentymile Lake up a 100-foot ridge to South Twentymile Lake. Long Lake is 200 yards down South's outlet. East Twentymile Lake may be reached by first going along the north shore of South Twentymile, staying 25 yards above the lake. Then climb .5 mile and 100 feet up towards a talus-topped hill northeast of the fissured row of cliffs. To return to North Twentymile (or for a short, steep route from North Twentymile to East Twentymile Lake), take a path down the southwest side of East's outlet until the route becomes too steep. At that point cut over to the south and drop down to the shore. Walking to the other three lakes will add about 1.5 miles to the 12 mile round trip to North Twentymile.

JOSEPHINE LAKE

31

Round trip: 1 mile
Elevation gain: 240 feet
Highest point: 7400 feet
Topo map: Victor Peak
Time: 2 hours
Access: Drive north of McCall on paved Warren Wagon Road past
    Upper Payette Lake and Secesh Summit to Josephine Lake Road
    at 19.6 miles. Turn left (north) on a primitive road and drive
    3.5 miles to the end of the road.
Difficulty: Easy

Slanting cliffs split by a double waterfall plunge into blue-green Josephine Lake on the south. Above the falls, a 400-foot dark grey cliff shadows a cirque above two tiny ponds. Left of this cliff, the

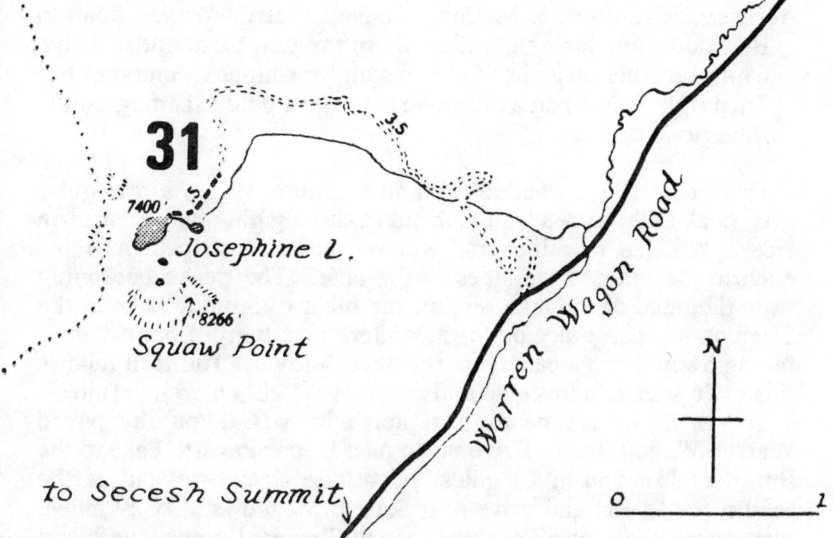

nipple-shaped highest nubbin on a light-colored ridge is named Squaw Point. On the west side of the lake, a band of cliffs resemble a row of toppled dominoes. Half way up the outlet, a branching waterfall foams into little pools.

To reach the trailhead, take the Warren Wagon Road north of McCall past Upper Payette Lake and Secesh Summit. At 19.6 miles, turn left (north) on the primitive and rocky Josephine Lake Road and drive 3.5 miles to the end of the road. 100 yards before the end of the road, an unsigned trail leads southwest up through logging slash, then angles left along the forest edge.

At .2 mile the route passes a pond in a meadow that is under cliffs divided by a snow-filled chute. At .5 mile the trail reaches the lake. The few campsites are all very rocky or slanting. A very steep path for experts only goes up the left side of the south inlet to two tiny ponds in a cirque. To see the waterfall on the outlet, on the way back take a path that begins about 25 yards from the trail at the meadow.

LOON LAKE   **32**

Round trip: 10.4 miles
Elevation gain: 340 feet
Elevation loss: 180 feet (return climb)
Highest point: 5840 feet
Topo map: Loon Lake
Time: 7 hours
Access: Drive north of McCall on paved Warren Wagon Road to
    Burgdorf Junction at 23 miles where the pavement ends. Drive
    6 miles further on a dirt road to a sign for Chinook Campground.
    Turn right (south) on a primitive road; go 1 mile to campground.
Difficulty: Moderate

From between a wooded hill and a granite ridge, a triangular grey peak and pleated wall look out at the big blue platter of Loon Lake. Wooded moraines and willows behind a strip of meadow enclose the other three sides of the lake. The peaks beckoning from the head of the lake remind the hiker of Stanley Lake in the Sawtooths. The quiet outlet meanders in a hairpin bend before falling away down a canyon to the Secesh River. The trail follows this river, which foams gold and green over light-colored granite.

To reach the trailhead, turn north in McCall on the paved Warren Wagon Road. Drive north past Upper Payette Lake to the Burgdorf Junction at 23 miles. Continue straight ahead as the road turns to dirt and drive past Secesh Meadows. At 29 miles, turn right (south) on a primitive road to Chinook Campground, and

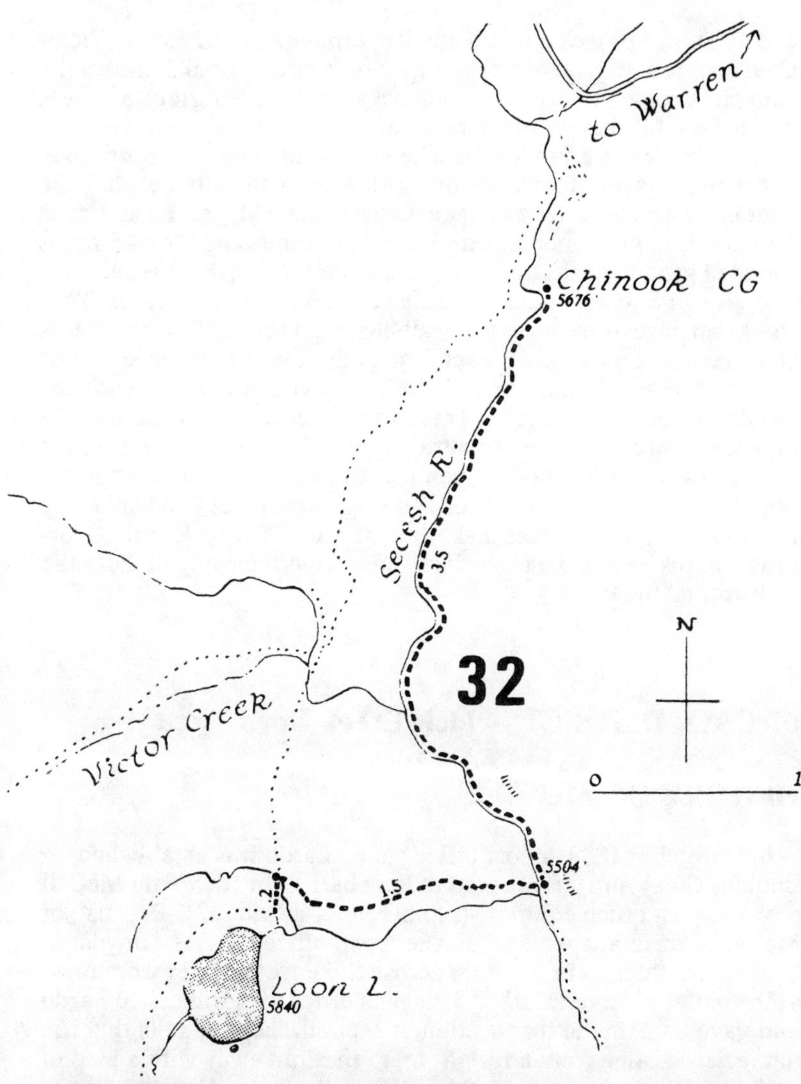

drive 1 mile to the campground, where the Secesh River Trail to Loon Lake begins. (A second trail to Loon Lake that follows ridges instead of the river is usable only in the fall or by horse parties because this trail fords the river.)

The trail starts beside the wide quiet river that flows over orange-tinted rocks. As the trail begins, a rounded peak looms ahead but is soon hidden by the green lace of lodgepole-covered hills. The trail gradually descends 180 feet in 3.5 miles to a steel suspension bridge over the river. At .7 mile the path crosses Alex Creek. At 1.5 miles, the route goes along an open, grassy slope and at 2 miles passes under a small overhang. At 2.2 miles, Victor Creek joins the river on the opposite shore. At 3.2 miles the canyon becomes more open and rocky. Here grey granite towers create fanciful shapes on the ridge across the river.

At 3.5 miles is a junction of the river trail with a trail up Loon Creek to the lake. Across the bridge is a tiny campsite beside Loon Creek. The route to the lake climbs the side of Loon Creek Canyon through lodgepoles growing in granite sand. At 4.5 miles rounded granite peaks and a pleated mountain appear ahead.

A sign at 5 miles points 1.5 miles back down to the river. Turn right (northwest) because the trail has been rerouted from what is shown on the topographic map. The path skirts a large meadow on the north side. At the head of the meadow is a junction with the alternate Loon Lake Trail. Travel south on this trail across the meadow. On the far side, this trail splits. The left branch leads to a large campsite at the big bend in the outlet, .2 mile from the junction with the alternate trail. The right one leads 7 to 9 miles up Loon Lake's inlet to Duck Lake and the Lick Creek Road. Overgrown paths lead down to the lakeshore from the camp or from the trail around the lake.

McCALL DISTRICT — Lick Creek Road Area

HISTORY OF McCALL

In November 1889, a post office called Lardo was established on Boulder Creek and later moved to Roseberry. In 1895 Tom McCall took the post office equipment to his hotel in McCall. Because of McCall's mismanagement of the post office, W. B. Boydstun became postmaster in his store across the Payette River from town at the outlet of Payette Lake. This post office was still called Lardo and gave its name to that section of McCall. Legend tells that the name Lardo came from a freight team that ran away with a load of lard and flour, thus thoroughly mixing the two. One old timer, Goldie Troen, remembered her parents talking about this when she was a little girl, so maybe it is a true story.

Tom McCall started the town of McCall in 1890 when he bought a log cabin from Sam Devers, a squatter, for a team, wagon, and harness. On the site McCall built a hotel and hired a railroad surveyor to survey and lay out the townsite. McCall also built a lumber mill, which later burned. McCall's son, Ben, built another mill on the east side of the lake. H. R. Hoff bought that mill and also built a flour mill. Both of these burned. Mr. Hoff and his son,

Ted, built another mill with Bert Mills. Mills sold his interest to Carl Brown in 1913. Although this mill burned too, it was rebuilt further up the lake.

The railroad reached McCall in June 1914, and the station there was named "Lakeport". Clem Blackwell, who had a saloon in the McCall Hotel, once received a letter from the railway agent, which said, "Your barrel of books is leaking!"

Local transportation was often by boat. Jack Wyatte built and ran the first passenger and freight boat, a sailboat. Later the steamboat, *Lyda,* took over this job. There is a modern legend of a sea serpent in the lake!

Lumbering continued to be the basic industry for the growing town. When Carl Brown and Ted Hoff split their lumber business, Hoff built a mill at Horseshoe Bend. In 1937 the town of McCall received 80 acres of land from Brown to develop a ski area, and Club Hill was built on this land. When Brown's mill burned again in 1940, he and his son, Warren, kept right on with their business. Later the mill was purchased and operated by Boise Cascade. The company recently sold the mill to developers to be made into condominiums and restaurants.

BLACKWELL AND CRYSTAL LAKES   33

Round trip: 11 miles (2 miles more for Crystal Lake)
Elevation gain: 2280 feet plus 360 feet to Crystal Lake
Elevation loss: 1250 feet (return climb) plus 620 feet for Crystal
Highest point: 7720 feet
Topo maps: McCall (20 foot contours), Fitsum Summit
Time: 10 hours
Access: Drive 2 miles east of McCall Golf Course on paved Lakeshore Drive to graveled Lick Creek Road. Go straight ahead (east) and drive 9.3 miles on Lick Creek Road.
Difficulty: Strenuous; cross-country from Fall Creek Saddle to Crystal Lake

At Blackwell Lake, a crescent-shaped island hugs the shore near a grey log cabin. Outcrops on the island are granite pebbles fused together, resembling a pavement of petrified eggs. A band of water lilies circles the deepest water beyond the island. The blue-green lake sprawls in woods below a rounded granite hill that is feathered with evergreens. Behind this hill another more pointed summit echoes the first. A 6-foot concrete and stone dam means that late in the season grey stumps and mud ring the lake, so this hike is best for late June and July. In October, huckleberry bushes at the lake turn red, mountain ash is orange, and other small

Payette Lakes from Fall Creek Trail

shrubs are yellow.

Oval blue-green Crystal Lake is in a basin of white granite benches. Trees grow on the benches around the east side, but on the southwest, granite sheets fall directly into the lake from a 600-foot peak. At the northwest end, granite slabs slant up to a tiny pond. This green pond perches in a hollow below three light-colored rock knolls that form stairsteps to a ridge on the west.

The trail to the Fall Creek Saddle has an excellent view of the canyon of the North Fork of Lake Fork. The view extends from the rugged grey cliffs and crumbled peaks surrounding Golden Lake across the canyon, north to the pointed, wooded peak between Duck and Hum Lakes beyond Lick Creek Summit. A row of granite knolls and cliffs forms one wall of the hanging valley the trail ascends. On an open grassy ridge beyond Fall Creek Saddle, the hazy blue arms of Cascade Reservoir spread out in the distance. Below the junction of the Fall Creek Trail with the Crestline Trail at 4 miles, the green shag of the peninsula of Ponderosa Park divides two blue wedges of Payette Lake.

The recommended route to Blackwell Lake is via the Fall Creek Trail from the Lick Creek Road. The old jeep trail from Lakeshore Drive is no longer open because of posted private property at the bottom. Due to thick underbrush in this area, skirting the private property to reach the jeep trail would be very difficult.

To reach the Fall Creek Trail, follow the Lick Creek Road and

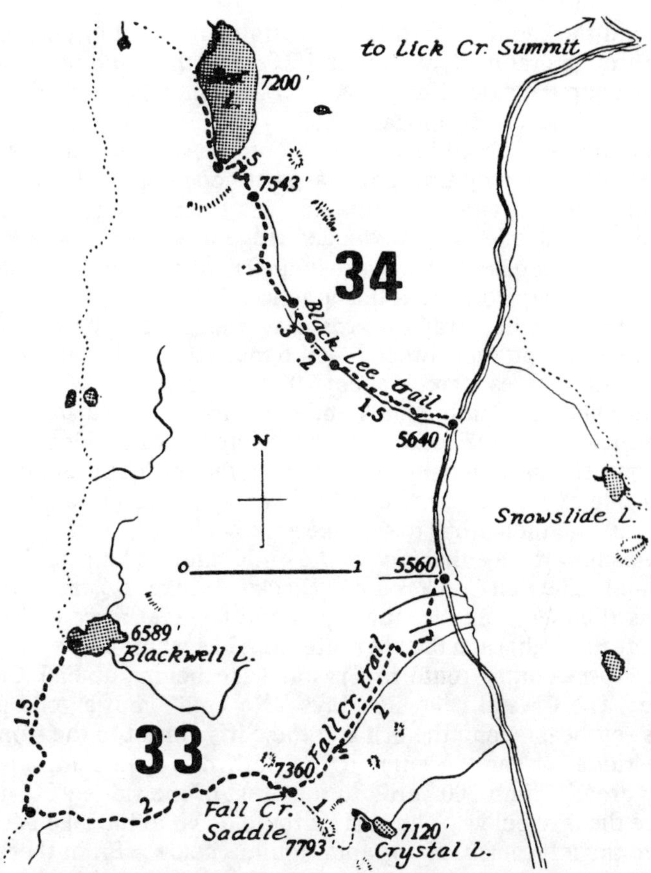

Boy Scout Camp signs on Lakeshore Drive from McCall until 2 miles east of the golf course. Go straight ahead on the graveled Lick Creek Road as Lakeshore Drive turns left. The trailhead is 9.3 miles up Lick Creek Road.

The Fall Creek Trail climbs south through a forest of grand fir, Douglas fir, and Engelmann spruce. The path crosses 3 small streams, and at .5 mile climbs southwest in small switchbacks through rocks and brush. As the trail climbs, subalpine fir takes the place of the grand fir. At 1 mile the trail levels in a large open area of grass and rocks. Here the route has already gained 1000 feet. Beyond this, the path enters the forest again along a stream. At 1.5 miles high cliffs border a flat meadow on the south. There are campsites here.

To find the trail at the end of the meadow, look for blazes and cut-through fallen logs. At 1.7 miles the path reaches an open rocky area and zigzags 300 feet up beside the south canyon wall to Fall Creek Saddle at 2 miles.

Beyond the saddle, the trail turns right (north) and goes up a ridge through granite boulders. In 150 yards, the route turns to go northwest up the side of the ridge. At 2.2 miles the path reaches an open hillside and disappears. Follow scattered blazes 200 yards west to intersect an old jeep trail. Continue west and then west-southwest on the jeep trail down a partly open spur of the ridge into the small canyon of Tyee Creek. The track crosses this creek **three times and follows a low wooded ridge to a junction at 4 miles** with the old jeep trail from Lakeshore Drive in a grassy saddle. The Crestline Trail begins at this junction.

Take the Crestline Trail towards Blackwell Lake. The path cuts downhill to the left (northwest). At 4.5 miles the trail, which is still an old road, crosses a creek about 200 feet below the saddle. On the other side, the path climbs and contours west of a sagebrush covered hill. Next the route enters the forest. At 5 miles the old road turns steeply downhill. At 5.2 miles the track circles the east (right) side of a hill of granite slabs. The way goes up to the crest of this hill and then drops to the lake at 5.5 miles.

Campsites are on either side of the outlet and, in late season, on the island. The Fall Creek route to Blackwell Lake is .7 mile longer and has 100 feet more elevation gain and 600 feet more elevation loss (return climb) than the old route from Lakeshore Drive.

The cross-country route to Crystal Lake begins at Fall Creek Saddle. The Crystal Lake sign says "No Trail", but a good path climbs southeast along the brink of the cliffs almost to the summit of the ridge. Near the summit the path disappears in a large grassy area. Climb 200 yards to the crest of the ridge at .5 mile and see the lake below. The easiest route down to the lake is via a gully to the left (north) of a granite tongue below. From there go further north to the tiny pond and down the right (south) side of its outlet. The lake is 1 mile from the saddle. Campsites are near the outlet where there is a small bay.

BLACK LEE TRAIL TO BOX LAKE
34

Round trip: 6.4 miles
Elevation gain: 1900 feet
Elevation loss: 340 feet (return climb)
Highest point: 7543 feet
Topo maps: Box Lake, Fitsum Summit
Time: 6½ hours
Access: Drive 2 miles east of McCall Golf Course on Lakeshore Drive. Go straight (east) on Lick Creek Road for 11 miles.
Difficulty: Moderate

Black tree-topped cliffs 600 feet high shadow a swampy meadow at the upper end of Box Lake. A 300-yard beach forms a wide white band between the meadow and the sparkling blue water. Stumps and silvered logs stick from the water because of a dam at the lower end. Four-foot boulders circle the lake except at the ends. Talus and brush straggle below jagged Beaverdam Peak, which sprawls for more than 2 miles along the east side of the lake. Box Lake, 1 mile long and .5 mile wide, is one of the largest backcountry lakes near McCall. In the fall the lake displays only three colors: the brilliant blues of the sky and the lake, the golds of aspens, willows, and dry grass, and the reds of shrubs and dried plants. The dark green firs and pines appear charcoal grey beside the bright fall colors.

The well-used trail to Box Lake is named the Black Lee Trail after the creek it ascends. A small unimproved campsite is at the trailhead, which is 11 miles up the graveled Lick Creek Road from McCall. The trail begins by switchbacking 800 feet in the first mile through a lodgepole-fir forest. At .7 mile the path straightens and climbs directly up. At 1.5 miles the route reaches a meadow and crosses the creek to another meadow. The path then runs through forest, crosses back over the creek at 1.7 miles, and comes out onto a brushy hillside. At 2 miles the route crosses back to the west side of the stream.

At 2.2 miles the trail climbs a sloping meadow, tufted with bunch grass, then passes granite outcroppings. A group of these pillars looks like a good spot for filming an Indian ambush. From this slope is a good view of the whole canyon of the North Fork of Lake Fork. Jagged peaks near Boulder and Louie Lake rise to the south, while right across the canyon, cliffs above Snowslide Lake create black shadows.

At 2.5 miles the trail traverses a grassy plot appliqued with wildflowers in July, then enters a wet meadow .2 mile long. Beyond the meadow, the route arrives at a notch at 2.7 miles and overlooks Box Lake. Distant mountains ramble beyond the lower end of the lake. One peak has two pointed ears and resembles the head of a bat. The trail hairpins down through brush to reach the lake at 3.2 miles. Two small campsites are on the east side of the beach, although the best sites are at the lower end of the lake where the ground is flatter.

SNOWSLIDE AND MAKI LAKES

35

Round trip: 8 miles
Elevation gain: 1980 feet
Elevation loss: 600 feet
Highest point: 7880 feet
Topo map: Fitsum Summit
Time: 4½ hours for Snowslide Lake, 7 hours for Maki Lake
Access: Drive 2 miles east of McCall Golf Course on Lakeshore
   Drive. Go straight on graveled Lick Creek Road to the trailhead
   at 12 miles.
Difficulty: Easy to Snowslide; cross-country for experts to Maki

Below an 800-foot wall of black cliffs, a shorter dark granite
knoll overhangs emerald Snowslide Lake. Across the lower end of
the lake from the trail is a white, rippled granite hill dotted with
trees. Granite slopes flank strips of forest and grass on the trail
side of the lake where dead logs like giant toothpicks point into the
water. Meadows studded with tiny lodgepoles and spruces hug
beaches of white sand at blue-green Maki Lake. A light grey peak
overlooks the lake from the northwest. A peak resembling a black
hood lurks in the distance to the south. Down the canyon, wooded
hills line the East Fork of Lake Fork.

To reach the Snowslide Lake Trail, go straight ahead (east) onto
the graveled Lick Creek Road 2 miles east of the McCall Golf
Course on Lakeshore Drive. At 8 miles, the road passes Slick
Rock, a grey dome of solid granite 800 feet high. The Snowslide
Lake Trail is 12 miles up the Lick Creek Road, 1 mile beyond the
Box Lake sign.

The trail to Snowslide Lake crosses the North Fork of Lake Fork
on rocks, then angles southeast and then south up through woods
and grassy areas. At a gully filled with aspens and brush at
.5 mile, the route turns straight uphill to the southeast. At 1 mile
the trail emerges from forest to go above another brushy area, and
crosses still more brush at 1.5 miles. The last mile climbs only
400 feet compared to the 800 feet of the first mile. The path
reaches the lake at 2 miles and passes three campsites. The trail
gets little use so take care not to lose it on the way back in the
woods above the highest brushy area.

From the upper end of Snowslide Lake, the trail up to Maki Lake
is well-defined to the summit of the ridge. The path winds up the
inlet of Snowslide Lake through a wildflower meadow under the
black cliffs. Near the top of the ridge, the trail climbs 400 feet in
.2 mile with no switchbacks. At the top of the ridge at 2.7 miles, a
sign for a trail down the East Fork of Lake Fork points northeast,
but the path is indistinct.

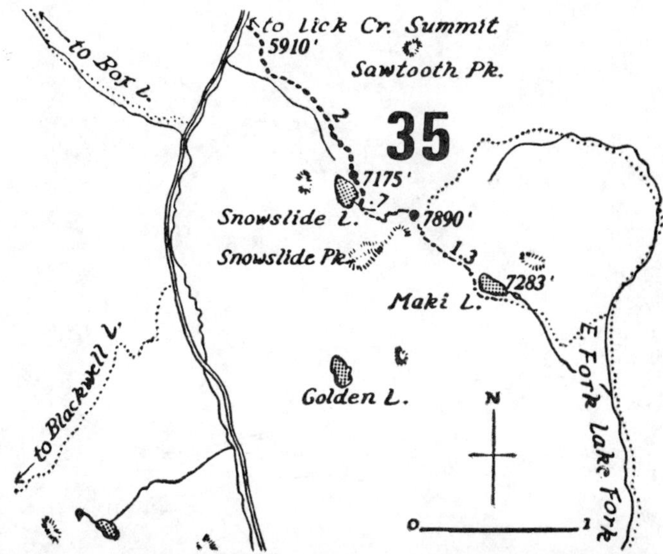

There is no sign for the route cross-country from the summit to Maki Lake. From the East Fork sign, turn southeast cross-country and follow the summit ridge southeast towards its low point. Maki Lake is not in the canyon just below the summit, but rather over this ridge to the southeast. Someone has cut a line of far-apart new blazes for the route. Keep well above the low point in the wooded ridge, almost at the edge of the rock slabs coming from the peak. The new blazes become more frequent 100 yards east of the rock slabs at 3 miles. The blazes and some rock cairns lead down the forested canyon parallel with a rocky ridge on the north to Maki Lake at 4 miles. There is little trace of a path. A compass may be necessary to find the route and pinpoint the location of the lake.

KRASSEL DISTRICT — Lick Creek Summit Area

DUCK LAKE

36

Round trip: 2 miles
Elevation gain: 300 feet
Highest point: 6840 feet
Topo map: Box Lake
Time: 2 hours
Access: Drive 2 miles east of McCall Golf Course on paved Lakeshore Drive. Go straight (east) onto graveled Lick Creek Road for 17 miles. The trailhead is 1.5 miles past Lick Creek Summit.
Difficulty: Easy

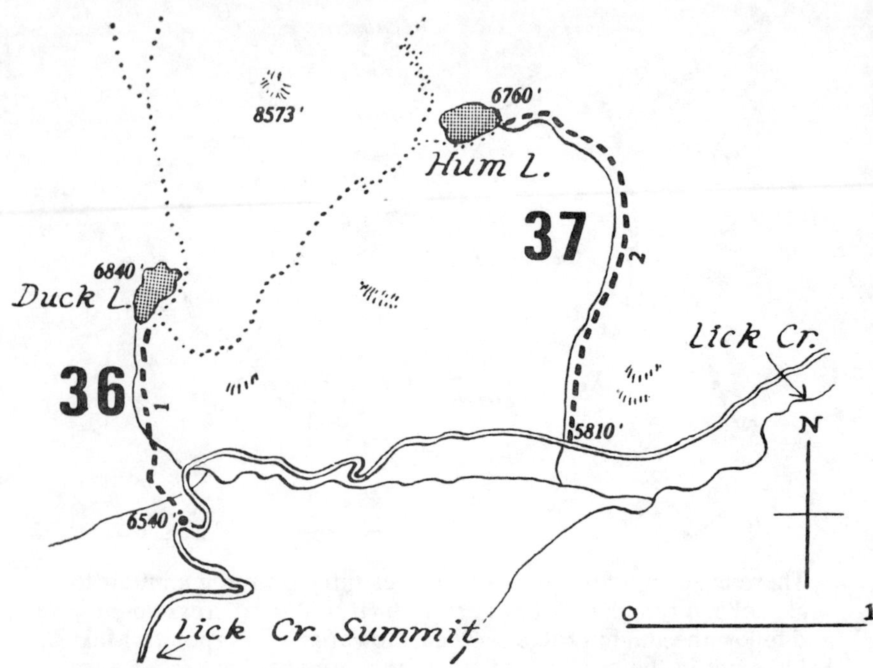

This is an easy hike to a wooded lake with a green flower-dusted meadow at the upper end. The drive up the North Fork of Lake Fork Canyon past sculptured granite Slick Rock and over Lick Creek Summit is beautiful, especially in the fall when aspens and larches tint the canyon gold. Towers and rock walls enclose the rugged canyon of Lick Creek where the hike begins. On the east side of Duck Lake, a mountain covered with woods and talus barricades this lake from Hum Lake.

To reach the trail, drive 2 miles east of the McCall Golf Course on paved Lakeshore Drive. When the drive turns north, go straight ahead (east) onto graveled Lick Creek Road. Drive 17 miles to a sign for Duck Lake. This sign is on the inside of the second switchback, 1.5 miles beyond Lick Creek Summit. There is only one small parking space.

The well-marked trail crosses a small creek on make-shift logs at 200 yards. The level path leads through a fir forest underlain by beargrass and grouse whortleberry. At about .5 mile, the path reaches the outlet of Duck Lake and switchbacks up it before crossing the creek on a big rock and slanting log. Some may prefer to wade these two stream crossings.

Next the trail leads gently along the stream to reach the lake at 1 mile near campsites. 100 yards along the lake is a junction with a trail that goes 2 miles over a divide to Hum Lake and the North

Fork of Lick Creek Trail. The trail along Duck Lake splits .7 mile north of the lake. One branch climbs over a pass into the canyon of Loon Creek to reach Loon Lake. The other goes along Twentymile Creek to the Warren Wagon Road at Upper Payette Lake.

HUM LAKE

37

Round trip: 4 miles
Elevation gain: 950 feet
Highest point: 6760 feet
Topo map: Box Lake
Time: 4 hours
Access: Drive 2 miles east of McCall Golf Course on Lakeshore Drive. Go straight (east) on graveled Lick Creek Road for 19.5 miles. The trailhead is 4 miles past Lick Creek Summit.
Difficulty: Moderate

Hum Lake lies deep in a bowl of 1500-foot rocky peaks. On the north, two ridges of brush, trees, and rock slabs lead to the lake. A trail goes over a pass between the two ridges to the Nork Fork of Lick Creek. South of the lake, a roof-shaped peak with 400-foot cliffs hangs at the end of a canyon. This peak hides behind a pointed hill of granite slabs and trees. The lower end of the lake holds a collection of dead logs against lush grass. In the fall, the blue water reflects the glow of small red-leaved bushes. To the west, a 2 mile trail climbs 1000 feet over a saddle to Duck Lake.

To reach the trailhead, drive 2 miles east of the McCall Golf Course on Lakeshore Drive. When the drive turns north, go straight ahead (east) onto graveled Lick Creek Road. The road climbs 900 feet in the last 3 miles to the summit at 15.5 miles. From the summit, narrow miniature Summit Lake glints 100 yards to the west. Beyond the summit the road makes 3 hairpin turns down into the canyon of Lick Creek, and winds along the edge of the canyon below 2000-foot rocky walls topped with spires. Just beyond a waterfall on Hum Creek at 19.5 miles is a parking space and sign for Hum Lake.

The trail begins 5 vertical feet above the road, runs 25 feet to the east, and then angles west above a granite outcrop. From there the path climbs 600 feet straight north in .2 mile. This section requires a very careful descent on the return. The hillside is studded with enormous ponderosa pines plated with rust-colored bark. In the fall the slope blazes with red leaves of huckleberries.

At .2 mile the trail levels and at .5 mile, it passes a flower-spangled meadow .2 mile long. Two tree-strewn rock slides come down to the trail at the edge of the meadow. From the upper end of the meadow, the wall of Lick Creek Canyon holds a pointed granite peak feathered with trees. The path crosses another meadow at 1.2 miles, and at 1.5 miles, the route turns west with the creek to wander through a third meadow. Beyond the third meadow, the path climbs through alders beside the creek, then in forest to the lake at 2 miles. Two campsites are near the outlet.

BOISE NATIONAL FOREST

CASCADE DISTRICT — West Mountain Area

BLUE LAKE

38

Round trip: 2 miles
Elevation loss: 400 feet (return climb)
Highest point: 7680 feet
Topo map: Smiths Ferry (15′)
Time: 2½ hours
Access: Turn left (west) at four-way intersection off Highway 55 8.7 miles north of Smiths Ferry. Drive 2.3 miles on paved road to a junction. Turn left (south) and drive 10.7 miles on graveled Snowbank Mountain Road to Potters Pond.
Difficulty: Easy

A little alpine lake is only 2½ hours from downtown Boise. Blue Lake near Cascade is 1 mile from the trailhead on the Snowbank Mountain Road. Two granite islands, which seem to have broken loose from a granite peninsula, float on the lake. Behind, grey granite knolls and cliffs sweep up to a wedge-shaped peak. Woods and meadows rippling with wildflowers surround the water. On the east side of the lake, the outlet cascades down a granite trough, alternating a thin shining sheet with a froth of white water.

To reach the trail to Blue Lake, turn left (west) at a four-way intersection 8.7 miles north of Smiths Ferry. Drive 2.3 miles on an oiled road to a junction. Turn left (south) on a gravel road signed for Blue Lake and Snowbank Mountain. Just beyond the junction, the road crosses old railroad tracks. The road winds through the wooded hills of a tree farm. After passing turnoffs for Grassy Flat and Tripod Reservoir, the track at 6.5 miles comes to a metal garage. Then the route enters an open grassy hillside sprinkled with trees. Soon the road looks down on Blue Lake sparkling below a wall of granite. At 10.7 miles, miniature Potters Pond winks in

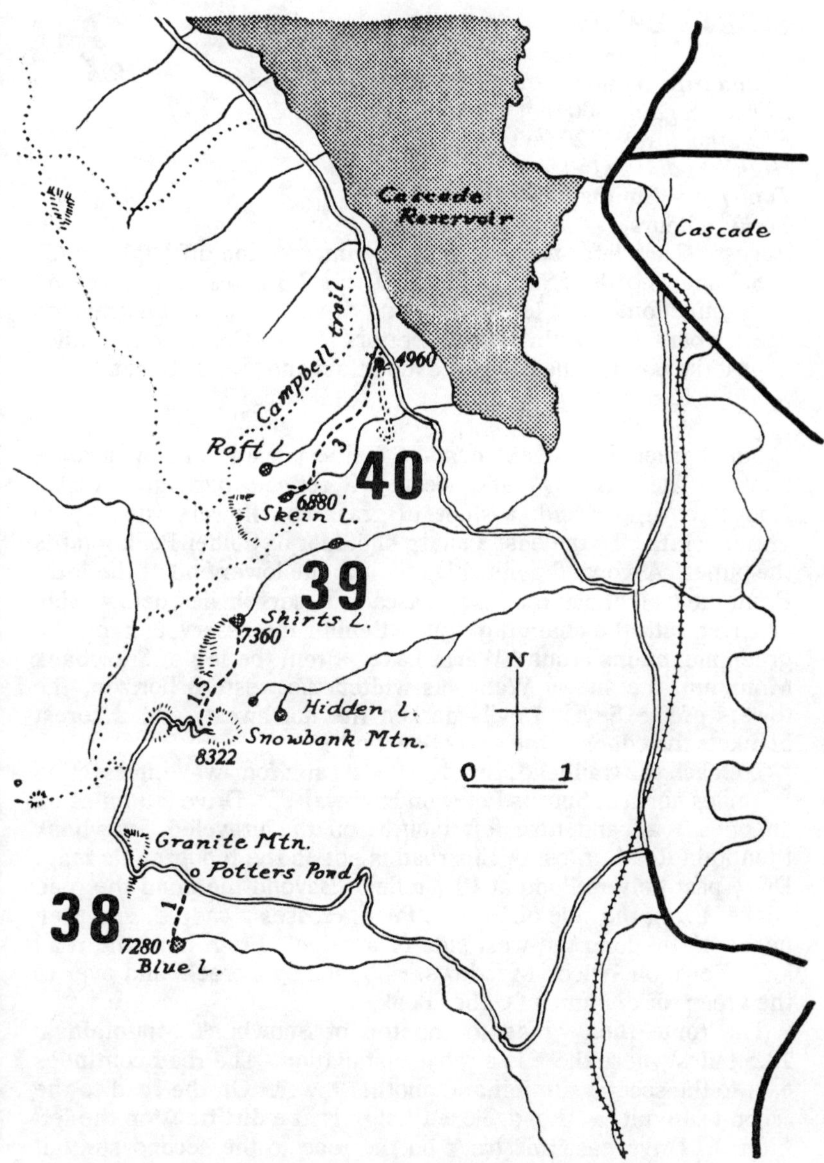

the grass. Most of this road is not on the topographic map.

Opposite Potters Pond the trail to Blue Lake leads south, winding downhill for 1 mile over meadows and across two streams. There are campsites at the lake, but the hike is so short it should be a day hike in order to prevent overuse.

SHIRTS LAKE

39

Round trip: 3 miles
Elevation gain: 400 feet
Elevation loss: 1120 feet (return climb)
Highest point: 8160 feet
Topo map: Smiths Ferry (15′)
Time: 4 hours
Access: Turn left (west) at four-way intersection off Highway 55
   8.7 miles north of Smiths Ferry. Drive 2.3 miles on paved road
   to a junction. Turn left (south) and drive 10.7 miles on graveled
   Snowbank Mountain Road to Potters Pond. Continue 2.7 miles
   past the pond to the top of the mountain and .5 mile beyond.
Ability: Expert

Small green Shirts Lake nests in feathery willows below granite
banks. The water is dark because it reflects dark grey rocks.
Above the upper end, a slope of grass and flowers runs up to
granite cliffs. To the east a sharp shoulder of Collier Peak guards
the outlet. A wooded peninsula juts into the lower end of the lake.
From the trail above the lake, Cascade Reservoir lies below, blue
or silver with the changing light. Behind the reservoir hang the
green mountains around Warm Lake. From the top of Snowbank
Mountain, the snowy Wallowas whiten the western horizon, the
towers of the Seven Devils darken the northwest, and a forest
blankets the edges of the spiky Sawtooths.

To reach the trailhead, turn left (west) at a four-way intersection
8.7 miles north of Smiths Ferry on Highway 55. Drive 2.3 miles on
an oiled road and turn left (south) on the graveled Snowbank
Mountain Road. Most of this road is not on the topographic map.
Drive past Potters Pond at 10.7 miles. Beyond the pond the road
snakes along the side of Granite Peak, crosses a saddle, and then
heads north along the west side of a ridge. From here the road
looks down on Wilson Meadows, ribboned by a creek, and over to
the green rocky hump of Gabes Peak.

The route then winds to the top of Snowbank Mountain at
13.5 miles where there is a radar installation. The road continues
east to the second summit and another tower. On the road to the
second summit, a "Road Closed" sign is at a dirt track on the left
(north). Drive past this track on the road to the second summit
about .5 mile to the third switchback (see map). At this switchback
a faint jeep track leads north and is the beginning of the unsigned
but blazed Shirts Lake Trail.

The track peters out in 100 yards in a grassy area. At the edge of
the grass, a poor trail goes down a tiny stream, which is usually
dry. After descending 720 feet from the top of Snowbank

Shirts Lake

Mountain, the path levels at a flat swampy meadow. Just before, look down to the east to glimpse tiny Lost Lake, which is similar to Potters Pond. Beyond the flat meadow, the trail climbs 400 feet north over a saddle. The route then descends a streambed to Shirts Lake at 1.5 miles. In late June, yellow dogtooth violets (glacier lilies) bring sunshine to the path. The lake has no good camping spots because of steep banks and willows.

SKEIN LAKE

40

Round trip: 6 miles
Elevation gain: 1920 feet
Highest point: 6880 feet
Topo map: Smiths Ferry (15′)
Time: 6 hours
Access: Turn left (west) at four-way intersection 8.7 miles north of Smiths Ferry. Drive 2.3 miles on paved road to a junction. Go straight ahead and at 5.2 miles on the gravel road, turn left (west). At 6.4 miles, turn west onto West Side Road and follow it. At 9.3 miles, turn left (west) on gravel road, and go .1 mile.
Ability: Expert

Two rounded peaks, the left one bristling with trees, guard dark green Skein Lake.   Wedge-shaped cliffs 200 feet high and rectangles of dark granite accent the face of the peak on the right, like giant bricks on end. Between the rounded peaks, light grey cliffs hang below the ridge top. Near the lower end of the lake above a lily pond, a tin-roofed log cabin stands beside a boulder as tall as it is. Skein Lake is best for early season because dead trees and muddy sand ring the water in late summer.

To reach the Skein Lake Trail, turn left (west) off Highway 55 at a marked four-way intersection 8.7 miles north of Smiths Ferry. At 2.3 miles keep right where the road passes a signed turn for Blue Lake and Snowbank Mountain at the end of the pavement. At 5.2 miles turn left (west) where the road straight ahead is signed for Cabarton West subdivision. Then at 6.4 miles, turn left (west) again to the West Side Recreation Area. At 7.3 miles the road becomes paved as it makes a right turn (north). At 9.3 miles a sign on the left (west) points to a short access road for the Skein Lake Trail. Drive up this gravel road for 200 yards until it turns right. Park here, but do not walk up this road, since it is a logging road.

To find the correct trail, look to the right side of the road at the turn where a narrow two-wheeled track covered with sticks and logs leads downhill to the north. Walk 100 yards along this track above some cabins to a four-way intersection of old roads. Make a left turn onto a road leading uphill to the southwest. In about 200 yards, this track joins another, continues uphill, and gradually narrows into a blazed trail. So many alders choke the hillside that at times they form a tunnel. The trail winds up the canyon of Campbell Creek.

At .7 mile the path crosses and recrosses the creek and then follows a steep ridge between Campbell and Skein Creeks. At 1.2 miles the trail climbs beside a tree-covered knoll. The route passes under huge ponderosa pines dripping with yellow green moss. At 2.2 miles, the path descends into the underbrush-filled canyon of Skein Creek, which it follows the rest of the way. There is no indication of a junction shown on the map with the Willow Creek Trail to Wilson Meadows. The Willow Creek Trail is not maintained but can be found with difficulty by walking over to Skein Creek once the trail enters the canyon and then taking an overgrown path up the creek to intersect the Willow Creek Trail.

At 2.5 miles the underbrush on the Skein Lake Trail thins until grassy slopes lie under scattered pines and firs. At 3 miles, the path passes a lily pond and ends at the old log cabin near a 6-foot high earth dam. Paths lead a few feet further to the lake. A small campsite is on the north side of the lake beyond the cabin.

CASCADE DISTRICT — Warm Lake Area

VULCAN HOT SPRINGS

41

Round trip: 2 miles
Elevation gain: 200 feet
Highest point: 5600 feet
Topo map: Warm Lake (15′)
Time: 2 hours
Access: 1 mile north of Cascade, turn right (east) off Highway 55.
Drive 25 miles on paved Warm Lake Road to information sign for
Warm Lake Recreation Area. Turn right (south) on dirt road and
drive past Stolle Meadows to spur road and campsites at
7.2 miles on right side of the road.
Difficulty: Easy

In a forest clearing, amid a cloud of steam, tiny hot springs
bubble up in little bowls of white rock streaked with orange algae.
In the spring, yellow mimulus and blue camas cover the grassy
bank around the springs. The water at the springs is too hot to
touch. On the stream formed by the hot springs, people have built
pools by damming the water with logs and plastic. The lowest pool
is about 15 feet square and 2½ feet deep with a sandy bottom.

The water here is still so hot that a person feels faint after a
10 minute dip. The water is easily clouded by algae and mud from
the bottom of the creek. Because of the high temperature, heavy
use, and less than sanitary conditions, bathing is not
recommended, especially for small children. Everyone visiting the
area should be sure to pick up all litter. The walk to the springs
makes a good conditioning walk or a place to go when the weather
is threatening. This hike is also open much earlier in the season
(by early June) than most in the area.

To reach the trailhead, turn east on the Warm Lake Road just
north of Cascade. The road is paved beyond Big Creek Summit at
16.8 miles (6594 feet) to Landmark. At 25 miles, just beyond a big
wooden map of the Warm Lake area, turn right (south) on a road
signed for Kinney Point and Warm Lake Lodge. The dirt road
passes several turnoffs, but keep straight ahead. At 6.1 miles the
way passes a road on the left to a guard station and comes out into
Stolle Meadows, which is a sea of blue camas in June. Across the
meadows rises the 2000-foot ridge of Cougar Rock, which is
covered with granite gnomes. At a second small meadow at
7.2 miles, a road leads to the right to campsites. Drive to the
campsites and look for a bridge across the river (South Fork of the

Salmon). The trail is not on any map and is not signed.

Start the hike by crossing this bridge, which is a flattened log with a pole railing. Beyond a small meadow the path crosses two more bridges. After the third bridge, the trail joins the track of an old road. The well-trodden trail leads gently up through a Douglas fir forest of slender trees growing in grouse whortleberry and serviceberry. At .5 mile the trail comes to the bank of the warm creek that leads to the springs. At 1 mile the path reaches the lowest pool in the creek. A campsite beyond the pool is very small and not recommended for camping because of the heavy use and short distance of the trail.

RICE LAKE, RICE PEAK, AND LONG LAKE   42

Round trip: 7.4 miles
Elevation gain: 2250 feet
Elevation loss: 960 feet (return climb)
Highest point: 8696 feet
Topo maps: Warm Lake (15'), Deadwood Reservoir (15')
Time: 7 hours
Access: 1 mile north of Cascade, turn right (east) off Highway 55 onto paved Warm Lake Road. Drive 25 miles to Warm Lake information sign. Turn right (south) on a dirt road and drive past Stolle Meadows to the junction with Cupp Corral Road at 8 miles. Go straight ahead and drive 6 miles on primitive Rice Peak Road.
Difficulty: Strenuous; cross-country from Rice Peak to Long Lake

The view from Rice Peak Lookout extends to a circular rim of mountains at the edge of the seen world. It includes the Sawtooths, the Salmon River Mountains, and the mountains near Cascade and McCall. The pale cream-colored peaks of the White Clouds back the blue scallops of the Sawtooths like ghost reflections. To the northwest, Warm Lake lies in a wooded basin like a blob of pale blue melted wax. Grass and willows are trying to erase shallow, light amber Rice Lake. A dark grey granite knoll is at the head of the lake, with a larger knoll on the right. Left of the knolls the Rice Peak Lookout sits on a hill of talus above a grassy ridge. Cross-country hiking and an old trail lead to a view of narrow blue-green Long Lake, afloat with logs and squeezed by forest. Behind the lake Rocky Peak forms a triangle of light-colored talus supporting two tiny black nubbins.

To reach the trailhead, turn right (south) off the Warm Lake

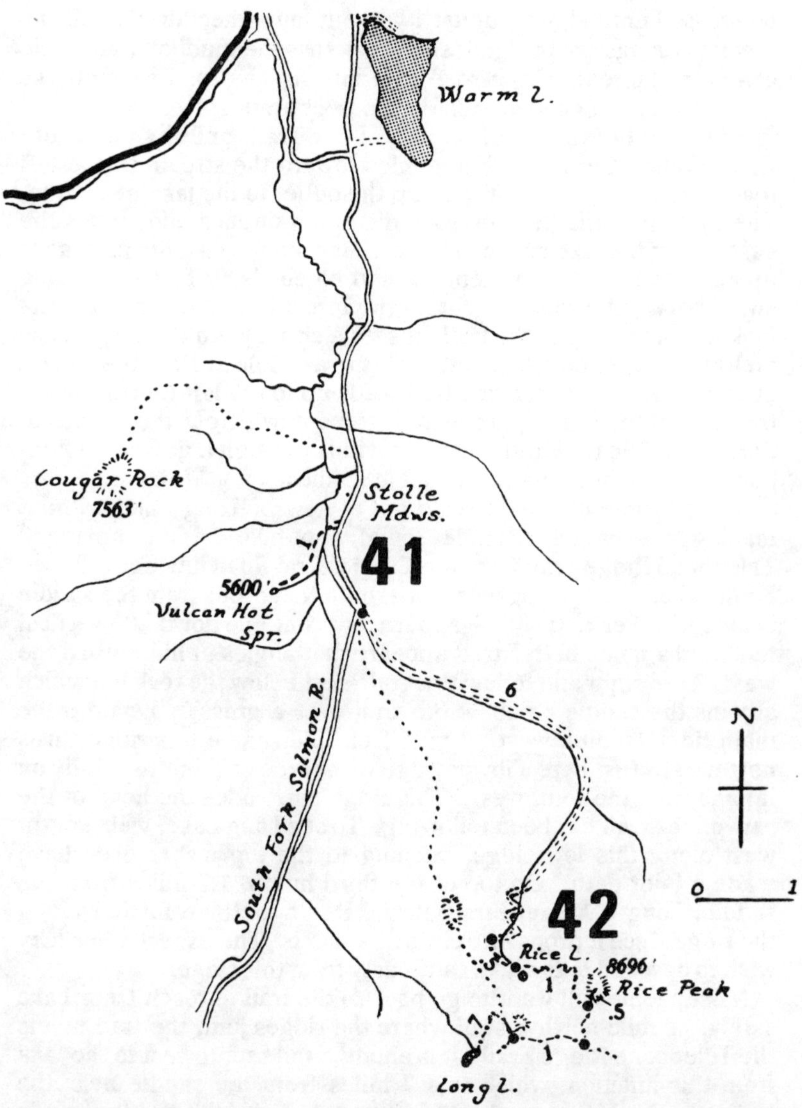

Road at the wooden Warm Lake Recreation Area sign 25 miles east of Cascade. At 5.5 miles the dirt road passes Stolle Meadows Guard Station and crosses the meadows. At 8 miles a road to the right (west) leads along the South Fork of the Salmon River to Cupp Corral. Take the road straight ahead signed Rice Peak Lookout. A ditch has been dug every 200 yards in this primitive road to drain it, so a high clearance vehicle is desirable.

At 4 miles the road comes to a muddy section that can't

be crossed until about August 1 without four-wheel drive. All the creek crossings are bridged, so once across the mudhole, a vehicle can go to the end of the road at 6 miles. The road switchbacks across an open logged area in the last rocky mile.

At the end of the road, the Rice Peak Trail, built by the Youth Conservation Corps in 1975, angles toward the stream to the left (east) through a fir forest, and up the outlet to the lake at .5 mile. The trail up to the peak crosses the outlet on logs and circles the east side of the lake past campsites. Beyond the lake the path goes up an open hillside of sagebrush and bluebells. After 4 or 5 long switchbacks, the route re-enters the forest and heads toward the lookout. At 1.2 miles the trail crosses a cirque with a spring below melting snow. The path climbs talus to a saddle at 1.5 miles. Here at an unsigned junction one trail leads up to the left (northeast) to the lookout and an apparent trail drops down from the saddle to the south. The trail to the lookout winds through a grove of white-bark pines to the manned lookout at 2 miles.

It is possible on this hike to get a view of Long Lake without making a separate 12 mile round trip hike on the unsigned Telephone Ridge Trail from the Cupp Corral Road junction. To see Long Lake, take the apparent trail south that drops from the saddle beside Rice Peak. It will disappear, but continue down 200 vertical feet until a much better trail appears that angles uphill toward the west. Turn right and follow this trail west below the rock hill which adjoins the saddle. Follow the trail over a grassy spur onto the main ridge leading west. 1 mile from the saddle this ridge turns northwest. Just here a lower ridge with three or more rock hills on it joins from the southwest. This ridge barricades the head of the canyon the trail has been following. To see Long Lake, walk south-west along this low ridge, keeping to the top where deer have made a faint path. On top of the third hump, 1.2 miles from the saddle, Long Lake appears below. Don't continue further along the ridge since it drops into cliffs at a notch. The expert hiker may wish to descend to the lake cautiously from this ridge.

Most people will want to go back to the trail to reach Long Lake safely. .2 mile northwest of where the ridges join, the trail meets the Telephone Ridge Trail. It is about .5 mile southwest to the lake from this junction, which is 1.7 miles from the saddle near the lookout. By this route the elevation loss from the saddle beside Rice Peak is 600 feet. This makes the total climb 2250 feet for Rice Lake, Rice Peak Lookout, and Long Lake, with a return climb of 960 feet. The distance to Long Lake by this route is only 3.2 miles compared to the 6 miles via Telephone Ridge.

BOISE DISTRICT — Bogus Basin Area

SHORT HISTORY OF BOGUS BASIN

Bogus Basin got its name because it once was the hideout of a gang of swindlers who made fake gold dust. Many people added other materials, such as gold-coated lead filings, to their gold dust in the 1860s. This led merchants to double their prices. Gold dust counterfeiting was such a problem that in 1864, the territorial legislature set a fifteen year prison term for anyone convicted of it.

In November 1866, John Page and John Watson were arrested in Boise for gold dust counterfeiting, while a third man, Thomas Murphy, escaped. Murphy, in a letter, called the *Statesman* editor a liar for reporting the bogus operation and threatened to sue. However, he was put in jail in Idaho City before he had the chance. None of the three men were convicted. Dust counterfeiting was still a problem until the First National Bank of Idaho was founded. Banks tended to stabilize the relationship between gold dust and currency.

Later Bogus Basin became a winter bonanza for southwestern Idahoans and tourists. Alf Engen selected a site for a ski area after snowshoeing into the area in 1937. A CCC camp prepared the area for skiing and a rope tow was installed. The road was a one-lane dirt road, so drivers were allowed to go uphill only until 2:30 p.m. After 2:30, only downhill traffic was permitted. Skiers used the old CCC building for a day lodge until the Bogus Basin Recreation Association built the Bogus Creek Lodge in 1962.

MORES MOUNTAIN

43

Round trip: 2 miles
Elevation gain: 550 feet
Highest point: 7237 feet
Topo map: Shafer Butte
Time: 2 hours
Access: Drive 16 miles up paved Bogus Basin Road and 3.6 miles on graveled Boise Ridge Road. Turn right (east) and go 1.7 miles on dirt road to a picnic area.
Difficulty: Easy

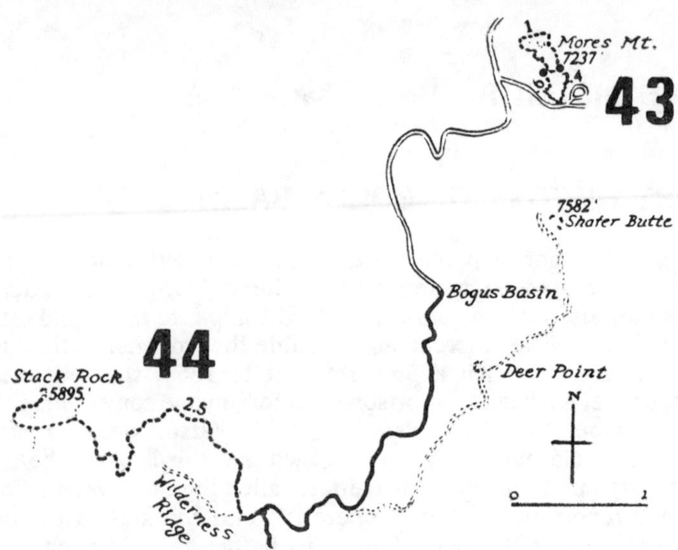

On Mores Mountain close to Boise, gnomes and fingers of rock punctuate the hillside, and weatherbeaten ponderosa pines hug granite outcrops. This hike has sweeping views of the Boise Ridge, the Boise Valley, and the summits of the Sawtooths. In June, so many wildflowers sprinkle the mountain they seem planted by a master gardener. The pungent scent of chapparal refreshes the air along the trail to the summit. The Youth Conservation Corps built this shaded, gradual trail in 1971 as a nature trail. A guide leaflet is sometimes available in a box at the beginning. To be sure of obtaining one, get one at the Boise National Forest office in Boise.

To reach the trail, drive 3.6 miles beyond Bogus Basin on the graveled Boise Ridge Road which continues beyond the parking area and goes around the bottom of runs serving the Bitterroot and Superior chairlifts. At a junction at 3.6 miles, turn right (east) on a signed dirt road and go 1.7 miles to the Shafer Butte Picnic Area. (The road straight ahead at this junction connects with the Harris Creek Summit Road between Horseshoe Bend and Idaho City.) Driving time from Boise is about 45 minutes.

Just across the road below the large parking area at the beginning of the picnic area, an old road, closed to motor vehicles, runs northwest up into the woods. Walk up this road to a box for leaflets and a sign that has a sketch map of the trail.

The trail winds gently up through trees and granite out-croppings. At the second outcropping, twisted pines frame a view of Shafer Butte and its ski runs. At .6 mile is a signed junction for an extension of the trail that circles the top of the mountain. This extension is a plant identification loop trail and is described in a separate brochure also available from the Boise National Forest. The loop has numbered stations and resting benches. It was constructed in 1975 by the Youth and Young Adult Conservation Corps. This trail is steeper than an unsigned path which turns left 100 yards further just before the main route goes downhill. This unsigned path is the other end of the loop. The hiker can take either trail or go back down. The next .5 mile of the unsigned path is through chapparal in the sun. At 1 mile, the path circles the top of the mountain just under the summit.

The mountain has a double summit. The eastern one is a grass and chapparal covered hill with a few big trees. The western summit is a rock outcropping with an excellent view. It is easy to leave the trail and go up 100 yards to either summit.

The route descends below the rocky summit through brush and across a little stream through the plant identification area to complete the loop at 1.5 miles. The downhill branch of the main trail zigzags through trees back to the old road. Follow the road south 200 yards back to the beginning of the trail.

STACK ROCK

44

Round trip: 5 miles
Elevation gain: 760 feet
Elevation loss: 640 feet (return climb)
Highest point: 5800 feet
Topo maps: Boise North, Cartwright Canyon
Time: 5 to 6 hours
Access: From Boise, drive 13 miles up paved Bogus Basin Road to Wilderness Ridge.
Difficulty: Easy (logging roads may be confusing)

The silver streak of Lake Lowell accents the view from this rock of the whole Boise Valley. To the northeast, 400-foot high Castle Rock echoes the pointed cap of Stack Rock. Bright blue royal penstemon and pale pink wild geranium brighten the route during June and July. The walk up to the 100-foot high granite out-cropping follows a chain of old logging roads that are closed to motor vehicles. This hike is not on a designated Forest Service trail. When near the solid granite rock, it resembles an old fashioned haystack. The firm granite makes it a good place for rock climbers to practice, although the rock shouldn't be climbed without ropes.

To reach the beginning of the hike, drive 13 miles up the paved

Bogus Basin Road from Boise. Park at the beginning of the ''private'' road to the Wilderness Ridge cabins. At 100 yards, a gate closes this road to motor vehicles because of the private property. Please observe all ''No Trespassing'' signs. Walk along this road for about .2 mile. Turn right (north) on an old logging road. Walk this road which winds along in the shade.

At 1.7 miles the logging road splits. Take the left branch west uphill beside a small creek. At 2 miles this branch intersects a jeep trail that approaches the rock from the north. Follow this jeep trail to the west and then north until the rock is seen ahead. At 2.4 miles, turn northeast on a path that reaches the rock at 2.5 miles. Return by the same route, although there is another way closer to the cabins. However, this route is not advised because it is almost entirely on private land.

BOISE DISTRICT — Arrowrock Reservoir Area

IRRIGATION IN BOISE VALLEY

Four federal laws helped lead to the development of irrigation in Idaho. In 1862 the Federal Homestead Act gave a settler 160 acres if he would cultivate and improve them. Settlers were irrigating land next to the Boise River on a small scale in 1863, and in 1864, they formed canal companies.

In 1877 the Desert Land Act provided 640 acres to anyone who could pay the low price and irrigate the land within three years. The construction of the New York Canal was begun in 1882 but not finished to Lake Lowell until 1909 and then only with the help of the federal government.

The Carey Act in 1894 encouraged state governments to develop irrigation projects. Extensive irrigation in the West began with the Reclamation Act in 1902, which allowed the federal government to build dams. Under this act, American Falls Dam was built in 1904 and Arrowrock Dam in 1915. The widespread settlement of Idaho began with irrigation.

SHEEP CREEK TRAIL:
Boise River to Devils Creek
(National Recreation Trail)

45

Round trip: 10 miles
Elevation gain: 1120 feet
Highest point: 4560 feet
Topo maps: Twin Springs, Sheep Creek
Time: 7 hours
Access: Turn right (northeast) on a gravel and dirt road 6 miles
north of Lucky Peak Dam on Highway 21. Drive 27.6 miles along
Lucky Peak and Arrowrock Reservoirs and the Boise River.
Difficulty: Moderate

In Sheep Creek Canyon, grey granite outcrops contrast with a
green jungle of Douglas fir, ponderosa pine, alder, serviceberry,
and chokecherry. Yellow arrowleaf balsamroot covers grassy hillsides in the spring. False solomon's seal, arnica, and bishop's cap
push up among the shrubs. Splintered remnants of wooden
mining flumes straggle on both sides of the lower part of the
canyon. Across the Boise River, snow patches the top of Thorn
Creek Butte in the spring. A 700-foot rock face just below Devils
Creek resembles a dinosaur with a spiky back. The Sheep Creek
Trail provides access to more than 50 miles of trail in unspoiled
wilderness at Boise's back door. Trinity Lakes can be reached by
hiking 20 miles of these little-used trails.

To reach the trailhead, drive on State Highway 21 northeast of
Boise to Lucky Peak Dam. Turn right (east) 6 miles beyond the
dam at the turnoff for Spring Shores Marina. Drive along the
shore of the reservoir on a gravel road 6 more miles to Arrowrock
Dam. Just below this dam, the road changes to a single lane dirt
road with turnouts. The track along the winding shore of Arrowrock Reservoir has no guard rails, so the recommended speed is
25 miles per hour or less.

At 12 miles beyond the dam is a junction with the Cottonwood
Creek Road, which leads 13 miles to Highway 21 near Idaho City.
Beyond the end of the reservoir at 13.7 miles, the route winds
along the Middle Fork of the Boise River. At 18.3 miles the road
passes the tiny resort of Twin Springs and its primitive hot springs
pool. The river runs through a gorge just before the road crosses a
bridge and reaches the trailhead at 27.6 miles.

The Sheep Creek Trail climbs through trees and bushes and
then crosses an open hillside that has several paths; keep on the
path closest to the creek. At .5 mile just above a rocky knoll is a
sign, "Sheep Creek Trail". From the sign, a branch of the trail
goes downhill to the creek. Follow the uphill path, which stays at

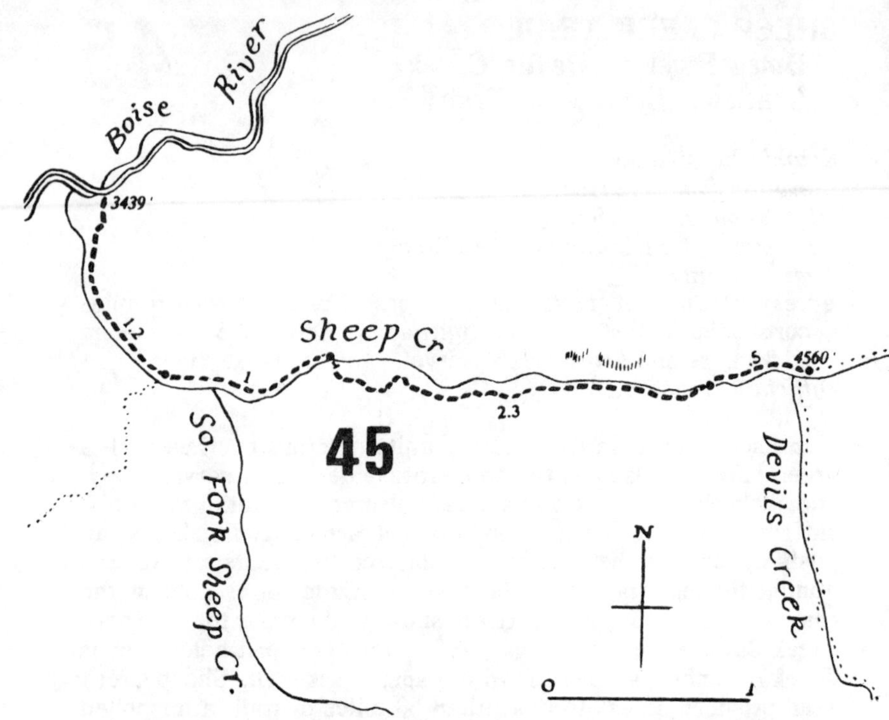

least 100 feet above the creek. The plants that at first glance seem to be poison ivy are really small chokecherries. Although rattlesnakes live along this trail, they come out mostly in hot weather. The route climbs gently, and is pleasant walking except for the lack of shade.

At 1.2 miles the trail descends to a junction for the Reed Trail to Corral Creek. At 2.2 miles the Sheep Creek route crosses the creek on a wooden bridge beyond a campsite and goes into the forest. The path switchbacks away from the creek. Then at 2.5 miles the trail runs along a steep wooded hillside as much as 200 feet above the creek. At 2.7 miles the route climbs around a little hill that has a view of the canyon in both directions. From the hill, a large rock face appears to block the canyon less than 1 mile ahead. At 3.7 miles, the trail descends closer to the creek, and at 4 miles comes right down to the bank across from the rock face. At 4.5 miles the path reaches a campsite in a small meadow filled with bitter cherry trees. Beyond the campsite the trail fords the creek. Those on foot can cross on a large log 75 yards downstream from the ford.

Downstream from this meadow stands a rock outcrop shaped like a hand with square fingers. The path meets the Devils Creek Trail at 5 miles on an open hillside.

The Devils Creek route goes southeast up to the head of Rattlesnake Creek and connects with a trail past North Star Lake to the Trinity Lakes. The main Sheep Creek Trail also leads to the Trinities via a trail near Smith Creek Lake. Both paths join and meet the Fall Creek Road near Trinity Mountain Lookout (see Smith Creek and North Star Lakes). By working with the topographic maps, the hiker can plan a loop trip on these trails through little-used wooded country.

COTTONWOOD CREEK (BALD MTN. TRAIL) 46

One-way distance: 9.5 miles
Elevation loss: 3800 feet
Highest point: 7515 feet
Topo maps: Arrowrock Reservoir Northeast, Twin Springs
Time: 6 hours one-way
Access: 1 mile east of Idaho City, turn southeast off Highway 21 onto dirt Bannock Creek Road. Drive 10 miles to Thorn Creek Butte Lookout for the top of the trail; for the bottom of the trail, turn east 7 miles south of Idaho City off Highway 21 onto dirt Thorn Creek Road and drive 10 miles.
Difficulty: Strenuous

As Cottonwood Creek falls 3800 feet from Thorn Creek Butte to the bottom of this trail, it tumbles through a green tangle of broadleaf trees and bushes. Aspen, red osier dogwood, water birch, and alder form thickets along the creek. The trail drops from the spruce-fir plant zone through the Douglas fir zone to the ponderosa pine zone. The view from the top of Thorn Creek Butte ranges from the snow-topped Sawtooths around to the hazy Boise Valley and the blue Owyhees. In June white blossoming shrubs and flowers such as scarlet gilia, larkspur, yellow mimulus, and forget-me-not turn the trailside into a parade of colors beside the foaming white creek. In late September when autumn hits this area, the trail is ablaze with red and gold. The lower part of this hike makes a pleasant walk in the spring or fall. In the early summer, start at the top of the butte and walk the whole trail down to the bottom for the unusual experience of an all-downhill hike.

To reach the top of Thorn Creek Butte, take the dirt Bannock Creek Road, which turns southeast 1 mile east of Idaho City. The various roads branching throughout the area are unsigned, but use of a map and driving the best road will get the traveler to the top of the butte. Neither the Forest Service map nor the topographic map shows all of these roads. Just beyond Mores Creek, the Pine Creek and Bannock Creek Roads both lead up to Thorn Creek Butte. The distance is about 10 miles to Bald Mountain Camp-

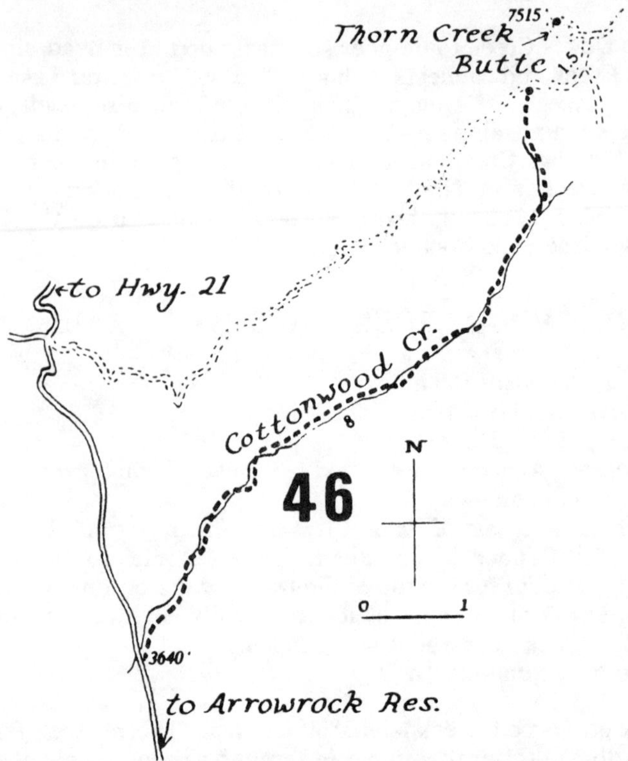

ground by either road. The top of the butte is 1.5 miles above the campground. To reach the bottom of the trail, drive up Highway 21 and turn east on the Thorn Creek Road 7 miles south of Idaho City. From here it is 10 miles to the trailhead, which is signed Bald Mountain Trail.

If hiking the trail from the top of the butte, hike down the lookout road 200 yards and take a blocked road to the right (southeast). At a junction with Forest Road 303 at .5 mile, take Road 303 (labeled 203 on Forest Service maps) south and then east along the top of a ridge. At 1.5 miles at a switchback at the head of a canyon, the trail signed Bald Mountain Trail leads south. At 1.7 miles the way crosses a tiny side stream into a forest of firs. At 2.5 miles, cross a rushing side stream where the canyon is full of aspens and alders. At 3 miles, the path comes to the East Fork of Cottonwood Creek and then crosses Cottonwood Creek to the west side.

At 4.2 miles the trail hopscotchs to the east side and then back after 300 yards. Ponderosa pines stand above the unrolling fronds of bracken ferns. At 5.2 miles the route passes to the east side again for another 300 yards. At 7 miles the trail returns again to the east side for .2 mile before crossing back. Now the ponderosa pines that hug the creek banks have trunks three feet wide. At

7.7 miles, the path jumps to the east side once more where the trail runs through a tunnel of alders. After .5 mile, at 8.2 miles, the route returns to the west side. Finally at 8.5 miles, the trail goes over to the east side once more and this time stays there. There are 10 crossings in all, and all crossings except the first and last must be waded in the spring. At 9 miles the path comes out into open chapparal and grass, follows a fence, and drops to the lower trailhead at 9.5 miles.

BOISE DISTRICT — Atlanta Area

ATLANTA HISTORY

Atlanta was founded in 1864 and named for a Civil War battle. In 1867 the miners brought in a stamp mill by pack train to process the ore, which was 75% silver. The Chinese in the camp named the peak above the town Greylock Mountain because they couldn't pronounce Grey Rock. Mining wasn't very profitable because a road from Rocky Bar wasn't built until 1878. Processing of Atlanta ore finally became effective in 1932 when an amalgamation plant was installed. This plant enabled Atlanta to produce the most gold of any Idaho area from 1932 to 1936. Antimony was mined from 1947 to 1953.

When two prostitutes, Annie and Dutch Em, walked from Atlanta to Rocky Bar to attend a dance in 1898, they were caught in a blizzard, and Dutch Em froze to death. Annie's feet were frozen and had to be amputated. Even though Henry Longhene started a fund to provide Annie with artificial legs, she always wore pegs, and thus became known as Pegleg Annie. She lived with Longhene for 22 years until he finally went back to Italy with her $10,000 life savings, earned by running a restaurant.

GROUSE LAKES
47

Round trip: 10.6 to 13 miles
Elevation gain: 3375 feet; 200 feet extra for Decker Creek Road
   (To see upper lake, add .6 mile and 130 feet gain)
Highest point: 8185 feet
Topo maps: Atlanta West, Atlanta East, Ross Peak
Time: 9 to 10 hours
Access: 1.7 miles west of Atlanta on Middle Fork Boise River
   Road, turn left (south) on primitive Yuba River Road. Drive
   2.5 miles to Decker Creek and turn east on very narrow Decker
   Creek Road and go .2 to 1.2 miles.
Difficulty: Strenuous

Along the trail to Grouse Lakes, a mosaic of wildflowers in lavender, blue, red, yellow, and white covers a series of big meadows. By early August the flowers are so thick it looks as though someone had taken a giant paint brush and painted the grass with red-orange, light blue and lavender. The highest meadow has so many tiny firs in it that the meadow from below looks like a green shag rug. A tangle of willows hides the upper lake's green water, which is across from a 50-foot dark grey rock knoll. To the right of this, 400-foot cliffs sweep up to a point and then down in granite waves. Between the lakes, the stream splashes down in little waterfalls. The lower lake is in a soft cushion of marsh.

To reach the trailhead, turn left (south) 1.7 miles west of Atlanta on the Middle Fork of the Boise River Road onto the primitive Yuba River Road. For directions for reaching Atlanta, see pages 81-82 in *Trails of the Sawtooth and White Cloud Mountains* by the author. Follow the Yuba River Road 2.5 miles south to a junction with the narrow and steep primitive Decker Creek Road. Leave passenger cars here. Up this road .5 mile, water seeps onto it to make a quagmire. In late August, two-wheel drive trucks can drive 1.2 miles east on the Decker Creek Road to the trailhead, but before that only four-wheel drive vehicles are suitable. Before July 15, only four-wheel drive vehicles should attempt the Yuba River Road because of mud. In May 1981, a bridge over the Yuba River at 1.5 miles was removed for repairs. Check with the Forest Service about the bridge before driving the Yuba River Road.

The Decker Creek Road leads along an open grassy hillside above the creek. 1 mile beyond the Yuba River-Decker Creek junction, a private road leads south over a bridge near weathered piles of boards that mark the sites of old cabins. At 1.2 miles the road switches back to the west abruptly, where a jeep track leads to a sign for Grouse Lakes.

The trail first crosses Decker Creek on small logs where some hikers may prefer to wade. The path leads south and then southeast through a Douglas fir forest to the first of several meadows at .7 mile. Watch for nettles along the trail, since by midsummer they are high enough to brush a hiker's hands. It is difficult to keep track of hiking progress with the topographic map because there are few landmarks. At 3 miles, the trail fords the creek to the west side to avoid an area of willows. At 3.2 miles the path returns to the east side on a network of small logs. Just before Senator Creek enters from the east is an unsigned trail junction marked with a cairn. This trail isn't shown on the topo map, but is on the Forest Service map. This trail allows a loop trip by a return down Decker Creek after going up to Grouse Lakes.

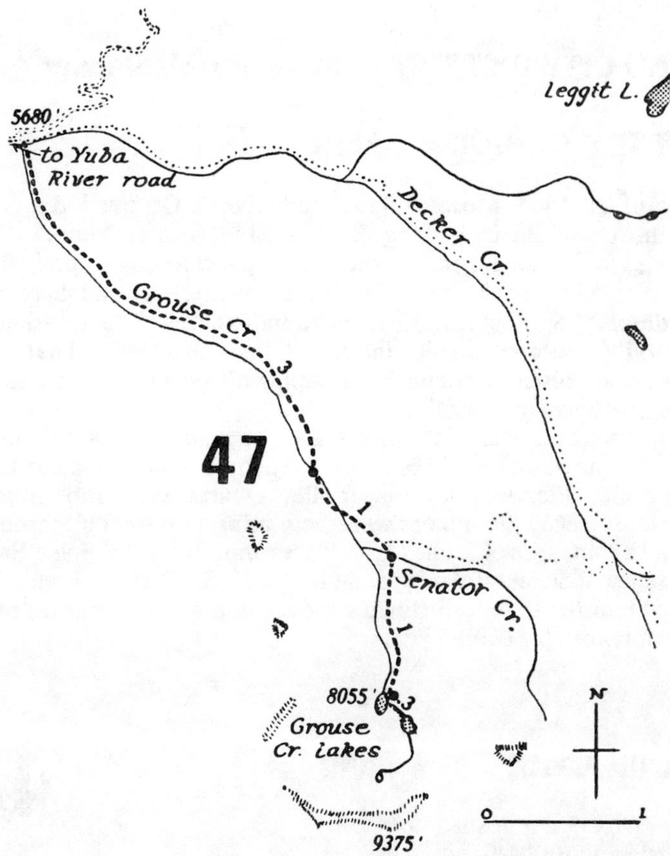

The trail to the lakes crosses Senator Creek in thick forest at 4 miles beside a large campsite 1700 vertical feet from the trailhead. The path traverses two small clearings, then comes out into a meadowy hillside .5 mile long splashed with paintbrush, bluebells, and yellow cinquefoil. Down the canyon are white sandy-sided peaks dotted with trees. There is one campsite where the trail reaches the lake at 5 miles with more small sites across the outlet on the west side.

To hike .3 mile further to the upper lake, follow a path around the east side of the lake until it ends in a marsh. Skirt the marsh to find the first inlet. Cross the inlet and follow it on the southwest side up a hillside of tiny firs to the lake. There are no campsites here due to the willows and swampy ground.

IDAHO CITY DISTRICT — Mores Creek Summit Area

HISTORY OF BOISE BASIN

In August 1862, Moses Splawn and George Grimes led a party into the Boise Basin looking for the Blue Bucket Mine. They explored to the north because they met a party led by Captain Tom Turner coming back from the Owyhees after an unsuccessful expedition. Splawn and Grimes found gold at the location of Centerville before hostile Indians killed Grimes. That fall, hundreds of miners went back with Splawn's party and established Idaho City and Pioneerville.

In the next ten years, the Boise Basin produced $100 million in gold. By the summer of 1864, 16,000 people lived at Idaho City, Centerville, Pioneerville, Placerville, Quartzburg, and smaller camps. By 1865, the miners were beginning to tunnel underneath the 249 businesses of Idaho City. Placer mining in the Boise Basin was the most successful ever done in the U. S. Parts of Idaho City burned four times, but the town survived and was the biggest town in the territory for twenty years.

JENNIE LAKE   48

Round trip: 9.2 miles
Elevation gain: 1940 feet
Highest point: 7850 feet
Topo maps: Bear River, Jackson Peak
Time: 8 hours
Access: Turn east on Atlanta Road at Edna Creek Campground, 18 miles north of Idaho City. Drive 6 miles on gravel road, and turn left (northeast) on dirt Crooked River-Bear River Road. Go 6.9 miles to jeep trail leading north.
Difficulty: Moderate

A 150-foot rounded knoll of grey granite, pitted by caves, guards the south side of dark green Jennie Lake. Behind the knoll a high, barren ridge holds 200-foot furrowed cliffs. To the east light grey towers decorate another set of cliffs above tiny shrubs that paint the canyon orange in the fall. Beside the knoll an inlet flows into the small lake through willows. Across the lake from the knoll, the outlet meanders through marsh grass. The topo map shows the

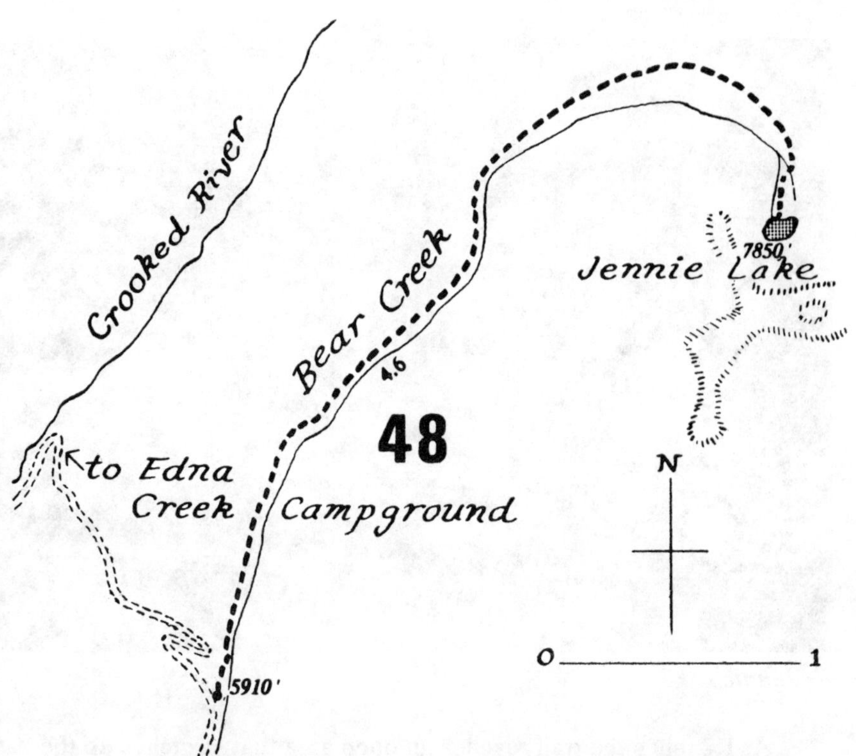

mountain wall behind Jennie Lake as wooded, but these hills and cliffs are mostly open. The trail is an old one that was rebuilt by the Youth Conservation Corps in the summer of 1980. The trailhead is only 2 hours from Boise, so the lake is one of the closest high lakes to that city.

To reach the trailhead, turn east on the graveled Atlanta Road at Edna Creek Campground, 18 miles north of Idaho City. At 6 miles, turn northeast on the dirt Crooked River-Bear River Road, which is passable for passenger cars. At 4.8 miles, this road crosses the Crooked River on a bridge. Beyond here the road climbs to a little summit at 5.9 miles. Then the route switchbacks downhill west and then back to the east to reach Bear Creek, a tributary of Bear River, at 6.9 miles. At this point a jeep trail leads north along the west bank of the creek. In 200 yards the jeep trail turns east to cross the creek over a culvert. Here the trail for Jennie Lake leads uphill to the left (north).

The trail climbs the canyon about 50 feet above the creek through lodgepole, spruce and fir. The way goes through shrub-filled clearings and open rocky areas. Soft ferns cuddle the creek as it flows over golden gravel. Lack of landmarks in the wooded canyon makes it hard to calculate hiking progress.

Jennie Lake

At 1.2 miles the trail reaches an open area that stretches up the side of the canyon. Then at 1.5 miles the trail levels as the route threads small meadows. The trail comes opposite two open grassy hills that are on the east side of the creek at 2.5 miles. Here the path is cut into the creek bank. At 3.2 miles the trail enters a series of large sagebrush and grass meadows below a sagebrush ridge. The trail through the meadows does not have a constructed tread. Instead blazes and rock cairns mark the way. The path disappears from time to time in the grass, so keep looking ahead to the next rock cairn.

At 4.2 miles the path comes close to a tiny stream (not the outlet) and turns west across the head of the canyon. After 200 yards the trail turns left (south) up along the side of a flat pale green outcrop. From here the route follows a small steep ridge up to the lake at 4.6 miles. The canyon makes a gradual semi-circle as it climbs, so the trail begins going north and reaches the lake running south.

MOUNTAIN HOME DISTRICT — Rocky Bar Area

HISTORY OF ROCKY BAR

Gold was discovered on the Feather River in the South Fork of the Boise River drainage in 1863. In 1864, a toll road was built to the settlements. Miners were working 53 arrastras in the area by then. One of the towns, Rocky Bar, was named the county seat of Alturas County, succeeding Esmeralda, another area settlement.

Arrastras ground ore by dragging heavy stones over a stone floor either by water power or horse power. Stamp mills weren't brought in until later. The gold at Rocky Bar was mostly in lodes. Miners there never were able to get enough capital to mine efficiently. Much of the mining had stopped by 1867.

The Alturas Hotel, with a gingerbread balcony, was the largest building in Rocky Bar. A fire destroyed most of Rocky Bar in 1892, leaving 150 people homeless. The most interesting part of Rocky Bar's history is the story of Spanish Town.

SPANISH TOWN

49

Round trip: 4 miles
Elevation loss: 800 feet (return climb)
Highest point: 6320 feet
Topo map: Rocky Bar
Time: 4 hours
Access: Drive up the rocky, dirt James Creek Road either 3.5 miles from Rocky Bar or 9.5 miles from Atlanta. The road begins 1.7 miles west of Atlanta. The trail starts just east of a switchback into the canyon with a waterfall.
Difficulty: Easy except for six creek crossings

At Spanish Town, a leaning log cabin, an old shack covered with galvanized steel, piles of silvered boards, and the rotting remains of log cabins stand as silent witnesses to past mining. This is an easy shaded hike downhill to an old ghost town that is mostly in ruins. Twenty-four historical sites have been inventoried.

Travelers as early as 1866 saw Spaniards or Mexicans mining here. The first settlers in Rocky Bar in the 1870s found the Spaniards' abandoned cabins. The legend is that these Spaniards mined here before the California gold rush. Probably no one will ever know where they came from or why they left. All materials

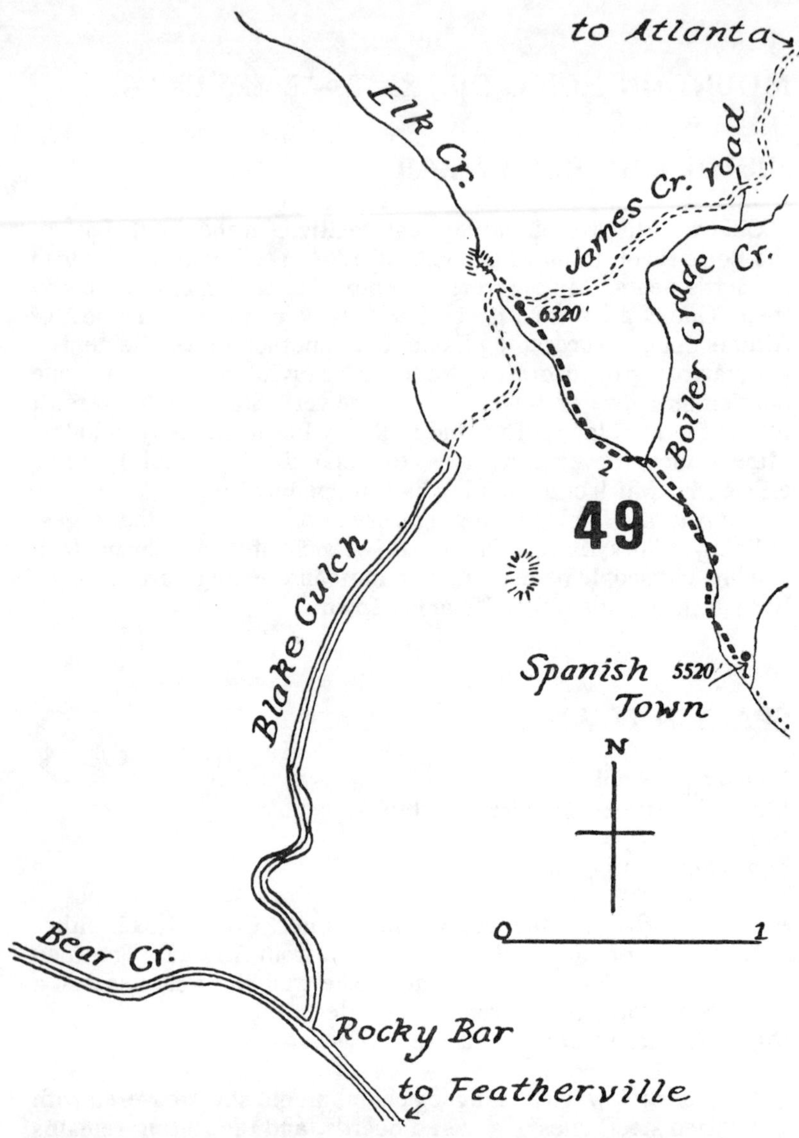

here are protected by the Antiquities Act, and there are heavy fines for anyone stealing or destroying any historical object.

The trailhead is 3.5 miles up the James Creek Road from Rocky Bar (9.5 miles from Atlanta). This road turns south 1.7 miles west of Atlanta off the Middle Fork of the Boise River Road. For directions for reaching Atlanta, see pages 81-82 of *Trails of the Sawtooth and White Cloud Mountains* by the author. Rocky Bar can be reached from Pine and Featherville. For directions for reaching Featherville, see the next hike. The road up the Boiler Grade over James Creek Summit is shown as primitive, but passenger cars can travel the rocky and airy dirt road after it has been scraped in the spring. 3.5 miles from Rocky Bar the James Creek Road switchbacks into a canyon where it crosses a bridge over Elk Creek. Above the bridge is a waterfall. The unsigned trail to Spanish Town begins as a jeep track about 200 yards up the Boiler Grade from the bridge. The trail leads southeast downhill through aspens away from the creek.

At .2 mile the jeep trail returns to the creek through a Douglas fir forest among 6-foot high blue delphiniums. The track has been washed out into a narrow path 200 yards further along the creek. Enormous ponderosa pines stud the hillside beyond the washout. At .7 mile the route hops the creek to the southwest side on logs. The trail crosses Elk Creek five times altogether and Boiler Grade Creek once. So many creek crossings may be a problem for beginning hikers, especially early in the summer.

At 1 mile, the path reaches Boiler Grade Creek and first crosses Elk Creek and then Boiler Grade Creek to the northeast side. At 1.2 miles the canyon becomes rockier where the trail goes back to the southwest side of Elk Creek. The trail returns to the northeast side for 100 yards at 1.5 miles before going back to the southwest. At 1.7 miles the route returns to the northeast side to stay. At a junction at 2 miles, take the signed Spanish Town Trail northeast 100 yards to the galvanized building and log cabin. Additional ruins are a few hundred yards up the East Fork of Elk Creek and also along the unsigned trail south of the junction.

MOUNTAIN HOME DISTRICT — Trinity Lakes Area

RAINBOW, HEART, LOOKOUT AND GREEN ISLAND LAKES   **50**

Round trip: 9.4 miles for all six lakes
Elevation gain: 1280 feet
Elevation loss: 1040 feet (return climb)
Highest point: 8400 feet
Topo map: Trinity Mountain
Time: 8 hours
Access: 2 miles east of Cat Creek Summit, turn north off U. S. 20. Drive 17 miles on a dirt road to Pine, and 8.5 miles on a paved road toward Featherville. Turn west on Trinity Creek Road and drive 13 miles on a dirt road to a road from Rocky Bar. Turn south and drive 3.2 miles on primitive road to Big Trinity Lake.
Difficulty: Moderate

Middle Rainbow Lake has its own 400-foot set of cliffs below the 800-foot ridge of charcoal grey cliffs that glowers above all three Rainbow Lakes. At the lakes, thick forest and green water contrast with these splintery dark cliffs on the south. From a saddle on the trail to this basin, nine lakes spread out below Trinity Mountain. Tumbled rocky peaks accent grass-covered green hills dotted with pines and firs. The region is unusual for Idaho because it has no sagebrush.

Of the three ways to reach Trinity Lakes, the easiest route is first to drive in from U. S. 20 past Anderson Ranch Reservoir. U. S. 20 runs from Mountain Home to Highway 75 south of Bellevue by way of Fairfield, and then east to Arco. Turn north 2 miles east of Cat Creek Summit off U. S. 20 and drive 17 miles on a dirt road to Pine. From Pine, drive along the South Fork of the Boise River on a paved road beside cabins and pine trees almost to Featherville. 8.5 miles from Pine, turn west on the dirt Trinity Creek Road, which winds up Trinity Creek and along canyon walls. The track is steep and rocky and is easier in a vehicle with a high wheelbase. 13 miles from the turnoff (sign says 17), the road intersects the Phifer Creek Road. Turn left (south) on this primitive road.

From here the first of the lakes, Little Trinity, is 3 miles further on a primitive road along the grassy crest of a ridge. .2 mile beyond Little Trinity is a turnoff to Big Trinity Lake where there are campgrounds. The grass-edged big lake stretches beside forested and granite-covered knolls. To reach the trailhead, drive south and west around Big Trinity Lake. Just above the campground on the south shore is a sign for the trailhead. (Other campgrounds are located at Big and Little Roaring River Lakes nearby.) The trail begins 100 yards along a road above the sign, .7 mile from the main road.

The trail first winds through meadows of lupine, paintbrush, and sulphur flowers and crosses a creek at .5 mile. The path switchbacks 800 feet to a saddle at 1 mile. Behind the lakes ahead, a ridge of dark grey cliffs rises to the left of the lookout-topped rocky cone of Trinity Mountain. A sea of peaks stretches south into the Smoky Dome area near Fairfield and north to Atlanta and Lowman.

The route zigzags down grass to a tiny creek at 1.5 miles (not on the topographic map) where a side path descends .2 mile to Green Island Lake. At 2 miles on the main trail, a sign for Lookout Lakes points to a sketchy side path that goes .2 mile up a stream to these lakes. Trinity Mountain Lookout hovers above the blue water of Big Lookout Lake, which a long-ago glacier carved out of the rock. Little Lookout Lake is only the eye of a marsh.

From the Lookout Lake Junction, the main trail climbs past a spring in a meadow and then down to a path to Heart Lake at

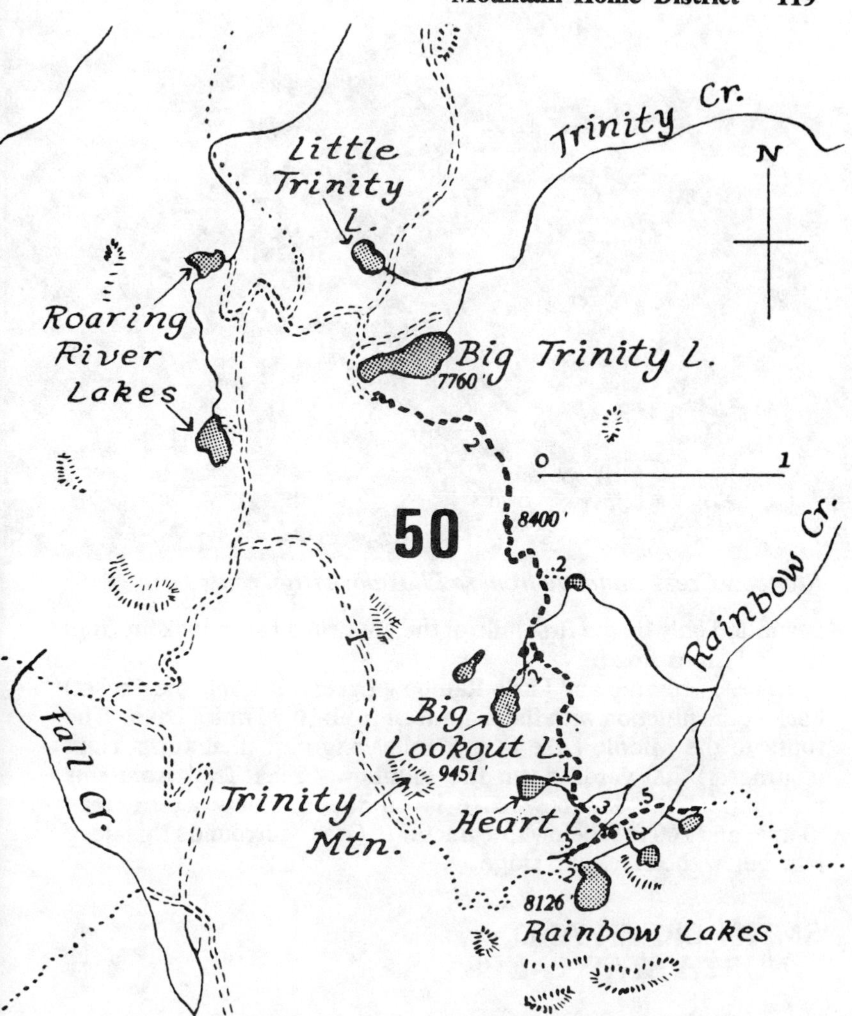

2.7 miles. Deep blue Heart Lake is just 200 yards up this side trail. On the side of this lake toward Trinity Mountain, trees divide white granite slabs above a grey cliff that plunges into the water. Beyond the Heart Lake Junction, the main trail drops to a junction with the Rainbow Creek Trail at 3 miles.

To reach Big Rainbow Lake from this junction, turn right (southwest) on the Rainbow Creek Trail and walk .3 mile until a pond appears through the trees on the left. Walk .2 mile around the left (northeast) side of the pond to the lake, which has a backdrop of two sections of cliffs on the ridge ahead.

The right branch of the Rainbow Creek Trail climbs 1100 feet in 1.5 miles from the junction and ends at the lookout road. The trail joins the lookout road 200 feet below the tower. Motor vehicles are

Rainbow Creek drainage from saddle above Big Trinity Lake

permitted only on the first mile of the spur road to the lookout from the Fall Creek Road.

To reach Middle and Little Rainbow Lakes, turn left (northeast) back at the junction with the main trail from Big Trinity Lake. The route to the Middle Lake is a .2 mile long path that turns right (southeast) 200 yards down the Rainbow Creek Trail from this junction. Little Rainbow Lake is on the Rainbow Creek Trail .5 mile and 200 feet below the junction. Grass surrounds this deep lake below the black cliff ridge.

SMITH CREEK AND NORTH STAR LAKES

51

Round trip: 10 miles
Elevation gain: 1080 feet
Elevation loss: 1060 feet (return climb)
Highest point: 8400 feet
Topo maps: Trinity Mountain, Prairie
Time: 8½ hours
Access: Turn north 2 miles east of Cat Creek Summit off U. S. 20 (west of Hill City). Drive 17 miles on a dirt road to Pine and then 8.5 miles towards Featherville on a paved road. Turn west on Trinity Creek Road and drive 13 miles on a dirt road to a road from Rocky Bar. Turn left (south) and drive 6.2 miles on primitive road to the third switchback on the Fall Creek Grade.
Difficulty: Moderate

The trail to Smith Creek and North Star Lakes leads along grassy hills which seem to be on an island in the sky, for they are so high above the surrounding country. Near the beginning of the trail, Trinity Lookout sits on top of a pointed tree-sprinkled hill. Waterfalls and sparkling streams thread meadows lacy with false hellbore. Lupine, paintbrush, and scarlet gilia cover the drier areas. Clumps of whitebark pine and subalpine firs dot the pale green hillsides. Smith Creek Lake nestles under green hills and rock benches. North Star Lake stretches between grassy ridges, a sapphire in light green velvet. Small peaks and delicate points create a backdrop. The trail near North Star Lake overlooks a faded quilt of green and gold fields on the flat shelf where the village of Prairie is located. This shelf falls into the canyon of the South Fork of the Boise that is below Anderson Ranch Reservoir.

To reach the trailhead, first drive up to Trinity Lakes. To reach Trinity Lakes, turn north 2 miles east of Cat Creek Summit off of U. S. 20 (west of Hill City). Go 17 miles to Pine on a signed dirt road. Continue 8.5 miles toward Featherville. Turn west on the dirt Trinity Creek Road and drive 13 miles to an intersection with the Phifer Creek Road. The Trinity Creek Road is the best and most direct of the three roads leading to Trinity Lakes. From this junction, it is 3 miles south on a primitive road to the lakes, and 5 miles to the beginning of the Fall Creek Grade at a junction with the road to Trinity Lookout. Drive 1.2 miles down the grade to the signed trailhead at 6.2 miles at the last of three sharp switchbacks.

The trail begins along one of the many contour terraces on this hillside. Then the path drops and crosses a side stream below a small waterfall at .3 mile. At .5 mile at a saddle, the route seems to go along the saddle and end. 100 yards before the end, the path makes a sharp turn north. It then descends a ravine into the canyon of Smith Creek. At 1 mile the way crosses two small streams and at 1.5 miles hops Smith Creek. The trail disappears in tall grass between these creeks.

At a junction just beyond Smith Creek, a poor trail turns north over a saddle into the drainage of Sheep Creek. The route to the lakes climbs the side of the main canyon of Smith Creek. At 2 miles the path ascends the outlet of Smith Creek Lake to the lake at 2.5 miles. On the topo map, the trail bypasses Smith Creek Lake, but this is not correct. The trail bypass shown on the map exists only as a faint path but can be used as a shortcut on the return from North Star Lake.

From Smith Creek Lake, the route circles the shoulder of the next ridge and rejoins the trail shown on the topo map at 2.8 miles. Next the trail curves into the canyon of Potter Creek and ascends a wooded hillside beyond to an open grassy slope. The path rounds a corner at 4 miles where North Star Lake appears. The route

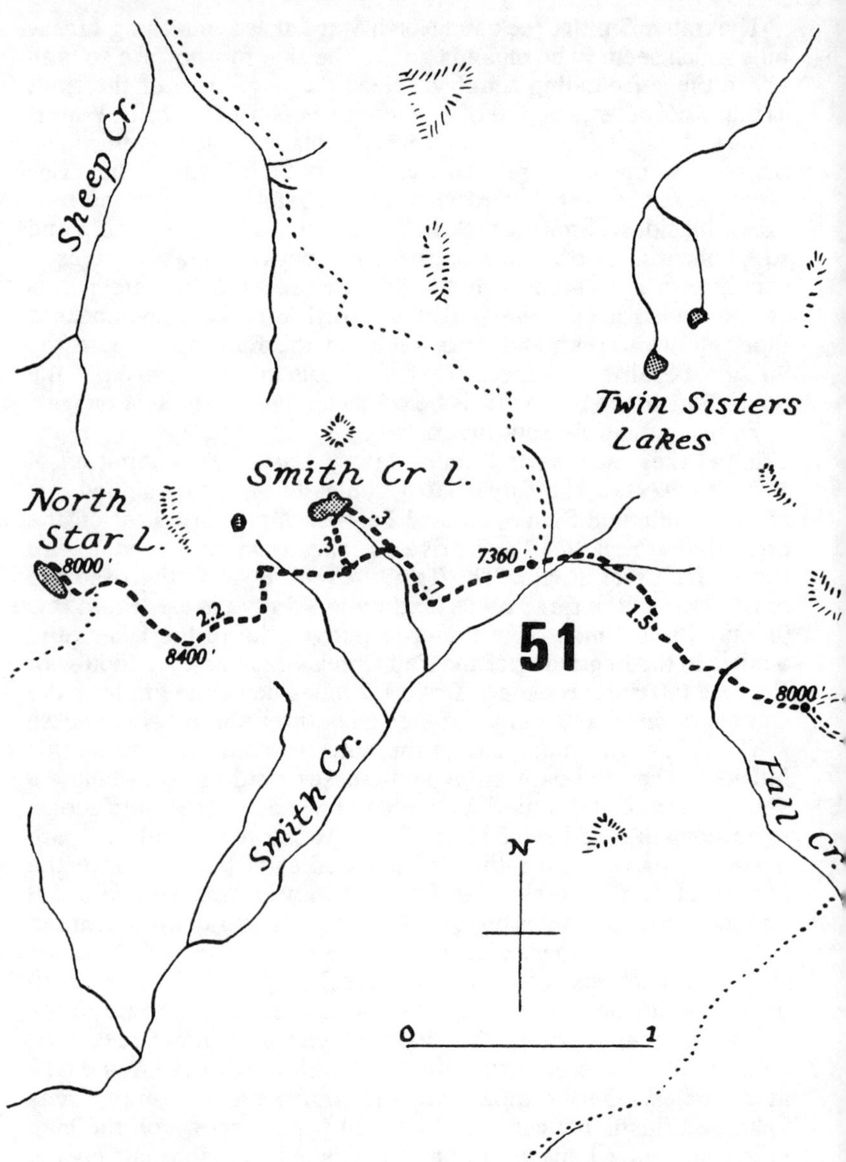

descends the hillside into a gully below the lake to an unsigned junction with a trail to Lava Mountain. The spur trail to the lake climbs 100 feet up a green hill to reach the shore at 5 miles.

LOWMAN DISTRICT — Lowman Area

RED MOUNTAIN LOOKOUT AND LAKES 52

Loop trip: 7.8 miles (1.4 miles extra to see highest lake)
Elevation gain: 2260 feet
Elevation loss: 100 feet (return climb)
Highest point: 8722 feet
Topo maps: Cache Creek, Miller Mountain East
Time: 7 hours
Access: At Lowman, turn left (north) on dirt Bear Valley Road and
  go 12 miles. Turn right (northeast) on Clear Creek Road and
  drive 7 miles on primitive road.
Difficulty: Strenuous; partly cross-country

Three of the Red Mountain Lakes nestle under 200-foot dark
cliffs below Red Mountain Lookout. The lookout perches on the
edge of the cliffs like a gull on a rock. From Red Mountain, the
hiker can see Trinity Mountain, Shafer Butte near Boise, Snowbank Mountain near Cascade, the Salmon River Mountains, most
of the Sawtooths and some of the White Clouds. Bunch grass and
flowers carpet the gentle side of Red Mountain between clumps of
lodgepole pine and subalpine fir. Pines, firs, red mountain heath,
white granite benches, and boulders enclose the tiny lakes. At the
lowest of the three lakes, a light red shoulder of Red Mountain
rises behind the waterlilies. This is the only view of the peak
where it looks red. Other tiny lakes are nearby, including Cat
Lakes and Lost Lakes.

To reach the trailhead, drive 12 miles up the dirt Bear Valley
Road from Lowman and then turn right (northeast) on the Clear
Creek Road. Drive 7 miles on this primitive road to a register box
for the Clear Creek Trail.

The first part of the trail runs in a deep, forested canyon beside
Clear Creek. At 200 yards, the trail crosses a side creek, Rough
Creek, and then a smaller creek at .5 mile. At .7 mile the path
leaves Clear Creek to climb a ridge through chapparal and
meadows. At 1.5 miles the trail reaches an open area and passes a
spring. At 1.7 miles is a junction with a side trail to Red Mountain
Lookout. (The Clear Creek Trail continues .7 mile east to a
junction with the Kirkham Ridge Trail leading from Miller
Mountain to Bull Trout Lake.) Turn north here and take the trail to
the lookout which climbs to the crest of a ridge and along it at the
edge of trees. Clark's nutcrackers may scold along the way. The
path angles northwest to a second ridge and switchbacks to a rocky

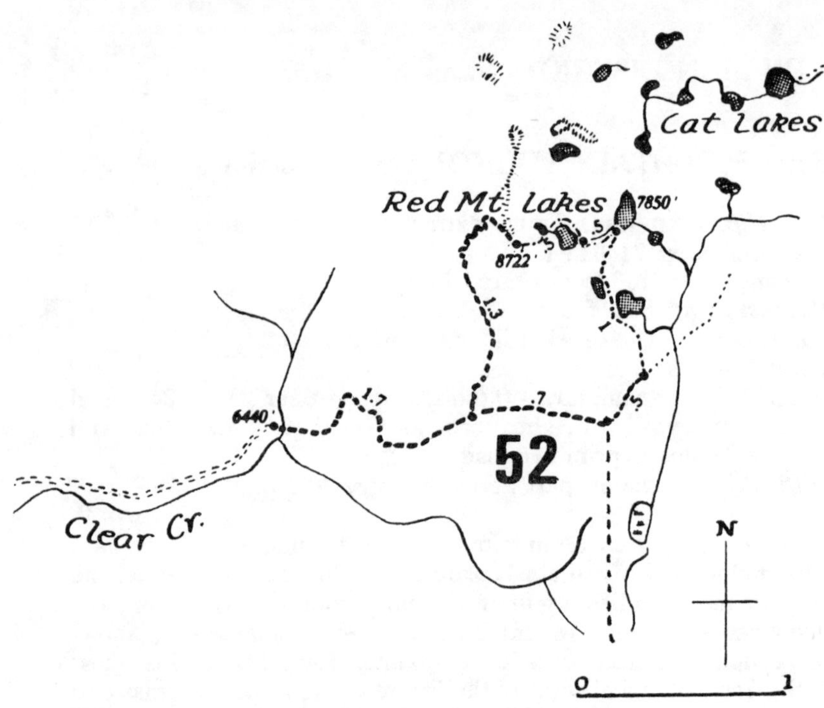

crest and the lookout at 3 miles.

From the lookout, all three lakes are spread out in plain view, so the easiest way to the lakes is to drop cross-country from the lookout. However, these routes are difficult. (To get to the highest lake, first walk .5 mile north along the lookout ridge to a wooded ravine. Descend the ravine as it angles .2 mile to the lake.) To reach the lake closest to the lookout, drop carefully down a rocky gully southeast of the lookout past a frog pond. Below this middle lake .5 mile from the lookout, a faint path leads down the outlet to the lowest lake at 4 miles.

To return to the main trail from the lowest lake, turn south through a boulder-filled gap and pass a shallow pond in the rocks. Then turn east down to a pond. From here angle south across an open hillside to the Kirkham Ridge Trail 1 mile below the lowest lake. Aim to join the trail .5 mile northeast of its junction with the Clear Creek Trail. This junction with the Clear Creek Trail is .7 mile east of the side trail to the lookout, at the 5.5 mile point on the loop hike. (The Kirkham Ridge Trail leads southwest from the Clear Creek Trail junction to Miller Mountain.) Another way to find Red Mountain Lakes is to take a faint path north 1 mile from this junction to the first of these lakes, but this path is hard to follow.

Lowest of the three Red Mountain Lakes

LOWMAN DISTRICT — Bull Trout Lake Area

KIRKHAM RIDGE TRAIL:
Bull Trout Lake to Cat Lakes and Link Trail   **53**

One-way distance: 9.5 miles (add .2 mile for Cat Lakes spur trail)
Elevation gain: 1360 feet
Highest point: 7670 feet
Topo maps: Bull Trout Point, Cache Creek
Time: 8 hours this section one-way
Access: Drive 1.5 miles north of Banner Creek Summit on High-
way 21. Turn left (southwest) on gravel road to Bull Trout Lake
and drive .7 mile to primitive Kirkham Ridge Trail Road. Turn
right (west) and go .5 mile to the road end. (See also Link Trail)
Difficulty: Strenuous

The green water of the lowest Cat Lake reflects dark firs and
pale granite knolls. Behind the trees two pointed peaks crowd an
orange shoulder of Red Mountain. A campsite is on the tiny
peninsula that juts into the lake from the east shore. The meadows
at Bull Trout Lake at the beginning of the trail sparkle with blue
camas and other wildflowers in season. Along the trail, a view of
the orange slabs and sand of Warm Springs Canyon is dramatic,

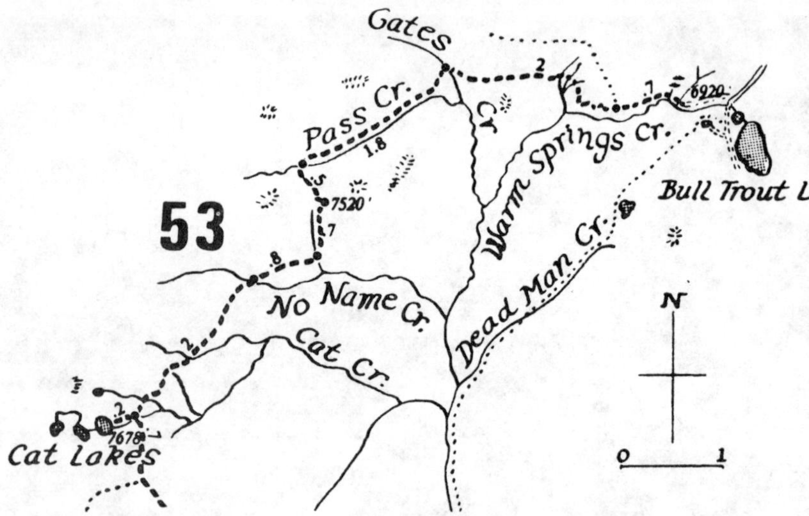

but most of the trail passes wooded hills. This trail provides the least strenuous access to the scenic but steep Link Trail. Part of the charm of this trail is in the solitude the hiker will probably find. This hike is good for early and late season because the highest point is less than 8000 feet.

To reach the trailhead, turn southwest 1.5 miles north of Banner Creek Summit off Highway 21 onto a gravel road to Bull Trout Lake. At 1.7 miles turn right (west) on a primitive road signed Kirkham Ridge Trail and drive .5 mile to its end. The trail starts at the edge of a flower meadow by crossing a swamp on flattened logs. Next the path winds along Warm Springs Creek through a lodgepole forest to meet a trail to upper Gates Creek at .7 mile.

At 1.5 miles the route crosses 3 small branches of Warm Springs Creek that run through sandy hills. Then the trail winds level through the woods before dropping 240 feet to a bridge at 2.7 miles over the branch of Warm Springs Creek called Gates Creek. From here the hiker can look down Warm Springs Canyon to orange talus and rock walls. On the other side of the bridge, the trail climbs 300 feet and at 3 miles begins to follow Pass Creek. At 4.5 miles, the route crosses to the south side of Pass Creek (campsites here) and climbs 100 feet to a wooded pass at 5 miles.

On the other side of the pass, the path switchbacks down across an open area with a view up Cat Creek Canyon. At 5.7 miles the trail reaches a large campsite, crosses a branch of No Name Creek, and enters a series of meadows. At 6.5 miles, there is another campsite where the route crosses No Name Creek. Beyond here, the trail climbs up and around the end of a hill and then down. At 7.5 miles the path crosses the first of three branches of Cat Creek. Just before a fourth cascading branch of Cat Creek at 8.5 miles, an unsigned path leads up the right (north) bank of this creek. This path climbs 200 feet in .2 mile to the first Cat Lake at 8.7 miles.

The Kirkham Ridge Trail continues from the Cat Lake junction by climbing gently along the head of Cat Creek Canyon with a view of nearby eroded gullies. .7 mile from the junction with the Cat Lake path, the trail drops to meet the Link Trail. From this junction, 9.5 miles from Bull Trout Lake, the hiker can see the southern Sawtooths around Graham.

LINK TRAIL:
Kirkham Ridge Trail to Warm Springs 54

One-way distance: 11.5 miles
Elevation gain: 2120 feet
Elevation loss: 3600 feet
Highest point: 8120 feet
Topo maps: Cache Creek, Bull Trout Point, Eightmile Mountain
Time: 2 days for this section one-way
Access: Reach the trail from Bull Trout Lake via Kirkham Ridge Trail or from Warm Springs Guard Station. To reach the guard station, turn left (west) 18 miles northeast of Lowman off Highway 21. Drive 2.5 miles on a dirt road.
Difficulty: Strenuous

The Link Trail has one of the best views of the whole serrated range of the Sawtooths. The view from the Link Trail includes more of the Sawtooths than is seen from Observation Peak in the range itself. For several miles the trail hugs the top of a narrow ridge. The Sawtooth panorama follows the trail like a giant mural above the canyon of Warm Springs Creek. Snow-filled canyons scar the dark blue faces of the enormous peaks.

Also near the upper end of the trail, Red Mountain presides over a complex of granite ridges, knolls, and lakes. For access to the upper end of this trail, see Bull Trout Lake. The lower end of the trail meets the Warm Springs Guard Station Road at the landing strip. To reach Warm Springs Guard Station, turn left (west) about 18 miles northeast of Lowman off Highway 21. Drive 1 mile to the guard station on a dirt road, double back as the road does and drive 1.5 miles further along the airstrip and across the end of it to the register box.

The upper end of the Link Trail turns south from the Kirkham Ridge Trail along a ridge above Eightmile Creek southeast of Red Mountain Lakes. Climbing 600 feet in 1 mile from this junction, the route contours in and out of gullies with a view of Red Mountain. At .7 mile the trail crosses an open area and then heads

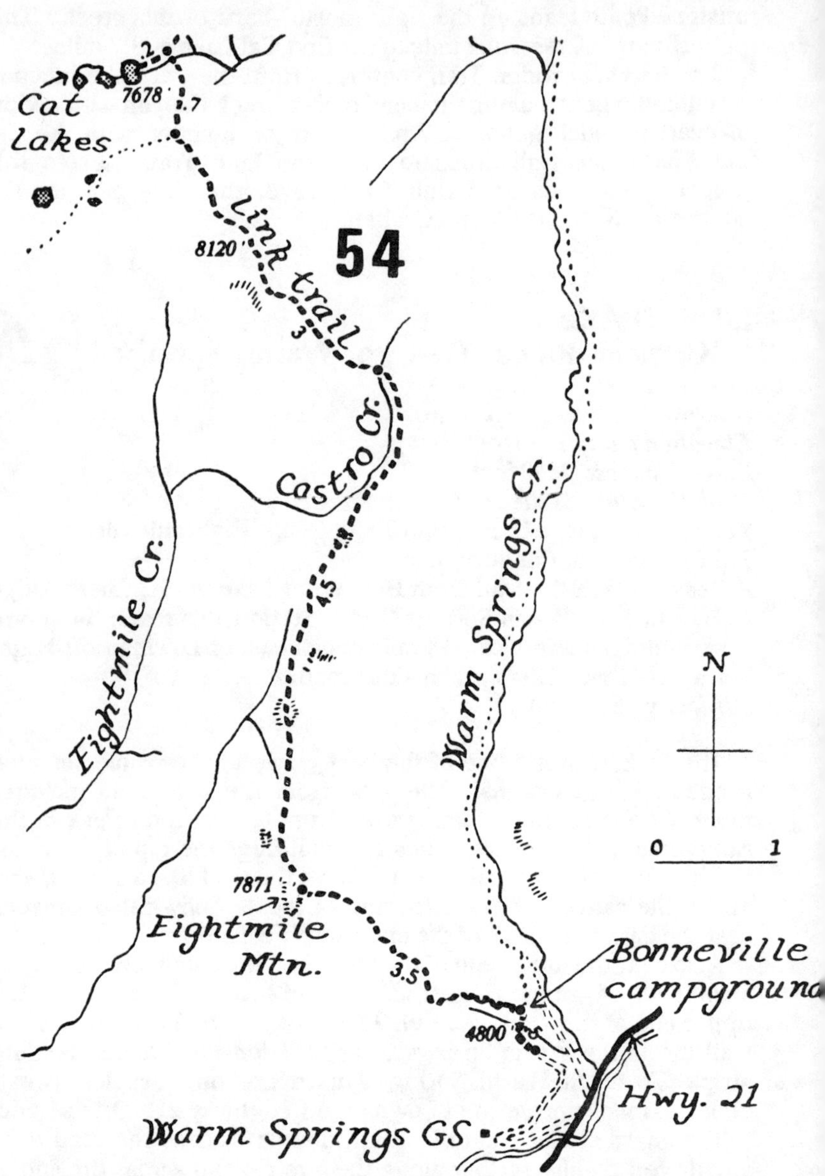

downhill at 1.2 miles. The route reaches a roof-edged saddle at 1.5 miles where the hiker gets a view of the Sawtooths.

From the saddle the path traverses southeast along the side of the next hill on the ridge. In early July, this section of the trail at 8000 feet may have snow on it. At 2.5 miles the trail heads southeast down a spur of this hill into the canyon of Castro Creek (a branch of the East Fork of Eightmile Creek) and crosses the creek on logs at 3 miles. A big campsite below the crossing is the only good one on the Link Trail because Castro Creek is the only dependable water source. There is one little stream that runs only in early season 50 feet below the trail at 6.5 miles.

From the Castro Creek crossing, the path climbs along the side of the canyon to a saddle at 4 miles where the Sawtooths appear again. Beyond here the trail climbs south up and down along the top of the ridge for several miles. The ridge varies from open and narrow to wooded and rounded. The canyon wall next to the trail has been eroded like a badlands so that bare striped rock is exposed. Use caution where the trail passes close to these eroded areas. At 6.5 miles, pine-needled areas under trees could serve as campsites within reach of the early season stream.

From here the trail climbs 160 feet almost to the top of the next hill, crosses an open area, and skirts the north side of Eightmile Mountain. At 7.5 miles the route crosses a saddle beside the top of this mountain, then switchbacks down the open side of the peak. The canyon of Grandjean and the Sawtooths behind it are very close. The trail drops down the southeast ridge of Eightmile Mountain in firs and brush. The trail climbs less than shown on the map in going up the west side of a hill.

At 9.2 miles the trail leaves the ridge to descend the South Fork of the Payette canyon wall next to Penrod Creek. At 9.7 miles, the trail zigzags down an open sagebrush and grass hillside to a junction with the Warm Springs Canyon Trail at 11 miles. Bull Trout Lake is 16.7 miles from here by the Warm Springs Canyon Trail, but that trail has a difficult creek crossing and no view of the Sawtooths. (The total distance from Bull Trout Lake by the Kirkham Ridge and Link Trails to this junction is 20.5 miles.) 200 yards below the Warm Springs junction, the joined trails cross Penrod Creek to a register box at a road at 11.5 miles from the upper end of the Link Trail at its junction with the Kirkham Ridge Trail. The road has come up 1.5 miles from Warm Springs Guard Station along an airstrip.

This hike description of the Link Trail begins at the upper end because the elevation gain is 2120 feet compared to 3600 feet in the opposite direction. The Link Trail and the Kirkham Ridge Trail make a fine three-day trip beginning at Bull Trout Lake.

BUREAU OF LAND MANAGEMENT

BOISE DISTRICT — Boise Area

EARLY EXPLORERS

In the report to General Macomb of his expedition, Captain Bonneville was the first to use the name "Boise River" in a written account. However, he may just have been using a name that had gradually become the established one. Lewis and Clark called the river by the Indian name of "Copcoppakark" (spellings vary). In the forty years after Lewis and Clark, fur trappers and explorers named many geographical features and passed on these names by word of mouth.

Robert Stuart wrote a journal of his 1812 expedition from Astoria to St. Louis on which he discovered the route for what became the Oregon Trail. He made that trek to give a report to Astor about the Hunt expedition. His account, which was published in French in Paris in 1821, called the Boise River the "Wooded River".

After Astor was forced to sell his first fur company to the British in 1813, Donald MacKenzie, who had been an Astorian, led three successful expeditions of trappers, including French-Canadians for the British Northwest Company, into the Snake River country.

Alexander Ross in 1824 called the Boise River "Reid's River", because John Reid had been killed by Indians there in 1814. Nathaniel Wyeth and William Sublette, who founded Fort Hall in 1834, called the river the "Woody River" and "Big Wood River".

In 1831, Army Captain Benjamin Bonneville, backed by John Jacob Astor, led a fur trapping expedition to the Rockies. Bonneville had experienced French-Canadian trappers with him, but he knew nothing of trapping, so the expedition was a failure. The French-Canadians are supposed to have exclaimed "Les Bois, Les Bois" when the expedition reached the Boise River.

Bonneville and his group wandered for three years, even though he had only a two-year leave of absence from the Army. The Army dishonorably discharged him when he returned a year late and refused to publish his journal. However, Andrew Jackson restored Bonneville's commission in 1836. Then in 1837, Washington Irving immortalized Bonneville and the "Les Bois" story in his book, *The Adventures of Captain Bonneville, U.S.A.* By 1843, many people were traveling the Oregon Trail.

RAILROADS

When the railroad came to Idaho, it closely followed the route of the Oregon Trail. The development of railroad lines aided in the settlement of Idaho. The connecting of the last two sections of the first transcontinental railroad with the golden spike at Promontory, Utah, in 1869 led to railroad development in Idaho. In 1878, the Utah and Northern built a line through Pocatello to Montana with the backing of Jay Gould of Union Pacific.

In 1881, Union Pacific started building a line from Granger, Wyoming along the route of the Oregon Trail to Huntington, Oregon. The line reached Montpelier in 1882. The Utah and Northern Company became part of this project, which they called the Oregon Short Line. At the time the line was built, a branch was constructed to Hailey and the next year was extended to Ketchum. The tracks had crossed Idaho to Huntington by 1884. The company laid the line as straight as possible, so the tracks bypassed Boise. New towns in the Boise Valley like Nampa and Caldwell sprang up along the rails. A company called the Idaho Central Railway built a spur line from Nampa to Boise in 1887. However, a through track wasn't put in until 1927.

OREGON TRAIL AT BONNEVILLE POINT 55

Through trip: 4.7 miles
Elevation gain: 20 feet
Elevation loss: 820 feet
Highest point: 3860 feet
Topo maps: Indian Creek Reservoir (20 foot contours), Lucky Peak
Time: 3½ hours one-way, plus shuttle driving time
Access: Turn off I-84 at Blacks Creek exit 10 miles southeast of Boise's Gowen Field exit. Drive 2.6 miles east on graveled Blacks Creek Road. Turn northeast and drive 1.5 miles to interpretive site.
Difficulty: Easy

After plodding westward through hundreds of miles of barren desert, the Oregon Trail tops Bonneville Point. From the point, the oasis of the Boise Valley extends to the horizon. Across the Boise River Canyon, trees fringe the top of Lucky Peak. In May 1833, Captain Bonneville's trappers first saw the Boise Valley from Bonneville Point and exclaimed "Les Bois, Les Bois!"

Hiking along the Oregon Trail near here makes the hiker feel like a pioneer. Even though a dirt road follows much of the trail, part of the original track still shows among the sagebrush as a

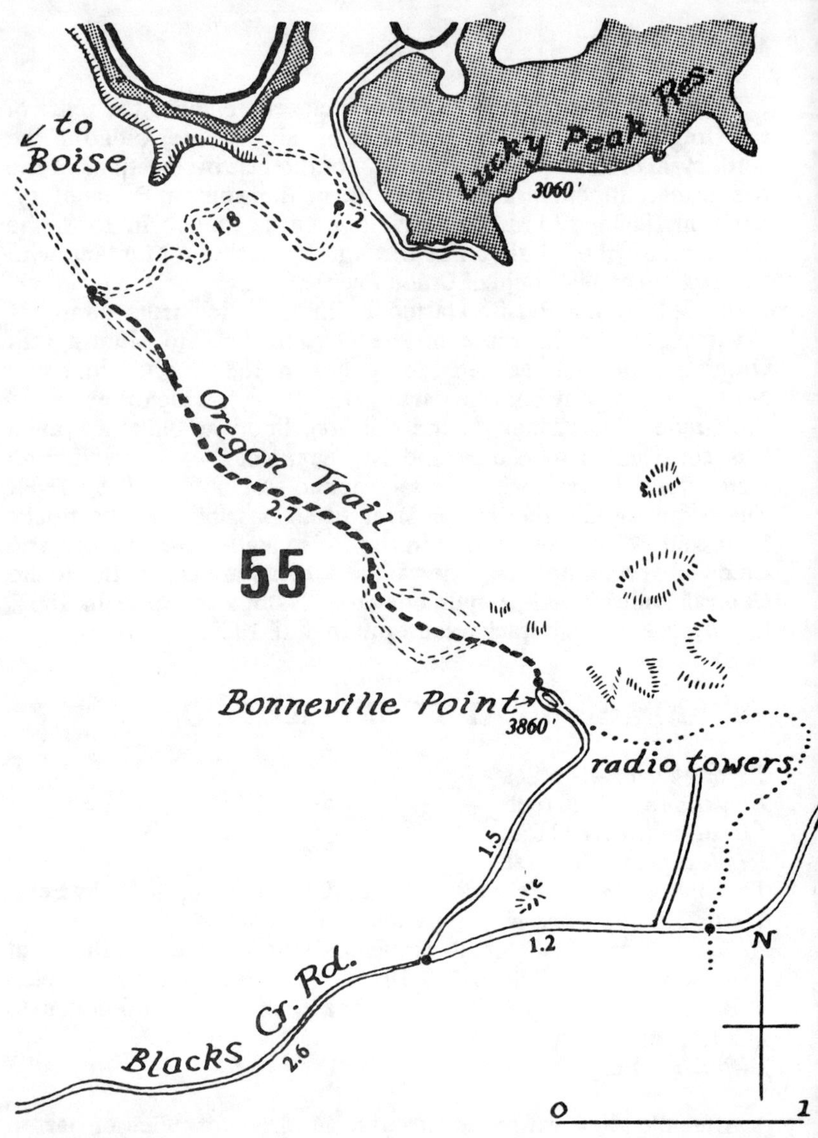

great groove in the land. The Bureau of Land Management has marked the route near Bonneville Point with 4-foot high cement posts. Near the end of the hike, blue Lucky Peak Reservoir floats below wrinkled velvet hills. The Oregon Trail has recently been made a National Historic Trail under the National Trails System.

To sense the drama for a pioneer seeing the Boise Valley for the first time, walk uphill along the 2.5 miles of the marked trail southeast of Bonneville Point below the radio towers from Blacks Creek Road to Bonneville Point. The easiest place to start hiking is at the Bonneville Point Interpretive Site or from where the Oregon Trail crosses Blacks Creek Road.

To reach Bonneville Point, go 10 miles on Interstate 84 towards Mountain Home southeast of Boise. Turn east and go under the overpass on the Upper Blacks Creek Road. After .7 mile, the road becomes gravel, and at 2.6 miles (sign says 3), it joins another. Turn left (northeast) here and go 1.5 miles to the interpretive site. (The road straight ahead from this junction crosses the marked Oregon Trail at 1.2 miles.)

As an American Revolution Bicentennial project, a pole fence, shelter, and Oregon Trail interpretive displays were put in at the site by the Bureau of Land Management. A picnic table with fireplace is available, and trees provide shade. A stone memorial commemorates Bonneville's discovery. The best time of year for this hike is May when the wildflowers, such as Mules ears, are at their peak.

To begin the hike towards the Boise Valley, follow the cement markers downhill from the northwest end of the site along a section of the original trail and across a fence to join a dirt road at 150 yards. At .4 mile, the dirt road splits. Take the left branch to follow the markers, which soon leave the road to descend a section of the original route. At 1 mile, the cement posts rejoin the road, and the two roads merge. The road passes a jeep track on the left at 1.5 miles and at 2 miles, descends beside a gully. At 2.2 miles the markers leave the road to climb along the side of a hill on the right. From the hill, the trail drops to rejoin the road at 2.7 miles near a junction with a primitive road heading northeast to Lucky Peak Dam. The last marker is at this junction. The hiker can continue northwest along the road which follows the Oregon Trail to the edge of Boise.

It is more interesting to follow the primitive road to Lucky Peak Dam northeast, contouring in and out of gullies. At 3.7 miles, the route runs above dark lava cliffs that brood over the Boise River Canyon and frame a slice of green Boise Valley. Across the river spreads the manicured grass of Discovery State Park, and to the right is the dam and reservoir. At 4 miles a gate blocks the road. Either crawl under the gate or open and shut it. At 4.2 miles, the road turns left and passes a track on the right at 4.5 miles. The route continues to the dam and boat launch at 4.7 miles.

The archeological site of the Foote House is near Lucky Peak Reservoir. Mary Hallock Foote lived in Idaho while her husband, Arthur, worked as the engineer for the original unsuccessful effort to build the New York Canal. She wrote and illustrated novels and short stories which told of life in the West.

HULLS GULCH (National Recreation Trail) **56**

One-way distance: 3.5 miles
Elevation gain or loss: 1200 feet one-way
Highest point: 5000 feet
Topo maps: Boise North, Robie Creek
Time: 2-3 hours one-way
Access: Drive to the end of Boise's 8th Street. The road turns
   from pavement to dirt with signs for the trail at 4 and 7 miles.
Difficulty: Easy

Next time family or friends want to go on an outing, why not go
to the unspoiled streamside and desert of the Hulls Gulch
Interpretive Trail only 15 minutes from Boise? Built by the Bureau
of Land Management and volunteer groups, the trail winds along a
rushing stream beside wildflowers, willows, and other shrubs. A
dark blanket of pines tops the Boise Ridge above. Below spreads
the whole Boise Valley. In prehistoric times this valley was a lake.
From the trail, little blocks of houses and buildings now seem to fill
the valley instead of water.

To reach the trail, drive to the end of Boise's 8th Street, where it
becomes a dirt road. This road climbs toward the Mile High Picnic
Area at the top of the ridge. The route passes the Boise Water
Company's roofed reservoir and a sandstone cliff that has been
pitted by swallows. The first large sign for the trail is about
4 miles up the road, and the second sign for the higher end of the
trail is at 7 miles. The easiest way to walk the 3.5 mile trail is to
use two vehicles and start at the second sign because then the
route will be mostly downhill. There is also a cutoff trail which
makes possible a 2.5 mile loop hike from the upper trailhead.
Directions are given from the upper trailhead.

This interpretive trail hike takes about 2 hours. If only one
vehicle is used, it will require an additional hour or more to walk
back to a car left at the trailhead. The trail is closed to motorcycles. A sign points to a separate track for them near the lower
end. The water in the stream is not drinkable, so carry water. The
trail is open all year, but it may be too hot most of the day in mid-
summer. During heavy spring and fall rains, the access road is
closed. There are no restrooms at the trailheads or along the trail.

From the upper sign, the trail slants down across a sagebrush
hillside towards two branches of the creek in Hulls Gulch. Near
the sign, the cutoff trail that makes possible a 2.5 mile loop hike
leaves the main trail. At about .5 mile, the path crosses above the
splashing of a small waterfall. Along the upper part of the stream
are old pipes which are remnants of the water system for Fort
Boise. The trail next crosses the southern branch of the creek,

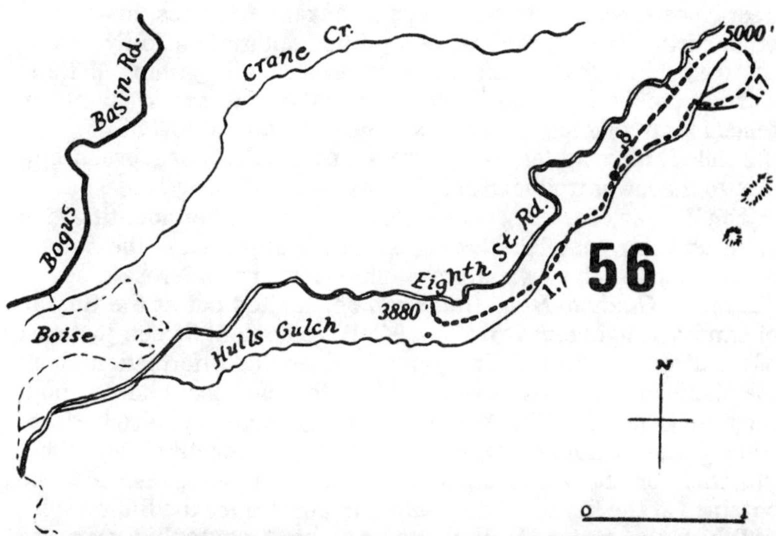

near a few ponderosa pine trees. Before man cut and burned the trees, the forest extended much further down than it does today.

Wildflowers decorate the ground along the trail in the spring. Some of these are yellow Mules ears, purple larkspur, and brilliant pink phlox. Miniature wildflowers an inch or two high keep the bolder ones company. Sagebrush, bitterbrush and grasses grow on the open hillsides. Due to overuse by man and his livestock, most of the Boise Front no longer has enough deep-rooted perennial grasses to prevent erosion. The Boise Front is a term for the hillside region above Boise and includes a 20-mile ridge of mountains from Harris Creek Summit to Shafer Butte and Shaw Mountain.

The trail soon crosses back to the northwest side of the creek on a bridge below the junction of the two branches. At 1.7 miles the path meets the return trail for the 2.5 mile loop near picnic tables. The route follows the creek most of the rest of the way. Granite outcrops of the Idaho batholith are just above the trail.   The stream, larger now, gurgles along over rocks shaded by trees and

shrubs. Some are willow, alder, hawthorne, red-ozier dogwood, syringa, and wild currant. In the fall the canyon glows with red and gold leaves and the golden flowers of rabbitbrush. The path crosses the creek to the southeast side on a bridge at about 2 miles and soon returns.

Other interesting plants and wildlife shelter here. Dense mats of miners' lettuce (*Montia perfoliata)* creep in the shade of the streamside trees.   This plant has edible round leaves and miniature white flowers rising from the center of each leaf. Mule deer come down to eat the foliage. Chukar partridges, hawks and other birds, lizards, rabbits, and ground squirrels also live along the trail. In a few places shiny green leaves in groups of three warn of poison ivy. Near both ends of the trail, areas have been fenced and planted to improve the vegetation for birds.   At 3.2 miles, the trail leaves the creek and climbs a sagebrush hillside to the lower trailhead at 3.5 miles.

The Bureau of Land Management has posted plant identification signs and thirty interpretive signs. These signs name the natural objects seen such as wheatgrass, ninebark, or ponderosa pine. A *Teacher's Guide to Hulls Gulch* can be checked out at the Bureau of Land Management Office at 3948 Development Street, just east of the airport in Boise. The guide has detailed information about the plants and animals as well as ideas for teaching children about their environment. The Bureau of Land Management also has pretrip meeting handouts and cassettes of all interpretive signs along the trail for the sight-impaired.   These cassettes can also be obtained at the library of the State Commission for the Blind.

The Hulls Gulch Trail is not on the topographic map, so distances between landmarks are estimates.

HISTORY OF BOISE CITY

The creation of Idaho Territory in 1863 and the beginning of Boise City resulted from the boom in the Boise Basin gold camps. Farmers began to farm the Boise Valley to supply the miners with food. Frank Davis built the first cabin in March 1863.

Major Pinkney Lugenbeel was dispatched with troops in 1863 to build a military post for protection of the Boise Basin travelers and miners from the Indians. On July 4, Lugenbeel found a site for the fort along the road from Boise Basin to the Owyhees. On July 7, area farmers met in the Davis-Ritchey cabin to form a town. Henry Riggs laid out the town and named it Boise.

To build the fort, Lugenbeel had to construct a mule-driven sawmill up Cottonwood Creek to get wood and dig a quarry to get sandstone. The officers soon sent for their wives, who led the social life of the growing town.

BOISE GREENBELT:
Glenwood to Barber Park

57

One-way distance: 10.6 miles (5 miles developed length)
Elevation gain: 140 feet
Highest point: 2760 feet
Topo maps: Eagle, Boise North, Boise South (20 foot contours)
Time: 6½ hours for entire distance
Access: There are several access points along the river, especially
   Veterans, Ann Morrison, Julia Davis, and Barber Parks.
Difficulty: Easy

During three seasons, a curtain of greenery hides urban Boise
from a person on the Greenbelt paths. The Boise Greenbelt is a
close-in linear park, but some of it seems remote from any city.
The blue and silver river meanders through the town forming
lagoons and islands that shelter ducks and other birds. Along the
banks, willows, wild roses, and currants tangle beneath tall
cottonwoods.

GLENWOOD TO VETERANS STATE PARK (2.7 miles)

Begin hiking this undeveloped private property section by
walking from Glenwood Road along the northeast side of the river
at the edge of the Plantation Golf Course. Beyond the Golf Course,
at 1 mile a dirt road goes past some new homes that face the river.
Detour around the homes on a street on the side away from the
river. Beyond the houses return to the dirt road as it follows a low
levee past an area of townhouses and an adjoining auto junkyard.

Next the dirt road goes behind a service building and becomes a
path. The path turns away from town towards the river into trees
and shrubs. It follows an elongated ridge of rocks through the
trees, then turns into a road again. Next this road passes a shed
and fenced well. From here the track continues along the river,
past a large open area at 1.7 miles with a view of Shafer Butte. In
the cottonwood trees, magpies have built their nests of sticks.
Beyond the open area, a grass-covered dirt road continues that
ends at a building lettered "Public Works".

To avoid trespassing on private land, walk northeast to Glendale
Street and follow it to Veterans State Park at 2.7 miles.

VETERANS STATE PARK TO MAIN STREET (1.2 MILES)

Veterans State Park is the beginning of public access. To go
from here to Main Street, the hiker may take either the Pica Pica
or the Typha Trail in Veterans Park. Both trails go around either
side of a large lagoon in the river. The walk of about 1 mile around
the lagoon is a pleasant one in itself, and is perhaps the best

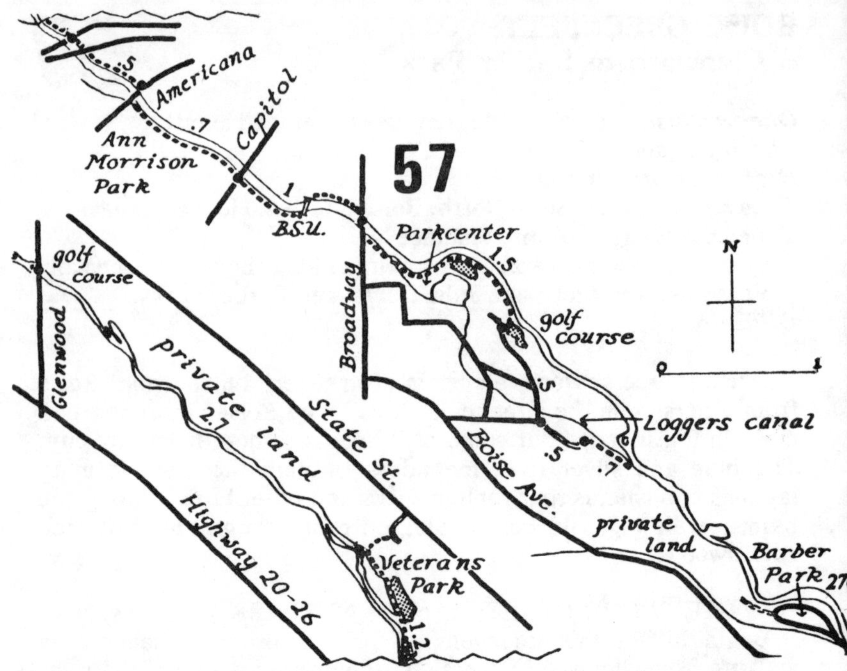

section of the Greenbelt. The route has numbered signs for a nature trail. Leaflets for the trail may be obtained by calling the Idaho Park and Recreation Department. Two swimming docks float at the south end of the lagoon. At the end of the lagoon at .7 mile is a restroom where the trails join.

Next the Greenbelt path leaves Veterans State Park as the trail crosses a creek on a bridge beside a low wooden dam in the river. Seagulls sometimes stand with their feet in the water on top of the dam. The route now follows the Boise River Greenbelt, sponsored and developed by the Boise City Park Department. The paved path is adjacent to a chain link fence of a gravel and asphalt plant and passes between a gravel pond and the river with a view of the hills. Just before crossing Main Street at 1.2 miles, the trail passes next to a car agency. At this point turn right to the nearest traffic light (Garden Street) to cross Main Street.

Follow Garden to Fairview and then walk back to the river on the downstream side of Fairview Bridge. The "loop" is a temporary recommendation until both Main and Fairview underpasses are complete. Fairview underpass work started in November 1980, and work on the Main Street underpass began the next summer.

MAIN STREET TO AMERICANA (.5 mile)

From Main Street to Americana, the paved path runs adjacent to the grounds of a motel, between Main Street and Fairview Avenue. Paving is now partially completed east of Fairview with the remaining path to be constructed after the Fairview underpass is completed. The path passes the foot of Fletcher Street and under a railroad trestle. East of the trestle, the paved trail loops out from the river, while an unpaved path runs right along the bank.

The route bridges a couple of lagoons and enters a mini-park of lawn and trees with picnic tables, barbecues, and seasonal use restrooms. Next the trail passes the Quinn Center Building and reaches Americana Boulevard. The path continues under the bridge to the southeast side of Americana at .5 mile. (For a through trip on the south river bank Greenbelt system, cross the river next on the walkway of Americana Bridge and enter Ann Morrison Park.)

AMERICANA TO 8th STREET/SHORELINE PARK (.7 mile)

To continue on the *north* river bank Greenbelt system, do not cross the river. Stay on the path and follow the river into Shoreline Park. At the foot of 13th Street, this park is opposite Ann Morrison Park and has observation decks and viewpoints to overlook the river and Ann Morrison Park. Shoreline Park has a bicycle and skate rental building with snack foods, which is open seasonally.

Continuing east from Shoreline Park, the Greenbelt forms a junction with Pioneer Walkway, which enters the Greenbelt from the north. (Pioneer Walkway can be followed south over the recently completed Pioneer Bridge into Ann Morrison Park.) Following the Greenbelt further east on the north side of the river will bring the path user to the 8th Street Bridge, just south of the Boise Public Library. Greenbelt users should carefully cross 8th Street and proceed on the east side of the bridge to return to the Greenbelt in Tourist Rest Stop Park.

AMERICANA TO 8th STREET/ANN MORRISON PARK (.7 mile)

The route from Americana to 8th Street in Ann Morrison Park is on the *south* side of the river and begins with a gravel path that comes down from the bridge past a low cement dam and crosses the spillway on a wooden bridge. The park has trees, shrubs, lawn, duck ponds, picnic areas, seasonal display fountain, floral beds, and restrooms. The gravel way continues along the river's edge past a parking area, riverstone beach, restrooms and a recently renovated playground.

Beyond the playground, the path skirts a cattail-edged pond at .4 mile and intersects with the Pioneer Walkway crossing the river from the north. The downtown buildings peer over trees from beyond the River Street District. The trail passes a picnic shelter and heads out of the park between buildings and the river to a parking lot beside the 8th Street Bridge at .7 mile.

8th STREET BRIDGE TO BROADWAY/JULIA DAVIS PARK

This section is 1 mile long. To go from the 8th Street Bridge to Broadway Avenue, first follow a paved path on the *south* side of the river which crosses under both the 8th Street and Capitol Boulevard Bridges. This area is "Tourist Rest Stop", one of the first stops available for early motor vehicles. This area is extensively planted with annual flowers and shrubs. Use caution when going under these bridges as the trail curves are sharp and oncoming cyclists or joggers can't be seen.

The route then climbs to the edge of Campus Drive at Boise State University. Opposite the BSU buildings at .5 mile, the hiker may cross the river to Julia Davis Park on a high arched footbridge. The walk on the *north* side of the river continues through the park and under the Broadway Bridge. The path on the north side of the river continues for another .7 mile and then ends in Municipal Park. To continue on the Greenbelt on the *south* bank, follow the path from Julia Davis Park under the Broadway Bridge; go up onto the bridge, and cross it. Construction began in November 1980 for a south bank underpass linking the BSU campus with the Greenbelt east of Broadway.

BROADWAY TO BARBER PARK (4.5 miles)

This section is partly developed. To begin the Greenbelt section on the *south* side of the river between Broadway and Barber Park, cross the parking lot for a bar just across the Broadway Bridge and follow the paved path again next to the river. If bicycling, beware of a speed bump in the middle of the parking lot! At the foot of Leadville Street, the path crosses Loggers Creek on a rustic wood bridge.

Beyond here, the trail runs along the river in a quiet, unspoiled area on a large island. The path comes out of the natural wooded area and then passes the Parkcenter office complex and ponds. Just beyond a gravel pond, the paved path ends at about 1.5 miles from Broadway. The paved path will continue east and split into a river front pedestrian route and a roadway-bike route.

For now, the cyclist must head towards Boise Avenue from the Parkcenter office complex, since private property blocks the public use of paths beyond this point. Follow M-K Parkway to the Myers Street Bridge over Loggers Creek. Then turn right and go west 3 blocks to Boise Avenue and follow Boise Avenue to Barber Park.

Future construction is planned through the subdivision adjacent to Parkcenter. Until this construction is completed, the hiker should find and follow the subdivision River Run Road to the south. (The land ahead to the east next to the river is blocked both by posted private land and by Loggers Creek.) Walk along River Run Road on a new bridge over Loggers Creek to Pennsylvania Avenue. Turn left (east) on Pennsylvania Avenue at 2 miles. This road becomes dirt and dead-ends at 2.5 miles. This dirt road and a path leading beyond it will be the Pennsylvania Avenue Greenway by 1983. The greenway will have a paved path and will terminate in a new park, Loggers Creek Park.

At present, to continue on foot beyond the end of Pennsylvania Avenue, follow a path along the creek from the Land and Water Conservation Fund sign at the end of Pennsylvania Avenue. This sign marks the location of the future 11-acre Boise City Loggers Creek Park. The path goes between the creek and a fence, then crosses a small canal on a bridge to the south, and joins a dirt road to the left (east). This road goes to the dam and headgate for Loggers Creek at 2.7 miles.

Development plans for Loggers Creek Park include a paved foot path through a tunnel under the Southeast Corridor Highway (M-K Parkway). Beyond the undeveloped Loggers Creek Park, all of the riverfront property is privately owned with no authorized public access. Negotiations are being held between some land owners and the Boise Park Department to acquire public property in the area. To continue to Barber Park, at present the hiker should retrace his steps back along Pennsylvania Avenue to the Myers Street Bridge. Go west 3 blocks to Boise Avenue, and follow Boise Avenue to Barber Park.

The main use of Barber Park is in the summer as the put-in point for people riding innertubes down the river. Beyond here, access has not yet been obtained for the remaining land along the river out to the Greenbelt destination of Lucky Peak Dam. However, the Bureau of Land Management has already built a 1.5 mile paved path between Diversion Dam and Discovery State Park on the north side of the river.

BOISE DISTRICT — Birds of Prey Area

HISTORY OF BIRDS OF PREY NATURAL AREA

In the 1840s, many parties who wanted to avoid crossing the Snake River twice used the south alternate of the Oregon Trail, which runs through the Birds of Prey Natural Area. After the Ward party was killed by Indians on the main Oregon Trail near Caldwell in 1854, Old Fort Boise, at the mouth of the Boise River, was abandoned. Military escorts were supposed to meet wagon trains, but they weren't always able to prevent Indian trouble. Indians attacked the Otter party on this route in 1860.

The completion of the Oregon Short Line tracks to Huntington in 1884 helped to supply the Silver City miners nearby. In 1901 Swan Falls Dam, the first dam on the Snake River, was built south of Kuna to provide electricity to Silver City. This dam stopped the salmon and steelhead runs on the Snake.

The fish were not the only important wildlife in the canyon. A nesting population of fourteen species of raptors that is of international significance lives in the canyon. Raptors are birds like eagles, falcons, hawks, and owls that catch their prey live. Golden eagles and prairie falcons are the most abundant species in the canyon. The Secretary of the Interior established the Birds of Prey Area in 1971 to protect these birds.

Recently the Bureau of Land Management has attempted to enlarge the Birds of Prey Area by 500,000 acres or more to cover the food supply of the raptors. Townsend ground squirrels are the main food supply, and they can't live in cultivated fields. A moratorium on new farms went into effect in 1975, but permanent status is needed. Secretary of the Interior Cecil Andrus enlarged the Birds of Prey Area by administrative order in December 1980; if Congress does not act on this, the enlargement will become permanent.

Two endangered species live in the canyon: the bald eagle and the peregrine falcon. The food supply here is unique because it is above the birds' heads. This enables the birds to conserve flying energy because they can coast back down to their nests with their heavy prey. The raptors hunt from two to ten miles on either side of the canyon. In addition to the birds and their nests, the area contains hundreds of unique Indian petroglyphs. This book does not tell how to hike to any because of the danger of vandalism.

BIRDS OF PREY AREA AT SWAN FALLS 58

Round trip: 5 miles
Elevation gain: 80 feet
Highest point: 2340 feet
Topo maps: Sinker Butte (20 foot contours), Wild Horse Butte
Time: 3½ hours
Access: In Kuna, turn south on a gravel road signed for Swan
   Falls. Go 18 miles to a dam; then go south of houses to a gate.
Difficulty: Easy but no signs

In the Snake River Birds of Prey Area 30 miles south of Boise, eagles and falcons soar and cry above the cliffs where they nest.

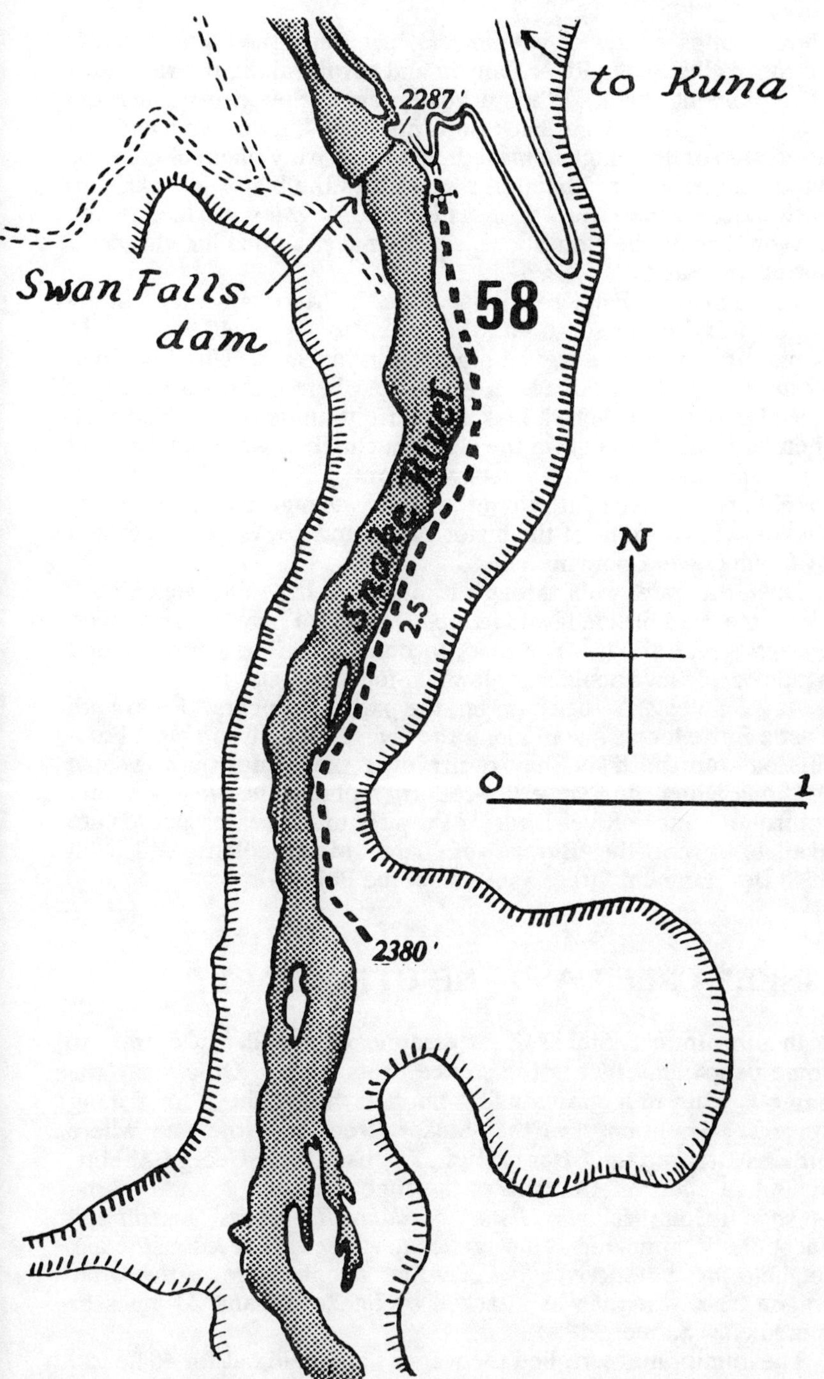
2287'
to Kuna
Swan Falls
dam
Snake River
58
2.5
2380'
N
0
1

Here clumps of desert wildflowers brighten green grass in the bottom of the Snake River Canyon and shrubs along the river give off a pungent smell. When a golden eagle flies close above the river, the light reflects back onto his light brown head and the underside of his wings to make him appear truly made of gold. A wide caramel-colored band of rock stripes the black lava cliffs on both sides of the river. It is usually 10 degrees warmer in the canyon than on the plain above, so this makes a good hike for early spring and late fall.

To reach Swan Falls from Boise, take the Meridian exit on Interstate 84 and drive south and then west to Kuna (10 miles). In Kuna turn south on a signed gravel road for Swan Falls and drive 17 miles to the edge of the canyon. Just before the road reaches the edge of the canyon, it makes two right-angle turns. The road then hairpins 1 mile down the cliff to a clutch of white houses and buildings beside the dam and power plant. Drive slowly, watching for children. Drive south from the houses to a gate and park here. Visitors are welcome at the historic dam and powerplant operated by Idaho Power Company.

Open the gate, walk through it, and shut it behind you. Walk along the road beside lava outcrops and past a lagoon surrounded by dark green reeds. The road becomes a trail at 1.5 miles and winds beside lava boulders below 300-foot black cliffs.

At 2.5 miles on a rock outcrop, the path disappears. From here Castle Butte looms ahead along the river like an iron ship. From this outcrop the hiker may return over the same route, or can continue along the river cross-country as far as he wishes before returning. Snake River Birds of Prey Natural Area brochures are available from the Bureau of Land Management Office at 3948 Development Street, just east of the Boise Airport.

SINKER CREEK AND THE OTTER PARTY

In late summer, Sinker Creek disappears for miles at a time, so some people say that is the source of its name. Others say the name is from immigrants using nuggets found there for fishing sinkers. Tradition says that Sinker Creek was the site where Indians attacked the Otter party in August 1860. George Abbott, an Indian agent at Umatilla at the time, gave an account of the episode in John Hailey's *History of Idaho*. Two boys, Joseph and Jacob Reith, appeared at the agency near the end of August to ask for help for the survivors. Forty-four people were in the Otter wagon train when it was attacked by Snake Indians 20 miles or more below Salmon Falls.

The immigrants corralled the wagons and held out for 48 hours.

Lack of water finally forced them to move. Six soldiers who had been discharged from Fort Hall were accompanying the train for military escort. As soon as the wagon train had to move on for water, they ran off. After the Indians killed or captured 22 members of the train, the rest of the party abandoned the wagons. Six weeks later, eighty soldiers from Walla Walla came to the rescue. The fourteen survivors scattered along the Owyhee River were very weak and had survived partly by cannibalism. The exact location of the attack was not mentioned in this account.

In Helen Nettleton's book, *Sketches of Owyhee County,* she gave evidence of her belief that the Otter party attack occurred near Bruneau. She believed that the Sinker Creek attack happened to a larger group about three years after the Otter party. She said that all record of this attack had been lost to history because the only survivors were two small children who were later adopted by Silver City families. She pointed out that the worst hill on the Oregon Trail Alternate was just below Sinker Creek, but this hill wasn't mentioned in the Otter story in Hailey's history.

Bureau of Land Management research indicates that the attack on the Otter party occurred near Castle Creek, a few miles east of Sinker Creek. Another party may have been attacked at Sinker Creek, since many wagon parts and some skulls were found there by early settlers.

MURPHY

Murphy, the nearest town to Sinker Creek, was founded as the terminal for the Boise, Nampa, and Owyhee Railroad to serve the Silver City mines. Plans called for the railroad to be completed to Dewey. The line reached the town of Guffey on the north bank of the Snake in 1898. Then in 1899, a steel bridge was built across the river and the railroad was extended to Striker Springs (Murphy). This bridge still stands and is being preserved by the Owyhee County Historical Society.

Recessions in the early 1900s caused a drop in mining, so the railroad was never completed to its Silver City destination. The town was named for an assistant engineer on the project who was a friend of Colonel Dewey's. Murphy served as a freight center for Silver City and the surrounding area, but the railroad tracks have long since been removed. The only reason Murphy still exists is because it became the county seat in 1935 after workers in a nearby CCC Camp voted for it over Homedale.

Oregon Trail ruts

OREGON TRAIL SOUTH ALTERNATE NEAR SINKER CREEK   59

Loop trip: 5.2 miles
Elevation gain: 580 feet
Elevation loss: 580 feet
Highest point: 3088 feet
Topo map: Sinker Butte (25 foot contours)
Time: 4 hours
Access: Turn left (east) off Highway 78 onto paved Murphy Flats
Road 3.2 miles south of Murphy. Follow arrows as road jogs. At
7.4 miles, the pavement ends. Drive .5 mile on dirt and then
turn right (south) and go .2 mile to a gate.
Difficulty: Moderate, but no signs

This hike into Sinker Creek Canyon and along a section of the
Oregon Trail South Alternate provides a taste of what the land was
like in pioneer days. 300-foot cliffs striped in rust, brick, and gold
guard the mouth of Sinker Creek next to the Snake River. Rock
outcroppings are scattered along the canyon like lava boats on a
rocky sea. A weathered cabin and leaning shed mark the site of a
homestead where Walt Disney made a movie about eagles. Access

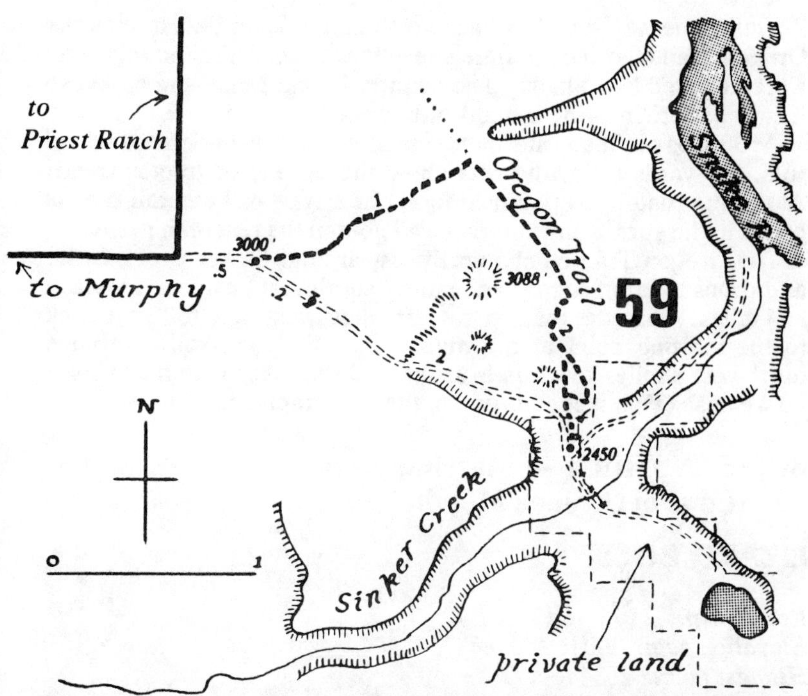

down the canyon to the river is blocked by posted and fenced private land, so binoculars are useful for viewing.

To reach the area, turn left off Highway 78 about 3.2 miles south of Murphy on the paved Murphy Flats Road and follow the road as it jogs left and then right. At 7.4 miles the pavement ends. Continue on the dirt road for .5 mile, turn right (southeast) and drive .2 mile to a gate. Park here off the road.

The first 2 miles of this loop hike follow a ranch road that descends a side canyon of Sinker Creek. Across the canyon at 1.5 miles, the Oregon Trail climbs a steep draw north of Sinker Creek. The elaborate rockwork visible along a rocky wall is not the Oregon Trail but was built to support a stage road. At 1.7 miles the road passes under gold-colored cliffs which are banded so that they look like giant garter snakes are embedded in them. At 2 miles, the track reaches the canyon bottom, with a view up and down Sinker Creek. The road continues to a ranch near a reservoir. A branch of the road turns left (northwest) down the canyon where a fence blocks its way (posted private land).

To reach the Oregon Trail, walk back up the side canyon on a faint path along the bottom of it. At 2.2 miles the Oregon Trail climbs the deep draw to the left (northwest) of the stage road seen from the route on the way down. Follow the stage road. At

2.5 miles the way switches back north and at 2.7 miles, it joins the Oregon Trail near the possible site where Oregon Trail immigrants were attacked by Indians. The country is sagebrush and rocks, so it isn't hard to imagine Indians hiding there.

At 3 miles the road runs over sandstone with well-defined wheel ruts. 15 yards later, the ruts show the outline of tractor tread! Along the road is a miniature forest of a type of horsetail that is green in the spring and summer and golden the rest of the year.

The Oregon Trail climbs northwest around Sinker Creek Butte and drops to intersect a road leading southwest beside a dry wash at 4 miles. Take the road to the left (southwest) and follow it back to the starting point at 5.2 miles. The Oregon Trail continues northwest 8 miles towards Murphy and the hiker may hike this if he wishes. (This section is not on the topographic map.)

BOISE DISTRICT — Marsing Area
(Edge of Owyhee Mountains)

LIZARD BUTTE

60

Round trip: .2 to 1 mile
Elevation gain: 200 to 400 feet
Highest point: 2634 feet
Topo map: Marsing (20 foot contours)
Time: 1 hour
Access: Drive west on U. S. 30 from Nampa. 3 miles south of Sunnyslope curve, turn east on gravel road. Walk or drive .2 mile and turn south on a dirt road and walk or drive .2 mile.
Difficulty: Easy

The view from Lizard Butte is prettiest in May when new grass tints the bases of the snow-capped Owyhees and the pastures on the nearby farms. At that time white and pink blossoms of the fruit trees of the Sunnyslope orchards cover the hills below the butte. From the butte on a sunny day, the Snake River is a shiny blue ribbon ornamented with islands. A cloudy day colors the river silver. Dark alcoves mark the locations of Jump Creek and Squaw Creek Canyons in the foothills to the south. The soft shapes of the Owyhee Mountains rise up behind these canyons. To see how the butte got its name, drive south of Marsing on Highway 78 for 3 or 4 miles. From this road, the black top of the butte forms a giant lizard with upraised head, splayed feet, and long tail.

To reach Lizard Butte, take the Karcher exit from Interstate 84 at Nampa; drive along Highway 30 past Karcher Mall to its intersection with Karcher Road. Drive west on Karcher Road (Highway 30) for 9.5 miles. At Sunnyslope the road makes a left

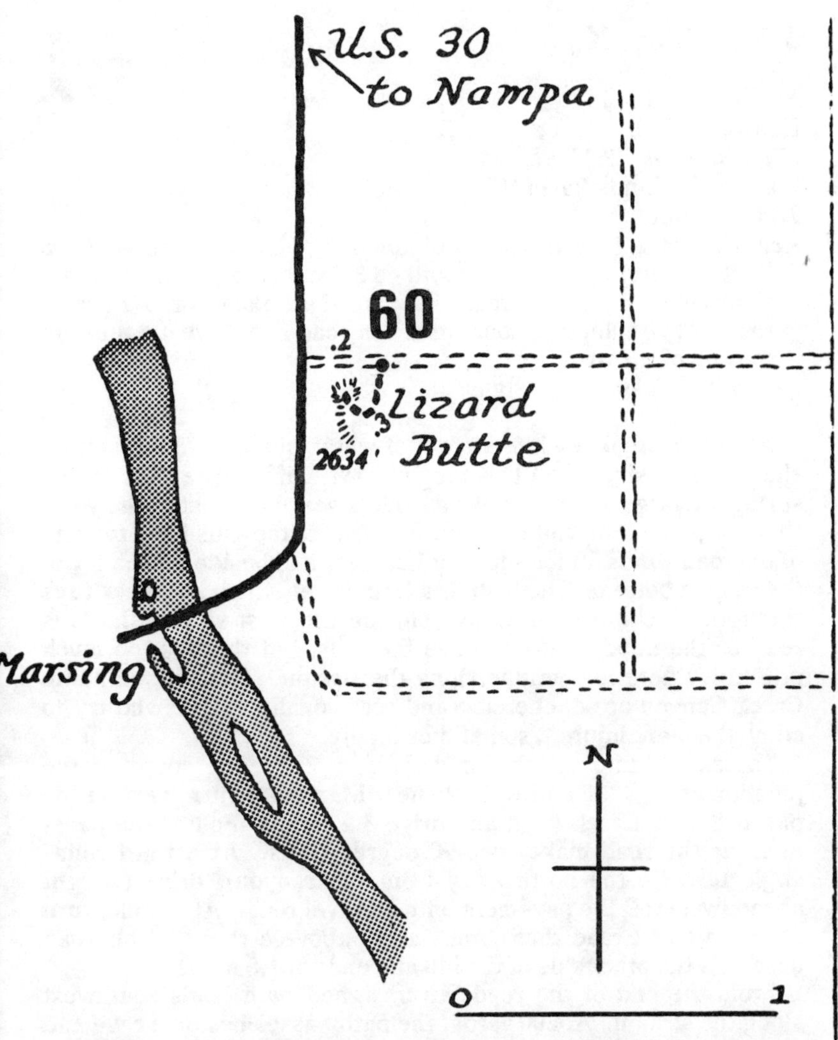

turn south.   Drive 3 miles south and turn left (east) on a gravel road just below the butte.

Walk or drive .2 mile east on the gravel road. Then turn south on a dirt road and hike or drive .2 mile to a cement stage which is used in the annual Easter sunrise services. From the stage, paths lead 200 yards to the 10-foot cross on the summit.

Depending on time and energy, a hiker can climb the butte from the bottom (round trip is 1 mile with 400 feet gain) or from the stage (round trip is .2 mile with 200 feet gain). Lizard Butte makes a rewarding ''mountain'' for small children to climb, although they MUST be watched carefully at the top due to the cliffs.

JUMP CREEK

61

Round trip: 1 mile
Elevation gain: 100 feet
Highest point: 2640 feet
Topo map: Sands Basin (15′)
Time: 1 hour
Access: Drive 2.6 miles south of junction of U. S. 30 and U. S. 95
    west of Marsing. Turn west and go 3.2 miles on paved road. At
    a corner in the paved road, keep straight ahead onto a gravel
    road. At .2 mile, turn south on a dirt road and drive 1.5 miles to
    the end of the road.
Difficulty: Easy, but no signs

At Jump Creek a white stream of water plunges 75 feet into a
shallow pool shadowed by orange-brown cliffs. The falls in the
spring are large and fluffy like a bride's veil, but most of the year,
they are just a thin white ribbon. The trail to the falls from the end
of the road winds under and over boulders and beside poison ivy in
the canyon bottom. The boulders form caves which the creek runs
through. A climb up a 20-foot cliff on the west side of the falls
reaches the upper canyon above the falls, but there is too much
poison ivy here to continue along the stream. The cliffs in Jump
Creek Canyon are dangerous, and occasionally people who try to
climb them are injured, sometimes fatally.

To reach Jump Creek Canyon, drive 2.6 miles south of the
junction of U. S. 30 and U. S. 95 near Marsing. Turn west on the
paved Poison Creek Road and drive 3.2 miles. Follow the pavement as the road makes two 90 degree turns. At a third right-
angle turn (to the north away from the canyon), drive straight
ahead (west) off the pavement onto a gravel road. At .2 mile, turn
south on a dirt road that climbs a hill above a ranch. This road
descends the other side of the hill and ends at 1.5 miles.

From the end of the road, an unsigned path leads southwest
along the stream. At 200 yards, the path passes beside a cave and
crosses the stream to the east bank. The route stays on the east
bank, winding over boulders and along to the falls at .5 mile.
Return the same way. Shower immediately after returning home
and launder all clothes worn because it is impossible to avoid
poison ivy on this hike.

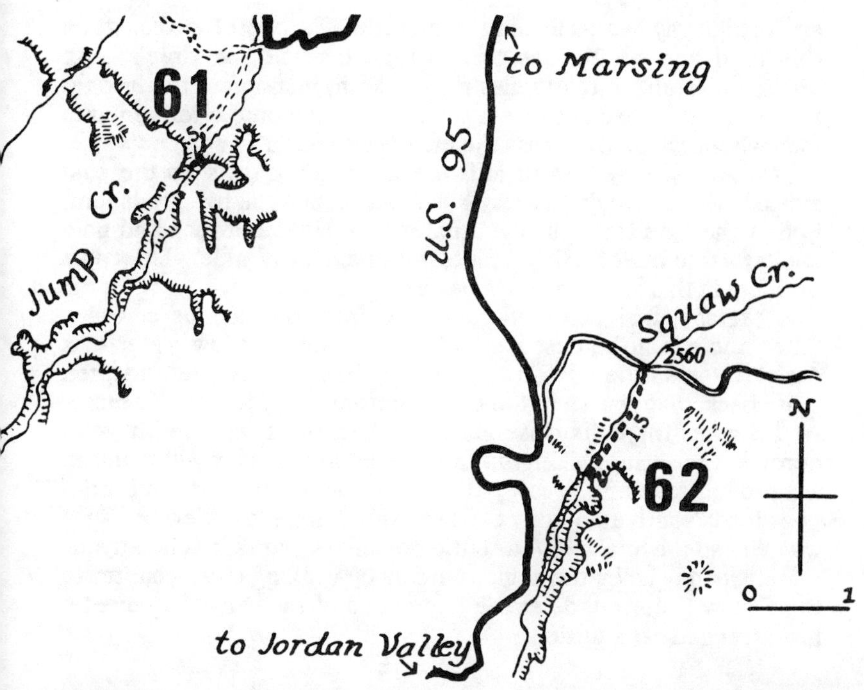

SQUAW CREEK

62

Round trip: 3 to 4 miles
Elevation gain: 240 feet
Highest point: 2800 feet
Topo map: Opalene Gulch
Time: 2 hours
Access: Drive 7 miles south of the junction of U. S. 30 and U. S. 95
near Marsing. Turn northeast on dirt Sommercamp Road and
drive 2 miles to a bridge.
Difficulty: Easy, but no signs

South of Marsing, Squaw Creek Canyon forms a narrow cleft
between 800-foot rust-colored cliffs. Cliff swallows swoop down
from nests among the towers, while caves pock the cliffs. In the
spring, red paintbrush and pink and white phlox accent the sagebrush. The traveler can glance down into the canyon from the
Squaw Creek Grade on U. S. 95, but he can get the best view of the
canyon from inside it.

To reach Squaw Creek, drive 2 miles west of Marsing on U. S. 30
and 7 miles south on U. S. 95. An unsigned road, the Sommercamp Road (with a stop sign), comes in at a sharp angle on the left

as the highway begins to climb the grade. Turn left (northeast) on this road and go 2 miles to a bridge over Squaw Creek. An unsigned primitive road turns right (south) just before the bridge. Don't take this road because a stream crossing on it often requires four-wheel drive. Go across the bridge and park.

Walk along a second primitive road which travels up the east side of the creek under a rocky bluff. At .2 mile the two roads join. Follow the road through sagebrush to a dilapidated rock and pole shelter cabin built by Boy Scouts years ago at .7 mile. Litter is a problem in this area, so take a bag and pick up some.

A sketchy unsigned trail continues from the shelter across a fence and along the east bank of the stream. At low water it is easier to cross the stream to the west bank for awhile and then cross back. Sagebrush in the creek bottom is ten feet tall or more. At 1.5 miles the cliffs close in, so walk in the streambed beyond here. In the spring, hiking up the canyon any further will result in a thorough soaking. A cow path .2 mile before the canyon bottleneck leads south up a gully 500 feet and .5 mile to a view of Highway 95 and the Snake River. Little poison ivy grows in this canyon.

Return may be by the same route or by walking cross-country to the Squaw Creek Grade at the upper end of the canyon to meet a pre-arranged car shuttle.

REYNOLDS CREEK

63

Round trip: 2.8 miles
Elevation gain: 180 feet
Elevation loss: 60 feet
Highest point: 2680 feet
Topo map: Wilson Peak
Time: 4 hours
Access: Turn west off Highway 78 about 17 miles south of Marsing. Drive 2.9 miles on dirt road.
Difficulty: Easy, but no signs

Resembling logs stacked vertically, 500-foot cliffs of rust-colored columnar basalt line the wide desert canyon of Reynolds Creek. The 300-yard width of this gorge leaves plenty of room for hiking. An elaborate old irrigation canal system of stones, built by the Chinese in the early mining and farming days of Owyhee County, provide good trails for 1 mile in the canyon.

Near the beginning of the larger canal is a hill topped with orange cliffs on a white base. Further up, the path passes right under an overhanging 400-foot cliff. A tangle of shrubs, trees, and poison ivy grows in the canyon next to the creek. The undeveloped canyon stretches about 9 miles from the mouth toward the hamlet

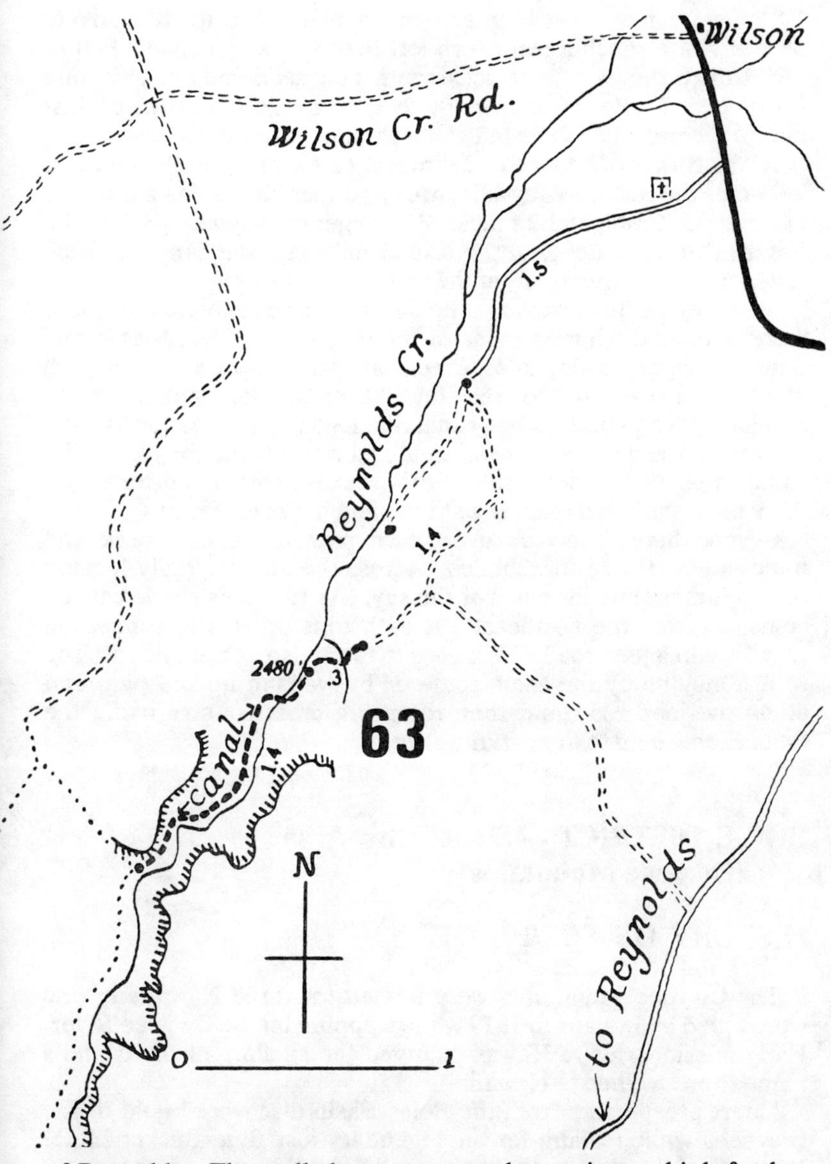

of Reynolds. The walls become more than twice as high further up, but they are not as close to the creek.

To reach Reynolds Creek, drive 17 miles south of Marsing on Highway 78 towards Murphy. The road passes a turnoff for Wilson Creek 4.9 miles beyond Givens Hot Springs. Turn right (west) 5.4 miles beyond Givens on Cemetery Lane, a dirt road. At .3 mile the road passes south of the Wilson Cemetery. At

1.5 miles, before a cattle guard and fence posted for the private property of a ranch ahead, turn left (east) on a dirt road. Follow the road to the east as it goes south and dead-ends at a mining prospect at 2 miles. Turn right (west) on a road that turns off just before the prospect and wind along through sagebrush.

At the corner of a fence at 2.4 miles, turn right (west) again. At 2.9 miles the road crosses a flat area and then drops down a ravine to Reynolds Creek at 3.2 miles. Passenger cars should park in the flat area and not descend the last .3 mile into the canyon. Hike mileage given here begins at the creek at 3.2 miles.

To begin the hike, walk .3 mile down the ravine to the creek and along a small ditch at the side of the creek for 100 yards to a tiny dam. Then cross Reynolds Creek on rocks and walk on a path along the east side of the creek for 300 yards. Here look up on the hillside above to find a stone canal that leads up the canyon. Climb 100 feet to the dry, overgrown canal and walk up the canyon on the canal bank. On the other side of the creek is another shorter canal. At .9 mile, the canal ends at a sharp bend in the creek.

Beyond here follow an overgrown path along the creek and under an overhang at 1.2 miles. Across the canyon, rusty-looking rock columns shut out much of the sky. At 1.4 miles a side canyon comes in from the northeast. A path runs up this to connect in .7 mile with a jeep road which goes to the Wilson Creek Road. The return may be by the same route or by walking up the path and along the jeep road and then returning cross-country using the topographic map to the parking area.

BOISE DISTRICT — Silver City Area
(Owyhee Mountains)

HISTORY OF SILVER CITY

The Owyhee Mountains were named for three Hawaiians who were killed by Indians in 1819 while trapping on the Owyhee River. Early missionaries to Hawaii changed the spelling of the island's name from Owyhee to Hawaii.

Later, prospectors from the Boise Basin discovered gold in the Owyhees while looking for the legendary lost Blue Bucket Mine. Versions of the story vary, but one tells of children in a wagon train collecting nuggets in a blue water bucket, putting a few away, and then forgetting about them until they got to Oregon. Some historians say the story probably originated with the Meek party who traveled the Malheur River to the Willamette Valley. In 1862 Captain Tom Turner unsuccessfully explored the south side of the Snake River as far as Catherine Creek looking for the nugget-filled creek.

In May 1863, Michael Jordan and W. T. Carson led twenty-nine men from Placerville in Boise Basin to the Owyhees in search of the Blue Bucket. They discovered gold on a tributary of the Owyhee River, which they named Jordan Creek. Two thousand miners followed, but they discovered the first party had staked all the good claims. Later in 1863, prospectors found silver there also.

The first settlement that grew up around the discovery was named Ruby City. Timber was scarce, so within six months the nearby hills were barren. Miners had to build stone and dugout houses. On December 31, 1863, Owyhee County was founded with the county seat at Ruby City. In 1864, the Orofino and War Eagle lodes were discovered. A new town, Silver City, sprang up near these discoveries. Colonel Dewey, Michael Jordan's partner, built a toll road between the two towns. The better buildings at Ruby City were taken down and moved to the new town, 1 mile up Jordan Creek. In 1865, the Poorman silver lode was discovered, probably the richest single lode ($4 million) ever found. A newspaper, the *Idaho Avalanche*, began in 1865 in Ruby City, and was the first newspaper in the state. In 1866, Silver City became the county seat.

Above Silver City, Fairview was a small town on the northeast slope of War Eagle Mountain. In 1875 members of the Fairview Miners Union held the mine superintendent captive for three weeks until company officials in San Francisco assured them they would be paid. This union was the first union in the Owyhees with 1500 members. Later that year, fire leveled the town.

Also on War Eagle Mountain, the two different groups who discovered the Poorman Mine quarreled over it. One group set up a cannon at the entrance so they could take ore out and send it to Portland. Eventually both groups sold out to investors after lengthy litigation. From this mine came some of the finest specimens of ruby and native silver ever exhibited. Ruby silver is silver and antimony sulphide occuring in red metallic crystals.

Additional trouble came to the Owyhee miners from the native Shoshone and Paiute Indians who were very hostile to whites. In 1864, Michael Jordan was killed in a battle with the Indians. He had flipped a coin with Colonel Dewey to see who fought the Indians and who stayed home. In 1865, the Army established a post, Camp Lyons, on the Owyhee-California Trail. The miners didn't think the soldiers were doing a good job of subduing the Indians, so the miners organized the Owyhee Volunteers. At first they had trouble finding any Indians to fight, but in 1868, the Volunteers, led by a man named Jennings, got trapped in a box canyon and had to be rescued.

A judge recessed a trial between rival claimants for the Poorman Mine so the participants could help with the rescue. By the time the rescuers got there, the Indians had left. The Bannocks under

Buffalo Horn went on the rampage in 1878 in a series of battles known as the Bannock War. Finally in a battle in the Owyhees between the troops of Captains Harper and Bernard and the Bannocks, Chief Buffalo Horn was killed and the Bannocks were subdued.

Bigfoot was a semi-legendary Indian or Indians who terrorized the Reynolds Creek and the Snake River ferry area and killed several stage drivers. There was a real Indian chief named Nambe or Nampuh (big foot) for whom the town of Nampa is named. In 1878, a man named William Anderson wrote a series of articles for the *Idaho Statesman* about the death of Bigfoot ten years before, at which Anderson claimed to have been an eye witness.

As he lay dying, Bigfoot is supposed to have confessed the story of his life to Anderson and to the highwayman, Wheeler, who had shot him. The tale was that Bigfoot was named Starr Wilkinson and was part Indian, 6'8" tall and weighed 275 pounds. He had gone west with a wagon train and fallen in love with a girl. When she rejected him for another, he killed her lover, and ran away into the mountains where he joined a tribe of Indians. He took an Indian wife and had at least one child. Whites killed his wife and kidnapped his son. An entertainer named John Kelley is supposed to have raised the boy and taught him to be an entertainer, too. Wheeler is supposed to have buried Bigfoot and to have promised him never to reveal the location.

The stagecoaches the Indians like to prey upon began coming into Idaho when the Idaho Territorial Legislature granted a road franchise to Michael Jordan, Colonel Dewey, and Silas Skinner in 1864. First Skinner built a road from Silver City down Reynolds Creek to Boise, crossing the rivers by ferry. (This was not the same route that today's road to Silver City takes.) By 1866 Skinner had completed a toll road from Silver City to Duncans Ferry on the Owyhee River. Freighters used 14-horse teams to pull the freight wagons up to 6300-foot Silver City, and stages provided passenger transportation.

Michael Jordan's partner, Colonel W. H. Dewey, was a colorful character.   He and Jordan had been partners on Nevada's Comstock Lode but had lost everything. Dewey bought the mine and town of Booneville in 1896, renamed it Dewey, and built a 20 stamp mill and a three-story hotel. Dewey made money in mining at Thunder Mountain as well as in the Owyhees and with his earnings, he built the huge Dewey Palace Hotel in 1903 in Nampa shortly before his death. Dewey once got into a fight with a miner he hadn't paid. The miner got even; during the fight, he secretly bit off Dewey's diamond stud.

Another important miner was Captain Joseph R. DeLamar, a former sea captain, who bought forty claims on Jordan Creek, 9 miles below Silver City. The settlement of DeLamar even had a newspaper, the *Nugget*. The area was dredged in the 1930s and today is the site of one of the largest open pit silver mines in the country.

Silver City was the nation's second largest silver producing area at the time when the Comstock Lode in Nevada was the first. Mining in the Owyhees continued on and off until World War II. Private owners are maintaining and restoring many of the old buildings in Silver City for summer homes.

AVONDALE BASIN

64

Round trip: 4.5 miles (.4 mile more round trip to summit)
Elevation gain: 1000 feet
Highest point: 6960 feet
Topo maps: Silver City (15'), Rooster Comb Peak (15')
Time: 4½ hours
Access: 4.1 miles south of Murphy on Highway 78, turn southwest on Silver City Road. Drive 5.4 miles on gravel and 12.3 miles on dirt. At 17.7 miles, turn northwest on DeLamar Road and drive 1.2 miles to Presby Creek.
Ability: Expert

In Avondale Basin weathered granite spindles and turrets cap scrub-covered hills. Green juniper and grey-green mountain mahogany clothe the hills beneath seamed and fissured granite sentinels. At the low point of the sloping basin, a tiny spring-fed meadow holds an old log corral. Old wagon roads leading into the area make an easy and pleasant loop hike. From the high point of the route, a wide panorama of wooded mountains with bare tops spreads out on either side of Silver City. The hiker can see Florida, War Eagle, and Cinnabar Mountains. Avondale Basin hasn't been mined, so it shows what the area was like before the miners came.

To reach these old tracks into Avondale Basin, take the road to Silver City, which turns southwest 4.1 miles south of Murphy off of Highway 78. At 5.4 miles the gravel road joins the dirt Rabbit Creek Road which has come directly from Murphy. From here, the dirt road is rough and steep. The route winds up and down over sagebrush hills with a view into the red-rimmed canyon of Sinker Creek.

At 10 miles the road reaches Scotch Bob Creek and follows it for 4 miles. Then the track heads up the spine of a ridge, and winds in and out of canyons to New York Summit at 16.6 miles, 3400 feet above Highway 78. Next the road drops to a junction with the DeLamar Road at 17.7 miles. Turn right (northwest) on the DeLamar Road and drive 1.2 miles. Park .2 mile beyond a road bridge over Jordan Creek, where undeveloped campsites mark an

View Northwest from above Avondale Basin

overgrown road leading uphill across the creek. (To avoid wading the creek at high water, walk back down the road to the bridge. Then walk up the other side of the creek on a path to find the old road opposite the campsite.)

Hike this overgrown wagon road along the right side of a tiny creek. The road crosses the creek at 200 yards, then heads northwest over to the small canyon of Presby Creek, which it follows. At .5 mile the track crosses this creek. The road is washed out in places but isn't hard to find. Cottonwood trees and willows throng the creek bottom, while juniper, fir, and mountain mahogany clothe the hillsides. When the road levels at 1 mile, rock outcroppings prickle the hilltops. At the head of the creek at 1.5 miles is a little meadow and silvered log corral. The jeep trail turns left (west) here before the meadow and follows a ridge.

For a closer view of the rock towers, cross the meadow to an old road which has come from New York Summit. Wind northwest up this road below a group of hills topped with rock towers. These rock towers are shown on the topo map only as circles since few of them are more than 80 feet high, and one contour line on the 15′ maps is 80 feet.

This road continues up Presby Creek, but at 1.7 miles, the road leaves the creek to climb the side of a ridge. On the ridge at 2 miles, the track intersects another jeep trail which has come up the side of Booneville Gulch. At this intersection is a fine view of hills around Silver City. Go .2 mile northeast of this intersection to the summit for a view to the north. The scene is interesting

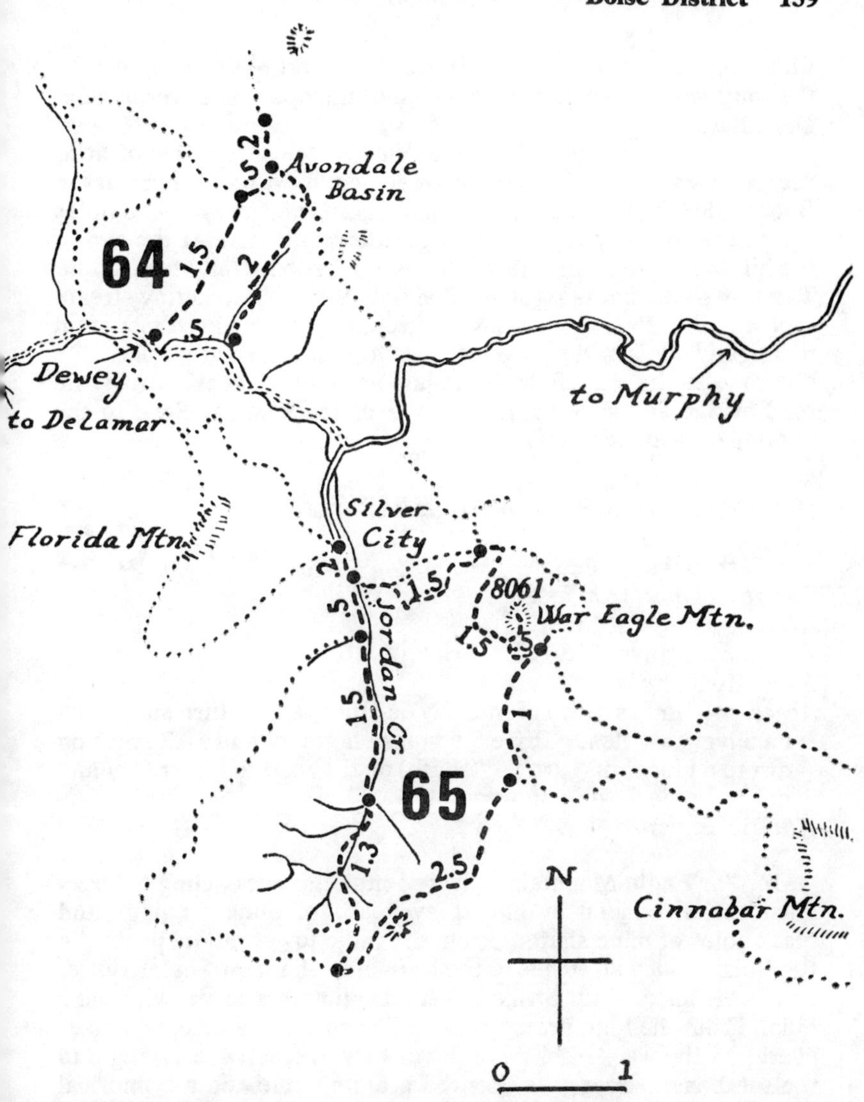

because the bare rounded hills contrast with boie wooded Silver
City peaks. Just below are two miniature reservoirs which hold
water only when the snow is melting.

To complete the loop hike, go back to where the Booneville
Gulch track joins the road. Take this track across the side of the
hill above aspen trees to a gate in a fence at a flat saddle at
2.5 miles. Here one jeep track turns left (south) along a fence
while another plunges straight ahead. (The track from before the
meadow and corral in Avondale Basin has come across the top of a

little ridge to join these other trails at this overgrown junction.) To the southwest, machinery raises dust in the open pit silver mine at DeLamar.

Take the track south along the fence. Below is a row of little rock needles splashed with lime green lichen. A creek murmurs in Booneville Gulch. This route is much more overgrown. At 3 miles where the roads split, take the right (lower) track. At the end of the hill the route turns left (southeast) but soon straightens again. The way switchbacks right at 3.5 miles, then follows a tiny stream (not on the topo map) down through juniper and mountain mahogany. When the road reaches Jordan Creek at 4 miles, the old mine at the site of Dewey is just across the creek. Cross the road bridge and walk back along the main DeLamar Road to the parking area at 4.5 miles.

JORDAN CREEK — WAR EAGLE MTN.

65

Round trip: 11.2 miles
Elevation gain: 1890 feet
Highest point: 8061 feet
Topo maps: Silver City (15′), Triangle (15′)
Time: 10 hours
Access: 4.1 miles south of Murphy on Highway 78, turn southwest on Silver City Road. Drive 5.4 miles on gravel and 12.3 miles on dirt to a junction. Turn left (south) on the road to Silver City and drive .5 mile to the campground.
Ability: Expert

On War Eagle Mountain, silvered mining shacks cling to rocky hillsides surrounded by light grey heaps of mine diggings and black holes of mine shafts. From the radio tower on the peak, the flat Boise Valley stretches to the hazy blue shape of Shafer Butte. In the distance, C. J. Strike Reservoir glimmers in wrinkled pink hills. From the high grassy ridge followed on this hike, the hiker overlooks the wooded basin of Silver City and can see Triangle to the southeast. Nearby, a fissured granite dome and a cylindrical peak circled with cliffs are two of the landmarks.

Although subalpine and Douglas firs grow on the cool north and west sides of the hills, mountain mahogany, juniper, sagebrush, and grass cover the south and east sides. Near the beginning of the trail, the round rocky top of Sawpit Peak overlooks Jordan Creek, which tumbles through thickets of willows. This hike is on some of the old wagon and mining roads that the Bureau of Land Management has proposed for a trail system around Silver City.

To reach the trailhead, travel Highway 78 and take the graveled and dirt Silver City Road 4.1 miles south of Murphy. Drive 17.6 miles over New York Summit to the junction with the

DeLamar Road. Take the Silver City Road to the left and drive about 1 mile to the campground just south of town.

From here, walk south on the road up Jordan Creek. At .2 mile, several jeep roads that come down War Eagle Mountain meet at the creek. The hike ends by coming down the northern one of these. An old clapboard house, shed, and barn are located 200 yards beyond the jeep roads. At .7 mile, the track crosses Sawpit Creek, where a branch road turns right (west) up this creek. At 1 mile the Jordan Creek Road runs in the creek for 50 yards but doesn't cross it. Beyond here the road has a bad washout, so driving beyond this point would be impossible, even in a jeep.

At 2 miles, the trail passes a flat fenced grassy area across the creek. At 2.2 miles the creek splits again and the road turns up the right stream. Do not take this. Instead, cross the right branch of the creek and find an overgrown track which goes straight ahead up the main stem of the creek. Almost immediately, the route crosses the creek, then returns in 200 yards.

At 2.5 miles the track hops Jordan Creek to the east side again. At 2.7 miles the way crosses the creek and goes uphill between two branches of it in the forest, climbing 800 feet in .5 mile. At 3 miles the track joins a better road at a switchback. Follow this road south diagonally up an open hillside. At 3.5 miles, this road intersects a third in a V. The new road leads back north along the top of a ridge. From the ridge the view includes all of the Silver City Basin, the red slopes of Cinnabar Mountain, and the flats and wooded hills around Triangle.

Follow this road north through a forest under the cylindrical cliff-sided peak. In mid-June, this section may still be under snow. At 4.7 miles the road comes out onto an open hillside and climbs along the east side of it. At 5.5 miles, the track passes through a fence on a flat saddle. At 6 and 6.2 miles are two branches of a road leading to Cinnabar Mountain. At 7 miles the track joins the radio tower road just above a saddle. Various jeep trails lead from the saddle past mines down towards Silver City. After climbing to the top of War Eagle at 7.5 miles, the hiker will notice a level road leading north between mines across the face of the mountain. This is the return route. To reach it, go back down the tower road and pick it up at the saddle at 8 miles. Turn left on this road and go past mine diggings for the Poorman Mine at 8.5 miles.

At 8.7 miles, the road goes above a mine dump, then below more diggings. At 9.5 miles, the track intersects the Linehan Flat Road in Webfoot Gulch where old roads run down both sides of the gulch from the junction. Turn left or take a short hike to the right to inspect Linehan Flat. The track on the north side of the gulch that crosses the creek right away and leads away from it is the most distinct. A granite dome guards the mouth of Webfoot

Gulch. This road passes old shacks at 9.7 miles and at 10.5 miles, it skirts a large mine shaft. Be careful! Next the way switches back to the gulch at 10.7 miles. At 11 miles, the road reaches Jordan Creek together with another track from the saddle. Hike back down Jordan Creek to the campground at 11.2 miles. Hikers may wish to camp overnight during this trip.

BOISE DISTRICT — Bruneau Area
(Edge of Owyhee Mountains)

HISTORY OF BRUNEAU

The Bruneau River was probably named for a Canadian trapper, Jean Baptiste Bruneau, who may have discovered it in 1815. The canyon varies from 600 to 1200 feet deep for 80 miles and is as narrow as .2 mile. A mixed outcast band of Shoshones and Paiutes who were friendly to the whites originally inhabited the valley where the Bruneau joins the Snake. Sagebrush grew only on the hills, while tall grass covered the valley floor.

The first settlers, John and Emma Turner, arrived in September 1869. Their daughter, Adelaide Turner Hawes, wrote a history of the Bruneau area, *The Valley of Tall Grass*. Abraham and Martha Roberson and their five sons had filed on land at Bruneau in April 1869, but didn't come there to live until the spring of 1870. Roberson had led two wagon trains across the plains and farmed near Boise for five years before coming to Bruneau.

The first store was three shelves in B. F. Hawes' adobe ranch house and was opened in 1875 by W. L. Ramsdell. B. F. Hawes' younger brother, Fletcher, started a school at this ranch in 1877. The school continued with other teachers after Fletcher was killed in the Bannock War the next year.

The Turners weren't home when the Bannock Indians raided the valley in the summer of 1878 because each summer they went to Tuscarora, Nevada to sell milk and butter to the miners and haul wood for them. Near Bruneau, twenty-six people took refuge in "Settlers' Cave" which had been dug in a sandstone and clay bluff on Roberson's ranch by his sons. The cave had a long hall, four small rooms, and a ventilation hole. Sentry pits were on top of the bluff. A friendly native, Bruneau John, warned the settlers so they could hide in time. For this he received a medal from President Garfield. Several people fled to safety at Silver City, although a few, like Fletcher Hawes, were killed at summer range camps.

An unusual early resident was Kitty Wilkins, known as the "Horse Queen of Idaho", who was the daughter of Bruneau ranchers. She ran horses loose in the desert and shipped them all over the country. She traveled with and took care of the horses she shipped, but always wore dresses and rode side-saddle even on the range.

BRUNEAU SAND DUNES

66

Loop trip: 5 miles
Elevation gain: 470 feet
Highest point: 2930 feet
Topo map: Sand Dunes (25 foot contours)
Time: 4 hours
Access: Turn left (east) 15.6 miles south of Mountain Home off Highway 51 onto Highway 78. Drive 1.8 miles and turn right (south) onto paved Bruneau Dunes Road. Drive 1 mile to Visitors' Center.
Difficulty: Easy

The Bruneau Sand Dunes are in the middle of high sagebrush tablelands like a misplaced ocean beach. The tallest dune is 470 feet and is the largest single sand dune in North America. Nestled beneath these smooth grey mountains of sand are shallow blue lakes, with edges rimmed with green bullrushes and grey-green Russian olive trees. The area is rich in wildlife, especially birds and lizards. Fishermen can catch blue-gill, sunfish, and large-mouth bass in the lakes. This state park features a short nature trail and a 5 mile hike that climbs the largest dune.

To reach the Bruneau Sand Dunes, take Highway 51 southwest from Mountain Home. Turn left (south) 1.2 miles west of Mountain Home when the highway does. At 15 miles, the road crosses the Snake River amid green sprinkler-irrigated fields. At 15.6 miles, turn left (east) at the Sand Dunes sign onto Highway 78. Turn right (south) at 17.4 miles onto paved Bruneau Dunes Road.

At 18.4 miles, the road arrives at the Visitors' Center where literature on the area is available. Displays of fossils, live lizards, and stuffed birds of prey surround a relief map of the dunes. The displays and literature tell that the construction of Strike Dam on the Snake River in 1952 raised the water table enough so that the lakes were created. There is information about Lake Idaho, which is the source of the fish and shell fossils found here. Pamphlets describe the different types of dunes like stellate and barchan. The Bruneau Dunes are unique because they have formed in the center, rather than at the edge of a basin. Organized groups can arrange for slide shows and talks on the dunes.

Idaho made the Bruneau Dunes a state park in 1968. Facilities include a picnic area, boat launch, and a large landscaped

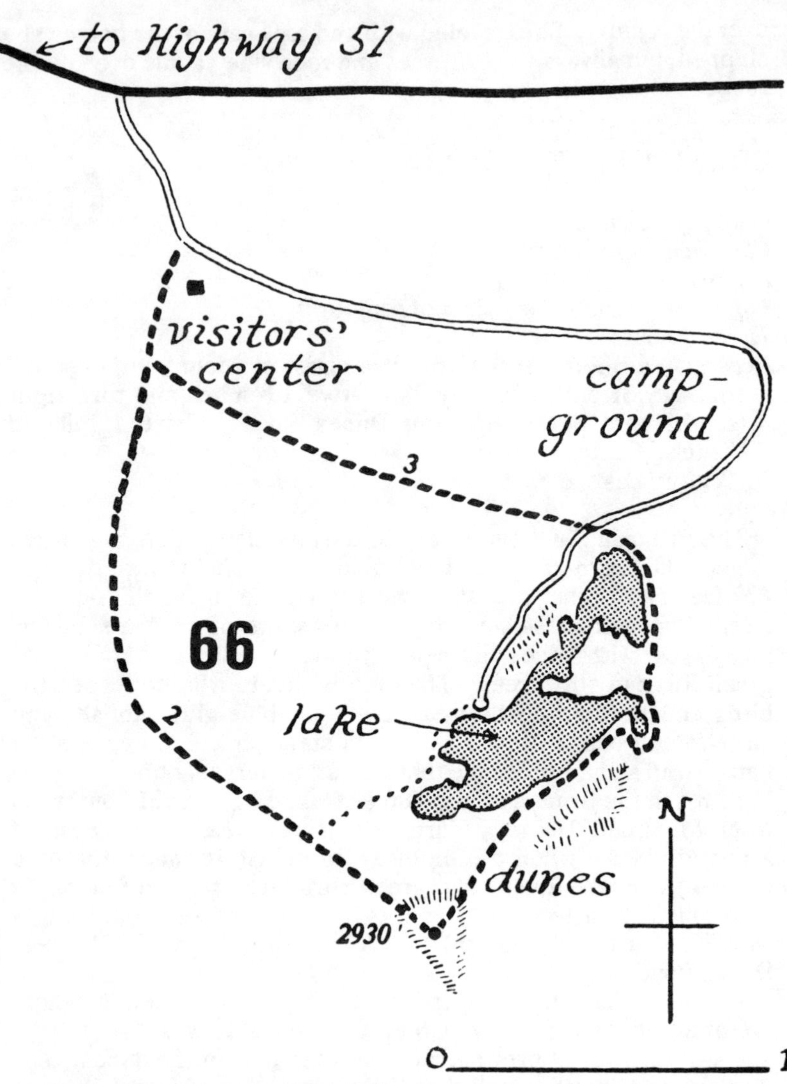

campground with hot showers.   Driving off-road is against regulations because it is very easy to get stuck in the sand.

A 5 mile trail starts at the information center and crosses sagebrush over to the lake area.   Then the route climbs the big dune, circles the largest lake, passes the picnic area and returns to the center.   Pick up a free copy of the trail map at the information center.   The hiker can find this trail from the picnic area, follow it around the lake and up the dune and come back by way of the boat launch.   Eight posts mark the trail, although the wind on the sand keeps any paths erased.   The short nature trail circles the picnic area and runs along the lakeshore.

People can go sledding on the back side of the big dunes. A flat bottom sled without runners works best. Skiers can even ski with an old pair of skis. The sand on the tiny dunes near the boat launch is not steep enough for sledding. Climbing the dunes is exhausting because of sliding back with each step.

Strong winds constantly sculpture and add to the dunes. On a windy day, the sand spins out from the crest of the dunes like ocean spray. Sometimes this sand fog is so thick that the top of the big dune is invisible from part way up the side. Circular winds that form between the dunes have blown pits in the back side of the big dunes.

The summer months are very hot, so use caution when hiking the 5 mile trail. In the summer, register with the ranger before the hike and check in when finished. Carry water and wear a sun hat. Spring and fall are the best months to visit the dunes, but the park is open year around. The lakes have larva of flatworms in the water. These larva can cause ''swimmers' itch'', which is a painful inflammation caused by the larva burrowing into the skin. Brisk toweling upon emerging from the water or showering immediately will prevent swimmers' itch.

INDIAN BATHTUB

67

Round trip: 3 miles
Elevation gain: 25 feet
Elevation loss: 125 feet (return climb)
Highest point: 2650 feet
Topo maps: Sugar Valley, Hot Springs (both 25 foot contours)
Time: 2 hours
Access: Drive 22 miles south of Mountain Home on Highway 51. Turn southeast on paved road and go 8 miles. Turn right (southeast) and cross a bridge. At 1.6 miles, turn left (south) on dirt Blackstone-Grasmere Road and go 3.5 miles. Turn left (east) on primitive road and go 1.5 miles to the road end.
Difficulty: Easy, but no signs

Hot water from a spring bubbling out of the base of 50-foot black cliffs fills three-foot deep Indian Bathtub. Although the Indians may first have dammed Hot Creek with rocks to make a swimming pool, white men added more stones. Petroglyphs are visible above the pool. Years ago, a unique species of wild orchid grew beside the pool, but they are no longer there. On either side of Hot Creek Canyon are desert tablelands covered with sagebrush and grasses. At the base of some of the cliffs, the rock is red where hot lava flowed over clay and baked it like bricks.

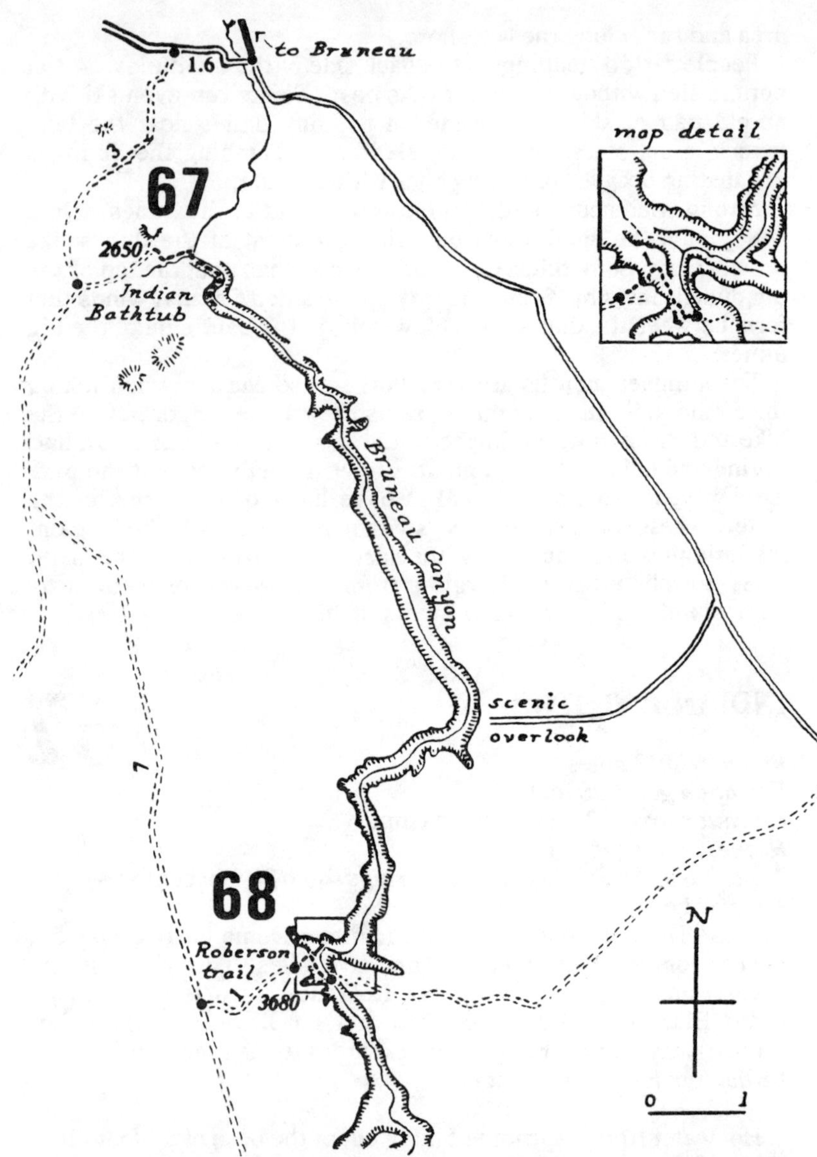

In the nearby Bruneau River Canyon, 200-foot black lava cliffs striped with pink hover over the twisting river.   The water murmurs clear in the fall but rushes cocoa brown with sediment in the spring.   Willows and cottonwoods stand on islands in the river waving branches toward the shore.   Netleaved hackberries and willows crowd entrances to tiny side canyons.   During winter, the greenish-white berries of poison ivy decorate leafless stalks like sinister grapes.   Emerald green junipers accent the Bruneau Canyon beginning about .5 mile above Hot Creek. Many varieties of plants and animals grow here because of the two side-by-side environments: streamside and desert. Wild roses grow next to sagebrush. A path leads down Hot Creek to the Bruneau River and up it for 1 mile or so.

To reach Indian Bathtub, take Highway 51 south out of Mountain Home. At 15 miles the road crosses the Snake River. At 22 miles, near the town of Bruneau, a paved road signed for Bruneau Canyon leads left (southeast). In 8 miles, turn right (southeast) on a branch road across a bridge over the Bruneau River. Beyond this turn 1.6 miles, turn left (southwest) up a hill on Blackstone-Grasmere Road. In 3.5 miles, turn left (east) onto a primitive road that leads downhill 1.5 miles and ends 200 yards from the Bathtub.

Climbing down directly to the tub is difficult, so take a path that circles from the end of the road east and south to the pool. Use caution in bathing, as the water isn't very clean and has biting bugs in it.

A path leads down Hot Creek on the north side .5 mile from the tub to the Bruneau River. From here a path goes 1 mile or more southeast up the river canyon before the way becomes overgrown with poison ivy. The canyon here is only 150 feet deep, contrasting with the 800-foot depth at the Scenic Overlook 8 miles south on the other side of the river. Many more little hot springs bubble along the river bank both north and south of Hot Creek.

BRUNEAU CANYON — ROBERSON TRAIL **68**

Round trip: 2 miles
Elevation loss: 640 feet (return climb)
Highest point: 3680 feet
Topo maps: Winter Camp and Big Hill (both 15′ with 40 foot contours); Hot Spring and Sugar Valley (with 25 foot contours)
Time: 2½ hours
Access: Turn southeast off Highway 51 on paved Bruneau Canyon Road 22 miles south of Mountain Home. Drive 8 miles and turn right (southeast) on a dirt road. Cross a bridge and at 1.6 miles, turn left (south) on dirt Blackstone-Grasmere Road. Turn left (southeast) at 5.8 miles, and turn left (east) again on Roberson Road at 10.4 miles. Drive to grassy area at 11.6 miles.
Ability: Expert

In the dark chasm of Bruneau Canyon, black columns of basalt, broken occasionally by horizontal bands of light red rock, form the canyon walls. Hot lava baked clay into brick to create these bands. From the bottom of the canyon, a 600-foot tower of dark basalt rises like a skyscraper to give the hiker on the Roberson Trail an idea of the depth of the canyon at the scenic overlook downstream on the other side of the river. Deep niches incise and furrow the canyon walls.

The gorge is so deep and narrow that some of it is in shadow all day. Green junipers drink the muddy river amid a jungle of wild roses, currants, and poison ivy. Spiky scouring rush and marsh grass elbow white sand beaches. In early spring the green grass creeps with tiny pastel desert flowers like pink phlox. The Bruneau River has been proposed for designation as a National Wild and Scenic River. The canyon is also being studied for possible wilderness status by the Bureau of Land Management.

To reach the trail, drive 22 miles south of Mountain Home on Highway 51. Turn southeast on a road signed for Bruneau Canyon and drive 8 miles to a junction. Note the mileage on the car's odometer here. Turn right (west) on a dirt road, cross a bridge over the Bruneau River, and turn left (south) just past a ranch, 1.6 miles from the junction onto the Blackstone-Grasmere Road. This dirt road winds up some low hills for about 2 miles and then drops down a steep grade. Near the bottom of the grade, at 3.5 miles, pass an unsigned primitive road leading left and down-hill to the Indian Bathtub. Continue through low hills to a place where an unsigned road turns left uphill at 5.8 miles. Take this turn (which is the main road) and continue winding uphill.

At about 9 miles, the road flattens and follows a fence on a plateau called the Miller Water Table. At 10.4 miles the track comes to an intersection where one road leads right at an angle through the fence. Take a primitive but smooth two-wheel way that leads to the left (east); drive to the edge of the canyon where the track ends 11.6 miles from the paved Bruneau Canyon Road. The end of the track is southeast of the trail beginning and isn't shown on the topo map.

Begin hiking by walking back along the road 250 yards. At this point, the road runs through a grassy area about 100 yards wide. Walk east-northeast down the lowest part of the grassy area to a V of sagebrush at the bottom and continue down a ravine. An overgrown trail runs just above the bottom of the ravine on the right (southeast) side.

Follow this trail as it switchbacks indistinctly across the hillside for 50 yards and then returns to the ravine, which curves east and ends in a dropoff. The trail leaves the ravine by turning southeast and traversing between two tiers of cliffs. Then the route contours a grassy hillside until the hiker can see more cliffs ahead. These cliffs are the end of a little valley that is south of the point where the road ended. The trail switchbacks below these cliffs through rocks and sagebrush to the Bruneau River at 1 mile. Here a wire ferry crosses the river at an old gauging station. A faint path runs both up and down the river from here.

The Roberson Trail is abandoned, so grass or rock covers the path all the way. The switchbacks through the rocks and brush are hard to find. This hike would not be good for children under eight because of the cliffs. There are no campsites at the river due to rough ground and poison ivy. The Roberson Trail crosses the river at the gauging station on an ancient wire ferry (don't use it!) and climbs the east wall of the canyon. A primitive road on the east rim of the canyon provides access to this trail, but is rougher than the roads on the west rim.

BIG JACKS CREEK — PARKER TRAIL   69

Round trip: 3 miles
Elevation loss: 600 feet (return climb)
Highest point: 4630 feet
Topo map: Big Hill (15′ with 40 foot contours)
Time: 3 hours
Access: Turn south 2 miles west of Bruneau from Highway 51 onto paved Grasmere Road. At 22.5 miles, turn west on a dirt road and go 4.6 miles. Turn north on a two-wheel track and drive 2.5 miles to a dry wash.
Difficulty: Easy, but poor trail and no signs

In the canyon within a canyon of Big Jacks Creek, 100-foot grey basalt cliffs rim the upper gorge above 200 feet of slanting talus. In the inner canyon, the blue-green creek hairpins back and forth from rock wall to rock wall across a wide band of green grass. Rows of brown obelisks of rock with niches between them serrate the top of the inner canyon walls. In the canyon bottom, clematis, wild roses, and scouring rush grow. From the upper rim, the winding inner walls form alternating intersecting lines resembling feather-stitching. Along the route, little barrel cactus grows under sagebrush or in holes in the rock. Prickly pear cactus is also found here. In mid-May, the barrel cactus blooms both pink and yellow.

To reach the Parker Trail, turn south on the paved Grasmere Road (Highway 51) 2 miles west of Bruneau. Drive 22.6 miles south to an intersection with two stop-signed dirt roads at the crest of a hill. Turn right (west) and drive 4.6 miles on this dirt road (the Wickahoney-Battle Creek Road). The Idaho Highway Department map has labeled Big Jacks Creek as Wickahoney Creek, but Wickahoney Creek is actually a tributary of Big Jacks Creek. At 4.6 miles, the dirt road makes a sharp left turn south where a two-wheel track leads north. The Bureau of Land Management calls a

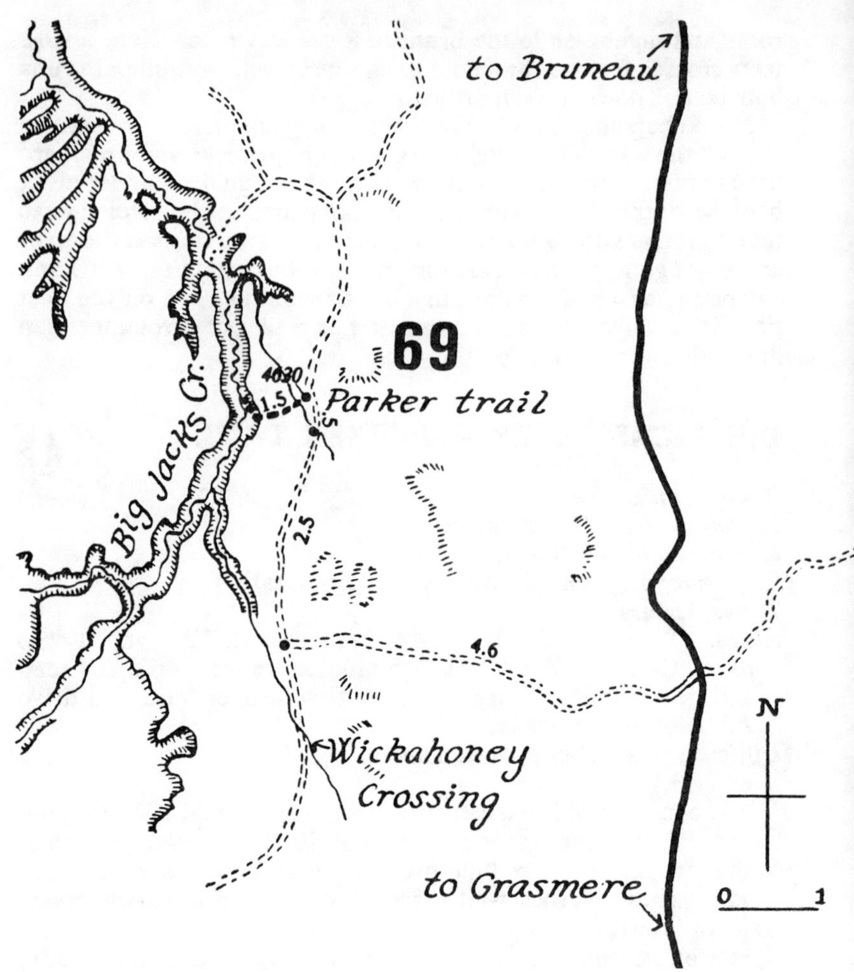

two-wheel track that is made only by the passage of vehicles a "way". Drive along this track 2.5 miles to a small dry wash. The track goes north .5 mile uphill where a branch leads .2 mile southwest to the Parker Trail.

These bways are rocky, so it is easier to park at the wash and walk .5 mile west along a cow path to intersect the track to the Parker Trail. The dry wash leads north and doesn't follow the track to the canyon. .7 mile from the dry wash, the track to the Parker Trail ends and becomes a steep, indistinct cattle trail. Continue down a gully until it turns into vertical cliffs at 1.2 miles. At this point, a faint trail goes slightly uphill to the north along the side of the gully. Take the path 200 yards to the brink of the inner canyon. The map incorrectly shows the trail from here going along a shelf.

Big Jacks Creek

Actually the trail drops to the creek immediately through grass and sagebrush. Look ahead for the most promising path to descend to the creek at 1.5 miles.

A faint path goes along the grass in the canyon bottom. However, in the spring wading the creek several times would be necessary to follow this path. To get a wider view of the Jacks Creek area from the top of the canyon, walk cross-country 1.5 miles north from the beginning of the Parker Trail along the canyon rim to the west side of a point where the dry wash joins the main creek. A desert pavement of rocks studded with barrel cactus and sagebrush lines this plateau. From the point, the traveler can look north and see the creek repeating the pattern of a canyon within a canyon for several miles, with the variation that some of the rock ahead is pink.

Many BLM "ways" explore the Big Jacks Creek area. The jeep track that intersects the way to the Parker Trail runs north a few miles along the canyon. Reaching the brink of the canyon from the jeep track in several places for a view would be possible on foot. The BLM has recommended Big Jacks Creek for study as a potential wilderness area.

LITTLE JACKS CREEK

70

Round trip: 2.4 miles (1.2 miles cross-country travel)
Elevation gain: 160 feet
Elevation loss: 240 feet
Highest point: 3780 feet
Topo map: Big Horse Basin Gap (20 foot contours)
Time: 3 hours
Access: Go 1.9 miles south of Grand View on Highway 78. Turn south on graveled Mud Flat Road. At 7 miles, turn left (southeast) on graveled Shoofly Cutoff Road and go 2.5 miles. Turn right (southwest) and go 7 miles on primitive road. Turn left (southeast) on another primitive road and drive 3 miles to the edge of a canyon.
Route: Partly cross-country with no signs

Grassy slopes slant between layers of grey-brown cliffs on the grass-topped hills that form the canyon walls of Little Jacks Creek Canyon. These layers form stairsteps that make the hills resemble wedding cakes before they are frosted. Where the trail described here enters the canyon, the layered hills above the upper canyon stop. From this point northeast, only the brown rock trough of the 100-foot inner gorge winds across the grass toward Grand View.

Willows, punctuated by occasional cottonwoods, have overgrown the canyon bottom. Between the willows, pure patches of poison ivy form thick sinister carpets. Red-banded trout in the creek hide under the overhanging willows. Horned lizards and prickly pear cactus live on the canyon rim. This little-used canyon is challenging hiking and is the deepest canyon in the Owyhees. Little Jacks Creek has been recommended for study as a wilderness area.

To reach the most convenient access point for Little Jacks Creek Canyon, drive southeast of Grand View on Highway 78 for 1.9 miles and turn south on the paved Mud Flat Road. The pavement ends at 4.3 miles just beyond the last farm. Continue on the gravel road to a junction with the graveled Shoofly Cutoff Road at 7 miles. Turn southeast, drive over a low ridge at 1 mile, and at 2.5 miles turn off to the right (southwest) on a primitive unsigned two-wheel track. Note that this track crosses Shoofly Road and that this turnoff is just before another road turns right (south) along a row of power poles. In about 2 miles, the primitive road crosses three deep seasonally-dry washes that will be a problem for passenger cars. At 6.4 miles, the way crosses a double-scraped track in the earth with a ridge in its middle (for a gas line). The road follows this strange track on and off until coming to a four-way intersection of ordinary two-wheel tracks at 7 miles. Turn left (southeast).

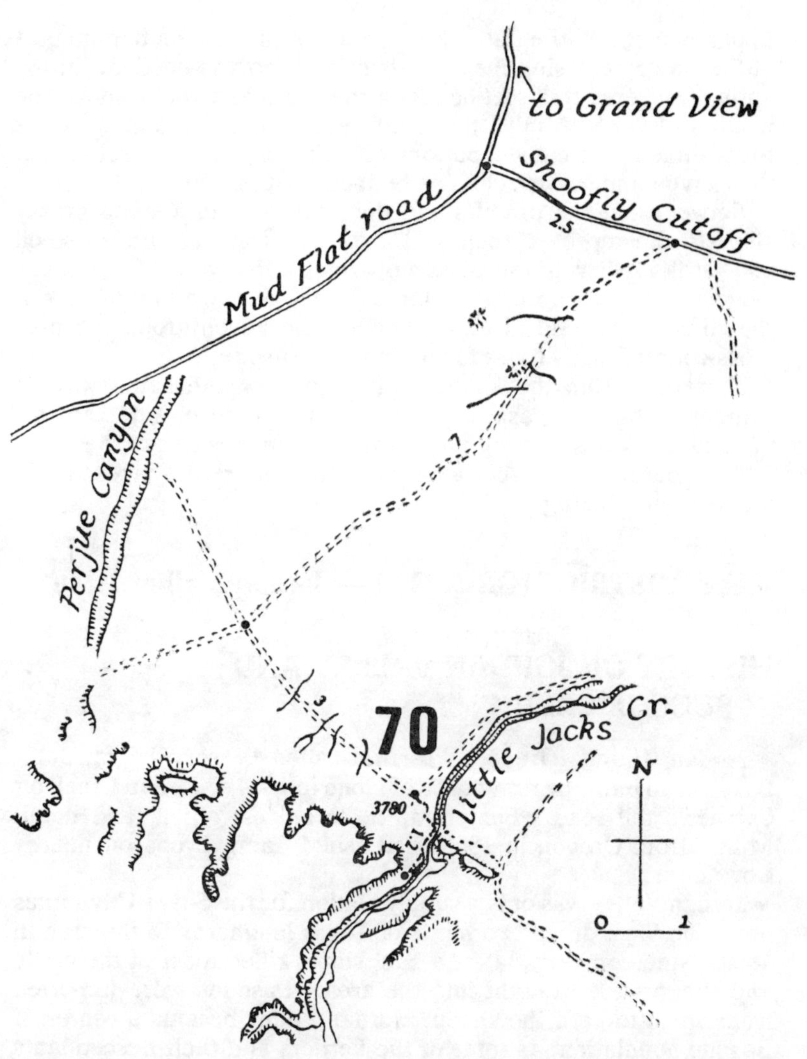

A hill to the southeast in the distance with a dropoff on the right
marks the access point. This track is rockier than the first and
crosses two deep washes. At 3 miles, this road makes a gradual
left turn. Here a jeep trail turns right (south). Park two-wheel
drive vehicles at this point and walk. The track turns east toward
the canyon and descends grassy slopes. At .6 mile the jeep trail
ends. Find a path that goes to the right from the end of the road
down to the canyon bottom at .7 mile. Across the canyon a trail
climbs to meet a jeep trail on the other side.

A cross-country route leads up the canyon to a viewpoint of the upper canyon. In the fall, hike right along the canyon bottom part of the way by crossing the creek back and forth as needed. In the spring, traverse this section along the grass and rocks above the willows. At about 1 mile, the shrubs and willows become too thick to continue in the canyon bottom. Climb along on the west side of the canyon under some cliffs on faint cow paths.

Between one set of cliffs and the next, ascend a steep grassy slope to the top of a knoll at 1.2 miles. The next grassy knoll 200 yards further up the canyon provides a fine view of the upper canyon. For a glimpse of the inner gorge, go down to the brink of the cliffs at the end of either knoll. The adventurous can hike cross-country many miles further up the canyon.

To return from the knolls, either go back the same way or contour along the grassy hills, going in and out of side canyons back towards the starting point. The distance is about the same either route. Be especially watchful for rattlesnakes while cross-country hiking.

VALE DISTRICT (OREGON) — Jordan Valley Area

HISTORY OF JORDAN VALLEY AND
SUCCOR CREEK

Jordan Valley (Oregon) was first called Baxterville, for John Baxter who built the first house of stone in 1864 at Jordan Creek on Skinner's toll road. Baxter ran a store, post office, and hotel. Militia from Oregon in 1865 established Camp Lyons on nearby Cow Creek.

Jordan Valley was only a supply station for the Silver City mines until Con Shea drove two herds of Texas longhorns to the area in 1869. Nineteen years later, a bad winter killed most of the cattle and sheep were brought into the area. Basques were imported from Spain to herd the sheep. Jordan Valley became a center of Basque population, as some of the herders and their descendants became stockmen themselves.

Two interesting people lived in the area in the early days. Jean Baptiste Charbonneau, Sacajawea's son, died in 1866 near the Owyhee River and is buried at the Inskip Ranch near Danner. Joe Monahan was an early miner at Ruby City who came to Succor Creek to be a cowboy and ranch hand. When neighbors laid him out for his funeral, they discovered Joe Monahan was a woman.

There have been four roads to Jordan Valley from the Boise Valley. The first was Skinner's toll road by way of Silver City. The second was the Poison Creek Road, which was built in the 1870s from the Snake River. The old stage station on lower Poison Creek is still standing. A stage station, the Rocks (named for two big rocks used for storing hay and grain by the freighters), was located at Rockville at the junction of the Poison Creek Road with Skinner's road down Jordan Creek from Silver City. A new gravel road was later built up Succor Creek and became the main highway to Jordan Valley until U. S. 95 was constructed about 1920.

Near Succor Creek and Jordan Valley, the 50-mile long Owyhee Reservoir on the Owyhee River was started in 1928 after twenty-five years of planning. Owyhee Reservoir, completed in 1935, brought widespread irrigation to Malheur County, Oregon.

JORDAN CRATERS (Oregon)   71

Round trip: 1 mile
Elevation gain: 100 feet
Elevation loss: 100 feet (return climb)
Highest point: 4600 feet
Topo map: Jordan Craters North (20 foot contours)
Time: 1½ hours
Access: Drive 37 miles south on U. S. 95 from the junction of U. S. 30 and U. S. 95. Turn west on a dirt road and drive 9 miles. Turn right and go 8 miles; then turn left (west) and go 7 miles. Turn left again (south) and drive 1.5 miles.
Difficulty: Easy, but no signs

Northwest of Jordan Valley, Oregon, near the Idaho border, Jordan Craters poke out of a 6-mile square of rough black lava. A path ambles up the side of the largest crater and down into its colorful center, where pink rock streaks the black lava. Bright green and orange lichens stripe the inside walls of the crater. The official name of the large crater is Coffeepot Crater. Several small craters cluster around the big one like coffee cups.

To reach Jordan Craters, drive south of the Marsing junction on U. S. 95 and up the Squaw Creek Grade. 37 miles south of the junction (2.5 miles south of Sheaville), turn right (west) on a dirt road. At 9 miles, take the right fork and drive 8 miles. Here, at 17 miles, turn left (west) and go 7 miles. At 24 miles, just beyond seasonally dry Coffeepot Reservoir, turn left (south) again and drive 1.5 miles to the end of the road beside the large crater. Most of these intersections are signed.

A path angles up the south side of the crater, circles the rim on the left and drops into the crater from the north rim. Only the surefooted should attempt to descend into the crater since the path is slippery. After descending into the crater, the hiker may want to

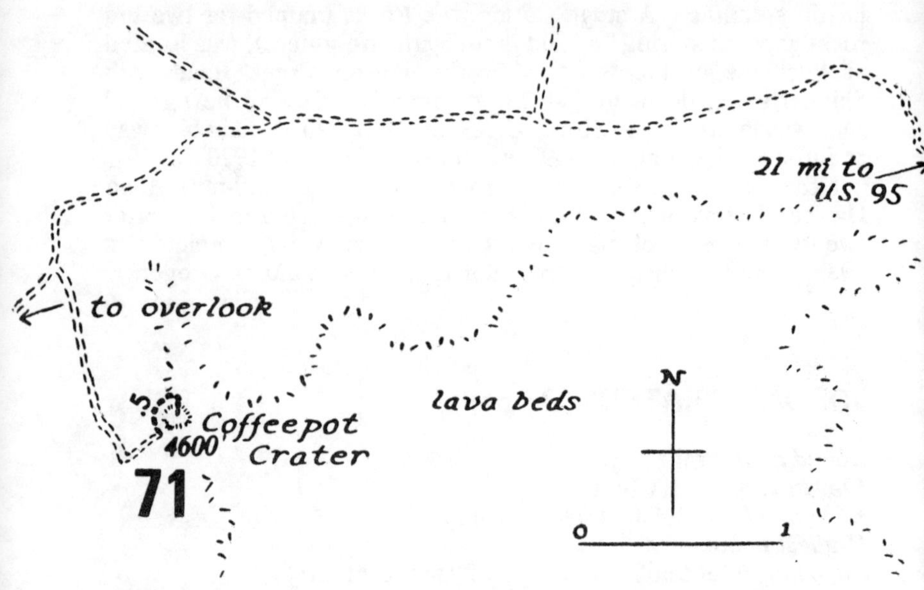

walk cross-country out on the lava fields to explore some small caves. However, be very careful because the lava is rough and has many sinkholes and dropoffs. It is best not to take small children or dogs out onto the lava fields.

Children will especially enjoy the small craters at the end of the road. The area is very similar to Craters of the Moon National Monument but doesn't have as many craters or lava tube caves. The road continues southwest beyond the turnoff for the crater at 24 miles. This road reaches an overlook at 29 miles. The view here of the canyon of the Owyhee River is of a deep rift in a vast area of desert tablelands.

THREE FINGERS ROCK (Oregon) 72

Round trip: 2 miles
Elevation gain: 700 feet
Highest point: 4828 feet
Topo maps: Three Fingers Rock, Pole Creek Top (both Oregon)
Time: 3 hours
Access: 5.1 miles west of Homedale, Idaho on Oregon 201, turn left (south) on Succor Creek Road. Drive 18.5 miles and turn northwest on an unmarked dirt road and go 3.5 miles.
Route: Cross-country with no signs

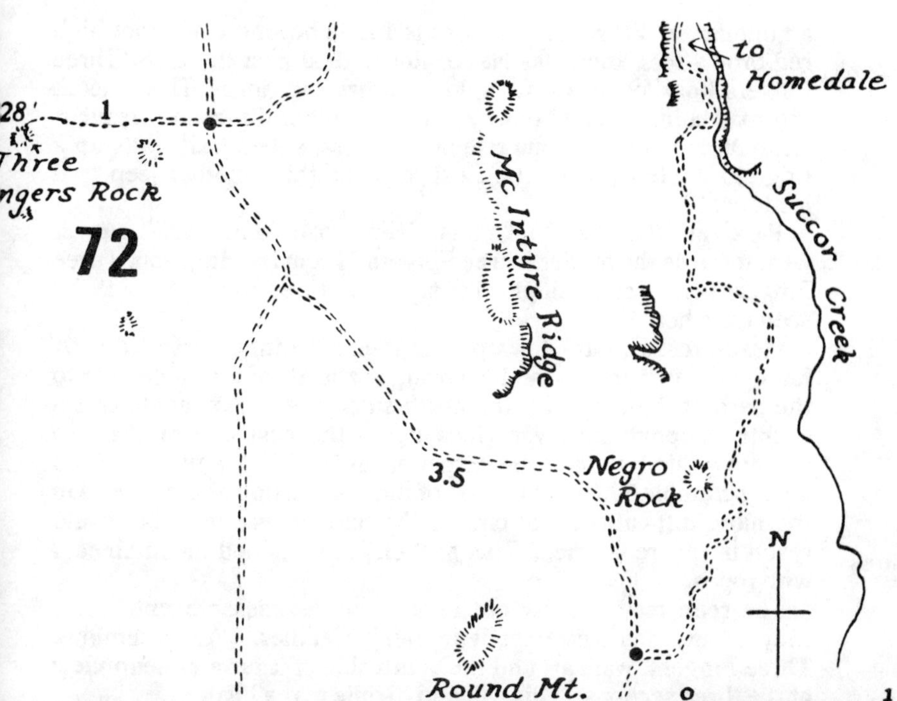

From the top of Three Fingers Rock, rows of buttes, rocks, and tablelands stretch to the Boise Valley and to the Owyhee Mountains. The 200-foot rock is split into three sections, 40 feet below the top. Green and orange lichens splash the walls below nests of hawks and eagles. The notches in the rock form little alcoves lined with grass. The top of the rock is the highest point for miles in every direction, so it is a landmark in the western half of the Boise Valley. The east section of the rock, which faces the valley, is easy to scramble up. From the access road along Succor Creek, 600-foot cliffs of brown rock tinged with orange rise to tablelands 1000 feet above the canyon floor. The best season of the year for this trip is spring when pink phlox, yellow balsamroot, and purple penstemon hide between the sagebrush among a fuzz of new green grass.

To reach Three Fingers Rock, drive west of Homedale, Idaho on Oregon Highway 201 past the Oregon state line at 3.5 miles. At 5.1 miles, a sign for Succor Creek State Park points left (south). Turn onto this dirt road and drive through Succor Creek Canyon where there are picnic areas, restrooms, and a campground. Beyond the campground, the road climbs 1000 feet up the side of the chasm.

18.5 miles from the highway, turn back north at a sharp angle on an unmarked dirt road. The turn is 1 mile beyond a 400-foot high red-brown rock known as Negro Rock. Just past the turn, Three Fingers Rock looms ahead, split into three sections. This smooth dirt road climbs up and down, passing another dirt road that turns left. On top of the second rise at 3.5 miles, a jeep trail leads up a ridge to the left (west). (Almost opposite this, another jeep trail leads east.)

Park at the base of this jeep road and walk up it west towards the hidden Three Fingers. From the ridge top, Three Fingers is a massive single cliff since the three-way split can't be seen from here.

Head cross-country towards the rock's slanting north side. A faint path leads from a muddy spring northeast of the ridge over to the base of the rock. On the north side of the peak, angle cross-country through grassy ravines up to the east one of the two notches. Climb to the little carpet of turf within the notch. From here, scramble 30 feet to the top of the east section of the rock. On the more difficult 40-foot cliff of the middle section, a fall could result in severe injuries. This section is for trained mountaineers with ropes.

The road may not dry out enough to be passable until after May 1, and don't attempt it in rainy weather. After climbing Three Fingers, walk around the south side of it for a closeup view of the three sections. This will add .5 mile to the hike.

JUNIPER GULCH (Oregon)   73

Round trip: 1.5 miles
Elevation gain: 360 feet
Highest point: 3720 feet
Topo map: Rooster Comb (Oregon)
Time: 1½ hours
Access: Drive south on U. S. 95 from the junction of U. S. 30 and U. S. 95 for 21.4 miles. Turn right (west) at McBride Creek and drive 8.8 miles to Rockville. 1.8 miles past Rockville, turn left (west) at Leslie Gulch sign and drive 10.5 miles.
Difficulty: Easy, but no signs

In Juniper Gulch, tiny caves that look like miniature cliff dwellings pit orange cliffs. In the spring, wildflowers accent sagebrush and scattered junipers. In the fall, rabbitbrush glows golden along the gulch. Nearby rock towers in Leslie Gulch and along Owyhee Reservoir blaze red and orange. The orange ridge to the left (west) is named The Yellow Jacket. This short walk up

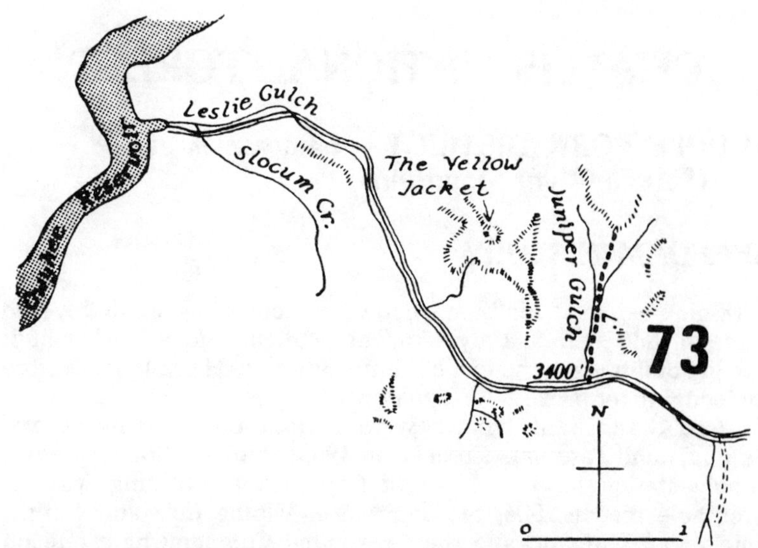

a side canyon from Leslie Gulch gives an intimate view of the rock formations found in the area.

To reach Leslie Gulch, drive south on U. S. 95 from the junction of U. S. 30 and U. S. 95 west of Marsing. Go 21.4 miles from the junction and turn right (west) at the sign for McBride Creek. Drive 8.8 miles on a gravel road to the old stage station of Rockville. Continue north 1.8 miles on the Succor Creek Road. Turn west at the sign for Leslie Gulch and drive 10.5 miles. Park at a picnic area with restrooms.

Ford the creek in Leslie Gulch and walk up a jeep road to the north. After 100 yards, this road turns into a trail. The path follows the east side of the gulch to a fork of two dry streams. Here the route heads between the streams on a flat area and peters out just under small cliffs at .7 mile.

CHALLIS NATIONAL FOREST

MIDDLE FORK DISTRICT — Seafoam Area
(Salmon River Mountains)

SEAFOAM HISTORY

Mining began at Seafoam when silver and gold were discovered there in 1886 by I. N. Daly and John Mullen. Mose Storher built two log buildings at the foot of Vanity Summit. He called this store and lodging for packers "Wagontown".

More than twenty mines were started on Seafoam, Float, Sulphur, and Josephus Creeks. In 1903, William Rideout built a supply station for the mines at Cape Horn. Mining was so profitable that in 1904, the Snowstorm Mining Company built a smelter at Seafoam, and the Greyhound Company built one on Sulphur Creek. In 1905, the Greyhound Company even constructed a rough toll road over Vanity Summit. Intensive mining continued into the 1920s, and some is still done today.

LANGER, ISLAND, AND RUFFNECK LAKES

74

Round trip: 5.4 miles
Elevation gain: 1280 feet
Elevation loss: 120 feet (return climb)
Highest point: 8240 feet
Topo maps: Langer Peak, Cape Horn Lakes
Time: 5 hours
Access: Turn north off Highway 21 onto Seafoam Road 18 miles northwest of Stanley and drive 7 miles on gravel road.
Difficulty: Moderate, but cross-country to Ruffneck Lake

Like a bottle cap on a pile of brown sugar, a lookout tower stands on the top of talus-sided Ruffneck Peak above blue-green Langer Lake. Nearby three other lakes are off the trail: Rocky, Island, and Ruffneck. The map shows the area as wooded, but rock outcrops and towers poke holes in the woods. 200-foot grey striped cliffs zigzag on an unnamed peak south of Island Lake. Next to the stripes, a grey rock tower peeks over a ridge from behind Ruffneck Lake. A round wooded island 100 feet across and shaped like a mushroom cap floats in Island Lake. Talus surrounds the milky-

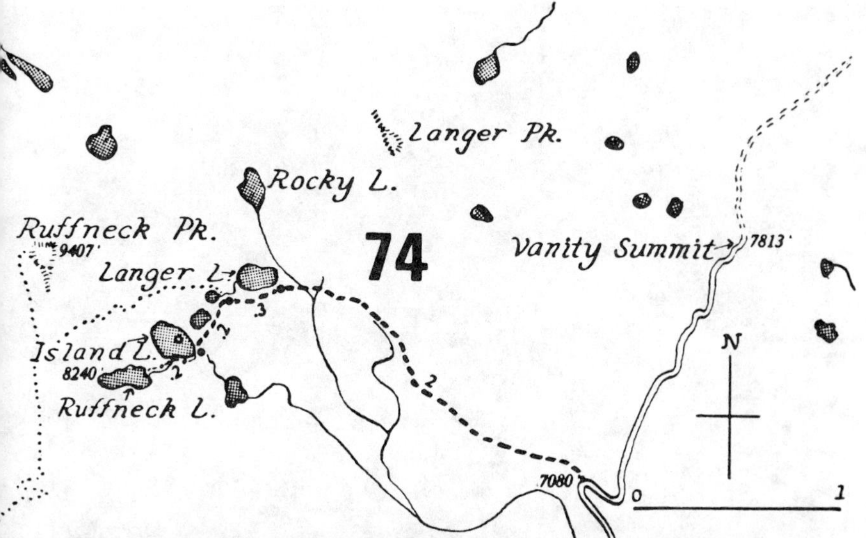

turquoise water of Ruffneck Lake.   By August this lake has a lowered waterline like a reservoir.

To reach these lakes, drive 18 miles northwest of Stanley on Highway 21. Turn right (north) on the graveled Seafoam Road and drive past the remnants of the old freight station of Wagontown. At 7 miles, park at the Langer Monument, which commemorates the death of a district ranger and two others in a wartime air search for a downed pilot.

The blazed Langer Lake Trail leads northwest into the River of No Return Wilderness just beyond the monument and climbs a wooded hillside 500 feet in the first .5 mile. Then the path levels but continues up the hillside. At 1.7 miles the trail crosses a stream that drains a swamp. 200 yards beyond, the route crosses the outlet of Rocky Lake and reaches Langer Lake at 2 miles.

The topo map has the names of Island and Ruffneck Lakes reversed. To reach Island Lake, go around Langer Lake on the main trail towards Ruffneck Lookout. At a small pond and sign for the Maishu Trail, turn left (southwest) on an unsigned path. Follow the path as it skirts another pond 200 yards from the turnoff and descends to Island Lake at .2 mile. The Maishu Trail runs 3 miles and climbs 1260 feet to the top of Ruffneck Peak.

The route to Ruffneck Lake goes up 200 feet in .2 mile along the left (east) side of Island Lake's usually dry inlet. An alternate route climbs a green patch to the right of talus on the far side of Island Lake and comes out on a ridge 100 feet above Ruffneck Lake. A route to Rocky Lake from Langer Lake leads .5 mile up the outlet of Rocky Lake. The main trail crosses this outlet 200 yards below Langer Lake.

Island Lake

SEAFOAM LAKES

75

Round trip: 6.4 miles
Elevation gain: 1360 feet
Highest point: 8160 feet
Topo map: Greyhound Ridge (15′)
Time: 6 hours
Access: Turn north off Highway 21 onto Seafoam Road 18 miles
    northwest of Stanley. Drive 10 miles on gravel and 4 miles on
    dirt to Seafoam Guard Station; turn left (west) and go 2.1 miles.
Difficulty: Easy, but cross-country to third and fourth lakes

   Misty green water colored like the inside of an ocean wave forms
four small lakes on Seafoam Creek. Above the first lake, three
dark grey peaks resemble three heads. A grey stripe across a buff-
colored cliff on the middle peak gives that head a pleased smirk.
The third of these peaks is smaller than the others and has fan-
shaped cracks. Rock benches climb the east side of the first lake to
two rock hills on a ridge to the left of the three dark peaks. From
the third and fourth lakes, the three peaks look triangular. The
second lake reflects the darker green of the woods around it. The
fourth lake sprawls among grass and red mountain heath under a
dark rock knoll next to the three pyramidal crags. The glowing

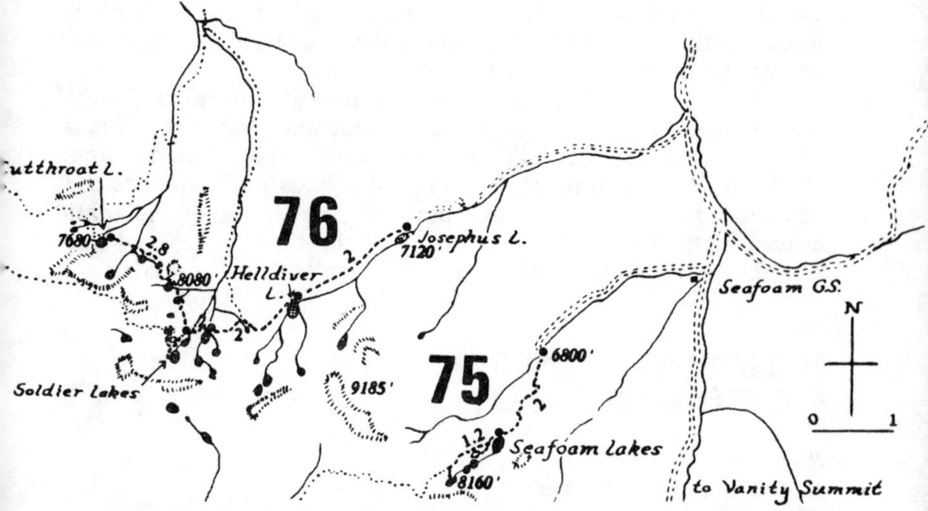

sea-green water of this lake holds tiny islands.

Even though four-wheel drive vehicles can drive to the first and second lakes, Seafoam Lakes is a good hiking destination. To avoid crowds, visit these lakes at midweek or in the fall, or make the destination the off-trail third or fourth lake.

To reach Seafoam Lakes, turn north on the Seafoam Road 18 miles northwest of Stanley and drive 14 miles (10 miles on gravel and 4 miles on dirt) over Vanity Summit to Seafoam Guard Station. 200 yards beyond the guard station, the signed Seafoam Lakes Road turns left (west). Drive 2.7 miles up this primitive road and park near the Fall Creek Trail sign unless in a four-wheel drive vehicle.

Ford Seafoam Creek and walk up the road. The road switches back at 200 yards, passes a mine road at .2 mile, and makes two sharp bends at .5 mile. A path leads from the end of the first bend up to the second and saves distance. Beyond these bends the road runs beside cliffs and alders below a pointed peak. At 1 mile, the track passes beside two mine sheds and zigzags up through rocks. At a fork at 1.5 miles, the left branch climbs boulders to a mine. The right (west) branch winds downhill to a ford at 2 miles where a track leads left 50 yards to the lake.

To reach the second lake, continue on the road beyond the ford. At 200 yards, a track dead-ends to the left (south) in the woods. Where the road splits 100 yards beyond, the hiker may take either branch, since these roads form a loop. The left fork leads up beside a mine and old ore cars. At the mine, the road jumps 6 vertical feet. The hiker can easily climb this. At 2.5 miles, the road turns back to the right (east) to return to the junction. At the top of the loop, the second lake shows through the trees 100 yards to the south. To get to the third lake, near the second, climb cross-country up the creek between the two lakes.

To find the fourth lake, go back down the right (north) fork of the loop for 100 yards until a blazed trail branches southwest. This is the Fall Creek Trail continuing to the Middle Fork of the Salmon. Walk up this trail through firs and lodgepoles until opposite the first one of the three dark grey peaks at 3 miles. Then cut south cross-country toward the middle one of the three peaks and find the lake at 3.2 miles. The fourth lake is .7 mile from the second.

HELLDIVER, SOLDIER, AND CUTTHROAT LAKES   76

Round trip: 16 miles
Elevation gain: 1360 feet
Elevation loss: 1040 feet (return climb)
Highest point: 8080 feet
Topo map: Greyhound Ridge (15′)
Time: 2 days
Access: Turn north off Highway 21 onto Seafoam Road 18 miles northwest of Stanley. Drive 10 miles on gravel and 7 miles on dirt, plus 4 miles on primitive road to Josephus Lake.
Difficulty: Strenuous

This hike tours a string of almost identical small lakes, no more than .2 mile across. The lakes march right along close together, all wearing the same uniform of green water, woods on one side, grey granite boulders and cliffs on the other. Variety lies in the size of the lakes, the color, and the backdrop. Colors range from emerald to dark green and olive. A small peak or a row of trees tops the cliffs. Most of the lakes have names, from General down to P. F. C., which is little more than a mud puddle.

To reach the trailhead, turn north on the Seafoam Road 18 miles northwest of Stanley. At Vanity Summit at 10 miles, the road becomes a narrow dirt road that plunges to the Seafoam Guard Station at 14 miles. Beyond the guard station, the track passes turnoffs for the Seafoam Lakes Road and Rapid River. Beyond the Rapid River junction, the road becomes primitive to Josephus Lake but doesn't require four-wheel drive. There's a small campground at Josephus Lake at 21 miles. Do not attempt to bring travel trailers to this campground. A horse trailer may be brought in with difficulty. Driving time from Highway 21 is 1 hour.

The trail begins at a register box and circles the northwest side of Josephus Lake. A sign at the trailhead says "Soldier Lakes - 5", but it is really only 4 miles. The River of No Return Wilderness boundary is just beyond the upper end of Josephus Lake. The trail climbs 560 feet up the canyon through woods in 2 easy miles, past the oasis of Mushroom Spring, to Helldiver Lake. The grey cliffs of Mt. Mills loom beyond a wooded ridge at the end of the lake. Just below the lake is a junction with a trail south to Fall Creek and Ruffneck Lookout.

The trail on to Soldier Lakes climbs 400 feet in a lodgepole-fir forest to a saddle at 2.7 miles. Then the route zigzags down to a pond and junction with the Soldier Creek Trail at 3.2 miles. Next the path circles the head of a canyon, crosses a boulder field, and arrives at the first lake at 4 miles. This round green lake, First Lieutenant Lake, nestles in woods with talus running up to grey granite cliffs of a small peak. The best of three campsites is off the trail beyond the inlet next to the talus. The second lake, Colonel Lake, is just over a 100-foot ridge from the first at 4.2 miles. Woods surround this lake, behind a strip of marsh grass.

There's a junction at Colonel Lake with the Patrol Ridge Trail. A side trip of 1 mile on this trail tours three more of the Soldier Lakes. The first of these, General Lake, at 200 yards, shines emerald green under a tree-topped rocky peak. The official trail (right branch) at an unmarked junction at General Lake circles the lake and goes on to Major Lake at .4 mile. This similar lake has talus and a big grey cliff. The left branch of the trail at General Lake leads 200 yards to the largest of the lakes. This unnamed lake of glowing green water is below a long, high ridge of cliffs. On the shore, a huge rock sits beside a spacious campsite.

Back on the main Soldier Lakes Trail at Colonel Lake, the trail on to Cutthroat Lake winds over a little ridge. The rerouted trail skips the third lake shown on the topo map. The next lakes on the trail are Sergeant at 4.7 miles, which resembles First Lieutenant, and Staff Sergeant at 5 miles, which wears the uniform of woods and talus below cliffs. Next the trail climbs 200 feet up a ridge to a saddle at 8080 feet beside a boulder field. On the other side, the trail zigzags down to tiny Second Lieutenant Lake at 5.5 miles. The trail continues to drop, passes near an unnamed lake at 6 miles, and at 6.5 miles reaches P. F. C. Lake, 480 feet below the saddle. P. F. C. Lake is a snow pond less than 25 yards long. From here the trail wanders over a ridge to Cutthroat Lake at 7 miles, where 300-foot gabled cliffs hang from a rounded grey peak.

YANKEE FORK DISTRICT — Basin Butte Area
(Salmon River Mountains)

HISTORY OF STANLEY

Fur trader, Alexander Ross, discovered the Stanley Basin on September 18, 1824. In 1832, Captain Bonneville took refuge from the Blackfoot Indians in the valley where he lived off mountain sheep for a month.

Two hundred prospectors soon arrived when John Stanley discovered gold in the basin in 1864. Beginning in 1866, miners on their way to Leesburg near Salmon passed by and some stayed to mine. By 1869, Stanley had a store and later became a crossroads for men on their way to the Yankee Fork, Loon Creek and other mines. From 1873 to 1895, several men discovered lodes or placers in nearby Kelly Gulch and Joes Gulch and started mining. Dredges were operated in the area; one was begun by the Sawtooth Placer Mining Company in 1890, and another by the Willis Dredge Company in 1909.

The first settlement was Upper Stanley, which was started by Arthur McGown, who built a cabin and sold beef to the miners. The store changed hands a few times, until one owner, Mrs. Benner, built a hotel there after the death of her husband. In 1902, Herbert Marshall built a hotel at the location of Lower Stanley. The two villages fought over the locations of the post office and school for many years, but finally both ended up in Upper Stanley.

HINDMAN LAKE FROM BASIN BUTTE 77

Round trip: 7 miles
Elevation gain: 400 feet
Elevation loss: 840 feet (return climb)
Highest point: 8400 feet
Topo maps: Basin Butte, Knapp Lakes
Time: 5½ to 7 hours
Access: 4.4 miles north of Stanley on Highway 21, turn right (east) on dirt Basin Butte Road and drive 11 miles to Hindman Lake Road, which is 1 mile below Basin Butte Lookout. Turn north on primitive Hindman Lake Road and drive 2.2 to 3.5 miles.
Difficulty: Moderate

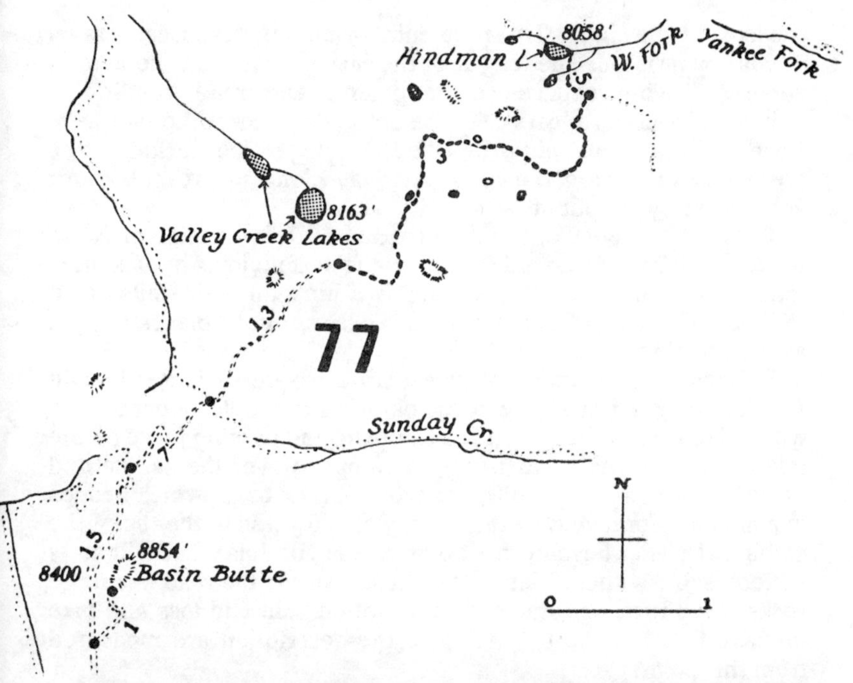

Above Hindman Lake, Cabin Creek Peak unfurls a wrinkled wall of burnt orange and grey stripes. The 1200-foot peak dwarfs the small green lake. To the northeast the top of Red Mountain resembles a pile of crumbled bricks. Around the 200-yard lake, wildflowers polka dot the grass, and springs arise from beds of soft moss. From the top of Basin Butte, the White Clouds' peaks spread out like a row of ghosts in the distance. The northern end of the Sawtooths seems next door. From just south of Stanley on Highway 75, the hiker may have noticed Cabin Creek Peak towering ahead on the north above wooded ridges.

To reach Basin Butte, turn right (east) off Highway 21 onto a dirt road across from the Stanley Lake Road turnoff 4.4 miles north of Stanley. At a turn for Cow Camp, keep straight ahead, but at a signed turn for Basin Butte at 2 miles, turn left (north). The road winds over sagebrush hills to a wonderful view of the Sawtooths at 3.5 miles. Much of the rest of the 12 mile road to Basin Butte climbs through woods. The road is narrow and gains 2500 feet in the last 8 miles. A passenger car should be able to drive to the top of the butte; watch the temperature of the car radiator. 2 miles below the lookout is a junction with a trail to Little Basin Creek, and a trail down the East Fork of Valley Creek to the Cape Horn Guard Station.

A primitive road to Hindman Lake turns left (north) 1 mile below the lookout at a sign, "This road built for mining purposes. Travel at your own risk". The length of the hike depends on the hiker's vehicle, driving experience, judgment, and road conditions. Drivers of passenger cars are wise not to drive the Hindman Lake Road. Future planning by the Forest Service includes the possibility of closing the road part way along to prevent motor vehicle use by the public.

The first 1.5 miles of the jeep road skirt the west side of Basin Butte. At 1.2 miles, an old road from the lookout joins it. The next mile drops 600 feet. At 2.2 miles is a junction with trails down Prospect Creek and Sunday Creek. There are good places to park at this junction.

The road next climbs northwest up a wooded hill 500 feet in 1 mile. At 3.5 miles, the track parallels a saddle between two wooded peaks. At this point is a campsite and parking place on the left. A path leads north from the campsite over the saddle and down 400 feet in .5 mile to Upper Valley Creek Lake, which nestles in a hollow. For a view of this lake, walk 50 yards to the top of the saddle. Driving beyond this point on the Hindman Lake Road is not advisable without four-wheel drive because the road has large rocks, deep ruts, and mud. The elevation gain and loss and hike mileage listed at the beginning of the description are measured from this point.

Continue by walking up the road, which climbs 120 feet in .5 mile. The track skirts the end of a ridge and drops 320 feet to some ponds at 1 mile. The road winds around the ponds in grass purple with elephant's head. The route then drops 200 feet, climbs 160 feet again, circles the end of another ridge, and descends 160 feet to intersect a trail down Basin Creek at 3 miles. On a ridge just before this junction is a spectacular view of Cabin Creek Peak and Red Mountain. The last .5 mile drops another 160 feet to the lake at 3.5 miles.

Beyond the outlet of Hindman Lake, the jeep trail continues north toward Cabin Creek Peak and then goes east below it 3 miles to mining prospects. At the lake, a foot and horse trail leads northwest 5 miles to Knapp Creek. Be sure to walk around the lake to see the springs, moss, and flowers at the west end, and to get an unobstructed view of the peaks.

Walking the whole jeep road would make the round trip 14 miles with a climb of 1320 feet and return climb of 1460 feet. It takes about 2 hours to drive in to the lake in a four-wheel drive vehicle from the turn at Highway 75. The hiker with a pickup without four-wheel drive will have a 7 mile round trip. Be sure to take the extra time to drive the 1 mile to the top of Basin Butte to see the view from the lookout.

HORSESHOE LAKE
(National Recreation Trail)

78

Round trip: 13 miles
Elevation gain: 1680 feet
Elevation loss: 640 feet (return climb)
Highest point: 8640 feet
Topo maps: Langer Peak, Knapp Lakes
Time: 10 hours
Access: 11 miles north of Stanley on Highway 21, turn right (east) and drive 5 miles on gravel to .5 mile west of Cape Horn Guard Station. Turn right (northeast) and drive 3 miles on dirt and 1.5 to 2.5 miles on primitive road to the beginning of a jeep trail.
Difficulty: Strenuous

A wooded peninsula splits the green water of Horseshoe Lake in the middle. An apple green carpet of grouse whortleberry underlies lodgepoles and firs on the peninsula. Willows cover a tiny island near the far shore below ramparts of a white and orange peak dotted with trees. Above the peninsula, three tiny lakes sit in a row south of the lake on a rock bench below a nipple-shaped peak. Beyond the lower end of the lake, the canyon of Loon Creek drops north toward the Middle Fork of the Salmon River. This trail continues down Loon Creek to the road from Yankee Fork at Loon Creek Guard Station. Horseshoe Lake provides access via rough cross-country travel to various lakes at the head of Loon Creek.

To get to the muddy Knapp Creek Road, first drive to Cape Horn Guard Station by turning east off Highway 21 at Trapp Creek Narrows, 11 miles north of Stanley and going 5 miles on a gravel road. To reach the trail to Horseshoe Lake, turn northeast on the new Knapp Creek Road .5 mile west of the guard station turnoff. The new dirt road goes out 3.1 miles before it rejoins the old track opposite F-82 Lake on the topographic map. From there on, the way is a rutted, bumpy primitive road.

At 4.5 miles, the road crosses a side stream in a mudhole. By August, a high wheelbase vehicle should be able to cross it. At 5 miles, the road enters a 1 mile long meadow. Half way along the meadow is another creek. Soon afterwards, opposite Elk Lake at 5.5 miles, the meadow becomes a swamp. The hike mileage at the beginning is figured from this point. Yellow butter 'n eggs and other flowers brighten the long meadow, which is between low wooded ridges.

Four-wheel drive vehicles can travel beyond the swamp to the end of the road shown on the topo map at .2 mile and up the jeep trail that ends at 2.5 miles. Early in the summer, it isn't possible to get beyond 5.5 miles on the Knapp Creek Road even with four-

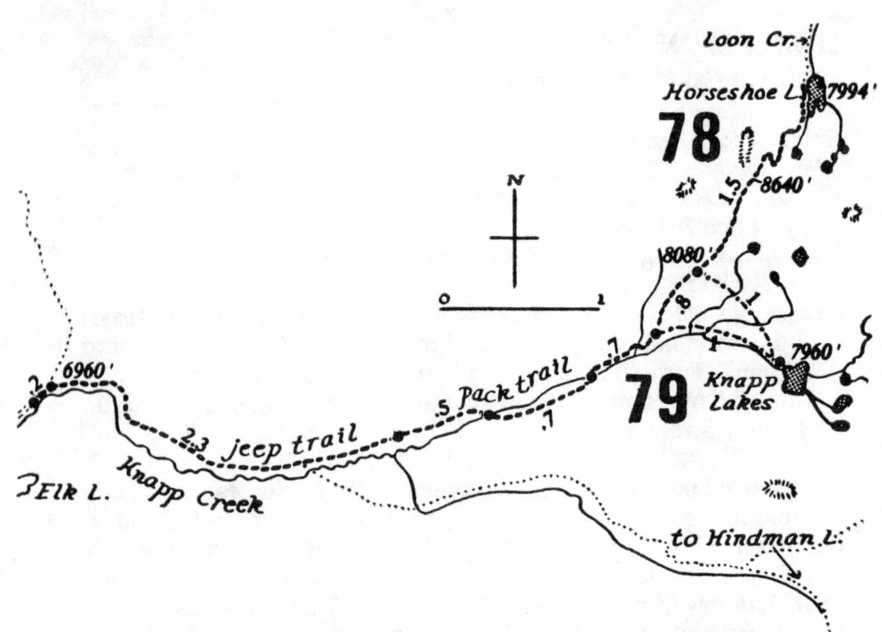

wheel drive. At .5 mile at the end of the meadow, just beyond the beginning of the jeep trail, is a junction with a pack trail to Winnemucca Creek. Beyond this junction, the jeep trail winds east up the canyon through forest and grassy clearings. At 2 miles, a pack trail branches southeast to Valley Creek and Hindman Lake. Due to trail rerouting, this junction is .5 mile west of the location shown on the topographic map. In the future, the Forest Service may close part of this road to motor vehicle use.

At 2.5 miles the jeep trail becomes a pack trail. From 3 miles to 3.7 miles, this pack trail has been rerouted to the south side of the creek. At 4.2 miles, the trail curves into a gully, crosses a side stream, and climbs out of the gully. The River of No Return Wilderness boundary is just before this gully. The gully marks the turnoff for a cross-country route up Knapp Creek to Knapp Lakes.

Beyond the gully, the Horseshoe Lake Trail climbs a wooded hillside to a burned-over ridge. From this open area at 5 miles, the striped cliffs of Cabin Creek Peak wrinkle ahead. The trail continues up through trees to a divide at 5.7 miles. Horseshoe Lake nestles 640 feet below in the trees, with a little rectangular pond perched on the rocks above. The trail switchbacks down to reach the lake at 6.5 miles. Campsites are located along the trail side of the lake and at the lower end.

With a four-wheel drive vehicle, allow 6½ hours for the round trip of 8 miles and 1400 feet gain to the lake.

KNAPP LAKES

79

Round trip: 10.4 to 11.4 miles, 2 to 3 miles cross-country travel
Elevation gain: 1120 feet
Highest point: 8080 feet
Topo maps: Langer Peak, Knapp Lakes
Time: 8 hours
Access: Reach the route from Knapp Creek Trail to Horseshoe
   Lake (see Horseshoe Lake).
Route: Cross-country

A "X" created by cracks in the rock of the grey face of an unnamed peak marks the location of Knapp Lakes. Cracks and dikes of darker grey fan out from the "X". East of the lakes, the crags of Cabin Creek Peak and the colorful ridge leading north to Tango Peak form a barricade. Small rounded hills covered with lodgepoles, firs, and grouse whortleberry line the shores of the largest lake.

Two routes lead to the first and largest (300 yards) lake. One way is to ascend the trail towards Horseshoe Lake beyond Knapp Creek. At a sign for Knapp Lakes in a burned-over area at 2.5 miles from the end of the jeep trail, take a compass bearing on the unnamed grey peak with the "X"and head towards it. Plastic markers and white strings are geologists' markings; do not disturb them. This cross-country pathless route is mostly level with little downed timber, but does have swamps. At a large stream, Knapp Creek, turn and follow the stream southeast up to the lake. Disregard any small streams connected with the swamps since they lead up to tiny ponds. The distance from the turnoff to the lake is 1 mile. Round trip distance is figured from the swamp 5.5 miles up the Knapp Creek Road.

The other route to the first Knapp Lake is to continue east where the trail goes north just beyond a side stream in a gully. This point is 1.7 miles up the Knapp Creek Trail from the end of the jeep road. This route follows Knapp Creek 1 mile to the lake and is .5 mile shorter than the first route. Stay within sight of the creek but out of its steep canyon. This route is rougher but easier to find. The first and largest lake has only a few campsites because of steep shores. To reach the upper lakes, follow streams from this lake by using the topo map. Only four of the other lakes are larger than 50 yards across.

YANKEE FORK DISTRICT — Yankee Fork Area

YANKEE FORK HISTORY

Mining on the Yankee Fork of the Salmon River began in 1870 when D. B. Varney and Sylvester Jordan found gold in the river. John Morrison discovered the Morrison Placer in 1873 and wintered there that year with forty-five others. In 1875, William Norton discovered the vein of the Charles Dickens Mine. He took out $11,500 with a hand mortar in thirty days.

In 1876, James Baxter, E. K. Dodge, and Morgan McKeim found the lode of the General Custer Mine. When miners moved into the area, packers began to freight supplies from Ketchum to the miners. The cost was from 5 to 15 cents a pound. Pack trains even carried in all the parts for the thirty-stamp General Custer Mill, including the ten-foot fly wheel.

Two towns, Custer and Bonanza, grew up around the mines. In 1878, Charles Franklin platted the town and sold lots in Bonanza, while Samuel Holman, the first justice of the peace, did the same for Custer. By 1879, a toll road had been built from Challis. In 1880, three changes of horses were required on the new stage line to get from Challis to the mines.

By the time the first women and children arrived, the town even had a newspaper, the *Yankee Fork Herald*. By 1880, the General Custer Mill was completed. Bonanza had eight lawyers and three doctors, but the only church was the Chinese one, which was called a joss house. (The name is pidgin English for a Chinese household deity.) In Bonanza many miners shingled their cabins with bark that had been peeled from live trees and flattened under rocks until dry. At one time George L. Shoup, who later became governor of Idaho, operated general stores in Bonanza and Challis and ran a freight line.

When the mines began to run out of high grade ore in 1888, mining declined. In 1888 at the end of the first boom, Arthur McGown and his family came to Yankee Fork, but stayed only a short time. In 1895, the Lucky Boy Mining Company was formed to reopen the General Custer Mill. This began a second boom which lasted until 1910. Many of those who had moved away returned, including Arthur McGown, who started several businesses. The final decline came when one of the Lucky Boy owners, Nick Trewick, got an option on the property and tried to get financing to dig a tunnel to solve hoisting and drainage problems. While he was gone, the mill closed for repairs and never reopened. By 1910, all the people had moved away.

However, during the Depression, several families moved into

the area to prospect and live in the abandoned houses. From 1939 to 1951, a giant dredge, owned by the Simplot Company, worked on the Yankee Fork and still sits in the river midway between Custer and Bonanza.

Edna McGown, the wife of Arthur's son, Tuff, recently helped Esther Yarber write two books of local history on the Yankee Fork and on the Stanley Basin. Since 1937, Tuff and Edna have lived summers and many winters at Custer doing a little mining, and they formerly were the caretakers for the museum and the town.

One of the most intriguing Yankee Fork stories is that of Lizzie King. In 1880, Lizzie's husband, Richard, died in a shooting incident. Charles Franklin, one of Bonanza's founders, befriended Lizzie afterwards, so was disappointed when she married a newcomer, Robert Hawthorne, instead of him. A week after the wedding, Hawthorne and Lizzie were both shot and killed at their home. No one was ever caught for the murders, but Charles Franklin acted very strangely after that and eventually moved to a prospect near Stanley where he lived alone. He was found dead a few years later with a locket containing a picture of Lizzie King in his hand.

CRIMSON LAKE

80

Round trip: 19.4 miles
Elevation gain: 2230 feet
Elevation loss: 300 feet (return climb)
Highest point: 8330 feet
Topo maps: East Basin Creek, Mt. Jordan, Knapp Lakes
Time: 2-3 days
Access: Drive 12 miles east of Stanley on Highway 75 to Sunbeam.
   Turn left (north) and drive 7.4 miles on pavement and gravel to
   Bonanza. Turn left (west) at guard station and drive 1.6 miles
   on primitive road to West Fork Campground.
Difficulty: Strenuous

On a calm day, blue-green Crimson Lake reflects the 400-foot cliffs and rock benches of two pointed red-orange peaks. Since the blue-green water mirrors peaks of its complementary color, red-orange, both colors seem more intense. The lake perches in a high canyon of orange rock peppered with dark green trees. South of the red-orange peaks, two 600-foot grey prongs of a spur of Cabin Creek Peak lean towards each other. Snow blankets the notch between them and climbs a split in the face of the right one.

Above the upper end of the lake, the tops of the light grey pinnacles on Cabin Creek Peak peer over the red-orange mountains. Woods surround the lake except at the upper end

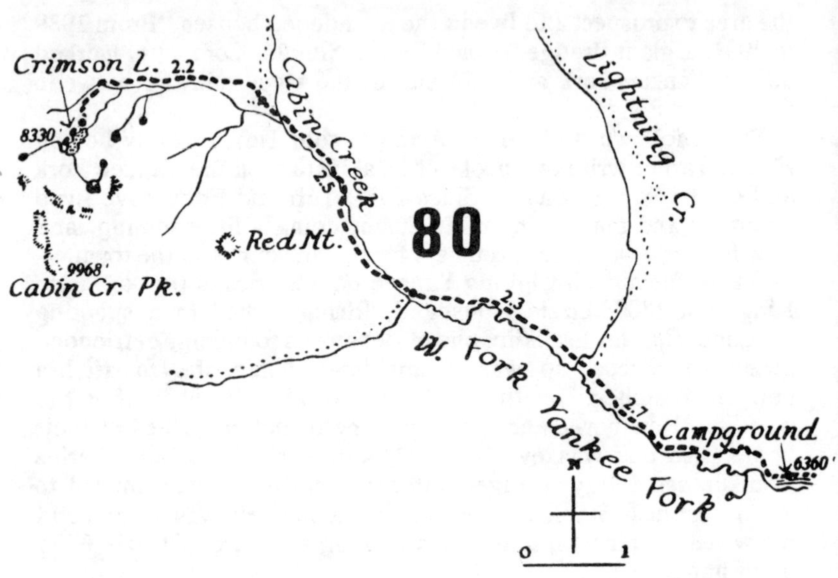

where a green meadow salted with tiny subalpine firs extends into an orange cirque. Three peninsulas with orange outcrops poke into the lake. Along the trail, bright red splotches and dark green trees accent the rounded salmon pink and cream-colored top of Red Mountain. No map shows a trail going to Crimson Lake from a junction of two branches of Cabin Creek, but there is an unofficial blazed trail.

To reach the trail, drive 12 miles east of Stanley on Highway 75 to Sunbeam. Turn north here and go up the Yankee Fork Road, which is paved for 3 miles, to Bonanza at 7.4 miles. Turn left (west) on a primitive road past the guard station and follow signs to the West Fork Campground at 1.5 miles, passing a sign for the West Fork Trail at 1 mile.

At the campground, walk north uphill 50 yards from a sign for the West Fork Trail. The trail starts in sagebrush and small stands of trees. The path climbs the side of the canyon to 300 feet above the creek at .7 mile. In an open area, the bright pink top of Red Mountain appears ahead to the northwest. The way passes behind a wooded knoll, then switchbacks down an open slope at 1 mile. The path crosses a tiny side stream in willows and descends through forest again to the West Fork at 1.2 miles. At 1.5 miles the trail comes to a junction with a trail that leads west along Deadwood Creek. The West Fork Trail goes through flat areas full of willows. At 2.5 miles the path circles the talus base of a 500-foot grey lava bluff. In a sagebrush flat beyond this, at 2.7 miles, is a junction with a trail north up Lightning Creek.

At almost 3 miles, the West Fork Trail fords Lightning Creek. North up the canyon, a burnt orange tooth sticks out of a brown and cream-colored peak. The way threads a narrow dry flat and then comes back beside the creek in grass and willows at 3.3 miles. Next the trail climbs out of this meadow into a lodgepole forest and edges the canyon wall at 4 miles. At 4.5 miles, the path crosses a mossy side creek. The Cabin Creek Trail turns northwest off the West Fork Trail in an open grassy flat at 5 miles.

The trail up Cabin Creek crosses to the west bank of the creek on logs at 5.5 miles. The trail disappears in grassy areas along here, so look for blazes. At the crossing of a side stream in an open area at 6 miles, the hiker can look up the canyon wall to Red Mountain. At 6.2 miles, avalance-strewn trees clog a meadow where the trail crosses back to the east bank of Cabin Creek. In early summer, wade the creek. Just beyond 6.5 miles, the way crosses another open area. At 7 miles, the trail passes a campsite.

The route climbs a narrow open area and then crosses the North Fork of Cabin Creek on logs at 7.2 miles. 100 yards beyond the crossing, a blazed spur trail goes 200 yards left (west) into the trees to a camp. Continue northwest up the main trail to an unsigned junction at the far edge of an open grassy area at 7.5 miles. The Crimson Lake Trail goes straight ahead here, while the main trail forks to the right. This junction is at the end of the first big switchback shown on the topo map beyond the creek crossing. It is essential to find this trail. Hiking cross-country to Crimson Lake from here is very difficult because the creek runs in a gorge higher up.

A sheepherder built the trail from here to Crimson Lake in his spare time. The trail climbs west-northwest up the canyon wall in the forest. At 8 miles the path comes to a talus slope, climbs the edge of it and crosses it. Then the route heads up a gully in the woods beside a tiny ridge that sticks out from the canyon wall. The path jogs sharply left 50 yards without blazes, and then continues up the left side of the gully going west.

Next the route comes down near the creek at the base of another talus area, and climbs the far side of the talus 100 yards before continuing its route along the canyon. At 8.5 miles, the way crosses an extensive open area and talus slope just below a big, knobby peak on the canyon wall. The trail enters the River of No Return Wilderness about here. It crosses three more narrow areas of talus, then climbs a wooded ravine and goes north of a tiny wooded hill at 9 miles. At the end of a level area beyond the hill, the trail turns left (southwest) downhill and crosses a creek.

On the other side, the route ascends a gully, and cuts to the right to follow the bank of the creek southwest. Beyond here, the path switchbacks south up a ridge that forms one side of the gorge of the outlet of Crimson Lake. After about 4 switchbacks, the trail reaches the top of the ridge above this gorge and follows the ridge 200 yards south to the lower end of the lake at 9.7 miles. The trail continues to the upper end of the lake along the west shore.

SULLIVAN LAKE (White Cloud Mtns.)   81

Round trip: 5.4 miles
Elevation gain: 1170 feet
Highest point: 6731 feet
Topo maps: Clayton, Potaman Peak
Time: 5 hours
Access: Turn south 2.5 miles east of Yankee Fork Ranger Station on a ranch road off Highway 75 at Sullivan Creek, about 17 miles east of Clayton; go 200 yards on a dirt road.
Ability: Expert

Pinnacles and cliffs splashed with orange and bright yellow-green lichen line the shrubby canyon of Sullivan Creek. From the trail, the hiker can look back down to the Salmon River Canyon and northwest to a brilliant red cliff in Potaman Creek Canyon. Near the lake, bitterroot blooms in early July. This flower's two-inch pink blossoms appear to rise out of the ground without leaves. At a ranch at the mouth of the canyon, logs enclose a gravel-bottom hot springs pool. Be sure to stop at the museum at Saturday Mountain Resort just west of Sullivan Creek to see historical pictures of the area. The lake is in the Sawtooth National Recreation Area, but the trail is not. Behind a fringe of grass, rounded hills covered with sagebrush and pines surround the lake.

To reach the trail, turn off Highway 75 about 2.5 miles east of the Yankee Fork Ranger Station and .5 mile before a bridge to the north side of the Salmon River. This turn is about 17 miles east of Clayton. Drive 200 yards to the ranch house to ask for permission to walk through the private land and to use the pool after the hike. Because of the low elevation and lack of shade, this hike is best for cool days in early summer and for fall.

Begin the hike by walking along the pasture to the hot springs at 200 yards. Join a jeep trail on the east side of the springs. The track passes an old cemetery and comes close to an operating mine at .7 mile. Turn west here and cross the creek to a trail that goes up the west side of the creek. At 1 mile, Potaman Creek joins Sullivan Creek from the southeast. At 1.2 miles, the path runs under colorful rock towers. The trail goes through two fences, crosses the creek to the east bank and soon comes back.

The path turns west at 1.5 miles to follow a bend in the creek.

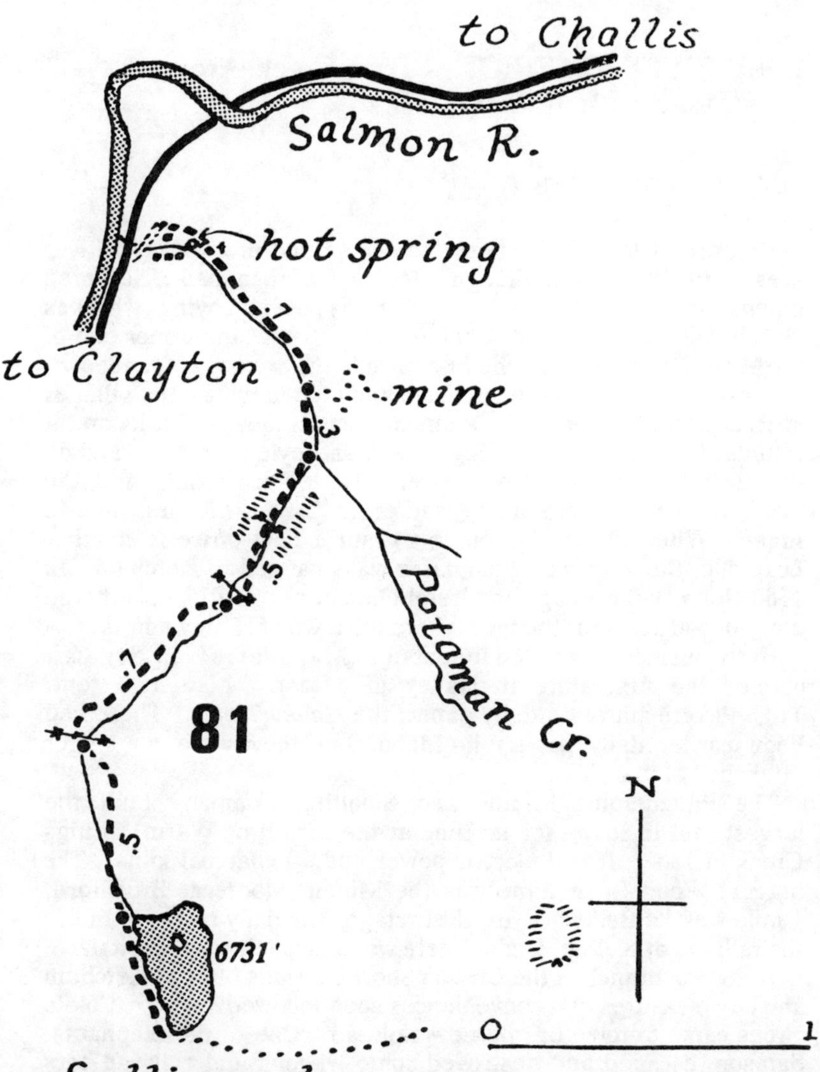

This section traverses a sagebrush hillside well above the creek. To find the trail here, go straight ahead as the trail crosses back to the west bank of the creek, and head 200 yards into the sagebrush. At 2.2 miles, the track crosses a tiny side stream in a ravine and then cuts back to cross a fence and then the creek. The next section of trail goes south along the east bank of the creek and climbs a pine-covered knoll at 2.5 miles. The trail meanders beside the stream, crossing once more to the west bank just before the lake at 2.7 miles.

LOST RIVER DISTRICT — Trail Creek Area
(Pioneer Mountains)

WOOD RIVER HISTORY

Because of Indian problems, no one settled in the Wood River area until 1879, even though Warren Callahan had discovered galena there in 1864. The first settler was Joseph Loving, who was closely followed by David Ketchum. In 1879, at the upper end of the Wood River, Galena, the first town in the area, was founded.

Prospectors found silver and lead and started mines and villages at Broadford, Bullion, and Doniphan near Hailey, at Muldoon, at Boulder City, up Warm Springs Creek on Boyle Mountain, and on the East Fork of the Wood River. Better processing and the availability of railroads made lead profitable for the first time in Idaho. When the U. S. wouldn't grant a post office to another Leadville, the town's original name was changed to Ketchum. In 1880, John Hailey, stage and freight line owner, filed a desert land entry of 440 acres for the land where the town of Hailey now is.

Early businesses started in tents. In May 1881, H. Z. Burkhart opened the first store in Hailey in a tent. Also in a tent, T. E. Picotte started a daily paper, the *Hailey Times*. There had been earlier daily papers in Idaho, but they were no longer published at that time.

The Philadelphia Mining and Smelting Company built the largest mill in Idaho for its time at the mouth of Warm Springs Creek in 1882. It had electric power and 20 charcoal kilns. The biggest Wood River mine was the Minnie Moore at Broadford, 1 mile west of Bellevue. By 1881, stages ran daily to Boise and to the railroad at Kelton, Utah. There was also a miners' hospital.

In 1883, a branch of the Oregon Short Line was built to Ketchum and city pleasures and conveniences soon followed. W. W. Cole's circus came to town on the new railroad. One of the elephants, Samson, escaped and destroyed some wagons and railroad cars before his owner stopped the rampage by putting a hot crowbar in Samson's mouth. The area had telephone service by 1883, when the Hiawatha Hotel was begun in Hailey. The Hiawatha, heated by natural hot water, wasn't finished until 1886 after eastern financier, Andrew Mellon, invested in it. In 1887, Hailey was the first town in Idaho to have electricity, which came from the Philadelphia Smelter in Ketchum.

The Triumph Mine on the East Fork of the Wood River was discovered in 1889 and proved to be more valuable than all the earlier mines by producing silver, lead, and zinc. Jay Gould, one of the owners of Union Pacific and an investor in the Wood River mines, brought a railroad car of friends and relatives to vacation in Ketchum in 1891. Inspite of the publicity, the mines were hampered by a collapse of the silver market in 1893. Only 200 people still lived in the area in 1900. It wasn't until 1957 that the Triumph Mine achieved full production, but that was short-lived. The Triumph Mill was sold in 1958 to a Cuban company who dismantled it and reassembled it in Cuba.

In 1884, H. C. Lewis built a toll road up Trail Creek from Ketchum to the Lost River, Bayhorse, and Custer. Near Trail Creek Summit, several mines were worked on the other side of the crest of the Pioneer Mountains from 1889 until about 1935. Some of these were the Phi Kappa and Black Rock Mines at the head of the Big Lost River, and the Copper Basin Mine.

Averell Harriman of Union Pacific hired Count Felix Schaffgotch in 1935 to select a place for a ski resort. Union Pacific built the Sun Valley Lodge in 1936 and the Challenger Inn in 1937 and installed the first chairlift in the world on Dollar Mountain. The lift had been invented by Jim Curran using the idea from hook loaders for bananas. Harriman imported the first Austrian ski instructors.

The movie "Sun Valley Serenade" made Sun Valley known world-wide, as did Ernest Hemingway's decision to live there. Hemingway spent some time in the Lodge in 1939, and after the war, he lived in Sun Valley with his fourth wife, Mary, for fifteen years until he accidently shot himself in 1961.

SUMMIT CREEK TRAIL

82

Round trip: 7.6 miles to saddle
Elevation gain: 1560 feet
Highest point: 9480 feet
Topo maps: Rock Roll Canyon, Phi Kappa Mountain
Time: 6 hours
Access: Drive 7 miles on pavement and 5 miles on gravel north-east of Ketchum on Trail Creek Road to Trail Creek Summit.
Ability: Expert

This hike leads to a saddle across from the orange and light grey wall of the Devils Bedstead. A grassy cirque clings to the front of the peak. On this mountain, a flat ridge drops in stairsteps to a notch with a triangular lump in it. To the right of the notch, a sliced-off point runs down a sharp ridge to a saddle of boulders. If a large devil tried to sleep on this mountain, he would find it most uncomfortable!

Behind the Devils Bedstead, a higher mountain rises from

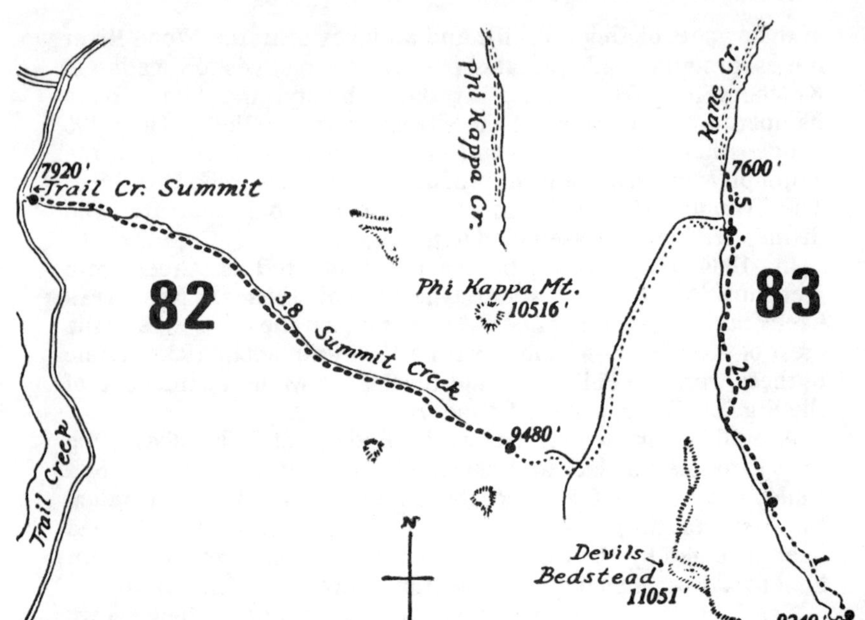

behind Kane Lake. This layered peak has a rounded top with a sheer drop on the side toward the Bedstead. The trail to the saddle treads meadows filled with paintbrush, cinquefoil, penstemon, and bluebells. The route passes springs hidden in moss. The round, notched leaves and delicate white blossoms of brook saxifrage grow in the moss. Scalloped rose-colored cliffs edge the upper canyon on the south across from orange talus shoulders of Phi Kappa Mountain. Back down Summit Creek, in the distance swell the high brown and pink points of the Boulder Mountains.

To reach the trailhead, drive 12 miles northeast of Ketchum on the Trail Creek Road to Trail Creek Summit. The first 7 miles are paved, but the last 5 miles are rough gravel. At the summit beside a Challis Forest sign are two tall snow markers with yellow diamonds on top. A jeep track beside the markers leads 100 yards northeast. Park here at the markers and walk along the track northeast down to the creek.

To find the unsigned trail, cross the creek to a path on the other side. The path switchbacks left and then back to the right (east) up the creek across an open grass and lupine covered hillside into the woods. At .5 mile the path comes to a flat, wet meadow. It is easy to lose the trail near the beginning of the meadow where two paths branch. Take the right less-used branch that goes to a blaze near the creek and crosses the creek.

Beyond the meadow, the trail runs in the woods, then comes into

the open at 1 mile. At 1.3 miles, the trail re-enters the forest.
Here two avalanche areas temporarily block the trail, so detour
around them. At 2 miles, the route follows a grassy hillside .5 mile
long. At 2.5 miles, springs bubble from moss under big firs. The
path at 3 miles crosses a side stream not shown on the map and
then climbs 200 yards along the left side of it.

At 3.3 miles the trail wanders into a clearing in the forest where
it is easy to lose the way. A blaze on the far side of the clearing at
the lower end marks the point to drop down and cross a stream.
Across the stream is a bigger open area where little trees have
been strewn about by avalanches. Cross this area of little trees, go
up the left side of it next to the forest, and the trail should
reappear. The trail winds through another small open area, then
makes a last zigzag up to the top of the saddle at 3.8 miles. Just
beyond the saddle in a little grassy valley is the best view of the
Devils Bedstead. The trail descends 3 more miles beyond here to
Kane Creek, reaching it .5 mile up the trail to Kane Lake.

KANE LAKE

83

Round trip: 8 miles
Elevation gain: 1640 feet
Highest point: 9240 feet
Topo map: Phi Kappa Mountain
Time: 6½ hours
Access: Drive 18 miles northeast of Ketchum over graveled Trail
Creek Summit to Kane Creek Road. Turn right (south) and drive
4.5 miles on primitive road.
Difficulty: Strenuous; partly cross-country

Across from 2000-foot mountain walls, mounds of turf carpet the
north side of milky turquoise Kane Lake. Among the turf in mid-
summer, buttercups, red mountain heath, and dwarf paintbrush
grow beside a tiny bubbling stream. On the south side of the lake
in front of a row of cliffs spotted with snowbanks, a point of rock
sticks up like a grey striped roof. Near this point a 300-foot waterfall splashes down a chimney in a black cliff. To the east, a second
waterfall glides, disappearing in the rock now and then to form a
unique dotted line. On the northwest down the canyon of Kane
Creek, the rugged wall of the Devils Bedstead crumbles.

To reach the trail, drive over Trail Creek Summit northeast of
Ketchum. The road is paved for 7 of the 12 miles to the summit.
Beyond the summit, drive 6 more miles to Kane Creek. Turn right
(south) on a primitive road and drive 4.5 miles to a ford of Kane
Creek. A vehicle with a high wheelbase is desirable. A jeep trail

Kane Lake

that is closed to motor vehicles goes .5 mile beyond the ford.

To begin the hike, wade Kane Creek and walk up the canyon on the jeep trail towards the headwall of peaks. At .5 mile, a trail to Summit Creek branches right (west). At .6 mile, the jeep trail hairpins left and ends. At the hairpin, the Kane Lake Trail goes straight south in woods up the canyon. The path climbs the side of a small ridge, then returns close to the east bank of the creek at 1.7 miles. Here the path hops the creek, and comes back immediately to avoid a section of high water under a cliff.

The official trail ends at 2.7 miles. The route from here winds through boulder fields without much of a path. Finally a path leads left (east) up a gully to avoid cliffs near a waterfall on the outlet. From the top of the gully, go south over rock benches and through meadows to the lake at 4 miles.

BOULDER LAKE

84

Round trip: 8 miles
Elevation gain: 2200 feet
Highest point: 9520 feet
Topo maps: Standhope Peak, Phi Kappa Mountain
Time: 7½ hours
Access: Drive 22 miles northeast of Ketchum over Trail Creek
   Summit to Copper Basin Road. Turn right (southeast) and drive
   2.5 miles to Wildhorse Creek. Turn right (south) and drive
   6.7 miles to a sign.
Difficulty: Strenuous

Boulders and flower-studded grass surround the blue-green water of Boulder Lake. Pikas scamper among the rocks giving insistent peeps. A striped grey and orange wall flanks the east side of the oval lake. Towers pointed and colored like termite hills of Africa top this wall. A knife-edged ridge of four jagged summits rises 1800 feet at the head of the lake. Light and dark grey stripe 800-foot cliffs on this ridge. To the west, a helmet-shaped summit near Washington Lake glowers behind an orange and white striped peak. Down the canyon from the lower end of the lake, a rose and light green tree-dotted ridge ends in an elephant-shaped hill.

The beginning of the trail is .2 mile north of the Wildhorse Campground. This campground is 2.5 miles south of Fall Creek on the dirt Wildhorse Creek Road. To reach the Wildhorse Road, drive 22 miles northeast of Ketchum over Trail Creek Summit. Turn right (southeast) on the Copper Basin Road, and turn right (south) again at 2.5 miles onto the Wildhorse Creek Road.

The trail begins by fording Wildhorse Creek. A path is found again at a sign in the middle of sagebrush on the other side of the creek. From the sign, the trail leads across the sagebrush flat, then switchbacks through a fir forest beside the canyon of Boulder Creek. At .7 mile, the trail runs along the edge of the 100-foot deep canyon.

At 1.5 miles, the path comes to an area of sagebrush, small firs, and aspens. At 1.7 miles, the trail crosses the creek to the east on logs. Now the route climbs beside a 20-foot chasm created by the creek in a crack in the bedrock. Beyond this, the trail zigzags along the edge of the forest and crosses the creek again on rocks to the west at 2.7 miles, 1400 vertical feet from the trailhead.

Unnamed peaks block the head of the canyon above as the route levels out into an upper valley. The trail threads rocks and sage-brush, then at 3.2 miles, it enters meadows that sparkle with red paintbrush, white bistort, and yellow buttercups. The trail may be confusing in the meadows, but is well blazed. At 3.7 miles, a

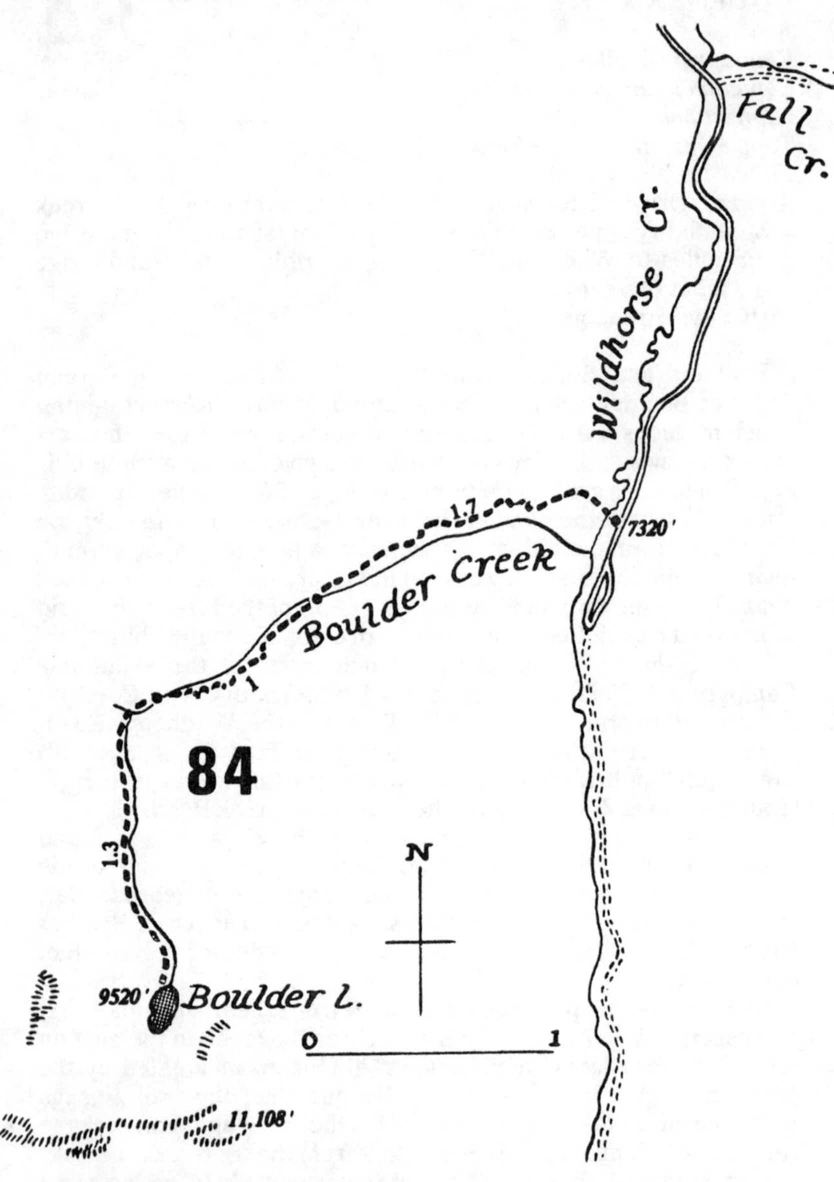

sketchy path climbs 300 vertical feet up the west side of the creek in the outlet's rocky canyon. The path reaches the lake at 4 miles.

MOOSE LAKE

85

Round trip: 10 miles
Elevation gain: 2255 feet
Highest point: 9455 feet
Topo map: Standhope Peak
Time: 8 hours
Access: Drive 22 miles northeast of Ketchum over Trail Creek
Summit to Copper Basin Road. Turn right (southeast) on a dirt
road, and drive 2.5 miles to Wildhorse Creek Road. Turn right
(south) and drive 4.5 miles to Fall Creek.
Difficulty: Strenuous

Jagged grey cliffs sweep up the the apex of a mountain wall
2300 feet above the head of Moose Lake. Below the wall two
sculptured granite ridges create giant rounded steps. Between
this wall and the granite ridges, small rocky peaks echo the higher
crags. The three lower ridges disappear on the west into a massive
mountain of grey granite. Above the little alpine upper lake that
hugs the east wall of the canyon, a throne-like rock tops a small
peak. Meadows, sifted with tiny flowers, and gnarled trees
surround this lake.

To reach the trailhead, drive northeast from Ketchum over Trail
Creek Summit. At 22 miles, turn right (southeast) on the Copper
Basin Road. At 2.5 miles, turn right (south) on Wildhorse Creek
Road and drive 4.5 miles.   Turn left (east) and drive
.3 mile to Fall Creek and park. South up Wildhorse Canyon, the
headwall includes a spire resembling the Matterhorn. The old
road shown on the topo map as going 2 miles further up Fall Creek
is closed to motor vehicles.

Begin the hike by wading the creek and walking up the old road
through sagebrush past a display of blazing star in season. To
save distance, take cutoff paths between road switchbacks in two
places. A trail turns south across the creek from the end of the
road at 2 miles. In the distance at the head of Fall Creek Canyon,
sharp peaks sit. A path up the south bank of Fall Creek also
reaches this crossing. This route passes the falls and has some
cross-country walking.

For the next mile, the trail wanders through level meadows
choked with willows. At a sign for Moose Lake at 3 miles, the trail
crosses Fall Creek on logs and turns southwest up the canyon of
the North Fork of Fall Creek. For 1 mile, the path climbs in four
large switchbacks not shown on the topo map. Across the canyon,
the light grey mountain wall behind Surprise Valley rises higher as
the trail climbs.

At 4 miles, the route levels to run along the creek across barren

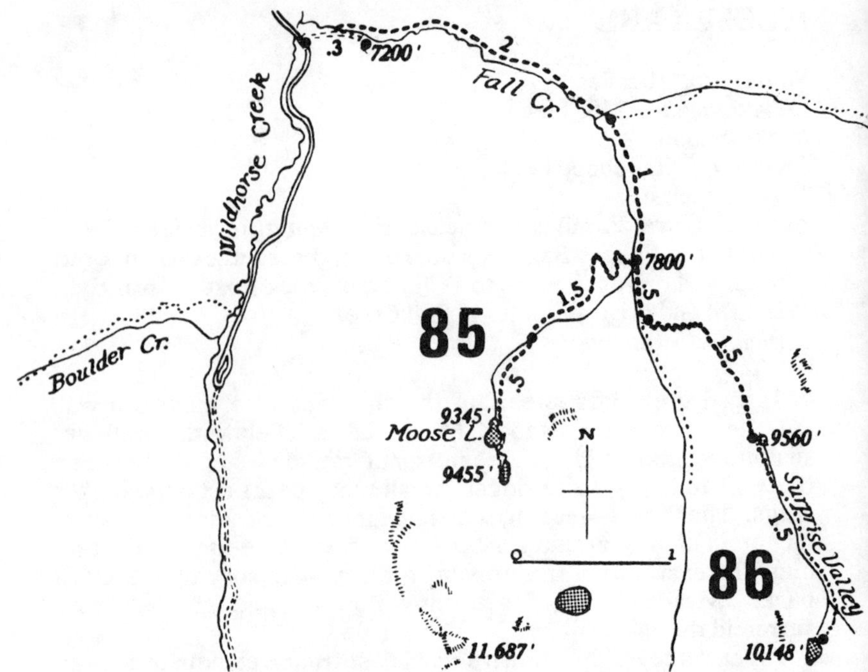

areas.   At 4.5 miles, the trail crosses the creek amid a cloud of
bluebells. Beyond here the path winds beside rock outcroppings
and a small meadow to the lake at 5 miles.   There are several
campsites. The higher lake can be reached by taking a path along
the east side of the lake to the inlet and walking up the inlet.

SURPRISE VALLEY AND LAKES

86

Round trip: 13 miles
Elevation gain: 2940 feet
This section: 3.5 miles and 2060 feet gain one-way
Highest point: 10,148 feet
Topo map: Standhope Peak
Time: 10½ hours to 2 days
Access: Drive 22 miles northeast of Ketchum over Trail Creek
   Summit to Copper Basin Road. Turn right (southeast) on a dirt
   road and drive 2.5 miles to Wildhorse Creek. Turn right (south)
   and go 4.5 miles to Fall Creek.
Ability: Expert

Just below Surprise Valley, a small, pale green lake floats on a
flat meadow under a double-pointed peak of slanting light grey

Surprise Valley

cliffs. The gables and towers of the cream-colored east canyon wall zigzag along up and down the canyon from this lake. Cracks running up at a 45 degree angle to the right decorate this wall, which is behind Bellas and Betty Lakes in Copper Basin.

Surprise Valley stretches up the canyon from the little lake. The .5 mile long valley contains stunted willows, scattered whitebark pines, squashy hummocks of turf, and a rainbow of wildflowers. Even in late August, the valley glows with paintbrush, cinquefoil, alpine sunflowers, and sapphire blue gentians. Talus rolls into the grass from a ridge of fractured cliffs hemming the meadows on the west. At the head of the canyon, rocks and tongues of grass run down to the pale green water of a second shallow lake. The wide triangle of Standhope Peak with crumbling grey cliffs etched with snow overlooks the lake. A few whitebark pines, flattened by the wind to shrubs less than four feet tall, cling to the barren benches. Flattened clumps of trees like these growing at timberline are called "krummholz", a German word meaning "crooked wood".

The trail to the first lake shows little sign of use, but the trail up to the valley and upper lake is non-existent; thus the hike promises solitude as well as scenery. At the west side of the first lake, the outlet has cut a gap in the canyon wall where this creek flows down into the canyon of Fall Creek. From this gap is a fine view across Fall Creek Canyon to jagged summits and dark cliffs.

For access directions for Fall Creek on the Wildhorse Creek

Road and for hiking directions for the first 3 miles of this hike, see Moose Lake. Beyond the Moose Lake junction at 3 miles, the Fall Creek Trail follows the creek at a distance through rocks and trees. The route climbs 250 feet before the unsigned Surprise Valley junction at 3.5 miles. The trail to the valley climbs 720 feet in .5 mile, zigzagging between boulders, small firs, and aspens. The path ducks under a high cliff, and at 4 miles, crosses a small round meadow near a spring. Beyond here, follow the faint trail with the aid of blazes and cairns. At 4.3 miles, the route enters a long narrow meadow where the first view of the cream-colored towers of the canyon wall appears. Beyond this meadow the trail wanders around boulders and trees to the first lake at 5 miles.

Beyond the first lake, only traces of the trail shown on the topo map exist. The route runs up between the talus and the stream on the west side of the creek at the west edge of the woods. Where the valley meadows begin at 5.5 miles, cross the creek to the left (east) side. Continue along the east edge of the meadow, staying in dry hillside grass where possible. At the upper end of the valley at 6.2 miles, the creek branches. The right (west) branch heads southwest up through a slot in the cliffs to the lake. The route circles left (east) into a small flat and crosses the west branch of the stream and then heads southwest up a slope of scree, dirt, and grass to the upper lake at 6.5 miles.

LOST RIVER DISTRICT — Copper Basin Area

BELLAS LAKES

87

Round trip: 6 miles
Elevation gain: 1600 feet
Highest point: 9440 feet
Topo map: Copper Basin (15′)
Time: 5½ hours
Access: Drive 22 miles northeast of Ketchum over Trail Creek Summit to Copper Basin Road. Turn right (southeast) and drive 11 miles to Copper Basin Loop Road. Turn south on dirt loop road and drive 6 miles to Bellas Canyon turnoff.
Difficulty: Moderate

Above the first Bellas Lake marches a row of jagged cream-colored cliffs with narrow black stripes. On the highest peak on this ridge, the black stripes form an eye and mouth for a mythical beast. On the west, two green meadows, each ribboned by an inlet, slope into the tiny green lake. A ridge of pleated cliffs hides behind a buff-colored rock knoll on the north. Behind the rock knoll, cream-colored talus leads to the top of Pyramid Peak. The

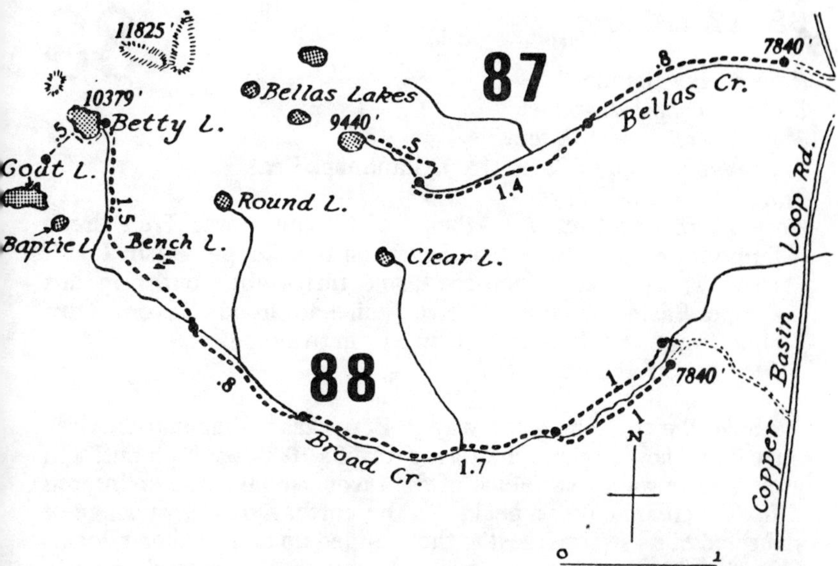

outlet below the lake tumbles beside the multiple trunks of white-bark pines to a grassy basin. Across Copper Basin, light green and copper peaks form a surrealistic mural.

To reach the trailhead, drive 22 miles northeast of Ketchum over Trail Creek Summit to the Copper Basin Road. Turn right (south-east) and drive 11 miles on a dirt road to the Copper Basin Loop Road. This road is muddy and hazardous early in the summer; inquire first about its condition before July 15. Take the south branch of the loop (turn right) and drive 6 miles to a sign for Bellas Canyon. Turn right (west) and drive .2 mile up a rocky track to the beginning of the trail.

The trail climbs along the stream through aspens and lodge-poles. Scarlet gilia, lupine, and yarrow lend Fourth of July colors to the way. At .8 mile, the path crosses the creek to the south bank on poles. The trail beyond the creek runs through large, dry meadows full of white mountain death camas, pale green elk thistle, blue whorled penstemon, and yellow cinquefoil. At 2.2 miles, the route enters a grassy basin containing clumps of tiny subalpine firs.

Here the path crosses the creek to the north bank below a fluffy waterfall. Next the trail makes a steep, wide switchback east through sagebrush. When the path returns to the creek, the way leads beside whitebark pines. Some of these are dead, and their twisted wood is dark gold. The path comes out into a flat meadow at 2.7 miles with a view of the white wall of peaks ahead. Then the trail climbs through a few trees to the first lake at 3 miles. The higher lakes may be reached by cross-country hiking.

BETTY LAKE

88

Round trip: 10 miles
Elevation gain: 2540 feet
Highest point: 10,379 feet
Topo maps: Copper Basin (15′), Standhope Peak
Time: 9 hours or 2 days
Access: Drive 22 miles northeast of Ketchum over Trail Creek
   Summit and turn right (southeast) on dirt Copper Basin Road.
   Drive 11 miles to a loop road, and turn right (south) on dirt
   Copper Basin Loop Road. Drive 7 miles to Broad Canyon. Turn
   right (west) and drive .5 mile up a primitive road.
Difficulty: Strenuous

Above the trail along the way to Betty Lake, diagonal crevices
filled with snow angle to the zigzag top of a 1000-foot high buff and
grey granite wall. Northeast of the turquoise lake rise splintered
cliffs of a cream-colored peak. To the north, a dark grey ridge of
slabs and talus sweeps west to the rounded tip of Standhope Peak.

Turf, rocks, and tiny alpine flowers such as pink kalmia
surround the above-timberline lake. A gap in a ridge on the south
shows the furrowed end of the rock wall. A .5 mile climb to this
gap presents a view of Goat Lake from above. This deep turquoise
lake sprawls on a shelf above the main canyon of Broad Creek and
below twin peaks on the end of the rock wall. Snow-filled fissures
join the pinnacles of the southern of these two peaks. A knife-
edged ridge attaches this peak to the triangular top and clawed
cliffs of the northern peak. Down the canyon across Copper Basin,
pointed copper mountains tint the sky.

To reach the trailhead, drive 22 miles northeast of Ketchum over
Trail Creek Summit. Turn right (southeast) on the Copper Basin
Road and drive 11 miles. Turn right (south) on the dirt Copper
Basin Loop Road and drive 7 miles to Broad Canyon. Turn right
(west) and drive .5 mile up the canyon on a primitive road to a "No
Motorized Travel" sign. The roads in Copper Basin can be muddy
and dangerous in early season. Call the ranger station in Mackay
if in doubt.

Park at the sign and begin hiking up the old road which soon
turns into a trail. The route climbs along the edge of a meadow full
of willows. At 1 mile, the path crosses to the north side of the
creek. Go downstream 100 yards to cross on a big log. There is an
alternate trail for this first mile. Turn right (north) from the "No
Motorized Vehicle" sign on a road that leads down into the
meadow. The road ends at a campsite beside the creek. A trail
starts here by crossing a log bridge. Then the path follows the
base of the mountain through a sagebrush flat and meets the other

trail just beyond the first creek crossing. This trail is useful in early season because of the bridge.

After the two trails merge, the trail passes through a series of dry meadows with a view of a pale pink and white ridge named the "White Mountains" on the south side of the canyon. At 2 miles the path is opposite a rose-grey rock knoll. The trail has climbed only 300 feet in these 2 miles. At 2.7 miles the route comes into a grassy area that slopes down to a creek crossing back to the south side. In early season, go upstream 25 yards to cross on a log.

The trail now begins to run underneath the 1000-foot row of cliffs. At 3 miles, the route reaches the head of the canyon. Rock benches form giant stairsteps that lead to the peaks at the head of the canyon. At 3.5 miles, the path crosses back over Broad Creek again to the north side, 1000 vertical feet from the trailhead. Early in the summer, this crossing will be a problem because there are no big logs. The high cliff wall continues to Goat Lake where the wall joins Standhope Peak.

Beyond this third creek crossing, the trail climbs an open hillside. 600 feet above the creek crossing at 3.7 miles, the path reaches a flat meadow with a swamp at the upper end named Bench Lake. Beyond here the way leads through whitebark pines, then ascends 200 feet in 200 yards over a bench. At 4.2 miles, the land flattens out again in another meadow where a bubbling stream meanders. At 4.5 miles the trail has climbed 600 feet from Bench Lake to a grassy basin with a good campsite at the end of the timber. There isn't much of a trail beyond this point.

The route to Betty Lake skirts the basin on the east and climbs 300 feet up a grassy ridge studded with rocks. The trail stays on the east side of the stream and does not cross as is shown on the map. The path disappears part way up the ridge, but the route to the lake at 5 miles is obvious. Baptie and Goat Lakes can be reached cross-country from the campsite in the timber by cutting across a bench to the southwest.

For a view of Goat Lake, climb southwest up a draw to a barren gap .5 mile and 400 vertical feet from Betty Lake. Horse riders would want to come to Goat Lake from below, but careful hikers could descend from this saddle to Goat Lake.

GREEN LAKE

89

Round trip: 8.4 miles
Elevation gain: 1600 feet
Highest point: 9600 feet
Topo map: Muldoon Canyon (15')
Time: 7 hours
Access: Drive 22 miles northeast of Ketchum over Trail Creek Summit to Copper Basin Road. Turn right (southeast) and drive 11 miles on dirt road to Copper Basin Loop Road. Turn right (south) and drive 10 miles on dirt. Turn right (southeast) and go 1.2 to 1.5 miles on primitive Muldoon Canyon Road. Four-wheel drive vehicles can drive 1.5 miles further to Green Lake jeep trail and up it for 2.5 miles.
Difficulty: Moderate

Charcoal grey peaks that are 1600 feet high and tinted rose and orange hem in Green Lake. Slanting, fissured cliffs on the south run up to a wedge-shaped peak. Below this peak, talus nibbles at the grass dusting the border of the milky, pale green lake. On the north, fractured rock bluffs and whitebark pines cover the bottom of an orange ridge of jumbled cliffs. Glacial debris mounds above the lake to the east. The only trees at Green Lake are a few whitebark pines, so the landscape is barren and strange. The high dark peaks cupping milky green water resemble a setting from another planet.

From the trail the sagebrush and grass lining Muldoon Canyon form a trough between rose-grey peaks. Near the head of the canyon, a black lava dome echoes the black peaks around Green Lake. An ore-loading bin and deep golden logs of a miner's cabin on Green Creek provide a pioneer setting. Above the cabin, twisted rails lead from a leaning shed to a tunnel in the cliffs.

To reach the trailhead, drive 22 miles to the Copper Basin Road northeast of Ketchum over Trail Creek Summit. Drive 11 miles southeast on the dirt road, and 10 miles south on the Copper Basin Loop Road. In early summer, Copper Basin Roads are very muddy; inquire first. Just beyond Starhope Campground, the road turns and goes north up the other side of the basin. 1 mile from the campground, take the primitive Muldoon Canyon Road. Drive 1.5 miles to a creek crossing. Mileage for this hike begins at this crossing. Passenger car drivers will want to stop where the road goes through puddles next to willows .2 mile before this point. Only four-wheel drive vehicles should attempt to drive beyond the creek crossing and then not until July 15. 1.5 miles beyond the creek crossing, walk up an unsigned jeep track that climbs southeast through sagebrush and then switches back to the north.

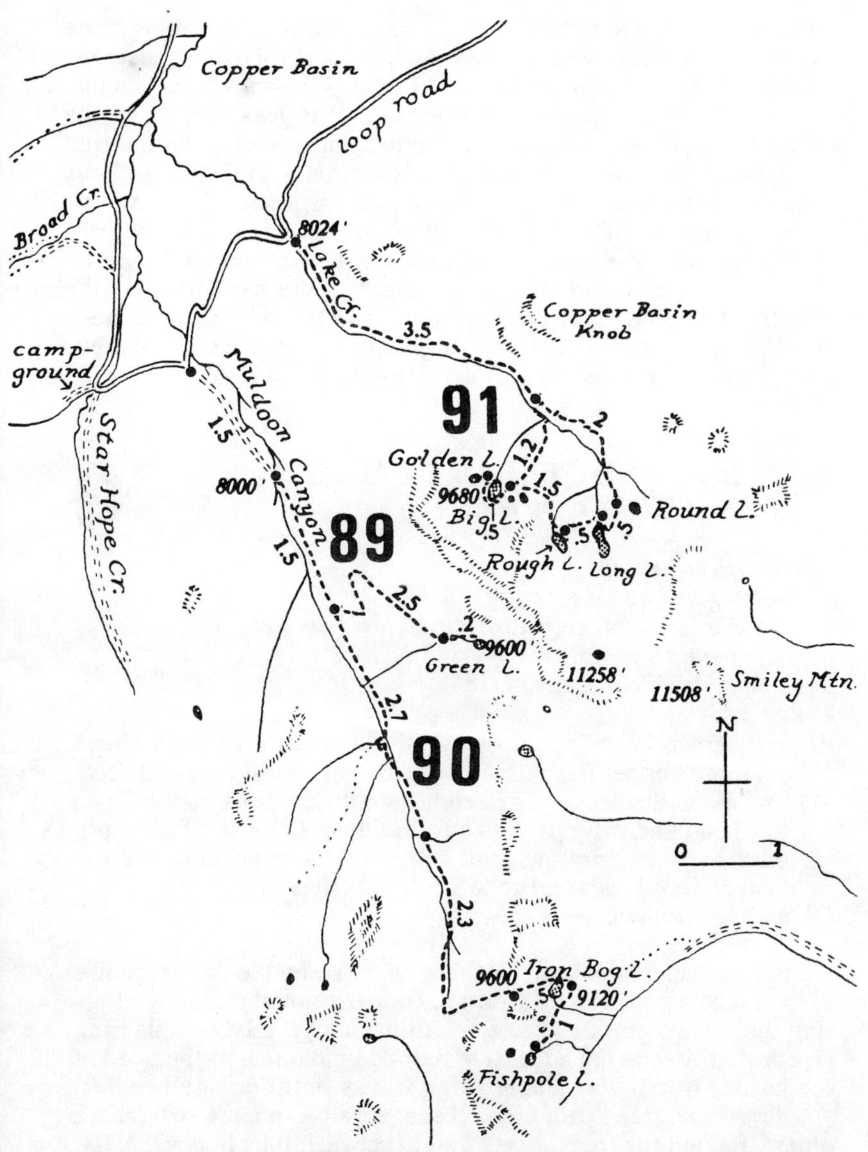

Near the end of a second switchback at 2.5 miles, the track passes an old ore-loading platform. The road next ascends a sagebrush ridge at the edge of the timber. Then the way branches twice; take either track. The jeep road winds south across the sagebrush to Green Creek at 3.7 miles. At 4 miles the track ends at a log cabin in a meadow. A few feet before the cabin, a road branches into the meadow and disappears. A few yards beyond this, a trail begins in the woods. This path passes a leaning mine shed and crosses Green Creek to the south bank. The creek tumbles 320 feet from the lake in .2 mile. The trail branches just beyond the crossing. Avoid the left path that goes straight up the edge of the gorge. In 100 yards, the two paths rejoin, and the trail cuts down the side of the gorge to cross back to the north bank above a waterfall. In late season, get drinking water at this crossing or from an inlet, because the lake tends to look murky.

Beyond this crossing, the trail runs in the stream for 25 yards. In early season, climb 20 feet at a notch in the rocks to avoid the water. When the path emerges from the water, it follows the creek to the lake at 4.2 miles. Signs of the species "Slobbus americanus" are very evident, so please pack out all litter.

IRON BOG AND FISHPOLE LAKES FROM MULDOON CANYON 90

Round trip: 16 miles
Elevation gain: 1840 feet
Elevation loss: 560 feet (return climb)
Highest point: 9600 feet
Topo map: Muldoon Canyon (15')
Time: 2 days
Access: Drive 22 miles northeast of Ketchum over Trail Creek Summit to Copper Basin Road. Turn right (southeast) and drive 11 miles on dirt road. Turn right (south) on dirt Copper Basin Loop Road and drive 10 miles to Muldoon Canyon. Turn right (southeast) on a primitive road and drive 1.2 to 1.5 miles. Four-wheel drive vehicles can go to 2.5 or 4.2 miles.
Difficulty: Strenuous

From above, Fishpole and Bobber Lakes resemble two turquoise eyes in a pale green face. Orange, copper-colored and grey crags ring the rolling grass and sagebrush basin of the lakes. Slanting layers of grey slate top a massive rounded mountain at the head of the basin. Nearby, a slender ridge waves burnt-orange needles.

Milky blue-green Iron Bog Lake sprawls among whitebark pines. Behind the trees, grass and sagebrush hills billow. A flat island made of a single slab of slate is in the lake. Northwest of the lake, little towers of dark grey and light orange march up the cliffs. Grey cliffs splashed with yellow green lichen drop down to the southwest edge of the lake. West of the pass at the head of Muldoon Canyon, a row of copper-colored battlements rises to a triangular summit. Part way up the canyon on the west wall, slabs of slate top a helmet-shaped black mountain. At the headwall of the canyon are a pointed peak and a row of jagged orange and black cliffs.

To reach Muldoon Canyon, drive 22 miles northeast of Ketchum over Trail Creek Summit to the Copper Basin Road. Turn southeast and drive 11 miles to the dirt Copper Basin Loop Road. In early summer, Copper Basin Roads are very muddy. Before July 15, call the ranger station in Mackay for the conditions before setting out. Turn south on the loop road and drive 10 miles to Muldoon Canyon.

Turn south on the signed primitive road and drive 1.5 miles to a creek crossing. Passenger cars should be left where the road goes through puddles beside willows .2 mile before this point. Only four-wheel drive vehicles should attempt to go beyond the creek crossing. The crossing looks flat and shallow, but the rocks are loose underneath. Those with four-wheel drive should not attempt the crossing before July 15. When this crossing is passable, four-wheel drive vehicles can be driven up to 4.2 miles further. Probably some drivers will want to park before the morass of mud and roots at Green Creek at 2.5 miles, or at the third crossing of Muldoon Creek at 3.2 miles. A crossing of Muldoon Creek at 3 miles is bridged, but the bridge is in bad repair. The crossing to the east at 3.2 miles is wide and muddy. Vehicles that make it across at this point can drive all the way to the end of the jeep trail at 4.2 miles. The track ends in a meadow below a sagebrush hill.

Mileage on this hike starts at the first crossing of Muldoon Creek at 1.5 miles. Copper Basin hikes are more scenic before mid-August, as most of the grass in the basin turns brown by then. Almost all of this hike is in the open with no shade, so it will be more pleasant on a cool day.

The road climbs and turns southwest past the bridged crossing of Muldoon Creek to the west at 3 miles. In 200 yards, a jeep trail continues west up a side canyon to a mine, but the Muldoon Canyon Road turns back down beside the creek. Those on foot will want to walk through a patch of trees to meet the road at the same elevation on the other side. At 3.2 miles just before the third crossing, the jeep track crosses a small deep side stream. Foot travelers will want to go 15 yards upstream to cross on a log. Wading will be necessary to cross back to the east on the track at the third crossing. As the track passes east of the black helmet-shaped peak, a series of small beaver ponds are strung on the creek like beads.

Beyond the end of the jeep trail at 4.2 miles, just before a small sagebrush hill in the center of the canyon, the unsigned pack trail first leads through a swamp towards large dead logs. The route is marked by an occasional post. Beyond this the trail goes through sagebrush and then crosses two swampy side streams. At

5.5 miles, the blazed trail climbs steeply to the left (east) of the main stream through woods. As the path climbs 400 feet in .5 mile, it crosses three branches of the main creek. When the trail reaches a shelf just under the row of cliffs at the head of the canyon, the route turns sharply left (northeast) beside springs bubbling out of moss. A sheep path leading west from the springs is not the trail.

The trail contours along a dry stony hillside towards a pass at 6.5 miles on the east wall of the canyon. The path disappears at the saddle but reappears 200 yards down the canyon towards Iron Bog Lake. The trail descends scree slopes past a level green shelf of wildflowers and whitebarks. Then the path goes through timber to Iron Bog Lake at 7 miles. To continue to Fishpole and Bobber Lakes, most hikers will want to take the trail which turns off the Left Fork of Iron Bog Creek Trail 100 yards below Iron Bog Lake. This trail crosses an open slope to the outlet, then passes two tiny ponds and a high rock knoll. Next the trail climbs sagebrush hills to Fishpole Lake at 8 miles.

Intrepid mountaineers can reach Fishpole Lake by climbing from the pass at 6.5 miles south .2 mile to a grassy saddle. This route then descends steep gullies and talus between cliffs to the lake at 7.2 miles. This route adds 160 feet to the elevation gain. Great caution is required, but not ropes. This saddle is a wonderful viewpoint for the day hiker who wants to see Fishpole Lake on the way to Iron Bog Lake but hasn't the extra time or energy to hike to Fishpole Lake on the trail. It is a 500-foot climb to return to the pass by the trail from Iron Bog Lake.

The distance to Iron Bog and Fishpole Lakes is much shorter from a primitive road up the Left Fork of Iron Bog Creek. This access makes the hikes only 4 to 6 miles round trip. However, the 8 mile primitive road up Iron Bog Creek and the Left Fork can be reached only from Antelope Guard Station. This guard station is 18 miles on a dirt road from the Arco-Mackay Highway (U. S. 93) or 23 miles from the Copper Basin Loop Road by way of Antelope Pass. The grade on the south side of Antelope Pass down to the guard station is also a primitive road. The dirt road to Antelope Guard Station from the Arco-Mackay Highway turns off U. S. 93 about 12 miles north of Arco. From the intersection of U. S. 20 and Highway 75 south of Bellevue (26 miles south of Ketchum), it is 64 miles to Arco.

Rough Lake

ROUND, LONG, ROUGH, BIG AND GOLDEN LAKES

91

Round trip: 13.7 miles (partial loop)
Elevation gain: 1680 feet
Highest point: 9680 feet
Topo maps: Copper Basin (15′), Muldoon Canyon (15′)
Time: 10 hours to 2 days
Access: Drive 22 miles northeast of Ketchum over Trail Creek
Summit; turn right (southeast) and drive 11 miles on dirt road.
Turn right (south) and follow dirt Copper Basin Loop Road
13 miles to Lake Creek.
Difficulty: Strenuous

From this loop trail, sharp white peaks behind Bellas Lakes in the distance contrast with folded orange and white rocks of Copper Basin Knob. Resembling pieces of licorice cake, tall peaks of crumbling black lava southwest of these five lakes face rounded hills of copper-colored talus.

Round Lake is beyond a swamp and boulder field below bare copper-colored and grey hills across from the wall of high black peaks that is southwest of all the lakes. Long Lake is amid granite benches and trees. Here three of the black peaks chimneyed with snow rise behind a glacier-sculptured rock ridge. Back down the canyon, a ridge of orange talus forms a lumpy backbone for Copper Basin Knob.

The pointed black lava mountains blotted with snow overshadow Rough Lake above granite benches and whitebark pines. At this lake north of the three main peaks, orange talus streaks a crumpled summit beside a row of cliffs that resemble the battlements of a castle. South of Big Lake, a black lava ridge looks like a monster with an ape-like head and triangular rump, with a backbone of enormous vertebrae between them. An orange dike in the rock of a sharp peak to the southwest is shaped like a boomerang. Sagebrush, grass, and whitebark pines grow around Big Lake and a swamp is at the upper end. Tiny tea-colored Golden Lake huddles under a bench of rock slabs below a peak with a blunt top and knife-like ridge. Pines cover rock peninsulas on the east side.

To reach the trailhead, drive 22 miles northeast of Ketchum over Trail Creek Summit to the dirt Copper Basin Road. Turn southeast and drive 11 miles to the Copper Basin Loop Road. Turn right (south) and follow the dirt road 13 miles to Lake Creek. An alternate route is to drive straight ahead 6 miles from the first loop road turnoff to the Copper Basin Guard Station. Turn southwest on the other end of the loop road and go 7 miles to Lake Creek. This takes as long or longer because this side of the loop road is rougher. Copper Basin Roads are hazardous in early season; inquire first.

An old jeep road leads through a gate and up Lake Creek Canyon, but is only open for .2 mile to motor vehicles. Most people park by the gate. The blazed trail and this old road don't always follow the same route. The trail first skirts a small meadow and then goes along the bottom of a prickly-looking ridge. Then the path climbs through trees and rock outcrops to reach a high sagebrush bench, which the trail follows for .5 mile.

At 1.3 miles, the route crosses a side stream and goes into the timber. At 2 miles the path skirts a large meadow. At 2.5 miles the trail wanders under rose and white cliffs on the side of Copper Basin Knob. At 3 miles the route passes a collapsing log cabin, then edges the east side of a long meadow. At the far end of the meadow at 3.5 miles, a sign points southwest for Big Lake where the Big Lake and Round Lake Trails meet to form a loop.

It is much easier to go to Round Lake first, because the climb to Big Lake from the junction is 960 feet in 1.2 miles, but the climb to the Round Lake turnoff is only 640 feet in 2 miles.

The unsigned Round Lake Trail crosses a stream at 3.7 miles and then bends left towards the canyon wall. At 4.5 miles, the path turns back towards the creek. At 4.7 miles at a small meadow, sharp black peaks laced with snow stick up to the southwest. The route crosses a boulder field and two streams at 5 miles and climbs a wooded ridge to the Round Lake turnoff at 5.5 miles. A sign points east 200 yards to the lake across a swamp and rocks.

To reach Long Lake, go .2 mile beyond Round Lake along the main trail, and take the left (south) branch of the trail at an unsigned junction to reach the lake at 6 miles. East of the lake, a big meadow contains two horse-tie racks. The main trail goes south along the east side of a long narrow tail of the lake. The trail crosses the outlet just below the end of the lake. The path then climbs 80 feet over a ridge to the west past some tiny snow ponds to a junction at 6.5 miles. Take the left (south) trail and climb 200 yards over a little hill to Rough Lake.

To go on to Big Lake from the junction, take the trail signed Golden Lake. This route descends to cross the outlet of Rough Lake well below the lake at 6.9 miles. Next the path ascends an open slope, then dips as it passes the tower-like end of a lava ridge. The path ascends a sloping meadow and passes a pale green pond at 7.7 miles with a view of the monster ridge. Beyond here, the trail passes a smaller pond, and reaches the lake at 8 miles. To go to Golden Lake, take a path around the upper end of Big Lake across a swamp to a sign for Golden Lake and climb over a little ridge to the lake at 8.5 miles.

To return from Big Lake to the beginning of the loop, turn north at the junction where the trail from Rough Lake reaches Big Lake. Stay on the trail that heads along a ridge top and avoid a path along the lakeshore. The trail drops down a hillside full of grass and buttercups and switchbacks through woods. Near the bottom of the main canyon, the trail crosses the outlet of Big Lake at 10 miles and skirts willows. The path threads the willows, crosses Lake Creek, and rejoins the main Lake Creek Trail at 10.2 miles. Returning via Lake Creek makes this hike 13.7 miles.

SAWTOOTH NATIONAL FOREST

KETCHUM DISTRICT — Trail Creek Area
(Pioneer Mountains)

PIONEER CABIN

92

Round trip: 7.4 miles
Elevation gain: 2500 feet
Highest point: 9460 feet
Topo map: Hyndman Peak
Time: 7 hours
Access: Drive 3.7 miles northeast of Ketchum on Trail Creek Road
    to Corral Creek. Turn right (east) and drive 3.5 miles on
    primitive road.
Difficulty: Strenuous

Pioneer Cabin

Pioneer Cabin is a rectangular, golden brown, board and batten cabin with a tarpaper roof. The cabin overlooks an orange and grey panorama of the Pioneer Mountains from a field of blue lupine. East of Pioneer Cabin, pleated grey Cobb Peak peers from behind the fluted sway-back top of Hyndman Peak. Handwerk Peak on the northeast clutches an orange double-pointed knob. The main ridge of this mountain points right at the cabin. On either side of this ridge, two U-shaped canyons ascend to a grooved headwall of small grey peaks. Between Hyndman and Handwerk Peaks, the corrugated mass of Duncan Ridge joins the headwall. From the trail below the cabin, successive blue ridges go off into the distance toward the Smoky Mountains. This view includes the pale green canyon and hills of Corral Creek which are ablaze with wildflowers in July.

To reach the trailhead, drive northeast of Ketchum on the Trail Creek Road 3.7 miles. Turn east and drive 3.5 miles on the primitive Corral Creek Road to the trailhead.

The trail crosses Corral Creek on a bridge, passes a register box, and follows a side branch of the creek in aspens and firs. At .5 mile, the path crosses a tiny side stream which is the last water on the trail in late summer. At .7 mile, the route crosses another smaller stream and goes into thick forest. The trail goes up in seven switchbacks, each 200 yards long. On the topo map, these are not shown as long as they really are.

At 2 miles the path straightens to follow a ridge up through open areas. Below on both sides, green grassy canyons follow the ridge. At 2.5 miles the trail flattens in a little basin often filled with

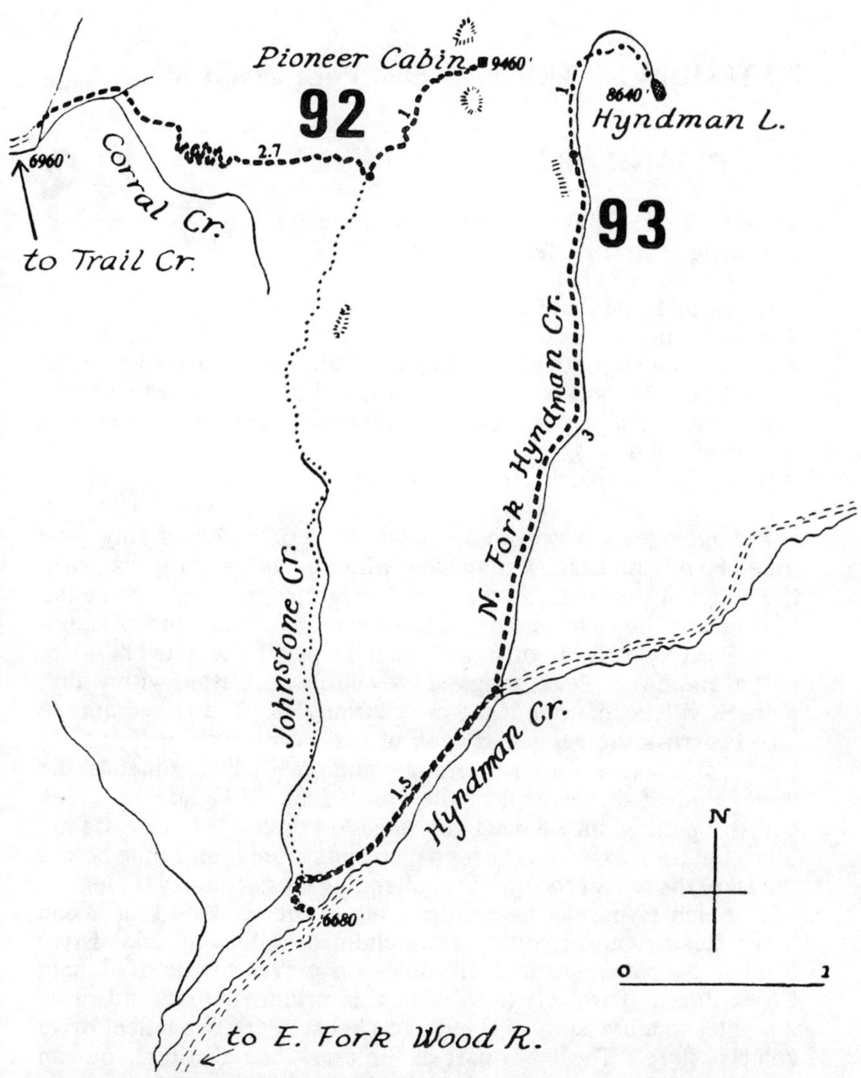

sheep. At 2.7 miles, the route reaches a junction with the Johnstone Creek Trail, 1900 feet above the trailhead. The unsigned trail up to the cabin turns south for 150 yards and then back to the northeast to follow a hilly ridge.

At the head of a tiny canyon, the route climbs between small grey and orange hills. Next the path edges talus as it follows a barren ridge towards orange crags in the distance. Finally the trail climbs the side of the ridge to a flat, grassy saddle. The cabin stands on the east edge of the saddle at 3.7 miles. Since the last 1.5 miles are not shaded, try to reach the cabin early on a hot day.

KETCHUM DISTRICT — East Fork Wood River Area

HYNDMAN LAKE

93

Round trip: 11 miles (2.5 miles cross-country)
Elevation gain: 1960 feet
Highest point: 8640 feet
Topo map: Hyndman Peak
Time: 9 hours
Access: 5 miles south of Ketchum on Highway 75, turn east on the East Fork Wood River Road and drive 8.5 miles. Turn north on primitive Hyndman Creek Road and drive 2.5 miles (4 miles with four-wheel drive).
Ability: Expert; partly cross-country

A huge meadow woven with wildflowers cushions tiny pale green Hyndman Lake. Orange and white boulders of quartz choke the outlet of the lake. To the east, the lumpy grey and orange top of Duncans Ridge meanders. The pale orange backbone of Handwerk Peak to the north turns grey as it drops off like a lovers' leap. Left of Handwerk Peak, a jagged grey cliff wall, netted with white, merges with burnt orange and cream triangles. The view from the lake is across the rugged canyon of the North Fork of Hyndman Creek to Pioneer Cabin. Orange and grey cliffs squeeze the upper end of the canyon of the North Fork of Hyndman Creek before opening into a vast dry meadow below Pioneer Cabin. Since the trail shown on the topo map ends more than 1 mile before the lake, the rest of the hike is challenging cross-country travel.

To reach Hyndman Lake, turn east on the East Fork of Wood River Road 5 miles south of Ketchum on Highway 75. Drive 5 miles on pavement and 3.5 miles on gravel to the Hyndman Creek Road. Turn left (north) on this primitive road and drive 2.5 miles to a crossing of Hyndman Creek. Park two-wheel drive vehicles here. The main part of the creek has a bridge, but an overflow of the creek beyond the bridge goes through river stones and mud. Four-wheel drive vehicles can go another 1.5 miles to the beginning of the trail, but hike mileage starts from the bridge.

This 1.5 miles of jeep road winds along the side of a sagebrush ridge above the creek. Up the canyon, grey cliffs of a peak ahead ripple to a rounded top. At 1.5 miles the road crosses the North Fork of Hyndman Creek, where a sign, "Dougan Pass - 4, Corral Creek - 6", points up the creek. Just before the creek a jeep track leads up to the left across the grass. From the end of this, a path goes uphill, through a fence, and into blazed aspen trees at

Hyndman Peak from Pioneer Cabin

1.7 miles. It is easier to connect with the blazed trail by going up this jeep track than by traveling along the creek.

After these aspen trees, the trail descends to the creek bank for 150 yards. Then the path winds along above the creek through sagebrush and aspens. Because of the large areas of sagebrush, this hike is best for a cool day.

A massive grey lava bluff overshadows the side canyon of Button Creek at 2.5 miles. At 3.2 miles, beyond a large sagebrush flat, the path enters mixed aspen and firs above a wide meadow and is more distinct. The trail disappears again at 3.7 miles in an open area, but cairns mark the way. Just beyond here, the route goes into aspens, firs, and shrubs on a steep hillside. This is shown as chapparal on the topo map. At 4.2 miles the path crosses a scree slope opposite a side stream falling down the canyon wall. This stream isn't on the topo map. Then the trail runs through plants and willows right beside the creek. Next the path climbs up and down where the trail has recently been repaired. At 4.5 miles in a talus field under cliffs on the canyon wall, the trail ends, even though the topo map shows it continuing .5 mile.

To continue cross-country to the lake, go gingerly down to the creek to go along under the talus and a washed-out section of the creek bank. In early season, the talus must be crossed due to high water. Once the trail ends, the way is rough with small logs, sticks, holes, and rocks hidden by plants, so be careful. Beyond the washed-out bank, climb up and walk along the top of the high, steep river bank. Traces of a path may occur occasionally. At 4.7 miles, a vast basin of sagebrush and grass opens on the west side of the creek opposite a wooded canyon wall on the east. At 5 miles where a small tongue of grass pokes up into the forest across the creek, drop down and cross the creek.

Climb this grassy tongue, then head northeast into the trees and go up a tiny ridge, shown on the topo map as the least steep route. After 400 vertical feet of this forest, the route reaches the talus at the outlet of the lake. Go around the talus to the lake at 5.5 miles.

JOHNSTONE PASS AND BOX CANYON LAKES   94

Round trip: 8 miles
Elevation gain: 2120 feet
Elevation loss: 440 feet (return climb)
Highest point: 10,000 feet
Topo map: Grays Peak
Time: 7 hours
Access: 5 miles south of Ketchum on Highway 75, turn east on the East Fork Wood River Road; go 5 miles on pavement, 5.5 miles on gravel, and 4 miles on primitive road to the road's end.
Difficulty: Strenuous

Spindles on a cream-colored mountain wall cluster above the west end of misty green Upper Box Canyon Lake. Curved bands of burnt orange accent the cream-colored wall. The lake is behind whitebark pines on a sandy bench. On the north, grey slabs cascade from a pointed peak. The trail up the open rocky East Fork of the Wood River Canyon to Johnstone Pass goes underneath dark red and light grey striped peaks. The route leads towards a pyramidal grey prong and the burnt-orange and cream-colored mountain wall. The trail up the canyon wall to the pass zigzags in accordion pleats to a notch in the rocks at 10,000 feet. From the notch, view the canyon of the Little Wood River and the black and copper-colored peaks in Copper Basin. Lower Box Canyon Lake is about 800 feet below the upper lake in timber below a tall peak faced with dark grey cliffs.

To reach the trailhead, turn east on the East Fork of Wood River Road 5 miles south of Ketchum on Highway 75. Drive 14.5 miles to the end of the road. The surface changes from pavement to gravel at 5 miles, and from gravel to primitive at 10.5 miles. Those with passenger cars may want to leave their vehicles just beyond the Mascot Mine at 14 miles. Before July 15, a wet area 1 mile before the mine and two small creeks near it may be problems.

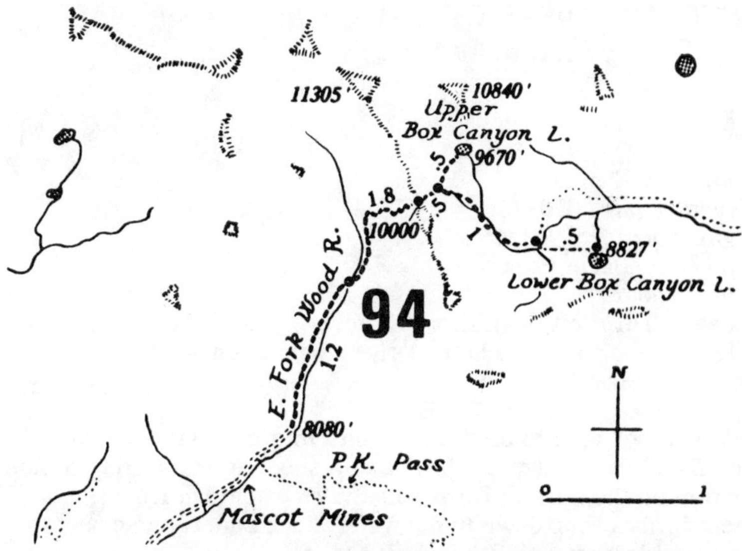

The trail begins at a register box and climbs along the west side of the creek. The path levels in a meadow at .2 mile below a striped dark red mountain splashed with white. At 1 mile, the route enters a patch of trees before crossing the creek in a flat, open area at 1.2 miles. Beside the trail, the stream swishes over bedrock among pink mimulus, bluebells, and cinquefoil. The path trudges up the creek among tiny firs for .5 mile as the hiker comes closer to the dramatic grey obelisk. Three waterfalls ribbon the granite slopes near this prong.

At 2 miles, where the trail begins to climb the sandy canyon wall, is a sign "Johnstone Pass - 1, Upper Box Canyon Lake -2". Above an abandoned ore car, the trail makes two long bends through a grove of whitebark pines. Then the route zigzags up the sandy gully that leads to a notch on the skyline. The hiker's feet slide back with each step in the sand. Gnarled whitebarks cling to the sculptured cream-colored outcroppings. As the trail ascends, the grey point sinks into the grey-striped canyon wall.

After climbing 1000 feet in 1 mile, the path threads the notch, then switchbacks down the other side. Next to a small stream at 3.5 miles, an unsigned path turns left (north) for the upper lake. This route heads 160 feet up a grassy hill to the lake at 4 miles. Several campsites are among the pines along the south shore. To reach the lower lake, descend Box Canyon on the trail for 1 mile, and head east .5 mile cross-country at a flat area to the lake. Going to the lower lake will add 3 miles to the round trip and 800 feet to the return climb.

KETCHUM DISTRICT — Wood River Area
(Smoky Mountains)

BAKER LAKE

95

Round trip: 2 miles
Elevation gain: 870 feet
Highest point: 8796 feet
Topo map: Baker Peak
Time: 3 hours
Access: Turn left (south) off Highway 75 at Baker Creek Road
   15 miles north of Ketchum. Drive 9.6 miles on dirt road.
Difficulty: Easy

A 400-foot rose-colored cliff slants into pink talus above oval blue Baker Lake. Trees, shrubs, and shooting stars grow beside the trail on the north. Terns sometimes catch fish from the lake. These birds swoop down to the water, duck under, and come up a few seconds later with fish in their beaks.

To reach the trailhead, drive 15 miles north of Ketchum on Highway 75. Turn left (south) on the dirt Baker Creek Road and drive 8.2 miles to the trail sign located 3.5 miles beyond the Norton Creek Road.

Across a branch of Baker Creek, the trail climbs west up sage-brush and lupine-covered ridges. Then the path goes through stands of firs and lodgepoles and across hillsides embroidered with flowers to the lake at 1 mile. On the way up the trail, the view southwest is up a canyon to the rounded top of Baker Peak.

Baker Lake makes an easy family outing. Start early since the trail is in the sun most of the way. Carry water to avoid 100-yard trips to the creek from the trail. Two or three over-used campsites show that this hike would be best as a day hike. The beginning of the road is in the Sawtooth National Recreation Area, but the rest of the hike isn't.

NORTON LAKES

96

Round trip: 4.4 miles
Elevation gain: 1460 feet
Highest point: 9107 feet
Topo map: Baker Peak
Time: 5 hours
Access: Turn left (south) off Highway 75 at Baker Creek, 15 miles
   north of Ketchum and drive 6 miles on dirt road. Turn right
   (northwest) and drive 1 mile on primitive road.
Difficulty: Moderate

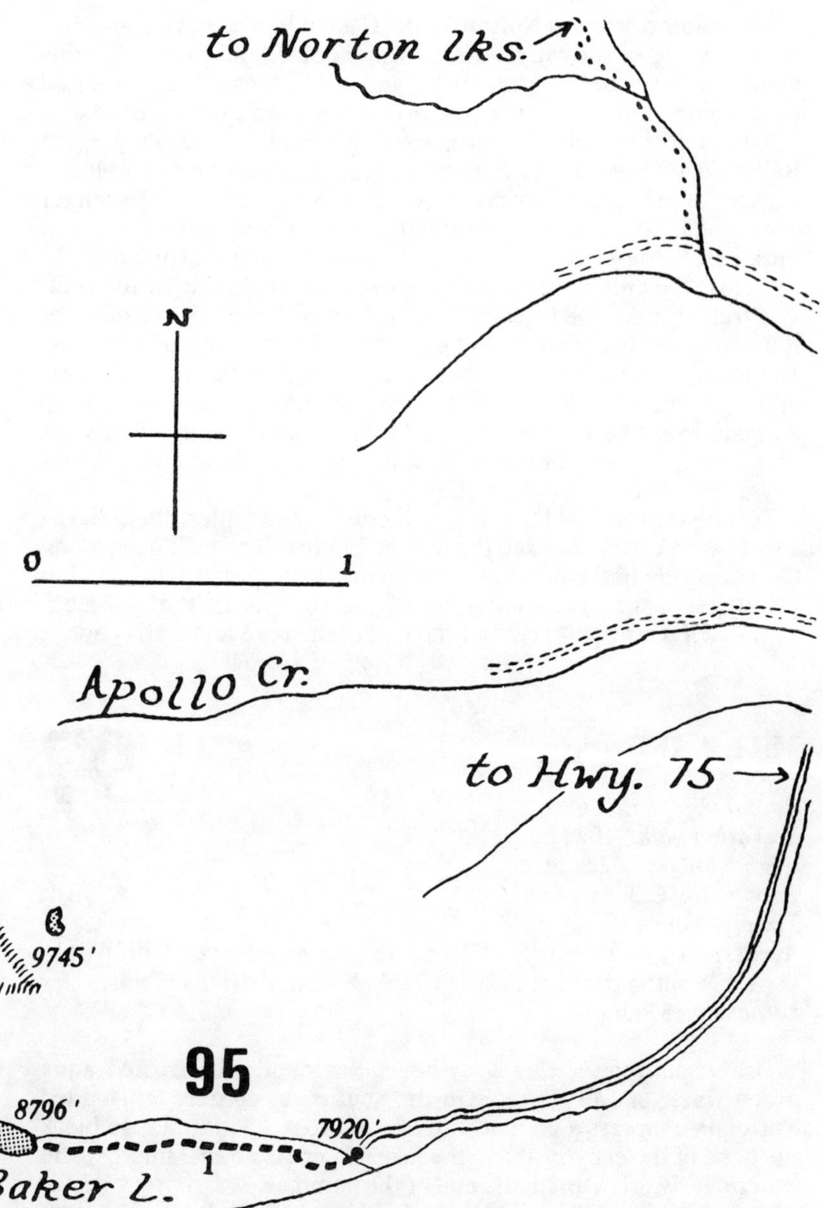

From above, lower Norton Lake resembles a great glowing emerald. On one side of the lake is a gravel beach. On the other side, white talus rises to a small peak. Along the inlet joining the two lakes grows a garden of bluebells, pink mimulus, and forget-me-nots. Talus and grass circling the highest lake lead to the richly-colored crags of Norton Peak. East of this lake, rock needles prickle on top of the canyon wall. Brown, buff, and rose stripe this wall. Along the lower trail, yellow seneca, blue whorled penstemon, and red paintbrush form a palette of primary colors.

To reach the trailhead, turn south off Highway 75 on the dirt Baker Creek Road 15 miles north of Ketchum and drive 6 miles to Norton Creek. Turn northwest on a primitive road. Passenger cars should not have trouble driving 1 mile further to the trailhead. Park before the road crosses the creek in a deep gravel gulch.

Across the creek, turn right (north) to the beginning of the trail. The trail ascends the forested west side of the creek. At .5 mile the route crosses a side creek and continues up a flowery hillside. At 1.5 miles the trail passes below talus and cliffs where pikas, making their plaintive cries of "peep, peep", live. These little animals look like miniature rabbits with smaller ears. Pikas cut grass for hay and store it both in and outside their dens. Their haystacks are occasionally as tall as 18 inches.

Just below the first lake, the trail crosses the outlet, then makes a wide switchback to reach the lake at 2 miles. The trail goes along the north side of the lower lake to the inlet and then up it .2 mile to the upper lake. The beginning of the road is in the Sawtooth National Recreation Area, but the rest of the road and trail is not.

MILL LAKE   **97**

Round trip: 4 miles
Elevation gain: 1020 feet
Highest point: 8222 feet
Topo map: Galena
Time: 4 hours
Access: 19 miles north of Ketchum, turn left (west) off Highway 75 onto primitive Prairie Creek Road and drive 2.2 miles.
Difficulty: Moderate

Driftwood upon a dark grey beach surrounds the frosted aqua green water of Mill Lake. On the southwest corner, talus-sided Norton Peak wears a pointed cap of solid rock. Square crags block the head of the canyon above the lake. There is no real inlet, so the water nearly dries up by the end of the summer.

To reach the trailhead, turn left (west) off Highway 75 about 19 miles north of Ketchum onto the primitive Prairie Creek Road and drive 2.2 miles. At the sign for Mill Lake, park and walk south on a jeep track that crosses Prairie Creek and goes into the forest.

At .5 mile the jeep trail crosses Mill Creek to the west. The jeep

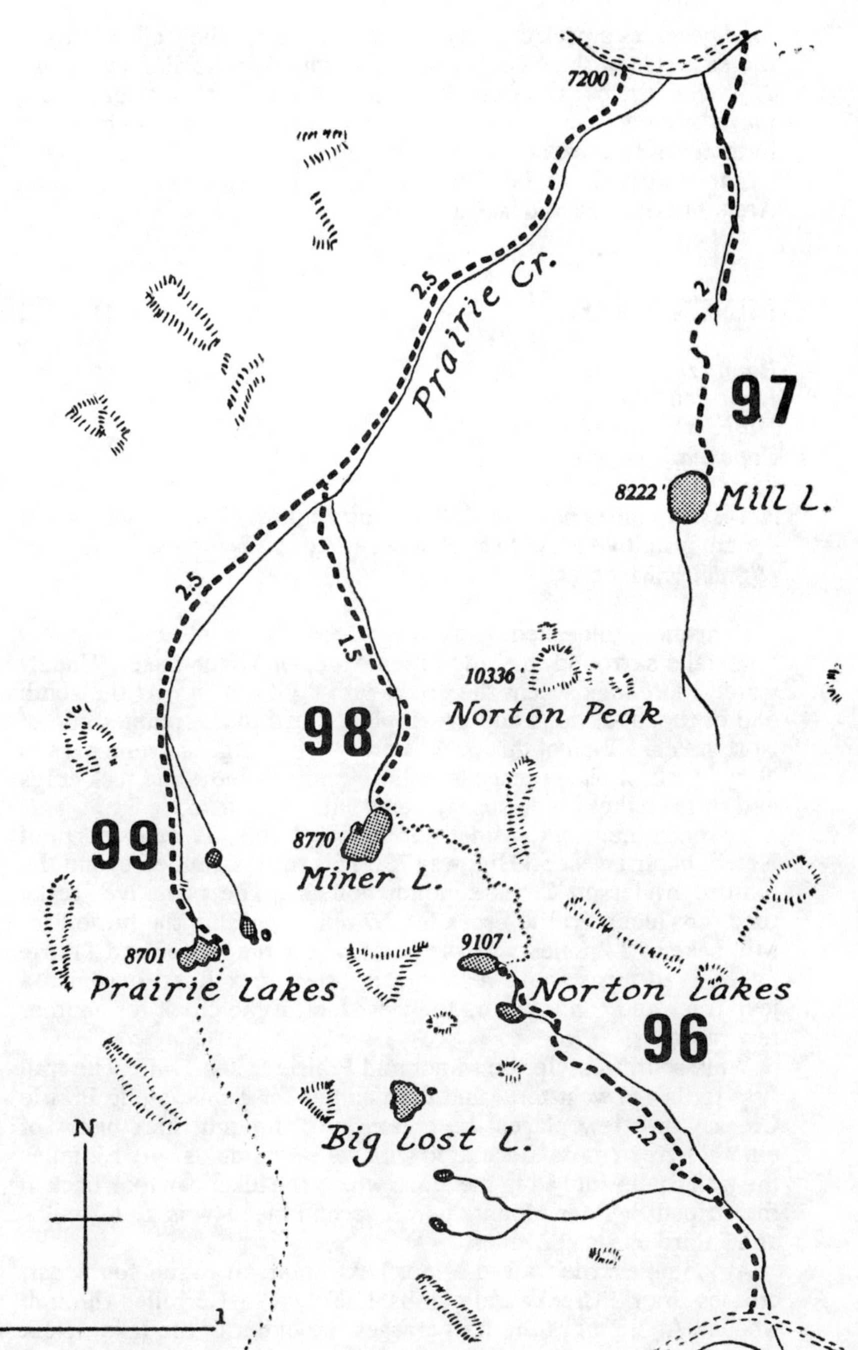
7200'
2.5
Prairie Cr.
2
97
8222' Mill L.
2.5
1.5
10336'
Norton Peak
98
8770'
Miner L.
99
8701'
Prairie Lakes
9107'
Norton Lakes
96
Big Lost L.
22
N
0   1

road becomes a pack trail at .7 mile. At 1 mile, the trail returns to the east side of the creek and enters a meadow of wildflowers. At 1.3 miles, the path crosses the stream, but here the stream is dry much of the summer. At 1.5 miles, the trail climbs through rocky hummocks and reaches the lake at 2 miles.

The Prairie Creek Road is in the Sawtooth National Recreation Area, but the trail and lake are not.

MINER LAKE   98

Round trip: 8 miles
Elevation gain: 1570 feet
Highest point: 8770 feet
Topo map: Galena
Time: 6½ hours
Access: 19 miles north of Ketchum on Highway 75, turn left (west)
   onto primitive Prairie Creek Road and drive 2.7 miles.
Difficulty: Moderate

Driftwood, bleached and silvered by the sun, and feathery horsetails surround the jade green water of Miner Lake. Underwater, more logs accent the green with light brown. At the south end of the lake, talus and green plants lead to the pointed top of Norton Peak. East of this peak, a primitive trail goes over a pass to Norton Lakes. Talus at the lakeshore congeals into solid rock crags and cliffs on the ridge above the east side of the lake.

To reach the trail to Miner and Prairie Lakes, 19 miles north of Ketchum turn west off Highway 75. This turn is 1 mile beyond the road to Anderson Creek summer homes. The primitive, rocky road runs along Prairie Creek for 2.7 miles, passing the turnoff for Mill Lake at 2.2 miles. At the point where the Miner and Prairie Lakes Trail turns southwest, the Prairie Creek Road becomes a jeep track and continues up the west fork of the creek for another few yards.

Walk southwest up the Miner and Prairie Lakes Trail. The trail first fords the west fork, and then climbs for 1 mile along Prairie Creek. In a few places the creek flows through thick banks of emerald green moss, decorated with yellow mimulus. At 1.2 miles the trail comes into a big meadow, where the hiker can look back at the striped Boulder Mountains. A second meadow is at 1.7 miles and a third one is at 2 miles.

At 2.5 miles, the trail to Miner Lake splits off to the southeast, crosses Prairie Creek, and climbs 1100 feet in 1.5 miles through woods. At 3.5 miles the trail crosses the outlet of the lake. Next the path enters a meadow of blue whorled penstemon and red paintbrush. The trail continues gently through forest and meadow below a talus ridge to the lake at 4 miles.

The Prairie Creek Road is in the Sawtooth National Recreation Area, but the trail and lake are not.

PRAIRIE LAKES

99

Round trip: 10 miles
Elevation gain: 1500 feet
This section: 2.5 miles with 1020 feet gain
Highest point: 8701 feet
Topo map: Galena
Time: 7½ hours
Access: 19 miles north of Ketchum, turn left (west) off Highway 75 onto primitive Prairie Creek Road and drive 2.7 miles.
Difficulty: Moderate

Logs thatched with bright green grass float on the apple green water of the largest Prairie Lake. The lake is so shallow that rust brown patches of lake bottom show through the pale green water. At the edge of the lake, a few silvered dead trees stand with their feet in the water. Twisted stripes of chocolate brown etch the face of a peak south of the lake. To the west, lime green grass splashes the rocks of a bare ridge. Furrowed and cracked buff-colored peaks line Prairie Creek Canyon below the lake.

For directions for reaching the trailhead and for the first part of the trail description, see Miner Lake. The trail to the lakes continues up Prairie Creek from the Miner Lake junction through forest and open hillsides and past granite spurs.

1.2 miles from the junction, the trail passes right under cliffs on the west canyon wall. At 2.2 miles in a swampy meadow, the trail crosses Prairie Creek, now tiny, to reach the lake at 2.5 miles. There is a large campsite on the south shore. Two tiny ponds are to the east over a rise 200 yards off the trail. A third pond hides .5 mile to the northwest. These ponds complete the Prairie Lakes.

The road is in the Sawtooth National Recreation Area, but the trail and lakes are not.

FAIRFIELD DISTRICT — Vienna Area
(Smoky Mountains)

HISTORY OF VIENNA AND SAWTOOTH CITY

In 1878, Levi Smiley and T. B. Mulkey discovered a quartz vein at the head of Smiley Creek and staked claims. Three settlements grew up as a result: Vienna on Smiley Creek, Sawtooth City on Beaver Creek, and Eureka in Alturas Lake Creek Canyon. In 1880, the owners of the Pilgrim Mine at Sawtooth City built a toll road over Galena Summit to the mine and brought in two mills.

The Vienna Mine was the largest mine in Smiley Creek Canyon. By 1882, there were fifty buildings in Vienna, including fourteen saloons and a sawmill. A twenty stamp mill was built that was a duplicate of the General Custer Mill at Custer. The Alturas Lake Creek Canyon area had several mines but no mill.

In 1883 and 1884, development was at its height after families began coming to live in these towns in 1882. In 1886, the road up Alturas Lake Canyon to Atlanta was widened. In 1892, a fire in the Silver King Mine at Vienna suddenly ended mining in the area, leaving 20,000 cords of cut and stacked wood in the canyon and near the mill.

SMILEY CREEK TRAIL FROM VIENNA TO DIVIDE BETWEEN SMILEY CREEK AND WEST FORK BIG SMOKY CREEK 100

Round trip: 6 miles
Elevation gain: 1440 feet
Highest point: 9040 feet
Topo map: Frenchman Creek
Time: 5½ hours
Access: Turn south off Highway 75 onto dirt Smiley Creek Road 200 yards west of Smiley Creek Lodge and drive 7 miles. The trail begins 200 yards beyond the turn for Vienna.
Difficulty: Moderate

At Vienna only one cabin, leaning with age, still stands. North of the cabin, an orange peak sprouts red and orange outcrops. At the divide between Smiley Creek and the West Fork of Big Smoky Creek, a granite ridge holds jointed pillars. South of here is the green and beige country of the South Fork of the Boise River. This

divide provides access via a moderately-used trail south down the West Fork of Big Smoky Creek and up Helen Creek to Snowslide and Paradise Lakes, about 7 miles from the trailhead. To the southwest down Emma Creek, the hiker can reach a road up the South Fork of the Boise at 5.5 miles.

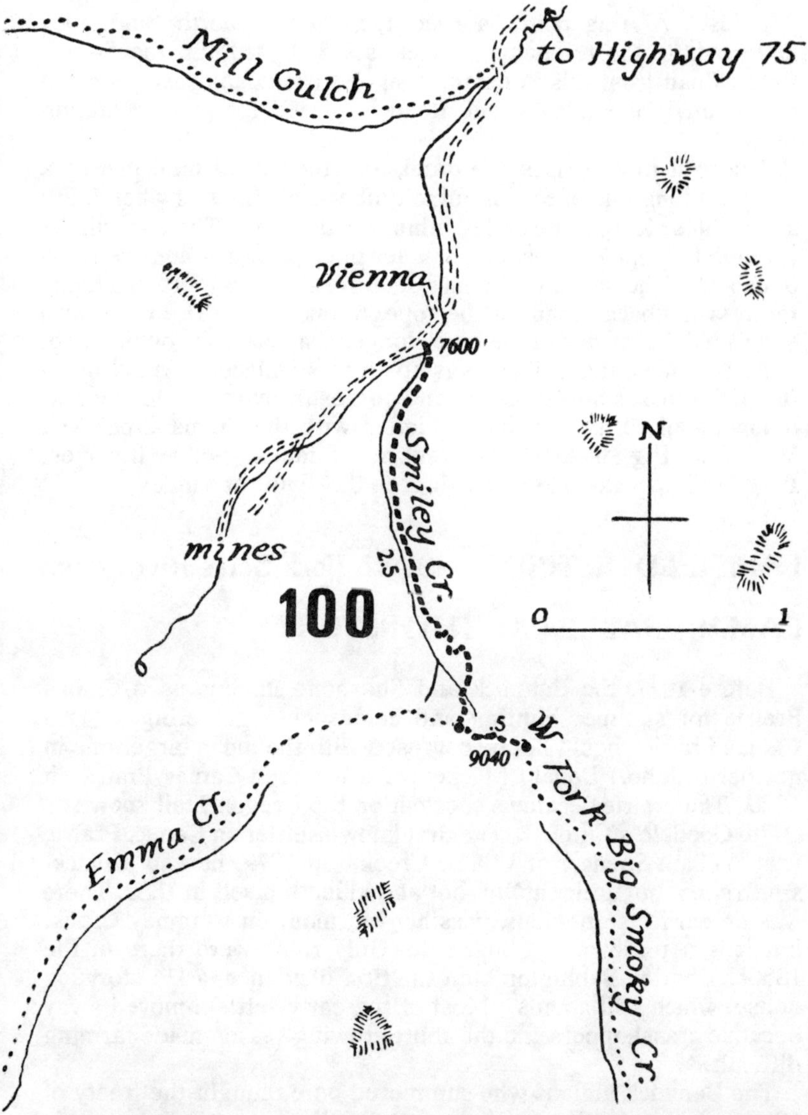

To reach the trailhead, turn left (south) off Highway 75 about 200 yards west of the bridge over Smiley Creek near Smiley Creek Lodge. Drive on the dirt road up the west bank of Smiley Creek for

7 miles.   At this point, a road turns right (north) and goes 200 yards to the remnants of Vienna.   200 yards up the Smiley Creek Road from this junction, a signed trail leads east.   Beyond this point, the Smiley Creek Road is posted for private mining property.

The trail first crosses the creek and then at .2 mile passes a 100-yard long pile of rotting mine timbers, abandoned when a fire at the Silver King Mine ended mining in the area.   The trail climbs through lodgepole pines past smaller piles of timber and the ruins of cabins.   The second mile has been rerouted so there are many more switchbacks than on the topographic map.   The route also stays on the east side of the creek longer than is shown on the map.

At 1.5 miles, the trail zigzags up a grassy hillside.   At 2.2 miles the path crosses Smiley Creek and passes through a little meadow below small cliffs to reach a junction with the Emma Creek and West Fork Big Smoky Creek Trails at 2.5 miles.   Follow the West Fork Trail up a steep forested slope to the divide at 3 miles.

FAIRFIELD DISTRICT — South Fork Boise River Area

CAMAS PRAIRIE (SOUTH) HISTORY

Before 1877, the Bannock and Shoshone Indians used Camas Prairie for summer hunting and camas bulb gathering.   (This Camas Prairie should not be confused with the much larger one in northern Idaho.) Donald Mackenzie discovered Camas Prairie in 1820.   The prairie became a shortcut on the Oregon Trail known as "Tim Goodale's Cutoff".   The first known settler on Camas Prairie was William Spencer at Willow Creek.   In 1879, he had a blacksmith shop, but accidentally shot and killed himself in 1880.   There was an earlier settlement, possibly Mormon, on Chimney Creek, but it is not known who made it.   Only ruins were there in the 1880s.   Charley Babington built the first residence, a 1½ story log house, which still stands.   Most of the early settlers moved away because grasshoppers and the short growing season made farming difficult.

The Bannock Indians who summered here thought the treaty of 1869 gave them rights to "Kamas Prairie".   Through an error this was written "Kansas Prairie", so the whites disregarded the Indians' rights because there was no Kansas Prairie in Idaho.   One reason the Bannock War occurred was that the Bannocks didn't like the settlers' pigs digging up the camas bulbs.

The first town was Soldier, 2 miles north of Fairfield, established by Jimmy Peck in 1880.   The first post office was at Corral.   Started in 1881, this post office is still operating.   Soldier was named after a party of soldiers from Fort Boise who once had camped there while controlling Indians. By 1910, there were 1800 settlers on Camas Prairie. The coming of the railroad in 1911 caused the town of Soldier to be moved south and it was rechristened "Fairfield". Camas Prairie later lost population and by 1970, it had only 700 residents.

ROSS FORK LAKES

101

Round trip: 24 to 25.5 miles
Elevation gain: 2400 to 3040 feet
Highest point: 8600 feet
Topo maps: Ross Peak, Marshall Peak, Atlanta East, Newman Peak
Time: 3 days
Access: Drive 18 miles north of Fairfield over Couch Summit or 25 miles east of Featherville along the South Fork of the Boise River (both are dirt roads). Then drive north over Fleck Summit 9 miles on dirt road and 1 mile on primitive road to Emma Creek.
Difficulty: Strenuous; expert ability for horse trail

Two points on top of 300-foot cliffs make the peak above the upper Ross Fork Lakes resemble a black cat. This peak is the highest point on a ridge of dark, jagged cliffs. The highest Ross Fork Lake sprawls in a swamp under a cirque below these cliffs. Below this lake the blue water of Ross Lake #4 laps whitened dead logs and green turf. On the west, rock benches fall into the water beside a high sandy ridge. The trail to the lakes passes through a series of dry meadows with a few scattered rocks and lots of wildflowers. Part way up the canyon, a peak in a side canyon resembles a big tooth stuck on the side of a wall. This tooth overlooks Ross Fork Lake #1.

Access to the lakes is from Ross Fork Basin, which is a level wooded area along the Ross Fork of the South Fork of the Boise. In the Basin, flats of sagebrush and grass interrupt the woods. Like a forest of granite Christmas trees, pointed outcrops stud sandy peaks along the canyon walls. The 100-yard wide river bed of white stones winds through the basin carrying the water of the Ross Fork.

To reach the Ross Fork area, drive 18 miles north of Fairfield over Couch Summit. The first 10 miles of the road are paved. Then drive north over Fleck Summit and along the upper South Fork of the Boise River. At 7.6 miles, the road passes the Methodist Camp. At 7.7 miles, keep straight ahead at an unsigned junction, and at 8.6 miles, keep right where the Bear Creek Road turns left. At 8.9 miles is a small campground. Leave passenger cars here. Beyond the campground the road becomes primitive and very rocky. At 10 miles (28 miles from Fairfield) is the Emma Creek Road junction and ford. The rest of the access depends on the type of vehicle and the driver's judgment.

Drivers of two-wheel drive trucks can take the right fork of the road north at the Emma Creek Ford. Then where this road rejoins the left branch at 1 mile at the base of a hill just past a smaller ford of Emma Creek, they can drive west and south back down the left branch to the signed intersection of the Ross Fork Machine and Horse Trails. Hike mileage starts here. This junction is .7 mile up the left fork from the big ford. (The horse trail is a jeep trail for the first .7 mile.) An alternative is to leave two-wheel drive trucks at the ford and walk .7 mile northwest up the left fork to the machine-horse trail junction.

Drivers of four-wheel drive vehicles can take the left fork of the road at Emma Creek Ford and reach the junction of the machine and horse trails. Then they can drive .7 mile west up the access track for the horse trail almost as far as a ford of the river. Or they may drive the machine trail north over a summit and north-west down to Johnson Creek at 3.2 miles. From here, a few four-wheelers late in the summer may wish to ford Johnson Creek and attempt to drive to the confluence of the North and South Forks of the Ross Fork.

The horse trail route is .7 mile shorter and avoids the 640-foot climb over the summit. However, the trail is suitable only for expert hikers due to the necessity of wading the river. This trail is blazed and maintained.

From the junction of the machine and horse trails, the jeep road to the horse trail turns left and goes another .7 mile to the edge of the river. The road first becomes a trail, skirts a talus slope, and then fords the river at 1 mile. By August 1, the water is still thigh deep. (See Stream Crossing section in the Introduction.) Early in the season, all hikers should walk the machine trail.

After crossing the river, walk 25 yards up a small creek that flows into the river opposite the crossing and find the trail. The trail is well-blazed and maintained, although the path disappears in some grassy places. The mostly level trail alternates between sagebrush flats and forest. 3.4 miles from the junction of the horse and machine trails, it crosses Little Bear Creek on rocks. The canyon at Little Bear Creek swings from a north to a northwest direction. Here the South Fork of the Boise splits into the Ross Fork and Johnson Creek. Just beyond Little Bear Creek are two old collapsed cabins.

The trail crosses a forested swamp before reaching Perkons Creek at 4.6 miles where there is no sign for the trail up Perkons Creek. At Bass Creek at 5.5 miles, just after crossing a small

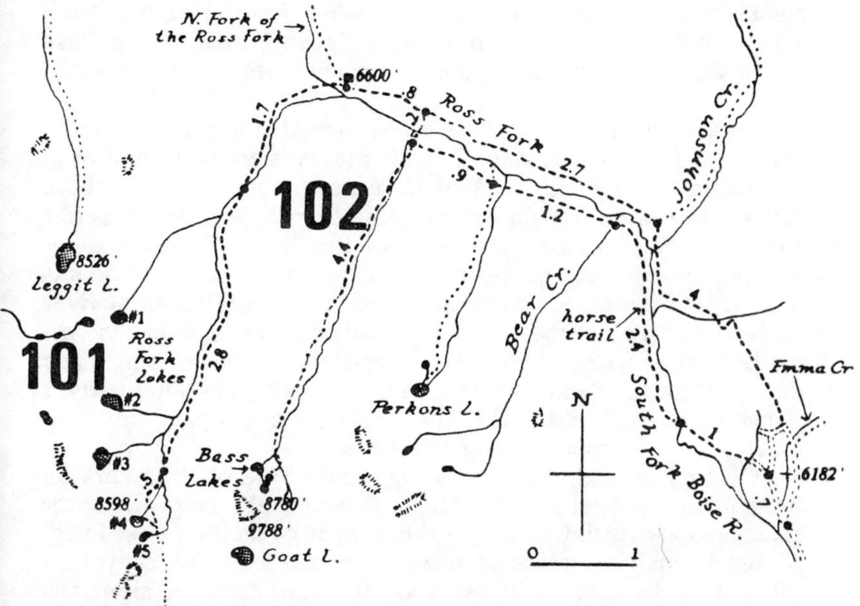

creek, the trail intersects the Bass Creek Trail in a sagebrush flat.
Turn north onto this path and cross the Ross Fork over river
stones. At 5.7 miles the Bass Creek Trail intersects the Ross Fork
Machine Trail at a sign. Follow this jeep track west up the Ross
Fork to an old cabin that squats beside the route at 6.5 miles near a
campsite. This cabin stands just beyond the point where the north
and south forks of Ross Fork join.

Near the beginning of the Ross Fork Machine Trail at .5 mile, a
side road leads left (northwest). At .7 mile at the base of Emma
Creek Canyon, two roads lead off to the right (east). The Ross
Fork Road rounds a curve to the left (north) and climbs a hill past
the Culver Mining Claim cabins and across sagebrush.

At a summit at 1.7 miles, 640 feet above Emma Creek, the track
enters forest. The route switches back twice, crosses a creek in
aspens, and drops downhill. At 2.7 miles, the jeep road flattens
and fords Johnson Creek at 3.2 miles. There is a footbridge with
railings suitable for horse or motorcycle. The fair road hairpins up
beyond the ford, then winds through trees to a signed junction
with a trail up Johnson Creek at 4 miles. At 4.1 miles, the track
passes a pole bridge across the river. This bridge hides in the
forest with no sign or blazes to show its location.

Beyond here the jeep trail runs along the edge of a sagebrush
hillside. At 5.5 miles a small road turning towards the river at a
post marks the trail for Perkons Lake. The track next fords a rocky
creek and winds through a muddy area. At 6 miles, the road

comes next to the river briefly, before reaching the Bass Creek sign at 6.7 miles. Between Johnson Creek Ford and the Bass Creek sign, the jeep track makes several detours to avoid downed timber.

To reach the lakes, continue walking along the jeep road past the old cabin. Distances on the trail up to the lakes are measured from this cabin. The South Fork of Ross Fork joins the North Fork 200 yards before the old cabin. This branch provides a better source of water in late season than the North Fork for those camping near the cabin. Beyond the cabin where the route seems to lead into the creek, cross the North Fork over yards of river stones. Just before the crossing, a blazed horse trail leads north up the North Fork. The blazed jeep road west of the crossing leads through a lodgepole forest. At .5 mile the track passes to the right of two cabins in the woods. The road becomes a pack trail at a washout .7 mile from the cabin at the forks.

At 1.7 miles, the trail crosses the South Fork of Ross Fork on rocks in a large open area that isn't shown on the map. Here the hiker can look southwest up the side canyon of the first Ross Lake. A sign beyond the crossing directs the hiker up this canyon to "Ross Fork Lake #1 - 2 miles". On the main trail the sign says "Ross Fork Lake #4 - 4 miles". The main trail returns to forest in 100 yards. At 2.5 miles, the route comes onto an open hillside. Most of the rest of the way, the trail goes through wildflower meadows sprinkled with trees. The last large open area at 4.2 miles before a second creek crossing is full of false hellbore and contains a campsite.

At 4.5 miles the path crosses back to the west side of the creek and then climbs straight up the stream 600 feet in a little over .5 mile. The trail climbs through forest with a view northeast of the Sawtooths near Alice Lake. At 5 miles the route switchbacks west and then south. Just before the path crosses the stream, turn right (northwest) up an open hillside on an unsigned trail to Ross Lake #4. The stream leads to swampy Ross Lake #5. The trail beyond the creek climbs over a 9200-foot pass west of Ross Peak and down Willow Creek to a trailhead near Featherville.

BASS LAKES

102

Round trip: 20.2 to 22.6 miles
Elevation gain: 2600 to 3240 feet
This section: 4.6 miles with 2200 feet gain
Highest point: 8760 feet
Topo maps: Marshall Peak, Newman Peak, Ross Peak
Time: 3 days
Access: Drive 18 miles north of Fairfield over Couch Summit or
   25 miles east of Featherville along the South Fork of the Boise
   River. Go over Fleck Summit and along the upper South Fork of
   the Boise to Emma Creek at 10 miles. With four-wheel drive,
   drive to Johnson Creek or perhaps Ross Fork Basin.
Ability: Expert

The milky turquoise water of Bass Lake #2 laps against a ledge
of 200-foot cliffs matted with tiny trees. Behind the lake, a high
wall of jagged dark grey and cream-colored cliffs hangs above a
cirque of talus. Horizontal fractures etch the cliffs. The lake is in a
grass carpet decorated with penstemon, elephant's head, cinquefoil, alpine sunflower, aster, and paintbrush. Looking down the
canyon from the ledge above the upper lake, a pointed sandy peak
with gabled towers guards the end of the wall of the canyon. In the
distance float cream-colored peaks at the head of Alice Lake in the
Sawtooths. A low grassy ridge divides the upper lake from the
lower. At the lower, deeper lake, silvered logs and a grass
peninsula poke into the green water from the outlet. At the upper
end, a rounded rock bench drops cliffs into the water.

The Bass Lakes Trail begins in Ross Fork Basin. For access
and for directions for reaching the Ross Fork Basin, see Ross Fork
Lakes. The last 2 miles of the Bass Lakes Trail does not have a
distinct path, but there are enough blazes and rock cairns so that
the experienced hiker can follow the route. This trail is being
considered for reconstruction, so in the future the trail should be
easier to follow.

From the Bass Lakes sign on the Ross Fork Machine Trail at
6.7 miles, a jeep track leads down towards a ford of the Ross Fork.
By August 1, there is hardly any water in the Ross Fork. A rock
cairn shows where the route continues on the south side of the
river. The trail goes south across a sagebrush flat, then climbs
through the trees along the northwest side of Bass Creek. At
.7 mile from the junction, the way passes above a small meadow
where the canyon becomes more open and rocky. At 1 mile, the
trail goes above a big meadow filled with willows.

At 1.5 miles the path flattens after a 600-foot climb in the
preceding .7 mile. On the canyon wall to the west, rock towers

resemble gnomes. At 1.8 miles the trail crosses the creek on rocks to the east. Just above the crossing, the canyon jumps 200 feet beside a little hill of talus. At 2.3 miles, the route crosses back through willows to the west bank of the stream. An old path angles left to an old camp beside the creek where the trail peters out in the grass. The trail to the lakes follows a line of rock cairns across the grassy hillside about 150 yards above the camp. Beyond here the canyon is open meadows with scattered stands of firs and lodgepoles. In the trees the trail is blazed, while in the open areas, scattered rock cairns mark the way. The route stays well above the creek.

At 3.5 miles the route comes out of woods opposite a peak that forms the end of the east canyon wall. In a swampy meadow, the path crosses a tiny stream where there are no cairns or blazes for 200 yards. Keep to the right (west) side of this meadow. Blazes begin ahead on large trees as the trail goes into a forest. The route angles east across the head of the canyon and becomes more distinct.

At 4 miles, the trail heads straight up a dry streambed and then switches back to the right (west). From here the mountains around Alice Lake shine in the distance. The trail levels beside the outlet of the upper lake, and then leads 150 yards along blazes on the west side of the creek to the upper lake at 4.6 miles. A campsite is located at the north end where the trail reaches the lake.

No spur trail leads toward a pass as shown on the topo map, although a connecting trail to Goat Lake is planned. To reach the lower lake, walk northwest 200 yards over a low grassy hill.

Appendices

A NOTES ON TRAILS NOT COVERED IN GUIDE

HELLS CANYON NATIONAL RECREATION AREA AND WILDERNESS

LITTLE GRANITE CREEK: Access from Potato Hill Trail. Trail begins at junction with Potato Hill Trail just above Hibbs Cow Camp and drops down Little Granite Creek and Granite Creek to the Snake River. 6 miles long. 6160 feet elevation loss. Steep and rocky but marked and maintained. Rattlesnakes and poison ivy in lower section. Only open July to October due to snow. Offers backpacker chance to go from Seven Devils Loop to the Snake River. More scenic than Stormy Point Trail.

STORMY POINT: Access from rough dirt road to Low Saddle from Lucile, Idaho. Trail begins at Low Saddle and drops to Snake River at mouth of Sheep Creek. 6 miles long. 3998 feet elevation loss. Steep and rocky for first 3 miles, then follows creek. Must wade Clarks Fork several times. After trail reaches Sheep Creek, it crosses Sheep Creek four times. Don't attempt to cross Sheep Creek at high water during May and June. A high water trail begins just below mouth of Clarks Fork that bypasses these four fords. Rattlesnakes and poison ivy in lower section.

MAIN RAPID RIVER TRAIL: Access from Rapid River Fish Hatchery. Trail begins at West Fork Rapid River Trail and continues to forest boundary and up river several miles. 3.4 miles to boundary, 400 feet elevation gain. Recommended for spring and fall, due to low elevation. View of few old mines.

SHEEP ROCK NATURE TRAIL (National Recreation Trail): Access from Sheep Rock Road which begins between Bear and Cuprum. Trail begins at Sheep Rock Road and makes a .5 mile loop. 22 numbered points and overlook of Hells Canyon, 5500 feet deep here.

RANKIN MILL: Access from Black Lake Road. Trail begins at Black Lake Road and connects with the West Fork of Rapid River Trail. 12 miles to Rankin Mill. 2100 feet elevation gain, 2900 feet elevation loss. Provides cross-country access to Ruth and Crystal Lakes. Old mill and cabin ruins in wooded canyon.

PAYETTE NATIONAL FOREST (Weiser District)

EAST BROWNLEE TRAIL: Access from near the summit of Highway 71, which goes from Cambridge to Brownlee Reservoir, by side road east past Brownlee Campground. Begins at road about 1.5 miles northeast of campground and continues over Cuddy Mountain to abandoned Buck Park Guard Station. 6 miles long. 3815 feet elevation gain. Maintained. View of the whole Brownlee Reservoir drainage. Flat alpine meadows in vicinity of Buck Park.

PAYETTE NATIONAL FOREST (New Meadows Dist.)

BIG HAZARD LAKE: Access from Hazard Lake-Elk Meadows Road. Begins at road and continues to Big Hazard Lake. .5 mile long. 50 feet elevation loss. Shaded trail to 1 mile-long lake in woods with view south to Bruin Mountain.

JOHN AND MARY LAKES: Access from Elk Lake Road is through private land and not recommended. Best to reach these lakes from trail past Twin Lakes. This makes John Lake 7.5 miles from the Clayburn trailhead and 880 feet elevation gain, 1680 feet elevation loss.

KENNETH LAKE: Access from Elk Meadows Road. Begins at Elk Meadows Road and climbs to Kenneth Lake. .2 mile long. 160 feet gain. Good shaded trail to small lake in woods.

PAYETTE NATIONAL FOREST (McCall District)

SHAW-TWIN LAKES: Access by jeep trail off Boulder Reservoir Road. Lakes have dams.

PADDY FLAT-LAKE FORK TRAIL: Access from Paddy Flat Road or Lick Creek Road. Begins on Paddy Flat Road and goes to Lick Creek Road. 9 miles long. 2180 feet gain, 2520 feet loss. Gives access to Boulder and Rapid Lakes when Boulder Reservoir Road is too muddy to drive. Passes Anderson Lake.

GOLDEN LAKE: Access from Lick Creek Road. No trail. 2 miles. 2200 feet elevation gain via cross-country travel.

VICTOR CREEK TRAIL: Access from Warren Wagon Road. Trail begins at Warren Wagon Road and continues to Loon Lake Horse Trail. 12.5 miles long. 2000 feet elevation gain, 2200 feet elevation loss. Provides access to Trail and Deep Lakes via cross-country travel.

CRESTLINE TRAIL: Across from Warren Wagon Road. Trail begins at Pearl Creek Road and continues to junction with Fall Creek Trail south of Blackwell Lake. Passes near Pearl, Heart, Brush, Squaw, Buck, and Blackwell Lakes. 14 miles long. 1180 feet elevation gain, 2240 feet elevation loss.

BROWNS POND: Access from Lick Creek Road. Jeep road begins at Lick Creek Road and continues to Browns Pond. .5 mile long. 200 feet elevation loss. 1 mile-long reservoir in woods with granite islands and a view of lower Lake Fork Canyon. Easy stroll for people staying at McCall. Best for early summer.

PONDEROSA STATE PARK: Access from Lakeshore Drive. Nature trails in marsh areas. Visitors' Center. View of Payette Lake.

BOISE NATIONAL FOREST (Cascade District)

NEEDLES ROUTE: Access from Warm Lake Road via Johnson Creek Road. Begins at Gold Fork Meadow, climbs Gold Fork Rock, and continues to East Fork Kennally Creek Trail in the Payette National Forest. 14 miles long. 1775 feet elevation gain, 3200 feet elevation loss. Poor condition, not well marked. No water first 9 miles. Close view of Needles Peaks.

CAMPBELL CREEK TRAIL: Access from West Side Cascade Reservoir Road. Begins at West Side Road, ascends to Wilson Creek Trail. Hiker can follow Wilson Creek Trail along top of West Mountain Ridge past Rock Lake to the Van Wyck stock driveway, then down stock driveway back to West Side Road. Length of through trip is 12 miles. 3200 feet elevation gain. Poor condition, not well marked.

COUGAR LAKES: Access from Kennally Creek Campground. Begins at North Fork Kennally Creek Trail and continues to

Cougar Creek Trail. 2.5 miles to lake from North Fork Kennally Creek Trail, 1600 feet elevation gain.

RIORDAN LAKE: Access from Landmark-Yellow Pine Road. 4 miles long. 1600 feet elevation gain. .7 mile-long lake in wooded hills.

CATON AND RAINBOW LAKES: Access from Landmark-Yellow Pine Road. 11 miles long. 5400 feet elevation gain to see both lakes. Remote, little-used country.

SUMMIT TRAIL: Access from Mud Lake Road. Begins at Snowshoe Cabin trailhead and continues to Meadow Creek Lookout Road. 12 miles long, 950 feet elevation gain. Passes near Pistol Lakes. Poor condition and not well marked.

BOISE NATIONAL FOREST (Emmett District)

TRIPOD PEAK: Access from Sagehen Reservoir. Trail begins at end of Joes Creek Road and continues to top of peak. 3 miles long, 2000 feet elevation gain. Lookout manned July-October. Good view of Sagehen and Crane Creek Reservoirs and surrounding mountains.

BOILING SPRINGS: Access from Boiling Springs Road. Trail begins at Boiling Springs Guard Station and connects with a trail along the Middle Fork of the Payette that continues to Clear Creek Summit. 14 miles long. 1900 feet elevation gain. Passes several undeveloped hot springs. Trail crosses the Middle Fork of the Payette River twelve times in the first 6 miles. These crossings *very dangerous or impassable* until August 1. Crossings are 1 to 3 feet deep in late summer.

LONG FORK OF SILVER CREEK - OXTAIL CREEK - BULL CREEK - SILVER CREEK SUMMIT LOOP TRAIL: Access from Silver Creek Summit. This loop at present lacks 3 miles of constructed trail between the Long Fork of Silver Creek and Oxtail Creek. This 3-mile section will be built in the future. In the meantime, either the Long Fork of Silver Creek branch, or the Silver Creek Summit-Bull Creek-Oxtail Creek branch of the planned loop provides fine hiking. Expert hikers may traverse the proposed section at present by cross-country travel along a ridge. The 21-mile loop offers rugged landscape and excellent views of a small lake and the Sawtooths. From the junction of Bull and Oxtail Creeks, the hiker can make a side trip of about 4 miles to Rice Peak.

WILSON MEADOW - POISON CREEK - SQUAW CREEK LOOP TRAIL: Access from Snowbank Mountain Road. Take trail down into Wilson Meadows and follow it north. At 1.5 miles pass a turnoff for the Wilson Corrals Trail. Continue on the Wilson Creek Trail. At 2 miles is a junction with the trail down Squaw Creek, which is the return route. At 3.5 miles is a junction with the Willow Creek Trail east down past Skein Lake. Continue on the Wilson Creek Trail and at 4.2 miles pass a turn-off to the east for the Campbell Creek Trail. At 5 miles turn northwest on the Poison Creek Trail. Greenfield Flat is at 6.5 miles. At 7.5 miles, the trail reaches the Squaw Creek Road. Go up the Squaw Creek Trail, which returns to the Wilson Creek Trail at 12.5 miles. From here it is 2 more miles back to the Snowbank Mountain Road for a round trip of 14.5 miles. Squaw Creek Canyon has many waterfalls and rock outcrops. View of Cascade Reservoir and Long Valley from Snowbank Mountain. Abandoned cabin at Greenfield Flat on Poison Creek. Old mine near Wilson Meadows. 2320 feet elevation loss, 2320 feet elevation gain. Little water from Squaw Creek Trail junction to Poison Creek.

BOISE NATIONAL FOREST (Boise District)

SWANHOLM PEAK AND WARRIOR LAKES: Access from North Fork Boise River Road via Trail Creek Road. Begins at primitive Horse Heaven Creek Road, climbs Swanholm Peak as a jeep trail 2.5 miles to peak, and continues past Warrior Lakes as a pack trail. 2 additional miles to lakes. 2500 feet elevation gain to peak, 620 feet elevation loss to lakes. Trail is poor.

BLACK WARRIOR TRAIL: Access from Middle Fork of Boise River Road. Begins at Middle Fork of Boise River Road, climbs Black Warrior Creek, and connects with the Neinmeyer Creek Trail. 11 miles long, 2700 feet elevation gain. Poor condition. View of old mines. Provides loop with Little Queens River Trail via Neinmeyer Creek.

BOISE NATIONAL FOREST (Idaho City District)

CROOKED RIVER TRAIL: Access from Idaho 21 near Edna Creek Campground. Begins at Willow Creek Road to Atlanta 1 mile east of Edna Creek Campground and continues to North Fork of Boise River Road. 12 miles long. 1460 feet elevation loss, 1000 feet elevation gain. Views of rugged canyon and rushing river. Do not drink the water without boiling, as upper part of Crooked River has roads along it. Through trip best for horse travel due to five fords of wide river, although hikers can safely ford river during August and September. Lower and upper ends of trail make good day hikes from early summer until it snows.

BOISE NATIONAL FOREST (Lowman District)

LOST LAKES: Access by way of Clear Creek (Bear Valley) and East Side Roads. Drive up Clear Creek Road towards Bear Valley about 16 miles. Turn right (east) on East Side Road for about 10 miles. Turn right (south) on a jeep trail for .2 mile to pack trail which goes to the left. It's easy to drive past the trail if the traveler doesn't watch closely. .2 mile jeep trail, .7 mile pack trail. Total elevation gain for both trails is 280 feet. Other lakes reached cross-country with compass from first. Small lakes in wooded country.

BOISE NATIONAL FOREST (Mountain Home District)

GREEN CREEK TRAIL: Access from road between Pine and Featherville. Begins at Warm Springs Bridge and leads to junction with Alpine and Rainbow Trails in Rainbow Basin. Mainly used by cross-country skiers, but provides access to Trinity Lakes area when roads still closed by snow. 4.5 miles long, 1900 feet elevation gain.

ROARING RIVER TRAIL: Access from Trinity Lakes. Begins at Trinity Lakes Guard Station and continues to the Roaring River Road. 8 miles long. 2740 feet elevation loss.

CROSS CUT TRAIL: Access from Tally-Baker Road. Begins 2 miles north of Lester Creek Guard Station (reached by Fall Creek or Sloans Gulch Roads near Anderson Ranch Reservoir) and connects with the Green Creek Trail. 6.5 miles long. 1600 feet elevation gain, 900 feet elevation loss. Good backpacking and day hikes, but not as scenic as Trinity Lakes.

CAMP CREEK TRAIL: Access from Pine-Prairie Road. Begins 2 miles north of Lester Creek Guard Station and connects with the Cross Cut Trail. 5 miles long. 1600 feet elevation gain.

BUREAU OF LAND MANAGEMENT (Boise District)

FLORIDA MOUNTAIN: Access from Silver City. This old road begins at campground south of city, climbs Florida Mountain to the summit and returns down Long Gulch to Silver City. 6 miles. 1600 feet elevation gain. Fine view of Silver City. Passes old mines. Best for late June and October. One of proposed hiking trails for Silver City area. Send to Boise District, Bureau of Land Management, 3948 Development Street, Boise, for map of these proposed trails.

SOUTH MOUNTAIN AREA: Access from Jordan Valley, Oregon. Hiking opportunities on a number of jeep roads in the area. Early day mining sites. Especially fine wildflowers in mid-June. Map available from Bureau of Land Management.

OREGON TRAIL NEAR CANYON CREEK: Access from Canyon Creek Road north of Mountain Home. The experienced hiker can follow the Oregon Trail several miles both east and west of Canyon Creek. Map available from Bureau of Land Management office.

THREE ISLAND CROSSING STATE PARK: Access from Glenns Ferry. 1 mile south of Glenns Ferry on West Madison Street. Two interpretive trails total .5 mile. Covered wagon rides available in summer. Located at Snake River crossing of the Oregon Trail.

CHALLIS NATIONAL FOREST (Middle Fork District)

MABLE LAKES: Access from Seafoam Road. Trail begins at Beaver Creek Campground and continues to Ruffneck Peak. First Mable Lake is at 4 miles after a 2000-foot elevation gain. Other lakes reached by cross-country travel. Small lakes in forested hills, except rocks around first lake.

VANITY LAKES: Access from Seafoam Road. No trail. Closest lake is .7 mile and 1000 feet elevation gain from road near Vanity Summit. Small lakes under rocky peaks.

MIDDLE FORK OF SALMON RIVER TRAIL: Access from Dagger Falls. Trail begins at Dagger Falls and follows the Middle Fork of the Salmon to Big Creek Bridge. The entire

80 miles of trail is in the River of No Return Wilderness Area. 2600 feet elevation loss from Dagger Falls to Big Creek Bridge. Campers may find the better camping locations occupied by boating parties who are assigned campsites and required by the Forest Service to stay at those assigned sites. Hikers may camp where they want. Avoid through trip in mid-summer due to high temperatures at lower end of canyon.

RAPID RIVER TRAIL: Access from Rapid River via Seafoam Road. Begins at end of Rapid River Road and continues to Middle Fork of Salmon River. 9 miles long. 1000 feet elevation loss. Necessary to hike 8 miles down to Indian Creek pack stock bridge to connect with Middle Fork Trail. 4 miles of this trail was burned by 1979 Mortar Creek fire.

CHALLIS NATIONAL FOREST (Yankee Fork District)

LIGHTNING CREEK TRAIL: Access from Bonanza via Yankee Fork Road. Begins at West Fork Yankee Fork Trail and continues to meet a jeep trail up Jordan Creek, passing Lightning Lake at 8 miles. 8.5 miles long. 2600 feet elevation gain. View of colorful peaks.

CHALLIS NATIONAL FOREST (Lost River District)

UPPER FALL CREEK TRAIL: Access from Wildhorse Creek Road. Lower part of trail covered in descriptions for Moose and Surprise Lakes. Upper trail begins at Surprise Valley Trail junction and climbs part way up to head of Fall Creek Canyon. About 2 miles long. 600 feet elevation gain. Fallen timber across trail. Little-used and poorly defined. Magnificent view of headwall of Fall Creek Canyon. Hiker can continue cross-country to head of canyon at about 4 miles.

NORTH FORK LAKE: Access from primitive North Fork of Lost River Road. No trail. 1 mile jeep trail, 3 miles cross-country travel. 1500 feet elevation gain. Little-used area. Excellent view of Ryan Peak in the Boulder Mountains.

SAWTOOTH NATIONAL FOREST (Ketchum District)

HIGH RIDGE TRAIL: Access from Lake Creek Road or Park Creek Road. Begins at Lake Creek Road, climbs to a saddle, and goes around the end of a ridge before dropping to the Park Creek Road. Requires car shuttle. 7 miles long. 2000 feet elevation gain. Challenging hike at high elevation with excellent views of the Pioneer and Boulder Mountains. Snow-free after mid-July.

HYNDMAN CREEK TRAIL: Access from East Fork of Wood River Road. Begins at Hyndman Creek Road, which has four-wheel drive access only. Will connect when completed with trail up North Fork Hyndman Creek and with Pioneer Cabin Trail. 2 miles to saddle with best view of peaks. 1800 feet elevation gain to saddle. 1.5 miles of trail beyond this point not yet built. Spectacular views of Hyndman and Cobb Peaks.

BIG WOOD RIVER TRAIL (National Recreation Trail): Access by footbridge from Lake Creek trailhead 3 miles north of Ketchum on Highway 75. Climbs 700 feet in 5 miles and provides access to the 40 miles of Adams Gulch and Fox Creek trail system.

SAWTOOTH NATIONAL FOREST (Fairfield District)

BIG SMOKY TRAIL: Access from Couch Summit from Fairfield or via South Fork Boise River Road from Featherville. Trail begins at Canyon Campground and continues to Chemetkan Campground at the south end of Sawtooth Valley. 20 miles long. 2920 feet elevation gain, 800 feet elevation loss. This is the most popular trail in the district. The route runs up Big Smoky Creek over the top of the Salmon River Divide and passes Skillern Hot Springs at 3 miles.

GOAT LAKE: Access from upper South Fork of Boise River Road. Trail begins at Bear Creek Road and continues to lake. 3 miles long. 1540 feet elevation gain. 2 miles of this is a jeep trail, and Bear Creek Road requires four-wheel drive.

PERKONS LAKE: Access from upper South Fork Boise River Road. Trail begins at Ross Fork Machine Trail and climbs to Perkons Lake. 3 miles long. 2100 feet elevation gain. Easy to find from horse trail on south side Ross Fork. Extremely steep last mile.

NORTH FORK OF ROSS CREEK - JOHNSON CREEK LOOP: Access from upper South Fork of Boise River Road. Four-wheel drive access to Johnson Creek. Trail begins at Ross Fork Machine Trail, goes up Johnson Creek and comes down the North Fork of Ross Fork. 15 miles long, including completing the loop on the Ross Fork Machine Trail. 2000 feet elevation gain, 1800 feet elevation loss. Provides access to Johnson Lake by cross-country travel. Connects with Alturas Creek Trail via .7 mile on old trail from upper end Johnson Creek.

WEST FORK OF BIG SMOKY CREEK TRAIL: Access from Big Smoky Creek Trail. Trail begins at Big Smoky Creek and climbs the West Fork to a junction at a saddle with the Emma Creek and Smiley Creek Trails. 6.5 miles long. 3500 feet elevation gain. Provides access to Snowslide and Paradise Lakes via trail from Helen Creek. Can be used to make loop from Chemetkan Campground on the Big Smoky Creek, West Fork Big Smoky Creek, and Smiley Creek Trails to Vienna.

WALLOWA—WHITMAN NATL. FOR. (Baker Dist.)

ANTHONY LAKES: Three short hikes beginning at or near Anthony Lakes, Oregon. Access by a 21 mile road from North Powder, Oregon (18 miles north of Baker on Interstate 84). Van Patton Lake: 2 miles, 1000 feet elevation gain. Hoffer Lakes: .5 mile, 280 feet elevation gain. Black Lake: 1.5 miles, 200 feet elevation gain. View of small triangular peaks with cliffs. Campgrounds at Anthony Lakes at base of ski area. No motor boats. Shorter driving time than McCall, Idaho from Boise area.

B DIRECTORY FOR NATIONAL FOREST AND BUREAU OF LAND MANAGEMENT OFFICES

Hells Canyon National Recreation Area (Wallowa Whitman National Forest), 3620B Snake River Avenue, Lewiston, Idaho 83501 (743-3648)

Nez Perce National Forest and Hells Canyon National Recreation Area (Salmon River District), Riggins Fire Center, Riggins, Idaho 83549 (628-3213)

Payette National Forest (Council District), 203 Illinois, Council, Idaho 83612 (253-4250)

Payette National Forest (Main Office and McCall District), McCall, Idaho 83638 (634-2255)

Payette National Forest (Weiser District), 27 W. Commercial, Weiser, Idaho 83672 (549-2420)

Payette National Forest (New Meadows District), New Meadows, Idaho 83654 (347-2141)

Boise National Forest (Cascade District), Cascade, Idaho 83611 (382-4271)

Boise National Forest (Emmett District), 1648 N. Washington, Emmett, Idaho 83617 (365-4382)

Boise National Forest (Boise District), 5493 Warm Springs Ave. Boise, Idaho 83702 (334-1572)

Boise National Forest (Idaho City District), Idaho City, Idaho 83631 (392-6681)

Boise National Forest (Lowman District), Lowman, Idaho 83637 (342-2744) summer only
(in winter:) 2645 N. Cole Road, Boise, Idaho 83704; 334-1055)

Boise National Forest (Mountain Home District), 2422 American Legion Boulevard, Mountain Home, Idaho 83647 (587-7961)

Bureau of Land Management (Boise District), 3948 Development Street, Boise, Idaho 83705 (334-1582)

Bureau of Land Management (Vale District), P. O. Box 700, Vale, Oregon 97918 (473-3144)

Owyhee County Sheriff, Murphy, Idaho 83650 (337-4222) for road conditions

Malheur County Deputy Sheriff, Jordan Valley, Oregon 97910 (586-2422) for road conditions

Boise Department of Parks and Recreation (Greenbelt), 1104 Royal Boulevard, Boise, Idaho 83706 (384-4240)

Challis National Forest (Main Office and Middle Fork District), Challis, Idaho 83226 (879-2285)

Challis National Forest (Yankee Fork District), Clayton, Idaho 83227 (838-2201)

Challis National Forest (Lost River District), Mackay, Idaho 83251 (588-2224)

Sawtooth National Forest (Main Office), 1525 Addison Ave. East, Twin Falls, Idaho 83301 (733-3698)

Sawtooth National Forest (Ketchum District), Sun Valley Road, P. O. Box 656, Ketchum, Idaho 83340 (622-5371)

Sawtooth National Forest (Fairfield District), Fairfield, Idaho 83327 (764-2202)

C GUIDE TO HIKES

EASY HIKES (Up to 7 miles with up to 1000 feet elevation gain)
Oregon Trail at Bonneville Point
Boise Greenbelt
Hulls Gulch
Spanish Town
Mores Mountain
Jordan Craters
Juniper Gulch
Lizard Butte
Squaw Creek
Jump Creek
Big Jacks Creek
Reynolds Creek
Birds of Prey Area at Swan Falls
Bruneau Sand Dunes
Blue Lake
Vulcan Hot Springs
North Fork Kennally Creek
Louie Lake
Snowslide Lake
Duck Lake
Hum Lake
Josephine Lake
Twin Lakes (Granite Mountain Trail)
Upper Hazard Lake
Scribner Lake
Seafoam Lakes #1 and #2
Baker Lake

MODERATE HIKES (7 to 10 miles with 1000 to 2000 feet gain)
Sheep Creek
Jennie Lake
Oregon Trail Alternate (Sinker Creek)
Box Lake
Boulder and Rapid Lakes
Loon Lake

Grassy Twin and Coffee Cup Lakes
Hard Butte, Twin, and Rainbow Lakes
Lava Butte Lakes
Rapid River
Emerald Lake
Hindman Lake
Langer, Island and Ruffneck Lakes
Norton Lakes
Smiley Creek
Miner Lake
Prairie Lakes
Mill Lake
Kane Lake
Bellas Lake
Green Lake

HIKES WITH CROSS-COUNTRY TRAVEL
Three Fingers Rock
Little Jacks Creek
Long Lake
Summit and Malony Lakes
Crystal Lake
Satan Lake
Knapp Lakes
Red Mountain Lakes
Seafoam Lakes #3 and #4
East, South, Long Twentymile Lakes
Kane Lake (last mile)

EXPERT ABILITY NEEDED (Route finding problems or treacherous footing)
Jordan Creek - War Eagle Mountain
Roberson Trail
Skein Lake
Blackmare Lake
Jughandle Trail
Maki Lake
Sullivan Lake
Shirts Lake
Ross Fork Horse Trail
Bass Lakes
Hyndman Lake
Summit Creek
Surprise Valley and Lakes
Avondale Basin

OPEN APRIL AND MAY
Sheep Creek
Rapid River
Hells Canyon
Lizard Butte
Hulls Gulch
Indian Bathtub
Jump Creek
Squaw Creek
Birds of Prey at Swan Falls
Big Jacks Creek
Oregon Trail at Sinker Creek
Oregon Trail at Bonneville Point
Reynolds Creek
Roberson Trail
Three Fingers Rock
Jordan Craters
Juniper Gulch

OPEN BY JULY 1
Spanish Town
Vulcan Hot Springs
Blue Lake
Skein Lake
Twin Lakes
Avondale Basin
Jordan Creek - War Eagle Mountain
Loon Lake

OPEN AFTER JULY 15
Surprise Lakes and Valley
Box Canyon Lakes
Six Lake Basin
Emerald Lake
Satan Lake

OVERNIGHT OR LONGER REQUIRED
Crimson Lake
Link Trail
Kirkham Ridge
Bass Lakes
Ross Fork Lakes
Hells Canyon
Northern Seven Devils Loop

LIKELY TO BE OVERCROWDED
Blue Lake
Vulcan Hot Springs
Round, Long, Rough, Big, and Golden Lakes
Bellas Lakes
Jump Creek
Indian Bathtub
Bruneau Sand Dunes
Boise Greenbelt
Hulls Gulch
Emerald Lake
Shelf Lake
Langer and Island Lakes
Seafoam Lake #1
Baker Lake

RARELY USED TRAILS OR CROSS-COUNTRY ROUTES
Link Trail
Kirkham Ridge
Long Lake (near Rice Lake)
Grouse Lakes
Sullivan Lake
Crimson Lake
Surprise Valley and Lakes
Iron Bog and Fishpole Lakes
Hyndman Lake
Bass Lakes
Smiley Creek
Shirts Lake
Satan Lake
Little Jacks Creek
Big Jacks Creek
Roberson Trail
Avondale Basin
Jordan Creek - War Eagle Mountain
Three Fingers Rock

ACCESS ROADS FOR TOUGH VEHICLES AND EXPERIENCED DRIVERS
Yuba and Decker Creek
Josephus Lake
Kane Creek
Knapp Creek
Muldoon Canyon
Black Lake
Little Jacks Creek
Hindman Lake

D   BASIC BACKPACKING EQUIPMENT

Clothing:
hiking boots (previously broken in)
*long pants
sweater
*wool hat
*rain jacket or poncho; micropore fabric is best
rain pants or chaps; micropore fabric is best
*sunglasses
mosquito headnet
wool boot sox
qiana or nylon sock liners (optional)
*long-sleeved shirt
*warm jacket
sun hat
complete change of clothes

General:
comfortable backpack
*flashlight
extra batteries and bulbs
*compass
*topographic map
plastic trowel
toilet paper
20 feet of 1/8″ nylon rope

Cooking:
backpacking stove
aluminum cooking pots (to fit stove)
utensils
folding plastic washbasin
biodegradeable soap
pot scrubber
spoon and plastic cup
extra fuel for stove
work gloves or pot gripper
*pocket knife
*firestarter
*extra food beyond needs of trip
*waterproof matches or butane lighter

Sleeping:
tent; breatheable fabric with waterproof rainfly, or single layer micropore fabric
foam or ensolite pad
down or Polarguard sleeping bag

First Aid:
mosquito repellent
sunburn cream
lip salve
*minimum first aid kit: prescription pain pills, moleskin, Bandaids, salt tablets, gauze, adhesive tape, antibiotic ointment, other items recommended by doctor

*essential items for every hiker

E   BIBLIOGRAPHY

Adams, Mildretta, *History of Rockville-Succor Creek*, Malheur Enterprise, 1967

Adams, Mildretta, *Historic Silver City*, Owyhee Chronicle, Homedale, Idaho, 1960

Bach, Orville, Jr., "Backpacking in Grizzly Country", *Backpacker*, February 1978, p. 45

Beal, Merrill and Wells, Merle, *History of Idaho*, Lewis Historical Publishing Co. Inc., New York, N. Y., 1959

Baker, Bessie, and high school journalism class, "New Meadows", unpublished paper, Caldwell, Idaho, 1945-1946

Beckwith, John, *Gem Minerals of Idaho*, Caxton, Caldwell, Idaho, 1934

Bird, Annie Laurie, *Boise, the Peace Valley*, Caxton, Caldwell, Idaho, 1934

Bradley, Jim, *Environmental Outfitting*, Moose Creek Ranger District, Nez Perce National Forest, 1975

Brosnan, Cornelius J., *History of the State of Idaho*, Charles Schribner and Sons, New York, 1918

Brown, Carl, "Burgdorf", unpublished paper, C.E.T.A., 1975

Brown, Vinson; Yocum, Charles; Starbuck, Aldene, *Wildlife of the Intermountain West*, Naturegraph, San Martin, California, 1958

Carrey, Johnny; Conley, Cort; and Barton, Ace, *Snake River of Hells Canyon*, Backeddy Books, Cambridge, Idaho, 1979

Corlett, John, "Idaho's Water", *Incredible Idaho*, Fall 1977, p. 19

Craighead, John J. and Frank Jr., and Davis, Ray, *A Field Guide to Rocky Mountain Wildflowers*, Houghton Mifflin Company, Cambridge, Massachusetts, 1963

Davis, Ray, *Flora of Idaho*, Wm. C. Brown Co., Dubuque, Iowa, 1952

Day, Ernest, *Stanley Basin and the Sawtooth Range*, Idaho Historical Society, Boise, Idaho, 1973

D'Easum, Dick, *Sawtooth Tales*, Caxton, Caldwell, Idaho, 1977

Defenbach, Byron, *Idaho, the Land and Its People*, American Historical Society, Inc., Chicago-New York, 1933

Elsensohn, Sister Alfreda, *Pioneer Days in Idaho County*, Vol. II, Caxton, Caldwell, Idaho, 1951

Endangered and Rare Species of Wildlife and Fish, Intermountain Region National Forests, not dated

Gibbs, Rafe, *Beckoning the Bold*, The University Press of Idaho, Moscow, Idaho, 1976

Goertzen, Dorine, *Boise Basin Brocade*, Capitol Lithograph, Boise, Idaho, 1960

Gulick, Bill, *Snake River Country*, Caxton, Caldwell, Idaho, 1971

Hailey, John, *History of Idaho*, Syms-York Co., Boise, Idaho, 1910

Hanley, Mike and Lucia, Ellis, *Owyhee Trails*, Caxton, Caldwell, Idaho, 1973

Hart, John, *Walking Softly in the Wilderness*, Sierra Club, San Francisco, California, 1977

Hawes, Adelaide, *The Valley of Tall Grass*, Caxton, Caldwell, Idaho, 1950

Henderson, D. M. et al, *Endangered and Threatened Plants of Idaho*, Forest, Wildlife and Range Experiment Station, University of Idaho, Moscow, Idaho, 1977

Higdem, Mary, "Geology of the Snake River Basin", Occasional Paper #14, Snake River Regional Studies Center, Caldwell, Idaho, November 1972

Idaho, An Illustrated History, Idaho State Historical Society, Boise, Idaho, 1976

Idaho Local History Bibliography, University Press of Idaho, Moscow, Idaho, 1976

Idaho Writers' Project, Idaho *A Guide in Word and Picture*, Oxford University Press, 1937

Kodet, Dr. E. Russel, and Angier, Bradford, *Being Your Own Wilderness Doctor*, Stackpole Books, Harrisburg, Pennsylvania, 1968

Larrison, Earl J., *Guide to Idaho Mammals*, Idaho Academy of Science, November 1967

Linder, Allen, and Fichter, Edson, *The Reptiles of Idaho*, Idaho State University Press, Pocatello, Idaho, 1969

Manning, Harvey, *Backpacking - One Step At A Time*, Vintage Books, New York, 1980

March, Bill, "How To Cross A River", *Backpacker*, April-May 1979

McLeod, George, *History of Alturas and Blaine Counties, Idaho*, The Hailey Times, Hailey, Idaho, 1938

Merrill, Bill, *The Survival Handbook*, Winchester Press, 1972

Miller, Donald, *Ghost Towns of Idaho*, Pruett Publishing, Boulder, Colorado, 1976

Miller, Nancy, "Mining in the Sawtooths: The Story of Vienna and Sawtooth City", *Idaho Yesterdays*, Spring 1965

Miller, Robert, *Guide For Using Horses In Mountain Country*, Montana Wilderness Association, 1975

Mining Industry of Idaho, *Annual Reports*, 1899-1979

Nash, Roderick, "Wilderness Is All In Your Mind", *Backpacker*, February-March 1979

Nettleton, Helen, *Sketches of Owyhee County*, Schwartz Printing, Nampa, Idaho, 1978

Oppenheimer, Doug and Poore, Jim, *Sun Valley, A Biography*,

Beatty, Boise, Idaho, 1976

Parsons, Donna, *Idaho, An Outdoor Classroom*, U. S. Office of Education, Blue Star Press, Nyssa, Oregon, 1968

Peterson, F. Ross, *Idaho*, W. W. Norton, New York, 1976

Preston, Richard J., Jr., *Rocky Mountain Trees*, Dover Publications, New York, 1968

Rollins, P. A., *The Discovery of the Oregon Trail*, Charles Scribner and Sons, New York and London, 1935

Rowland, Frank, *Founding of McCall*, Caxton, Caldwell, Idaho, 1960

Ryan, John F., *A History of Camas Prairie*, Camas County Historical Society, Fairfield, Idaho, 1975

Sisk, Lizzie, untitled manuscript containing reminiscences of pioneer days in Long Valley, undated

Snake River Birds of Prey Natural Area, United States Department of the Interior, Bureau of Land Management, 1979, pamphlet

Snake River Birds of Prey Study Area: Summary Report, Department of the Interior, Bureau of Land Management, 1979

The Snake River Country, The American Wilderness Time-Life Books, 1974

Sparling, Wayne, *Southern Idaho Ghost Towns*, Caxton, Caldwell, Idaho, 1976

Strahorn, Carrie, *Fifteen Thousand Miles By Stage*, G. P. Putnam and Sons, New York, 1911

Thurston, Mary, "Roseberry - The Town That Isn't There", *Incredible Idaho*, Spring 1975

Udvardy, Miklos D., *The Audubon Society Field Guide to North American Birds, Western Region*, Alfred A. Knopf, New York, 1977

Walker, Eugene, *A Geologic History of the Snake River Country of Idaho*, Idaho Historical Society, September 1963

Waterman, Guy and Laura, "Dogs on the Trail", *Backpacker*, August 1977

Weis, Norman, *Ghost Towns of the Northwest*, Caxton, Caldwell, Idaho, 1971

"Wilderness Manners", (pamphlet), U. S. D. A. Forest Service, Northern Region, Missoula, Montana

Wilkerson, James A., MD, *Medicine for Mountaineering*, The Mountaineers, Seattle, Washington, 1969

Williams, Milt, "Wildlife of Idaho", *Idaho Heritage*, June-July 1976

Yarber, Esther, *Land of the Yankee Fork*, Sage Books, Denver, Colorado, 1963

Yarber, Esther, and McGown, Edna, *Stanley-Sawtooth Country*, Publishers Press, Salt Lake City, Utah, 1976

Files of the Idaho Historical Society, Boise

Acknowledgments

I would like to thank all those who helped me with this book. This guide couldn't have been written without the help of my family. I would particularly like to thank my youngest son, Stuart, who was my companion on most of the hikes. My husband, Wayne, my other children, Doug, Leslie, Neal, and Hilary, and my parents, Wallace and Eleanor Cathcart, also hiked with me and provided transportation. So did members of the Mountain West organization in Boise and various other friends.

Offices of the Sawtooth, Challis, Payette, and Boise National Forests, and of the Hells Canyon National Recreation Area, and offices of the Bureau of Land Management in Boise and in Vale, Oregon provided trail information and edited the completed hike descriptions. In particular I want to thank Wally Larsen of the Fairfield Ranger District in the Sawtooth National Forest; Butch Harper and Tom Farr of the Ketchum District, Sawtooth National Forest; Fred Salinas and Grant Thorson of the Lost River District, Challis National Forest; Clifford Mitchell of the Middle Fork District, Challis National Forest; Guy Pence formerly of the Yankee Fork District, Challis National Forest; James Arp of the Payette National Forest; Rich Belnap of the McCall District, Payette National Forest; Roger Schumacher and Craig Frank of the New Meadows District, Payette National Forest; Monte Florence of the Weiser District, Payette National Forest; Robert Carpenter of the Boise District, Boise National Forest; Stephen Butler of the Idaho City District, Boise National Forest; Jack Smith formerly of the Lowman District, Boise National Forest; Walter Tegge and Chuck Arendts of the Mountain Home District, Boise National Forest; Val Simpson and George Buckley of the Cascade District, Boise National Forest; William Cardwell of the Emmett District, Boise National Forest; Wally Meyer and James Gabettas of the Boise District, Bureau of Land Management; Fearl Parker of the Vale District, Bureau of Land Management; John Cooper of the Boise Department of Parks; and Art Seamans, Pat Ormsbee, and Jonathan Klein of the Hells Canyon National Recreation Area.

I would especially like to thank Ace Barton, one of the authors of *Snake River of Hells Canyon*, for editing the sections on the Hells Canyon and Seven Devils areas and providing information about them. I would also like to thank Bob Kline of Idaho Mountain Search and Rescue, who edited the chapter on safety, and Todd Graeff, trails coordinator for the Idaho Department of Parks and Recreation, who edited the chapter on low impact camping. In addition, I want to thank Mary Ann Cameron for her editing of the entire manuscript.

Margaret Fuller

About the Author

Margaret Fuller was born and raised in Palo Alto, California. While growing up, she hiked extensively in the Tahoe, Muir Trail, and Mt. Lassen areas in California. In 1956, she received her B. A. in biology from Stanford University, where she was active in the Alpine Club. She has lived in Idaho since 1957.

Margaret and her husband, Wayne, an attorney, have five children, ages 15 through 26. In 1973, she earned her Idaho elementary teaching credential and has done part-time teaching. She serves on the Idaho Commission on Women's Programs. At present, she is a writer and homemaker.

Mrs. Fuller has had articles published in *Scenic Idaho, Incredible Idaho,* and *Idaho Citizen* magazines. Besides hiking, backpacking, writing, and photography, her hobbies are alpine and cross-country skiing and sewing, especially of outdoor gear.

In 1979, Margaret's first book, *Trails of the Sawtooth and White Cloud Mountains,* was published by Signpost Books. This is a sequel to that book, written partly because so many people have asked her for information about hiking in Idaho areas other than the Sawtooths. In doing research and taking pictures for the two books, Mrs. Fuller has hiked more than 1500 miles on Idaho trails.

Index